Soviet Radio and Television Netw

Number of Wired Speakers (In Republics; in Oblasts i...

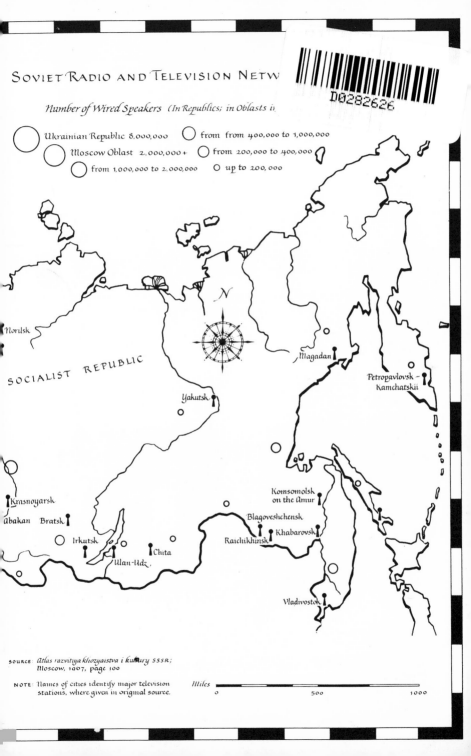

- Ukrainian Republic 8,000,000
- Moscow Oblast 2,000,000+
- from 1,000,000 to 2,000,000
- from from 400,000 to 1,000,000
- from 200,000 to 400,000
- up to 200,000

N

Norilsk

SOCIALIST REPUBLIC

Magadan

Petropavlovsk - Kamchatskii

Yakutsk

Krasnoyarsk

Komsomolsk on the Amur

Abakan   Bratsk

Blagoveshchensk

Irkutsk

Khabarovsk

Raichikhinsk

Chita

Ulan-Udz

Vladivostok

SOURCE: Atlas razvitya khozyaistva i kultury SSSR; Moscow, 1007, page 100

NOTE: Names of cities identify major television stations, where given in original source.

Miles

0   500   1000

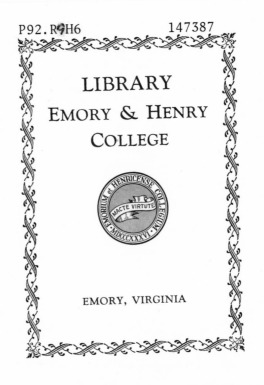

MASS MEDIA
IN THE SOVIET UNION

MARK W. HOPKINS

MASS MEDIA
IN THE SOVIET UNION

PEGASUS · NEW YORK

To
Marijean

PREFACE

A BOOK is infected with the author's prejudices, and it is only fair to suggest to the reader what they are, for they inevitably must influence research and judgments. This is especially true, I think, in writing about the Soviet Union. While I have attempted to remain dispassionate in describing and assessing the Soviet mass media, my own thoughts on the Soviet system have, I am sure, prevented complete success. There are many facets of Soviet society that I have found, from personal experience, to be demeaning of human life. The intrusion of the political bureaucracy upon the individual citizen's personal acts and conscience is, I think, the most conspicuous and pervasive. There are other characteristics of contemporary Soviet life, however, that I have come to admire. A belief in the worth of man, a respect for human emotion, a disdain for affectation and falseness in human relations, a resistance to placing the acquisition of things and position above the enrichment of the human spirit—all these I have sensed in my contacts with the Soviet people.

As regards the Soviet press specifically, my judgments are influenced by American values. It seems to me that the press should voice the fullest range of thought. When the press is managed by special interests, the inevitable consequence is suppression of "dangerous" ideas, and therefore the denial of individual liberty. Thus, whether the press is privately or state managed, it ideally should be *considered* public property existing to provide a forum for the variety of human experience. The ideal has never been achieved; and many times it conflicts with other essential goals of a society. But it is the objective that those who are franchised to manage the press should, it seems to me, strive toward.

The Soviet press as a whole is still too much the voice of special interests. And these—Soviet party-state bureaucracies—

exhibit a chronic fear of unregulated thought, which is reflected in the administration of the mass media. Many Soviet journalists have become imbued with the same attitude. Even the most idealistic—those who do in fact believe that the press exists to serve the people—are compromised. Yet I think there are Soviet journalists, too, who quietly attempt to enlarge the range of opinion in the press, who value the right of an individual to voice his personal hopes and grievances without fear of reprisal.

That the Soviet press was and is the victim of Stalinist attitudes is beyond doubt. The Stalinist heritage is the context within which human diversity struggles for expression in the Soviet Union. But one must make this judgment with humility. It is all too easy to condemn from afar where one is not exposed to the consequences of one's attitudes. And it is all too human to imply in a discussion of the Soviet press that it is inferior to the American way. I believe that the press, as it has developed in the United States, has yielded principles that well serve human society, foremost the principle that no one man, or one society, or one historical era possesses the truth. But the American press has its faults, too. It remains, it seems to me, too much a commercial enterprise. As economic forces compel ever greater centralization of information processing, there is a real danger that the American press will find increasing benefit in endorsing stability, rather than in leading innovation.

It is not therefore unreasonable for American journalists to consider the Soviet experience in managing a state-owned press. We may learn from Soviet mistakes as well as from accomplishments. As the American press grows into larger and larger corporate institutions, it seems also to draw away from human contacts—a phenomenon by no means unrecognized. Possibly the Soviet experience with readers' councils and special departments to handle readers' requests and complaints contains something of use to the American press. We may also witness in the Soviet press the consequences that flow from the uniformity and centralization of information, and from the management of information for what presumably or allegedly are overriding national requirements.

At various points throughout this book, I have referred to the American mass media. I have not attempted a comparative treatment, but only to draw parallels or note contrasts where they seemed to me helpful in understanding the Soviet press system. Nor can this work possibly be offered as a complete description of Soviet mass communications. I have not dealt, for example, with the system of oral propaganda, although this is of considerable importance in the formation of attitudes in the Soviet Union. Nor is there sufficient discussion of the content and functioning of the national language press. Finally, the focus of this book is on the Soviet newspaper press, which has throughout Soviet history been dominant in the mass media. Most of what is said about newspapers and the work of Soviet newspaper journalists applies also to the Soviet magazine press and to radio and television. Yet the latter especially deserve increasing separate attention for the changes they are effecting in Soviet society.

Not only the contemporary electronic media and the national language press, but the history of the Soviet press offer opportunity for further profitable investigation. And I hope that this book will stimulate additional study, as I have been stimulated by those who have done research before me on the Soviet press; here Alex Inkeles and his *Public Opinion in Soviet Russia* must be mentioned.

Occasionally, I have used information from my own discussions with Soviet journalists, and from my personal observations of Soviet journalistic practices. In this, I must simply ask the reader to trust that I have presented facts and opinions accurately. Though I have not wholly relied on personal experience to describe any single segment of the Soviet press, it seems to me that such experience can help in understanding how the Soviet mass media actually work, in contrast to how they should work. The second is frequently what is offered by official Soviet documents on the press; a reading of these alone as an accurate description of what exists can, I think, be deceptive.

I am, in any case, grateful to many Soviet journalists who have given me insight into their work and the workings of the Soviet press. Gratitude is also due Soviet journalism educators for the guidance and help they have given me at various times. Much of the initial research for this book was done in 1963–64 in the Soviet Union under the auspices of the Inter-University Committee on Travel Grants, and with the financial support in 1962–64 of the Ford Foundation's Foreign Area Fellowship Program. I am greatly indebted to both institutions.

I am also indebted to *The Milwaukee Journal*, which has provided me time and resources to write specially on the Soviet Union since 1964, and to travel extensively in the country in

1965 and 1967. My contact with the Soviet Union in these ways is reflected throughout the present study.

This book also would have been less than it is without the contributions of Professor John A. Armstrong and Theodore Shabad, both of whom read large parts of the manuscript and drew on their own exacting knowledge of the Soviet Union to make corrections and thoughtful suggestions. Invaluable too were comments of Professor Ralph O. Nafziger, who applied his devotion to clarity of thought and his broad knowledge of international communications to the entire manuscript. To all three I express my thanks, not only for constructive criticism, but for their personal interest and limitless encouragement in producing this book. Wherever it has failed in accuracy of fact or logic of judgment must, however, be my responsibility.

Finally, there would have been no book at all without my wife, Marijean, who not only typed the bulk of two drafts of the manuscript while keeping together a home for four children, but managed it all with cheer.

Mark W. Hopkins

Shorewood, Wisconsin
March 1969

GENERAL NOTE

THROUGHOUT this book, the Russian words *"raion,"* meaning district, and *"oblast,"* translating as region, are used when referring to Soviet administrative units. *Oblasts* are subdivisions of republics. In turn, *raions* are parts of *oblasts*. The larger Soviet cities are also divided into *raions*.

In transliterating Russian into English, the Russian letters ий are represented by *ii*; the я by *ya*; ы by *y*; and ю by *yu*. The Russian "e" occurring at the end of some nouns and adjectives and at the beginning of other words is ordinarily represented by *ye*. The Russian soft sign, usually indicated in English by an apostrophe, has been dropped altogether. Where customary American usage dictates otherwise, the exceptions have been made.

All dates, before and after the 1917 Bolshevik Revolution, are according to the Gregorian Calendar. In the nineteenth century it was 12 days ahead, and in the twentieth, 13 days ahead of the Julian Calendar, which was used in Russia until 1918.

CONTENTS

TABLES

CHARTS

MAPS

ILLUSTRATIONS

MASS MEDIA
IN THE SOVIET UNION

CHAPTER 1

THE PRESS AND SOCIETY

Ever since their formative years after the Bolshevik coup of 1917, the Soviet mass media have been cast as a "people's press." Soviet newspapers, magazines, radio, and more recently television are the extensions of Everyman. They stand, they are told, in the rank and file, amplifiers of workers' and peasants' grievances and aspirations. Their strength, they are reminded, is drawn from the people, a magical word in Soviet revolutionary tradition and present-day political lexicon that abstracts mankind's virtues. Almost every issue of *Pravda*, official newspaper of the Soviet Communist Party, carries a front-page photograph glorifying the common man. The picture might be of a rugged Russian construction worker against a backdrop of a new factory's steel-latticed superstructure. It might show the soft, pastoral face of a young girl, her hair swathed in a surgical cap, her sparkling eyes intently focused on a chemist's flask. Whoever, the portrait is *Pravda*'s testament to the people, in a now mechanical exercise that is somewhat analogous to the American newspapers' puffs of local civic leaders.

In Soviet editorial offices, the sheer quantity of letters from readers, regardless of content, is considered a measure of the bonds between people and press. Not unlike his American counterpart, the Soviet editor counts it an accomplishment when he has successfully engaged faceless bureaucracy in the cause of a wronged individual. The Soviet journalist's professional ethics are saturated with his responsibility to the people. That Soviet mass media do not always play this role brilliantly, and that they indeed often undertake it with lackluster and even cynicism, does not obscure the fact that in theory they are allied with the masses.

What lends an unreal air to this commitment is the Soviet mass media's role as spokesman for the Communist Party.

Even before the Bolshevik Revolution in November, 1917, the
Russian revolutionist Vladimir Lenin wielded newspapers as
instruments of political leadership and organization in the same
way the partisan political press was used here before and after
the American Revolution. A newspaper, Lenin wrote in his own
revolutionary times, was needed "to concentrate all elements
of political dissatisfaction and protest, to fertilize the proletarian
revolutionary movement." [1] Joseph Stalin, during his quarter-
century rule, made the Soviet mass media virtually a parrot
of his thoughts by putting full weight on the partisan political
nature of the press. In the hands of the Communist Party and
Soviet state, he said, the newspaper was "the means to maintain contacts with the working masses of our country and rally
them around the party and the Soviet state." [2] Nikita Khrushchev, though far more sophisticated than Stalin in techniques
of persuasion, and more permissive of conflicting opinion, nonetheless had the Soviet politician's penchant for managing news.
"As soon as some [Communist Party] decision must be explained or implemented," he told a conference of journalists
in Moscow, "we turn to you, and you, as the most trusted
transmission belt, take the decision and carry it to the very
midst of the people." [3]

From the American vantage point, there is a conflict between
the two fundamental roles of the Soviet press. American press
theory is weighted with a journalist's obligation to stand some-
where between the people and the government, protecting the
former from arbitrary power of the latter. So it seems the
crudest hypocrisy for Soviet journalists to speak of their commitment to the people when Soviet mass media issue a torrent
of government statements and interpretations of events with
rarely a critical objection from journalists themselves. The
standard, not too profound American retort to this arrangement is that the press cannot serve two masters simultaneously.
Either it is publicist for the government, or voice of the people.
Criticism of political leaders then becomes one gauge of the
American mass media's worth as defender of the common man;
and the Soviet mass media's conspicuous refusal or inability to
make any but the most commendable and favorable statements
about Soviet political authorities seem at once proof of a kept
press.

Soviet press theory squares the circle. It maintains, in harmony
with general Soviet political ideology, that the people and the
government are one. They have no essential differences of goal.
The government—specifically the Communist Party, which

remains the effective government in the Soviet Union—draws its power from the people. Armed with principles of Marxism-Leninism, as the Soviet rhetoric goes, the party directs and leads the people in the building of a new society. If one accepts unanimity of Soviet government and people in objectives and attitudes, it follows that the Soviet mass media simply circulate information in a homogeneous society. Or to put it another way, as Soviet theorists do, if a state-owned press opposes the government, it simultaneously opposes the people, an illogical act on the face of it.

To understand more fully Soviet press concepts, forgetting for a moment what exists in practice, we must touch on Marxist thought. It contends among many things that a given society's institutions evolve from its economic structure. Government, law, education, commerce, and the arts are all fashioned by a dominant class. That class in turn derives its power from ownership of the means of production, and maintains its superior status by manipulating all institutions. Thus, in contemporary Soviet press theory, the American mass media are described as functionaries of capitalists. Being owners of newspapers, magazines, radio, and television, capitalists easily manage public opinion for their own purposes, according to the most bald Soviet critique. By contrast, it continues, the Soviet mass media are publicly owned and *a priori* identify with public interests. In the somewhat stilted Soviet political vocabulary, this view may seem hopelessly simplified and obsolete. "From the first days of its existence, the Soviet press has served the worker class and expressed the thoughts and hopes of the broad masses of workers," Soviet journalists are instructed. " . . . The bourgeois press serves the class of capitalists. It is not concerned and by its very nature it cannot be concerned with the interests of the workers, with whom it has no ideological or organizational connections." [4]

The notion of ownership influencing mass media's performance is by no means alien to American discussions of the press. Proponents of publicly financed television fault commercial broadcasting for catering more to sponsors' wishes than to the needs of the public.[5] Nor is the idea uncommon elsewhere in the West. The publicly owned British Broadcasting Corporation is one ready and conspicuous example of an attempt to free the mass media from undue influence of narrow interest groups.

This, of course, was one stated goal of Bolshevik revolutionaries. But when we survey the structure and operation of the Soviet mass media today, it is apparent that something else exists. Instead of being the independent champion of that mystical and awe-inspiring force called the people, the press is bound to Communist Party and government bureaucracies which oversee the mass media to achieve certain objectives. These are not necessarily to the disadvantage of the mass of the Soviet Union's 239 million people. The Soviet press, for example, is enlisted in campaigns to educate people in basic hygiene. It disseminates information nationwide on new government programs, such as pension or educational reforms, that affect the lives of millions of Soviet citizens. But likewise, and to the disservice of the Soviet population, the mass media deliberately conceal or misinterpret certain information. They offer virtually no facts or analysis, for instance, how major decisions are arrived at in the Soviet political hierarchy. There is no attempt by the Soviet press to judge independently the qualities of men who direct the nation. Information about the world beyond Soviet borders emerges in the press decidedly and inevitably with a pro-Soviet bias.

This is to say that the Soviet mass media reflect a particular social system in which theory and practice do not always correspond. The Soviet political system falls far short of the democratic socialism that was once envisioned. Under the impact of Lenin's revolutionary doctrines and Stalin's totalitarian practices, Soviet society has been molded into a highly structured, minutely organized society focused on defined goals. The Soviet press, of course, has not been exempt from this process.

However, in assessing the Soviet mass media as they actually exist and function, two factors must be kept in mind. First, the Soviet press is, it should be obvious, one of many institutions in a vast and complex society, and necessarily interacts with all of them. This is not to ignore the fact that the Soviet press is first and foremost beholden to the Communist Party and government bureaucracies, and that all Soviet institutions—government, law, education, industry, commerce, agriculture, and civic organizations—are intertwined with the Communist Party apparatus. What takes place in Soviet society, however, is an interplay of forces within the established framework.

The Soviet printed press over the years has been one means by which a predominantly illiterate Soviet population was taught to read, and by which it has acquired much of the information necessary for daily living in a nation being transformed from an agrarian into an industrialized, urban society. Having aided in raising the educational level of its audience, the Soviet press was then challenged to alter its content to appeal to a far more sophisticated and discriminating readership than existed fifty years ago. To cite another example, Soviet political managers have become aware, along with politicians of urban nations the world over, of television's extraordinary potential for creating a favorable image of things and people. Thus, for instance, national Communist Party meetings have been televised. Soviet political leaders themselves have addressed the nation via television. In February, 1965, Premier Alexei Kosygin in a televised report to the Soviet people discussed results of his visits (just concluded) to North Vietnam, North Korea, and Communist China.

Though Soviet sociologists shy away from exploring attitude changes as a result of television exposure, we know from American experience that television has placed a premium in American politics on personal style and appearance. There is no reason to doubt that Soviet citizens, seeing their own political figures perform on television, form a different impression of these men, good or bad, than they had before. Clearly, Soviet leaders are not apprehensive of being turned out at elections, whatever their electronic image. But they are concerned with broad public attitudes and support. And to the extent that they use the television medium to form these, they must expose themselves, and all the telltale personal mannerisms, voice tones, and facial expressions that in the printed press can be concealed. Television, then, makes it incomparably more difficult for Soviet politicians to sustain an image of human perfection, as the Soviet propaganda apparatus was able to do with Joseph Stalin, who was presented to the Soviet population through media much less revealing of human frailty.

As one other instance of the interplay of Soviet mass media with other social institutions, the Soviet press has often taken an active role in the dispensation of justice in Soviet courts. It is not uncommon in ordinary trials (excluding blatantly political trials) for Soviet newspapers to agitate publicly in support of or against the accused, prior to a court judgment. In recent years, however, the Soviet legal profession has turned particular attention to fair trial and impartial adjudication. With this turn in legal ethics, the Soviet press has been berated for generating mob passions and in fact interfering with justice.[6] The demand, if not yet the universal result, is that Soviet mass media assume a more responsible role in educating their audiences in the Soviet legal process.

As these various examples imply, the Soviet press does not

exist in a vacuum, nor does it function purely as publicist for the Soviet political establishment. Being pervasive, as well as persuasive, in Soviet society, the mass media's structure and functioning are altered to some degree as other Soviet social institutions change.

The interaction of the mass media with the legal system, commerce, education, and what we would call big government is not so evident in the Soviet Union as in the United States. The major American mass media—the large newspapers such as *The New York Times*, or magazines such as *Life*, as well as the national broadcasting networks—are relatively autonomous in American society. Although the national American press is a business enterprise whose development has paralleled that of American business and industry generally, it enjoys considerable financial independence. It operates in a pluralistic society in which many special interests compete rather openly for influence and gain. Development and conflict of opposing ideas, and competition among individuals and institutions, are still regarded as basic American values. In these circumstances, the major American mass media visibly conflict with other social institutions.

Soviet society, particularly its political leaders, places a premium on public harmony and unanimity, regardless of what private controversies or dissensions exist. National goals are characteristically formulated by the Communist Party hierarchy. The Soviet mass media and other social institutions are not always in harmony with particular policies. But where conflict exists, it is moderated if not concealed by the overriding quest of the leadership for public unity. Thus, the Soviet press, while it influences and is influenced by other organizations, offers less public documentation of the interaction than the American mass media. Still, it would be deceptive to say that the interplay is nonexistent simply because it is not always clearly demonstrated.

A second general concept germane to the Soviet press is the unpredictability of the mass media in society. Regardless of the conscious deliberations that went into the formation of the Soviet mass media, they do not always do what is expected of them. Indeed, they have produced unexpected consequences for Soviet social managers.

It takes no special knowledge to recognize that the effects of mass media anywhere are not wholly subject to scientific analysis. In contemporary times, television has burgeoned into an industry of still incalculable consequences for the political and economic structures of modern, industrial nations. Its readily acknowledged capacity to influence popular tastes and attitudes on a mass scale has made television a boon to commerce. It has altered family relationships in the United States and radically changed the conduct of American campaigns and government. Of particular concern and fascination to social scientists, televison seems to form an unreal world in which people are never participants, but always spectators to events and experiences presented two-dimensionally in otherwise familiar surroundings. Among other suppositions, in the words of Gunther Anders, "the real world is forfeited." [7]

Before television, the newspaper and magazine press and radio all shaped American and other societies, and continue to do so, in ways that were hardly predictable. The American newspaper as it evolved into a mass consumption product revised marketing and production methods of industry; this process in turn continued to shape the American press so that today upward of three fourths of American newspaper content is allotted, in the form of advertising, to information on products, commerce, industry, and attitudes.

Radio broadcasting, which for the first time in man's history made it possible to expose masses of illiterate people to alien ideas, has had equally unforeseeable and unplanned effects. Today, the battery-powered transistor radio—compact, inexpensive, requiring no costly and elaborate power networks—opens immense opportunities to educate and influence millions of people in backward, illiterate nations, and, far superior to newspapers, is a genuine vehicle of social revolution.[8]

Soviet political leaders have been no more capable of predicting the precise effects of mass media on popular thought and attitudes than anyone else. Generally, in fact, they have held a rather unsophisticated view of what roles the mass media play in society. For a good share of Soviet history, they have looked on the press as a bullhorn, ignoring its more subtle uses in mass persuasion and education, and seemingly unconcerned until recently with the process by which people become aware of and accept new values.

Meanwhile, the Soviet mass media have matured into large, sometimes unwieldy institutions, which within the framework of the highly integrated Soviet society can be said to have an existence of their own. In this view, the Soviet press is not simply a "transmission belt" carrying information and ideas from one point to another, as an apolitical piece of machinery. Rather, Soviet mass media create their own image of Soviet society, and they serve many different functions beyond those traditionally assigned roles as the people's voice and political house organ.

Before describing these functions, we should put the Soviet press into both the physical and social contexts. These provide the general boundaries within which the mass media perform: they dictate limitations on what the press can and cannot do, regardless of ideals and theory.

The Soviet Scene

The Soviet mass media are spread over a huge nation covering a sixth of the world's land surface, or about three times the area of the continental United States. The Soviet Union's sheer size has always presented formidable obstacles to development of an effective mass media network. It has meant enormous difficulties in distributing newspapers and magazines, in supplying newsprint and printing equipment—particularly in early years when the Soviet transportation system was small and backward. The Soviet geography has also made radio broadcasting and television costly means of communication. Both radio and television have been dependent in their growth, of course, on the progress of Soviet electrification. As a result, for decades, areas of the country were not reached at all by radio, and huge sections are yet beyond television broadcasts. Television, as highly as it is now prized by the Soviet government as an instrument of mass persuasion, certainly has been retarded because of the expense of constructing transmission systems, whether cables or relay towers.

Added to the Soviet land mass as a physical barrier to enlargement of the press network is the harsh climate of much of the country. This, too, has held back extension of the Soviet transportation system, including highways and rail and air lines, and of electrification, given their costs weighed against other national needs. Thus, dissemination of the printed press, and to some extent the growth of radio and television, have been restricted by conditions over which the Soviet government has no control, or which it has altered only at great cost. These are not profound observations. But in the continental United States we have grown accustomed to a well-developed transportation and distribution system. When discussing mass media, for one thing, we generally ignore the influence geography has on them. The obstacles that Alaska's geography poses to mass communication development are similar to those in a good share of the Soviet Union.

As in Alaska also, the Soviet population is concentrated in a proportionately small area. Only about 10 per cent of the Soviet Union's 239 million people live in Siberia and the far east. Approximately 70 per cent live in the western segment of the country, including the Urals region and the Caucasus. The grouping of the Soviet population obviously somewhat offsets the geographical problem. The bulk of Soviet citizens can be reached by the printed press and radio and TV broadcasting with a network that covers an area roughly equal to that of the continental United States. Of course, building a mass media system in this land area alone has been no minor undertaking; extending the system to encompass the remaining 30 per cent or so of the population has been the especially costly part, and was accomplished in slow stages.

What must also be kept in mind in surveying Soviet mass media is the multi-national character of the country. It is divided into 15 national republics, the Russian Federation being by far the largest. Many nationalities have their own autonomous republic or region within one of the 15 major republics. Of the total Soviet population of 209 million at the 1959 census (the most recent), 114 million, or a little over half, were Russian. There were about 37 million Ukrainians, the second largest nationality group; 8 million Byelorussians; and 16 other nationalities comprising a million or more persons. Beyond these, numbering in hundreds of thousands, sometimes in groups only of hundreds, were about 100 other nationalities.

A persistent and forceful policy of the Soviet government has been to unify these nationalities. Several particularly—Ukrainians, Estonians, Latvians, and Lithuanians—exhibit separatist tendencies to the present day, although their republics are politically and economically integrated with the entire Soviet structure. All the same, two forces are at play. The central government, the Communist Party, is constantly working at national harmony and stability among ethnic groups, which in times past especially has meant Russification of huge regions. On the other hand, various nationalities with old and deep cultural traditions seek to preserve their heritages.

What this has produced, as in the United States though for different reasons, is a multi-national press. All central publications and radio and television programs are produced in Russian, the official national language. However, each republic has its own native language newspapers, magazines, and broadcasting. These are by no means independent of the national government. Indeed, one of the ever-present apprehensions of the central party apparatus is that of native language publications encouraging, or at least not dispelling, nationalistic tendencies.[9]

Therefore, whether a newspaper, for instance, is published in Russian or a native language, it is an integral part of the mass media network. Nevertheless, the operation of a national press system in a multi-national country causes certain difficulties. For one, much information, because it is originally transmitted in Russian, must be translated into 57 other languages for newspapers and 44 for magazines.[10] This carries with it the customary risks of distortion and misinterpretation. There is a more subtle issue. To minority nationalities, statements and proclamations from the central government must *sound* Russian, no matter how they are presented by the Soviet mass media. As a means of persuasion, the Soviet press then faces difficulties common to multi-national and multi-racial countries. They might be likened to the American newspapers' difficulty in reaching American Negroes. The newspapers generally are products of another sector of American society—the white middle class—and as a result, their content often is irrelevant to the Negro. The Soviet press, too, may well fail to reach segments of its audience because of cultural differences.

Whatever the Soviet mass media's success in communicating, the multi-national character of the Soviet Union unmistakably influences the performance and structure of the country's press. It ranks with Soviet geography and climate and population distribution as one of the given quantities. So, when we talk about the Soviet mass media in their habitat, it is a misconception to imagine *Pravda* against a background of Red Square and the Kremlin, just as it is misleading to think of the American press in terms of *The New York Times* or NBC-TV against New York's skyscraper silhouette. The Soviet mass media is simultaneously the 4-page, tabloid-size newspaper published in a cotton town in central Asia, the daily Ukrainian language paper in the republic capital of Kiev, the local radio station program in Russian coming from a loudspeaker in a student dormitory at Leningrad University, the Radio Moscow folk music hour drifting out of a shortwave set in the Siberian city of Irkutsk, or finally a color TV broadcast in Moscow itself.

The Soviet System

To place Soviet mass media, secondly, into some sort of social milieu, they function in an often corporate-like atmosphere. The general scheme is a government-managed press; analogously, it is a composite of several mass communications variants or off-shoots operating in the United States. Traces of the American corporate public relations function can be detected in the Soviet mass media: the corporation house organ comes very close in terms of purpose and content to Soviet newspapers. Techniques of American advertising, as in the attempt to form opinion through repetition of slogans, are present in the Soviet press system. The Soviet press also shares with the American religious and labor press the inclination to judge events from an ideological or class point of view. And in terms of general management and subordination of the mass media to a single directorate, the Soviet press is not unlike—searching for an approximate American counterpart—the United States military base newspaper. But such comparisons are somewhat deceptive right off. The Soviet mass media function in a considerably different political and cultural community than American, of whatever type. If it shares characteristics of a variety of American mass communications, the Soviet press all the same has its own personality traits and eccentricities.

A predominant one is its attachment to the Soviet political establishment. Through interlocking directorates, in which many Soviet journalists are simultaneously editors and Communist Party members, the mass media are in the first instance responsible to the party apparatus, from the very pinnacle to the base. The party appoints and approves newspaper and magazine editors, and radio and television broadcasting managers. Other arrangements further determine the roles and content of the mass media. A censorship agency checks the mass media, not as rigorously as in the past, but it is a restraining influence even if a given editor never seriously errs in his judgments.

There are also purely economic institutions and patterns in Soviet society that shape the press system. All printing plants, printing equipment, newsprint production and allocation, all means of communications (telegraph, radio, cable lines, railroads, trucking, etc.), all press distribution channels, and all communications industries (radio and TV manufacturers, for instance) are state owned. Their general and specific development is part of overall economic plans, along with steel production, housing construction, shoe manufacture, and thousands of other industries. Thus the mass media, like any Soviet enterprise, are intertwined in a vast economic system. Newspaper and magazine budgets are incorporated into a financial sheet of one or another Soviet organization, including the Communist Party. The same is true of radio and television broadcasting. There is no exact counterpart to such economic dependency among American mass media. Perhaps the closest is the American government, which publishes periodicals edited by government employees and printed on government presses at government expense.

Being wholly in the state sector, Soviet mass media are oriented in quite another direction than a press system, such as the American, which is financially allied to a private economy. For example, until the late 1950's, the Soviet press was almost oblivious to costs, to whether it was financially solvent or showed a profit. Even now, many Soviet newspapers are state subsidized, and the broadcasting industry is almost entirely government-financed. Hence, the motivation of Soviet journalists to satisfy audience tastes and demands comes from sources other than monetary. Or, to put it another way, Soviet newspapers have survived, even flourished in terms of circulation, far beyond the point where they would have withered and died in a competitive, private economy.

The Soviet mass media's primary or screening audience in the past and present alike has been composed of Soviet political managers, the Communist Party apparatus of perhaps 200,000 or 250,000 members who alone among the party's complement of 14 million members function full-time as management for Soviet society. This is not to exclude other significant and influential groups in Soviet society, such as the government ministerial bureaucracy, the military, the industrial managers and economists. They, too, are special audiences of the mass media. Given their importance in Soviet economic and political affairs, they directly or indirectly affect the content and emphasis of the Soviet press. Soviet armed forces, for example, have their own mass media network, which concerns itself primarily with military affairs. A number of Soviet periodicals are devoted predominantly to problems of industrial management, economic theory, finance, and manufacturing.

However, the common denominator in Soviet society is the Communist Party apparatus. In that organization, lines of political and economic authority and responsibility intersect. The party's select politburo formulates major policy, in all spheres, foreign and domestic, political and economic. Clearly, the 11 politburo members are not autonomous. They react to events, as well as initiate policies. They refer, if not defer at times, to the Central Committee, a larger group of party members drawn from provincial party organizations, government administrative agencies, the military, and security police. The politburo works within the framework of reports and counsel from political and economic advisers. Nonetheless, the global decisions rest with the politburo. And multitudes of lesser decisions in the daily political and economic management of the Soviet Union are made in Communist Party committees, from the national Central Committee down to the republic, *oblast, raion,* city, and village levels.

In political matters, the politburo establishes guidelines of Soviet foreign policy, and often enough quite specific policies, much as the American President and his cabinet and advisers deal with foreign crises arising from wars, military provocations, international commerce and finance, and political coups. Within the Soviet Union, the Communist Party apparatus is the dominant and seldom-challenged voice in such inexact matters as cultural policy, literature, arts, and what in a broad sense are national purposes, values, and beliefs. Under these last falls the propagation of Marxism-Leninism as a philosophical interpretation of what makes society change and progress (or regress), of the relationship between the state and the people, the interconnection of economics and politics, of the artistic function in society, or the international function of socialism and communism among other social systems. Being the only Soviet political organization, the Communist Party exercises the power and prerogatives that American corporate management does *within* the corporation, or that the high command does in a military organization.

Nonetheless, within this social framework, and subject to influences of geography and peoples, the Soviet press performs several broad functions. They can be discussed under six general categories: a political press; mass mobilizer; keeper of the morals; public forum and social critic; educator and reporter; mass entertainer and merchandiser.

A Political Press

In many ways, the Soviet journalist occupies a position similar to an American corporate vice-president for public relations or advertising. The Soviet newspaper, because of its involvement with the political system, has an overriding inclination to defend, explain, and promote management's—the party-government apparatus—policies and views. The Soviet editor, himself a member of the management team, is especially concerned that his publication win acceptance from his peers and superiors. This means, of course, that he constantly gauges shifts of thought and emphasis among those who make political and economic decisions, and tries to tailor his publication to parallel these changes.

The Soviet mass media's overall performance is always being
judged by the Communist Party apparatus, among other audiences. In turn, the Soviet journalist corps is acutely sensitive to
party reactions, much as the American advertising agency account executives are attuned to the likes and dislikes of clients.
Or, to draw another comparison (indicated earlier), the Soviet
mass media operate somewhat like the newspapers of the American labor unions or religious denominations. These publications,
like the Soviet mass communications, are financially dependent
on organizations that strive toward particular objectives shaped
by a particular ideology. Editors of labor union newspapers are
not only predominantly occupied with news and interpretations
of the labor movement, but are inherently disposed toward promoting labor, and making value judgments in terms of what is
good or bad for labor. Even given the American journalistic
ethics that assign priority to factual, impartial reporting of an
event, the labor press views developments within American society from a wholly different perspective than does, for example,
the large metropolitan newspaper, which has a different audience and economic arrangement. Similarly, the religious press is
allied with organizations propagating distinct systems of thought.
The religious press, of whatever denomination, is at once a
channel of information on theological matters, on administrative
questions, and on purely lay issues. Editors of Protestant, Catholic, or Jewish newspapers may quite naturally vary in their
interpretations of what is important, of what represents change
or progress; but most are not fundamentally in disagreement
with the philosophies of their sponsors. Within a general, changing framework of values and beliefs, and within a defined organization, the religious press is sometimes simply a mouthpiece. In other instances, it can be an innovator of ideas and
critic of doctrine and authorities.[11]

The Soviet mass media perform in similar circumstances.
But to these must be added the fact that the American religious or labor press operates in a pluralistic society. Other
segments of mass communications in the United States reflect
clearly different values and beliefs. Other special interests—
political parties, business, government—as well as the mass
popular press, continuously challenge narrow presentations
or doctrinally distorted views of American society. The Soviet
mass media for most of their history have not had to share
the marketplace of ideas. Indeed, they have operated as if
no market existed at all. In recent years, however, the Soviet
press has started adapting to a sort of international pluralism

of ideas. As world communications have expanded, and with development of global broadcasting via satellites, Soviet authorities have become aware of increasing competition from beyond Soviet boundaries. Somewhat like a religious press network, the Soviet mass media are confronted with dissemination of information within the Soviet Union by sources that take substantially different points of view. The most conspicuous examples are radio broadcasts by the United States and Communist China. International TV broadcasting presents even greater problems to Soviet authorities, in their own concern with purity of doctrine, as they look to the future.[12]

The Soviet government more rigidly and successfully restricts the interplay of different ideas among the Soviet people than a given religious organization can among its adherents. But denial of information is achieved only in a society which is severely repressive throughout. In recent years, the Communist Party has tended to emphasize the function of the mass media to counter foreign opinions and information rather than attempt to insulate the Soviet people from other worlds of thought.[13] This is not so much of its own choosing, but rather because in adopting some policies, and recording progress in some areas, the Communist Party has had to react to developments which were unforeseen or minimized. For example, after the Soviet government ceased jamming most foreign radio broadcasts in 1963, there was bound to be a change in Soviet mass media content, depending on the extent of penetration of foreign interpretations of events into Soviet popular thought.

Nonetheless, it is clear that the Soviet press is allied with a political order in Soviet society whereas, by contrast, the mass American press is an adjunct of an industrial order.[14] Therefore, evolution of the Soviet political system paces development of the mass media: the broad national objectives of the political structure simultaneously are those of the press. Soviet society's industrial, agricultural, military, educational, and cultural institutions interact with the mass media, as was proposed earlier, but these institutions also are part of the Soviet political order. The Soviet political structure, in this sense, is not simply the Communist Party apparatus, but the whole governing, decision-making bureaucracy. The central party has a commanding voice in this structure, as the board of directors does in an American corporation, or the chiefs of staff in the armed forces. Its authority has outer limits, defined not so much by regulation or law, though these are factors, but by past practice, by assessments of what is possible in given circumstances, and by generally accepted norms of administration and management. These in turn have been and are being shaped by those large forces operating in a given social structure, such as industrial development, urbanization, and rise of educational levels. The party's dominance in Soviet society has given the Soviet Union certain forms (collectivized agriculture, for instance, and nationalized industry), but the political structure, and the Communist Party apparatus specifically, has not therefore been immune from the effects of its own initiatives and accomplishments.

In this constant evolution and interaction of Soviet social institutions, the Soviet mass media take on assorted political responsibilities and duties. In Soviet writings, these are propounded as principles, as American press theory describes performance of the mass media in their own political-economic circumstances. For instance, one Soviet reference for journalists[15] lists the following: (1) Party orientation (*partiinost*), which may be interpreted as conscious acceptance that the press is a politically partisan institution, and that it therefore expresses party philosophy and goals; (2) high level of ideology (*vysokaya ideinost*), which suggests that the mass media should be spiritually reinforced with the ideology of Marxism-Leninism, in perhaps the same way that the Catholic diocesan newspaper should not only reflect interests of the Church, but should be permeated with the spirit of Christianity; (3) truthfulness (*pravdinost*), an obligation to transmit information truthfully; (4) popular orientation (*narodnost*), which reminds the Soviet press of its responsibilities toward the masses, and simultaneously of the people's access to the publicly owned press; (5) mass character (*massovost*), which not only maintains that the Soviet press serves the masses, but functions amid them; and (6) criticism and self-criticism (*kritika* and *samokritika*), which calls upon the press to criticize failures and faults of the Communist Party, the government, and their agencies, as well as to criticize its own performance.

In Lenin's words, which are reprinted in virtually all Soviet discussions of mass media's functions, the press also is a collective propagandist, agitator, and organizer.[16] In the context of the times—the words were written in 1901—Lenin was arguing that a newspaper could be an organizational center of a political party, as well as an instrument of persuasion. To mention one more set of guidelines, the Soviet press has been given these characteristics: (1) differentiation, to serve various categories of readers, (2) purposefulness of content, especially in discussing problems of socialist development, (3) close association with readers by means of letters and news notes, and (4) organization of public affairs discussions.[17] These are all rather sweeping assignments for Soviet mass communications. It seems axiomatic, as with all large principles and purposes, that they can be interpreted to cover a multitude of sins and virtues.

How much criticism should there be, and toward whom should it be directed? When and how extensively should public discussions of government proposals be conducted? To what degree should the mass media side with the masses, if popular interests seem to conflict with Communist Party objectives (as clearly they did, to cite a gross example, in Stalin's blood purges before and after World War II)? One may say, in the Soviet context, that the political order answers these questions to its own satisfaction. But suppose the Communist Party apparatus exercises the most self-protective policies as far as mass media's performance is concerned. One danger, as the American government has discovered in far less expert and intense management of the news, is a "credibility gap." The mass media lose their effectiveness as molders and shapers of opinion. Or suppose press criticism of government policies is merely given lip service. As a society becomes more complex and less subject to close central command, which is the observable process in the Soviet Union, the lack of vigorous public criticism of policy implementation permits error to multiply.

In other words, given its general principles and its alliance with the political order, the Soviet press must constantly strike a balance among conflicting responsibilities. When national goals, for example, are clearly set and their achievement is imperative (victory in war is an instance), a dissenting, critical press performs a disservice. However, when uncertainty arises, or when alternative objectives of roughly equal merit exist, the mass media may be useful as an independent judge. That is the American viewpoint. The American mass media are regularly more the critic of national policy than the Soviet. The rationale is that public exposure and critical analysis of government decisions, among others, will reveal human flaws and right the wrongs. Needless to say, governments look on this press function with mixed feelings. They would prefer mass media to be constructively critical, or even to promote national policy.[18] The Soviet political order can and does of course enlist the mass media in its causes, far more comprehensively than the American. But Soviet authorities, too, value the critical function of the press.

Mass Mobilizer

Mass communications by their nature deal with a mass audience. The Soviet press from its origin was considered a mass press by the political bureaucracy, regardless of the fact that only one out of four people could read when Lenin's Bolsheviks seized power in November, 1917. As mentioned earlier, one characteristic of the contemporary press is *massovost* (mass character). National Soviet newspapers such as *Pravda, Izvestia,* and *Komsomolskaya Pravda* are published in millions of copies. Size (ordinarily only six pages) is sacrificed to mass dissemination. As a stopgap, before sufficient funds were invested to produce large numbers of standard radio receivers, most of the Soviet Union was wired for sound; loudspeakers carried central broadcasts among the Soviet population. Beginning with the prerevolutionary Bolshevik press, the objective always was to reach the mass audience of workers and peasants, rather than a select strata of the powerful and influential. The reason was evident. The Bolshevik Party, among other political organizations fomenting revolution in czarist Russia, aimed to rally the masses to assume power. Bolsheviks were not concerned with changing attitudes of existing authority.

After 1917, the Soviet press switched roles, naturally enough, and became champion of the government. More than that, the Soviet mass media took on the function of mobilizing the nation for cataclysmic changes in the Russian social structure. This function was pronounced in the 1930's, when enforced collectivization and brutally demanding rapid industrialization were begun under Stalin's direction. The mass media rallied the Soviet people during World War II in their battle against Germany, and after the war, in their massive reconstruction efforts.

Soviet mass communications retain their mobilizing function. From one point of view, it is a heritage of Soviet social revolution, of industrialization, of Soviet economic development under a supremely powerful, centralized political organization. As we study ways by which underdeveloped nations of Latin

America, Africa, or Asia tackle their problems of modernization, we see the mass media cast in the same role as they have
been in the Soviet Union. Wilbur Schramm, writing of the
mass media's uses in development, observes:

> Communication development is not *really* in competition with
> industrialization, agricultural modernization, educational de-
> velopment, health improvement, community development, the
> growth of nation-ness, broad participation in public affairs,
> or any of the other great goals of national development. . . .
> It is the servant and ally of each of these.[19]

Schramm sees the mass media as "agents of social change,"
which aid in the transition from old values and relationships
to new ones.[20] Other analyses similarly propose deliberate and
planned use in developing nations of mass media as instruments
of change and modernization.[21] Or to put the matter in a
different perspective, mass media are not only catalysts of
development, but are in themselves one index of progress.[22]

There obviously are differences in how the mass media are
used in mobilizing a nation for one or another purpose. But
it is not difficult to find instances of any press system allied
with the government at one time or another. In the United
States, the press has helped mobilize the nation in time of
war.[23] In other cases, the American press summons its
audience to support various "good causes"—charity drives,
urban renewal, antipoverty and welfare programs, and plans
for combating air and water pollution. The motivation is sometimes the mass media's sense of responsibility, of an obligation
to a society in which they must exist, or of their own economic stake in the cause (newspapers generally approve of
modernizing downtown areas, for example).

Turning to the Soviet press, voluntary cooperation with the
political order is less an issue than it is with the American
mass media. The political bureaucracy can decide to emphasize
(or minimize) an event, a plan, a policy. Thus, for example,
when a five year program for agriculture was adopted by the
Communist Party in 1965, it was automatic that the mass
media, as an ally of the party, publicized the new program
in the most favorable light. The cost, originally about $78
billion, was equated with new farm equipment, more rural
housing, an improved food supply, and a generally higher
standard of living for the entire Soviet population. These themes
appeared in reports from the printed press, radio, and tele-

vision. In subsequent treatment, as the farm program was implemented, the mass media focused on improved conditions
on collective farms and gains in agricultural production, re-
lating these to the general plan. The press attempted to create
an air of optimism and progress and to show that the farm
program was working.

The same approach is made to all fundamental (and some
not so fundamental) Soviet policies. The press tries to enlist
the broadest possible public support, usually by portraying
the new policy as beneficial to the masses. Two things should
be said about Soviet campaigns to mobilize popular opinion
and participation. First, they occur in an atmosphere of little
or no dissent. There is no mulling and pondering in the press
over the wisdom of the basic policy once it has been adopted.
And, second, the policies themselves are not necessarily irra-
tional or unwise.

Related to such Soviet mass media campaigns are those to
create popular acceptance of innovation, of change in habitual
ways of doing things, of new relationships. When the Soviet
economic reform was adopted in 1965, an instant problem was
popular understanding of the word "profit." For years, the
Soviet mass media had associated this with capitalist systems,
and thus given it a highly unfavorable connotation. Profit was
synonymous with "greed," "exploitation," "rich," "injustice,"
and "imperialism," among other negative words in the Soviet
Union. The Soviet press was now faced with the task of turning
"profit" into an acceptable, positive idea. One tactic was to quote
from Vladimir Lenin's prodigious writings—undisputable authority. The Soviet mass media recalled Lenin's approving remarks on profits in a socialist society. Further, the press
explained at great length the different uses of profits in a
socialist and capitalist society (profits line the pockets of the
rich in capitalist, but finance public welfare programs in socialist society). And, lastly, the mass media attempted to discredit
the foreign interpretation (not only western but Chinese, as
well) that Soviet emphasis on profits evidenced a rebirth of
capitalism.

In Soviet history, this one example of the Soviet mass media
paving the way for innovation is of course miniscule. The
press has been instrumental in altering public attitudes toward
farming and manufacturing methods, industrial management,
distribution, work, and economic planning, to name a few of the
areas radically affected as the Soviet Union developed an in-

dustrial, urban, planned society. The mass media similarly have worked for popular acceptance of the Communist Party's dominant place in Soviet society, of Stalin as an infallible leader, of the imprisonment and execution of millions of Soviet citizens, and of persecution of religious believers, among other categories of dissenters from established norms of thought and behavior. These items scarcely exhaust instances in which the Soviet mass media have prepared or conditioned popular opinion. And to mention them is not to imply that the Soviet press has always been successful. It has not. Nor has it always been totally employed in sharp changes in Soviet society. In the political sphere, for instance, the Soviet press infrequently or only very subtly forecasts the coups and power struggles that have occurred in high political councils. It is most often brought into political affairs of this type after the fact.

However, it remains true that in the violent, stormy course of Soviet development, the mass media have served innovation, whether wise or not. The American press performs an identical service, less consciously and less purposefully. Articles discussing, for example, the present and probable future impact of automation on American society in effect help prepare people for disruptive changes in their lives. The basic assumption is that automation is both desirable and inevitable. The mass media argue industry's cause and create public acceptance. The American government, in cooperation with or by manipulation of the press, bends public opinion to certain plans or policies. James Reston, going back into recent history, suggests that the favorable publicity given to the Marshall Plan, when that program of European recovery was proposed, was a major factor in its adoption.[24] American Presidents, most emphatically from President Franklin D. Roosevelt's years onward, have been ever conscious of the mass media's power in preparing for and accustoming the public to new ideas, and they have sought to use that power.[25]

Closer in style and method to the Soviet mass media's part in social innovation and change is American advertising. Advertisements are in large part concerned with altering habits, forming new attitudes, gaining acceptance for new procedures and products among a mass audience. The daily routine of the American housewife has been revolutionized not just because there are more machines to replace hand labor, but because advertising encouraged American women (and men) to mechanize the home. Indeed, the popular understanding of "new" (a new product, a new way) as synonymous with good, favorable, or beneficial, for example, owes much to advertising. The Soviet mass media are fond of the word "new" as well. "Innovators" among Soviet workers are applauded in the Soviet mass media. The "new" farm technique is labeled as such, and presented favorably against old methods. New architectural and clothing fashions, construction procedures, factory assembly-line improvements also are surrounded with the aura of optimism and goodness. That is, the Soviet press, not unlike American mass media, particularly advertising, tries to eliminate a major obstacle to innovation, the very fact of newness with its inherent challenge to familiar routines.

Keeper of the Morals

On a much broader scale, the Soviet mass media are the carriers of values, beliefs, and ideals. The press conveys to the general public what is considered correct behavior and morality. Obviously, the mass media are not alone. The Soviet educational system operates in the same areas. An individual Soviet citizen also is influenced by his friends, fellow workers, by what he reads and sees elsewhere than in the mass media. What the press does, daily, is remind of and reaffirm values or ideals.

In Soviet society, these frequently emit from the political bureaucracy. As one consequence, the stated morality or behavior in the Soviet press often sounds unreal. It strikes the foreigner as "propaganda," in the sense of being fictitious or deliberately deceptive. The primary purpose is not to distort, but rather to propagate, to propose to the Soviet mass audience what attitudes or behavior *should be*, rather than to say what *is*. A typical statement in Soviet newspaper editorials begins, "All the Soviet people unanimously approve of . . . ," followed by a decision or action of the Communist Party. What is being said, quite obviously, is that all Soviet citizens *should* approve of the action. Whether they do or not is quite another thing. In other stock phrases, the Soviet press condemns, criticizes, cautions, rejoices, accepts, and rejects on behalf of the whole Soviet people.

The press talks of the "new Soviet man" as if he were flesh and blood. Such portrayals of the ideal man are similar to instructions and illustrations given American soldiers. Army publicists know that no soldier ever matches the model, in behavior and dress, but he *should*. Accounts in the Soviet mass media of criminal trials, of hooliganism, currency speculation, pilfering, lying, cheating, loafing, drinking, wife beating, profiteering, slandering, and brawling are all lessons in how one should not behave, and Soviet press reports ordinarily are bluntly explicit in saying so. They draw a moral from the tale. In hundreds of redundant reports, the Soviet mass media sketch pictures of the worthy citizen, husband, wife, worker, Communist Party member, collective farm chairman, factory manager, schoolboy, writer, artist, government bureaucrat, and even the national leader.

Among the model citizen's attributes, besides honesty, patriotism, love of labor, and the like, is an immersion in Marxism-Leninism, an acceptance of the Soviet Communist world view. Hence, the Soviet mass media continuously restate the Soviet political-economic doctrines, and is enjoined to explain reinterpretations of them. For example, in 1956, when Khrushchev revived "peaceful coexistence" as a cornerstone of Soviet foreign policy, the mass media set about to explain its place in Marxism-Leninism. But more than this, the Soviet press transmits year after year, generation after generation, the Marxist-Leninist formulas and doctrines as the intellectual or spiritual context in which Soviet citizens must live. In the same way, though less intensely and blatantly, Americans are reminded of the mainstream of American thought and ideals. The mass media in the United States educate successive generations in the principles of political democracy and a capitalist economy. American press editorials and many "news" stories remind citizens of how a democracy operates, and what the ideal citizen does. Clearly, there are large differences between Soviet and American press performance in this area. The American press is not so heavyfooted. American ideals are not so structured and organized, nor do they emanate so consistently from a single point as the Soviet. The Soviet mass media tend to preach from a pulpit, taking their authority from the scriptures, and lacing their sermons with moral truths of Marxism-Leninism.

Still, the Soviet press serves to "socialize," to inculcate and perpetuate a particular set of values. What makes the Soviet mass media distinctive in this function, compared with the American, is not only the conscious, concerted way they go about the job. It is the fact that the press generally excludes consideration of other value systems. For example, the mass media propagate a materialistic view of the world (in the philosophic sense), but prohibit favorable presentation of Christian or Islamic philosophies.

The Soviet press also operates to legitimize the existing government structure. This is hardly surprising. The Soviet political order must continuously justify its claim to govern. Unlike the former Russian monarchy, Soviet political leaders do not take their authority or moral guidance from God. And since the Communist Party politburo is not popularly elected, it must rationalize its commanding position. Hence the party's assertion that it most perceptively of all interprets the scientific doctrines of Marxism-Leninism, and that it is entitled to govern by its special knowledge. The Soviet mass media reinforce the assertion with endless descriptions of what the party has accomplished, armed with Marxism-Leninism. As a whole, these are simplified, if not crude. Moreover, the press creates a credibility gap, for in excessive praise and glorification of the party, it presents a public image that rarely conforms to reality. Likewise, no one attaches much credence to the corporation house organ's profile of the board chairman.

Public Forum and Social Critic

Within a rather vaguely defined framework, the Soviet mass media provide a forum where conflicting ideas and views are proposed to the public at large, or to special interest groups. The tendency over the past few years has been toward greater discussion of controversial matters, and the Soviet press is more interesting as a result. It would be wrong, however, to suppose that the mass media have always been docile transmitters of proclaimed truth. Before 1917, aspiring revolutionists, among them the Bolsheviks, battled over ideas, policies, and tactics in their newspapers. And after the Bolsheviks took power, the Soviet press was full of controversy. It began to subside in the late 1920's, as Stalin's power grew, and then died in the 1930's, coincident with industrialization, and particularly Stalin's purge trials and mass repression. Revival came in the mid-1950's. The useful date is 1956, when Khrushchev delivered the celebrated anti-Stalin address at the Communist Party's 20th Congress. Increasingly, after that, the Soviet mass media have tested the limits of open discussion.

The change should be seen in the context of other developments in Soviet society. Khrushchev's broadside attack on Stalinism loosed pent-up forces. The Soviet literary "thaw" began. Soviet courts and law were reformed. Powers of the Soviet internal security police were reduced. The fear and apprehension that characterized Stalin's rule began to fade. People began to speak their thoughts more openly; an atmosphere receptive of public criticism began to form. At the same time, the Soviet economy was gradually recovering from the war. Soviet industry became more diversified, automated, and complex. And, too, the Soviet population expanded, from about 198 million in 1956 to 239 million at the end of 1968. A new generation arose, with new views. Educational levels moved up.

The Soviet mass media have reflected these developments, and have shared in them. One result is enlargement of the public forum in the press. Soviet newspapers, magazines, and radio and television also serve more effectively now as critics of society. And more noticeably than in the past, they have become defenders of the innocent, channels of popular grievances, and voices of reform. Suggestive of these changes among journalists' views is a statement by a Soviet editor at a Moscow conference:

> During the years of the personality cult [Stalinism], we lost the habit of debating, of exchanging opinions. We lost the habit of good, fruitful discussion when some question arose. I am speaking of a businesslike argument from which the truth emerges. . . . The chief thing is that we must foster within ourselves the desire to discuss more frequently in newspapers questions that are not clear.[26]

In Soviet society, the public forum becomes increasingly valuable. If the Soviet press of the 1930's was primarily a mobilizing force for industrialization, the press of the 1960's participates more and more in problem solving. This change mirrors Soviet society. There were relatively few alternatives available or allowed in the 1930's; dissent and discussion delayed and detracted from relatively simple goals. But management of the Soviet planned economy is altogether a different matter when ten instead of two alternative solutions are possible for a given problem. Largeness and diversity work against central decisionmaking. In American business, one-man direction gave way to team management as the single factory grew into the huge corporation. Task forces, study groups, and specialists all become essential in isolating problems, and then resolving them. In similar circumstances, the Soviet press serves the purposes of a "brainstorming" conference.

The Soviet economic reform was preceded by a long debate among specialists. It began in 1962, with an article in *Pravda* by Yévsei Liberman, a Kharkov University economist. A lull followed. Then, in 1964, *Pravda* published an article by a well-known Soviet scholar, Vadim Trapeznikov, who proposed, like Liberman, the use of tax rates, incentives, flexible prices, and profit index to manage the increasingly unwieldy Soviet economy. Quite formally, *Pravda* announced that Trapeznikov's article opened up general discussion, and invited assorted specialists to contribute their views.[27]

There were other press debates over Soviet economic management, and it is now commonplace for Soviet newspapers and periodicals to allot space for advocates of various economic proposals, both for industry and agriculture. Clearly, there are off-limit areas. And many discussions in the Soviet mass media are generated in the political bureaucracy, or by some faction in the bureaucracy. We would know a lot more about the workings of Soviet society if we knew precisely, for instance, how a given article like Liberman's or Trapeznikov's gets into the Soviet press. Who suggests that Liberman or Trapeznikov write it? Who decides that such ideas as theirs should be opened to debate at a particular time?

In any case, we can see a relation between Soviet social developments and the functions of the mass media. As a marketplace of ideas, the press serves several purposes. First, it subjects broad schemes to the test of analysis and criticism before they are officially adopted, if they are. The bugs are worked out. Possible effects and repercussions are pinpointed. The start of the economics debate by Liberman, only to be broken off for two years, suggests that opposition had to be overcome in some quarters before the discussion could be resumed in public. Second, the political establishment does not become clearly identified with a proposal until it has been refined, and until it has gained a currency. Third, public discussion draws many people into the decision-making process, giving them a sense of participation in affairs of state.

Soviet leaders need public support, advice from specialists, and some understanding of a problem's dimensions. They unquestionably try to manage exchange of opinion in order to generate popular acceptance of new concepts. But management of opinion is a difficult art, and is imperfectly practiced, as contrasted to sheer suppression of opinion. It is hard to steer discussions and debate into predetermined channels without emptying them of creative thought. And of course at some point imaginative discussion becomes more valuable to political management than the recitation of stale formulas. The problem is identical to that of the American business executive. While "yes men" are useful in establishing a power base, they are not of much help in resolving complex problems. Creative, independent minds are. But they also resist impediments to free discussion.

Two kinds of debate and discussion occur in the Soviet press. One is the open controversy. Besides the one on economic reform, there have been others on farm problems, city planning and development, air and water pollution, education, law, crime prevention, the arts, and the role of the press itself.[28] In these discussions, there is clear give and take. One view clashes with another. Two or more interest groups are at odds. The second type of dispute, more difficult to detect, takes place in upper echelons of power. In these controversies, so far as we can fathom them, basic foreign and domestic policies are challenged or formulated through speeches, reports, and editorial statements appearing in newspapers and periodicals.[29] In the fall of 1967, for instance, there were some sparks over the financing of Soviet rural renewal, with subtle differences of opinion appearing in *Kommunist*, the Communist Party's leading theoretical journal, in its newspaper *Pravda,* and in the government paper, *Izvestia*.[30] Differing from open discussion, the debate-by-innuendo involves major political authorities and is conducted in an Aesopian language understandable fully only to the informed.[31]

However conspicuous or concealed the discussion, it is nonetheless evident that the Soviet mass media have become a forum for opposing views. Indeed, western analysts of Soviet affairs identify certain publications with particular interest groups or attitudes. The Soviet literary monthly *Novy Mir* unquestionably represents the "liberals" or "progressives" of the Soviet literary community, for instance, while another journal, *Oktyabr*, speaks for the "conservatives" or "traditionalists."

Along with greater discussion has come a more critical press. The two are closely related, of course. Much debate in the Soviet press simultaneously challenges entrenched practices and viewpoints. But as a social critic, the press is also the watchdog. Throughout Soviet history, this has been one of its assigned tasks, though the energy and independent initiative have not always been there. Broadly speaking, the mass media focus on policy implementation, rather than on policy itself. And as critics, the big, important newspapers like *Pravda* and *Izvestia* range more freely than the local weeklies. In either case, the press searches for flaws in the social machinery. It exposes corruption, incompetent management, and inept government. The national press, because of its prestigious position, takes on government ministries for backsliding on new policies or production plans. The regional press directs its fire toward local government, industry, and agriculture. Acting on "signals"—news tips and complaints—from readers, newspaper correspondents investigate allegations of injustice, highhanded bureaucracy, and bungled planning. The press does not get consistently positive reactions. The undying complaint of political leadership, which has a vital stake in exposing weaknesses, is that large and small bureaucracies pay only lip service to press criticism. Yet the Soviet mass media, somewhat as in the United States, are an outside check on performance of other social institutions.

Their contributions to society in this job are fairly familiar. As critic, the press spots symptoms of what may be serious problems. It maintains broad surveillance over government programs, and in effect reports back on their success or failure. Further, the mass media provide a channel for popular grievances, also obviously a form of criticism. These Soviet social managers need to know if they are to maintain some national harmony and stability.

The quandary from the political leadership's point of view is always how to channel criticism, how to limit the mass media's independent probing of society's anatomy. One can argue that the Soviet press, out of its alliance with the political bureaucracy, is effectively compromised. In some particulars this is true. The Soviet editor, like the corporation vice-president for public relations, generally has the political management's outlook. But the picture is not so neatly drawn. The Soviet political bureaucracy is not a single glacial mass moving inexorably in one direction. Nor does the Soviet journalist corps march robot-like to commands. There are divergencies of opinion within political ranks, and inevitably therefore in the Soviet press. The government hierarchy then can only set down general operating procedures for the press, and from that point reward and punish performance.

Thus, as social critics, Soviet journalists acquire a sense of what is fair game for public attack, and what areas are reserved. In the latter—immune from open, concerted press criticism—are current political leaders, the Communist Party as an institution, the military machine, communism as a system, Soviet foreign policy, and some standard values or ideals (unity of the party and people, the collective, and patriotism, for example). At the other extreme, bureaucracy, corruption, failure to reach production targets, inefficient management, poor consumer service, and the like, call down the wrath of the Soviet press as instantly and automatically as American newspapers descend on congressional junketing or pilfering from public funds. In between are gray areas. In recent years, the Soviet press has raised doubts about conventional attitudes toward labor mobility, performance of the Soviet parliament, crime prevention, and computerized economic planning. In probing these areas, the Soviet press is less the watchdog than the critic at large. Its role here has enlarged to the degree that Soviet society has become more complex and less responsive to central commands.

Educator and Reporter

The business of mass communications is to disseminate information within a society. Some information moves from the field to command posts, from the mass population to decision-making centers. Some moves from institution to institution, and from one interest group to another. Every society needs information, and the more integrated its economy and politics, the more it takes on the look of the modern, urban nation— large cities, massive industry, disciplined work force, rail and road networks, and so on—the more information required. And the reverse; without a constant flow of information, the modern urban nation cannot be built. Schramm, in his studies of information in developing countries, suggests:

> It is generally the increasing flow of information that plants the seed of change . . . by keeping the *national* goals and the *national* accomplishments always before the public—thus modern communications, widely used, can help to weld together isolated communities, disparate subcultures, self-centered individuals and groups, and separate developments into a truly national development.[32]

From its beginnings, the Soviet press has been engaged in this process. By the mid-1920's, after the Bolshevik Revolution and the civil war, the Soviet state was made up of dozens of separate nationalities, a generally illiterate peasantry, a factory work force with primitive skills, and the forerunners of new institutions (national planning agencies, for example) about which people knew very little. Given the broad national objectives of industrial development and establishing a new political system, the overriding challenge was to impart to the population the attitudes and skills necessary to achieve these goals.

Once a revolutionary remaking of a society is set in motion, the need for information burgeons. The peasant who farms as his father, and his father before, who consumes much of what he grows, and sells the remainder in his own village, neither demands nor needs much knowledge. But introduce a tractor into this setting: the peasant suddenly needs technical information. He must know how to repair and maintain the machine, how to use it effectively. The tractor implies an exchange of goods between far separated points, between city and village. Whether he owns his own land or manages state farms, the peasant needs information about finance and accounting as the farm changes into a business. The new information abets changes that demand still more information. As long as a society is expanding, developing, thrusting outward, the flow of information grows. It can reach the point, as it has in the United States, where whole industries are occupied in the electronic filing, cataloging, and retrieving of vast stores of information.

The mass media do identical work. They collect information about things, events, and people, and distribute the findings in appealing, easily digestible form to a mass audience. Clearly, there are varied forms. Foreign analysts are impressed, generally unfavorably, by the Soviet mass media's practice of instructing their audiences in what to think or how to accept information. Sometimes instructions seem to outweigh information. Or perhaps it is that the same instructions are so consistently repeated. Yet, in whatever form, the Soviet press devotes most of its time and resources to disseminating information.

A major segment is educational or instructive. *Pravda* is the only leading world newspaper in which a tenth of a given day's issue may be devoted to a single factory's experience with a new cost accounting procedure, or to a state farm's experiment with an incentive system. The equivalent in the American press would be half a dozen pages in a major newspaper describing a business group's success in downtown renewal. Soviet mass media, probably to the great boredom of many of their audience, issue a stream of "how to" articles and broadcasts. One can learn how to manage a farm, how to increase labor productivity, how to improve customer service in a department store, how to enter a university, or how to construct an apartment building.

Such information comprises in effect a vocational school in which the uneducated are taught to live and produce in an industrializing society. That such information appears in the mass media reveals the priorities established by the party-government apparatus for the press. While light, entertaining articles rate higher in Soviet audience surveys, the political leadership obviously regards the mass media as more important for the skills and methods they can impart. It is concerned at every point, including the press, with directing popular attitudes and habits in the direction of a modern society that functions smoothly and harmoniously. By widely disseminating instructive information, the press helps create mass standards and procedures among citizens.

Other information provided in the Soviet press falls into the category of "useless" facts—isolated statistics, little-known events or places—which is the kind of material published as "fillers" in American newspapers. To mention briefly some other groupings, one finds in the Soviet mass media information on "peoples of other lands," products and technology, strange occurrences, the weather, scientific discoveries, and new books, plays, and films. This potpourri hardly exhausts the list. It merely suggests the wide range of necessary and useful information that flows from one point to another in Soviet society through the mass media.

A share of the flow is "news," factual reporting of events within the Soviet Union and abroad. Much of this information, as mentioned before, is also interwoven with interpretation, bias, and opinion. And for that, it presents a particular and often grossly detached picture of reality, much like American television commercials. The new model automobile, adorned with an attractive girl, rolling effortlessly through a wooded countryside, is not what most people know. All the same, the television viewer receives information, at the least what the new car looks like. Soviet audiences are exposed to an enormous amount of information the same way. They are also offered information of a purely utilitarian, pragmatic nature. Changes in transportation schedules, new work regulations, alterations in pension or medical programs and the like are all facts that help people in their daily routines.

A particularly noticeable category of Soviet mass media information is "nonnews" or "noninformation." American audiences are accustomed to the mass media announcing what has changed since yesterday, how the world is different today, and how it may alter tomorrow. Some of the most important "news" in the Soviet press, by contrast, tells the people that nothing has changed, that all is well with the world. For example, Khrushchev's removal from power created anxiety in the Soviet Union. What course would the new leadership take? Apprehension was quelled a few days later when *Pravda* published an editorial that reaffirmed decisions of the 20th Communist Party Congress in 1956 and the 22nd in 1961. This editorial told the Soviet people that the new leadership would follow policies on "peaceful coexistence" and the "cult of the individual." In short, Khrushchev's overthrow was not a neo-Stalinist coup. A part of the Soviet mass media's daily outpouring is of this nature. It merely conveys, in repeating certain phrases and ideas, a sense of stability and calm. In 1963, when the Soviet Union suffered an especially bad grain harvest, there were shortages of food throughout the country and the Soviet Union ultimately had to import foreign grain. The press, however, revealed nothing of the grain problem at the time. There were no alarming articles, no excited news reports. During the Cuban missile crisis in 1962, the tone of the Soviet press changed only slightly, although for a few days the Soviet Union and the United States bordered on nuclear war. Or, as a last example, when Soviet-led forces invaded Czechoslovakia in August, 1968, the Soviet mass media understated the huge military movement to the extent that it appeared that a small force had entered Czechoslovakia at the request of the Prague government.

It should be emphasized that not all information concerning important events is presented in tranquil terms in the Soviet press. However, the mass media are consciously used at times to prevent public excitement and agitation.

Mass Entertainer and Merchandiser

Like Soviet public life, the mass media seem everlastingly serious, and often just plain ponderous and dull. They preach and sermonize. Soviet journalists consider "sensationalism" cheap, profit-hungry journalism. What Soviet journalists are discovering, however, is that one does not have to be dull to treat important, serious topics. And gradually, over the last few years, Soviet journalists have tried to liven up the mass media. One compelling reason is that some initial readership and viewership studies suggest poor audience reaction. Another, less measurable, quantity is the change of Soviet society. A postwar generation wants diversion and entertainment. There is more time and money to devote to these. Clothes fashions, touring, hobbies, sports, hair styles—in contrast to steel production quotas, Marxism-Leninism, and agricultural technology—interest Soviet men and women the greater their leisure time and incomes.

Thus, along with the weighty subjects, the Soviet mass media offer an increasing amount of light reading and entertainment. A segment of most national newspapers, even *Pravda*, is devoted to sports. They traditionally have published feuilletons, and among the foreign journalists most frequently reprinted is the American satirist Art Buchwald. Soviet periodicals do much more now with women's fashions than ten years ago. Light fiction and poetry, most of it undistinguished, are fairly standard in Soviet newspapers.

Soviet television got off to a bad start in a way because it mimicked the printed press. Thus, there are bland, scripted round-table discussions that sound like a *Pravda* editorial. Documentaries take Soviet television viewers through a paper-making process. Films glorify the Soviet Revolution. But there is a clear awareness that programming must be improved. And there is some feeling that Soviet television should, after all, provide sheer entertainment, as well as information and education. One can read into this ulterior motives. Television, and the printed media, will be more influential and persuasive if they hold audiences. American newspapers share this attitude, of course, and American television is largely entertainment for the obvious reason that it attracts an audience for commercials. From this point of view, the Soviet mass media have a message, too, and the political bureaucracy has reason to present the message attractively. There is nothing inherently different between promoting the idea of consumption and the concept of collective labor. American advertising has been considerably more successful than Soviet, but the mass media in both countries (and elsewhere of course) are engaged in the same work.

While the Soviet press has long been a merchandiser of ideas, it has little experience or inclination toward merchandising products. The Soviet mass media are just beginning to be transformed by commercial advertising as we know it, and to affect the Soviet economy in return. Development of advertising has been retarded because of the longtime prevalence of a seller's market in the Soviet Union. However, as consumer goods become more plentiful, managers of consumer industries and retail trade networks are wrestling with the problems of sales. They are therefore turning to the mass media, partly to create demand and partly to inform the buying public of what goods are available where. As the consumer goods industry becomes larger and more varied in the Soviet Union, the mass media will be increasingly used as merchandisers. In turn, Soviet editors and broadcasters, we can suppose, will be under still further pressure to produce newspapers and programs that will attract an audience. One probable consequence of the existing trend is that the Soviet mass media, now wholly dependent on subscription income and government subsidies, will become more closely associated with the state-owned industries and retail agencies. Of course, such an alliance would constitute a radical change for the Soviet press. And it should be emphasized that in the context of Soviet society, new commercial relations of the mass media do not imply absence of political or government management.

In general, what we can see is the Soviet mass media moving away from the most detailed direction by the political bureaucracy toward something like the enlightened American corporate house organ that feels less compelled to praise management. To see how the mass media arrived at this point we should go back in Soviet history in more detail. From the history of the Soviet press, one can understand what was envisioned by the Bolsheviks, what was instituted by Stalin, what was changed in the Khrushchev years, and thus why the Soviet mass media perform as they do today.

CHAPTER 2

FROM REVOLUTION TO REFORM

OF THE THREE Soviet leaders—Vladimir Lenin, Joseph Stalin, and Nikita Khrushchev—whose thoughts and actions have had a strong impact on the Soviet press system, Lenin ranks first by far. There are perhaps three reasons for his overriding influence. First, he was certainly more a theoretician than either Stalin or Khrushchev and his interpretations of the role of the press in achieving and maintaining political power proved of lasting use. Second, by his own journalistic career as well as by his writings, Lenin cast the model for a Soviet centralized press system and so exercised the influence of precedent. And third, deliberate deification of Lenin after his death in 1924 made his views on the press, and most other subjects, sacred writ.

It was Stalin's lot to use Lenin's theories in practical matters of establishing a new state. His contribution to press theory was small, as it was to Marxism-Leninism in general. To Stalin goes the dubious credit of exaggerating the most restrictive interpretation of the role of a publicly owned press in Soviet society, and of developing a network of newspapers, under strict government censorship and Communist Party control, to propagate state policies and mobilize a people. If Lenin supplied the ideas, Stalin applied them. It was he who really built the mass media structure, incorporating, as it turned out, dullness, conformity, and purposefulness.

Khrushchev, too, had nothing strikingly original to propose to Soviet press theory. But in contrast to Stalin's scorn for dissension, which resulted in a mouthpiece press, Khrushchev's more flexible nature led him to loosen controls, so that to some extent the Soviet press became a marketplace of ideas. While never denying that the press was an arm of the party, Khrushchev acknowledged implicitly that it was a social force in itself and that by serving, within bounds, as a forum for discussion, it could contribute to social development. In one sense, Khrushchev turned the clock back to the 1920's, when a debate raged over the functions and form of the Soviet press system. Stalin won that debate simply because he won the concurrent political battle and achieved a position from which he could institute the repressive elements of Lenin's press theory. Khrushchev in a way reopened the discussion in the 1950's, but by then the press had become rooted in its ways and so the issue was not what form the Soviet press should take, but in which direction it should develop.

Lenin: A Rebel Press

It is inaccurate to refer to Lenin's "theory of the press," as if it were an academic treatise. His collected writings on the press, which fill a book of more than 700 pages (including, however, some very inconsequential observations and communications),[1] are more in the realm of operating principles. He worked them out during his career as a revolutionary, often to justify or plead for certain political actions. Thus, Lenin's press theory is actually a conglomeration of essays or a few paragraphs of editorials written in the heat of battle. For this reason, it is deceptive to isolate Lenin's concepts of the press from his general political philosophy. The former were a facet of the latter. Lenin's thoughts on the press were never far removed from practical politics. He seldom spoke about the ideal press of the future, but rather of what sort of newspaper should be published at the moment, how it should be directed, and what function it should serve.

As a Marxist, Lenin held the customary view that a society's economic system, dominated by one class, chiefly determined its legal and political institutions. In the Marxist interpretation, capitalists comprised that class in nineteenth- and early twentieth-century Russia. In Lenin's view, they therefore managed the press in a loose-jointed arrangement that assured press loyalty to monarchy and capitalism. Russian newspapers and journals were, in fact, private enterprise. But it was gross exaggeration to suppose that they therefore unanimously endorsed the existing social order, for they did not.[2] What one could say was that the mass press was tied in with the Russian economic and political structure, and that the Russian government regularly tried to suppress opposition newspapers and periodicals.

Lenin's view that the press served the dominant class was not original to him. But it was of singular importance to later Soviet press development. For from it sprang two ideas. First, it was considered entirely justifiable (as well as politically expedient) after the 1917 Bolshevik seizure of power to deny elements loyal to the old order access to the press. The press had passed into the control of the proletariat. Second, freedom of the press was interpreted from another point of view. It was not only a matter, the Bolsheviks said, of everyone's right to say what he would in the press, but of management of the economic structure of the press—of newsprint production and allocation, use of printing equipment and buildings, and distribution. The two were inseparable. He who owned the means of producing newspapers determined who said what to whom. In his early years, Lenin *acted* as if he believed this. But only in 1917, just before the Bolshevik Revolution, did he put the idea explicitly. It is worth quoting Lenin liberally because in one form or another the idea of economic guarantees of press freedom appears throughout the history of Soviet mass media development.

> Capitalists call "freedom of the press" that state of affairs when censorship is removed and all parties are free to publish any newspaper. In this very thing there is no freedom of the press, but freedom for the rich, the bourgeoisie to deceive the oppressed and exploited masses. . . . Publication of a newspaper is a large, income-producing capitalist enterprise in which the rich invest millions and millions of rubles. "Freedom of the press" in a bourgeois society consists in freedom of the rich systematically, unceasingly and daily in the millions of copies to deceive, corrupt and fool the exploited and oppressed masses of the people, the poor. It is asked, is it possible to fight this howling evil and how? The means is state monopoly of private advertising in newspapers. . . . It will be said, but this is destruction of freedom of the press. That is not true. This would enlarge and restore freedom of the press. For freedom of the press signifies that all opinions of *all* citizens may be stated. And now? Now only the rich and the large parties have this monopoly.
>
> Besides with publication of large Soviet [workers' council] newspapers, with all the advertising, there would be full guarantee of expression of opinion to a very much greater number of citizens, say, to every group collecting a certain number of subscriptions. Freedom of the press would in this case become a great deal more democratic, would become incomparably fuller. . . . State authority in the name of the Soviets will take *all* printing plants and *all* paper and distribute them justly, first to the

government in the interests of the majority of the people, the majority of the poor, especially the majority of the peasants . . . second, to the large parties, polling, say, in both capitals a hundred thousand or two hundred thousand votes; and third, to the smaller parties and to any groups of citizens, attaining a certain number of members or collecting a certain number of subscriptions.[3]

Lenin never quite formulated the particulars of a government-owned press. He simply envisioned a general scheme, derived from Marxist programs, by which the masses would be assured access to newspapers. And, once the Bolsheviks were in a position to put the ideal into practice, politics interfered. From the beginning of Lenin's career as a revolutionary, the quandary was the same. Revolution in his mind demanded disciplined thought and action. In the main, Lenin tended toward unanimity of opinion rather than diversity. This was scarcely compatible with the pluralistic press he talked of in 1917.

The Russia of Lenin's lifetime, beginning in 1870, was an empire dying. Revolution and reform were the talk among Russia's young intellectuals in St. Petersburg, Moscow, and in the provinces. Marxists feuded with other factions of socialists. Constitutionalists, monarchists, populists, and anarchists mingled and contended in an undercurrent of rebellion. There was an electrifying awareness that an old system was giving way. One broad political movement battled for reform, for constitutional democracy; a second for revolution, for a wholly new social order. Lenin joined with the second. In the mid-1890's, as a young lawyer, Vladimir Ilich Ulyanov became active in St. Petersburg Marxist circles. Russia's industrial revolution was under way. Worker discontent generated demands for shorter working hours, higher pay, and welfare benefits. Nicholas II was crowned czar in 1894 and pledged to preserve autocracy. The inability of this gentle man to move forcefully and rapidly toward reform created its own political reaction.

Marxists, among others, agitated for civil rights, economic welfare, and overthrow of the monarchy. In St. Petersburg, Lenin helped establish a Marxist political organization, the League of the Struggle for the Emancipation of the Working Class. The league made plans to publish an underground newspaper, *Rabocheye Delo*. But in December, 1895, just as the first issue was ready for printing, police arrested nearly all of the league leaders, including Lenin. He later reminisced that the newspaper was intended to draw information from broad ranks of workers and unite their "strike campaign with the revolutionary movement against autocracy."[4] The consequence for Lenin of the newspaper project was 14 months in a St. Petersburg jail, and three years exile in a Siberian village, Shushenskoye. There, until his return to European Russia in 1900, Lenin busied himself with completing his first major work, "The Development of Capitalism in Russia," corresponding with friends and family, reading and planning his future political career. Toward the end of 1899, Lenin began formulating a scheme for a national or all-Russian newspaper. The impetus was a proposed revival of *Rabochaya Gazeta*, defunct newspaper of the Russian Social-Democratic Labor Party. Formed in 1898 to unite Russia's disjointed Marxist organizations, the party itself was still far from a going concern.

Lenin argued that a newspaper could be the center of revolutionary thought and action. The newspaper, in Lenin's view, was simultaneously an institution and a means of communication and persuasion. There was no single body of theory that could be presented consistently to the working masses and make them conscious—a favorite word of Lenin's—of their political and economic interests in overthrowing autocracy. These were not original thoughts. As in American revolutionary times, journalism and partisan politics merged in Russia. *Rabochaya Gazeta* had said in one issue: "We think that our newspaper is needed now not only because it will discuss all questions about the labor movement here and abroad, but because it will unite Russian workers. . . ."[5] What separated Lenin's concept from current political journalism was its particular emphasis on the newspaper and its staff as a cohesive political organization. Thus in three articles written for *Rabochaya Gazeta* (which never was revived), Lenin pledged: "We will readily devote space in our newspaper for articles on theoretical questions, with the invitation to all comrades to discuss debatable points openly."[6] And at another point, he contended that the chief means to develop a political program and tactics was "a party organ published regularly and linked with all groups . . . without such an organ, local work will remain provincial. The formation of a party—if this party is not properly represented by a well-known newspaper—remains to a significant degree just words."[7]

These ideas carried over as Lenin made plans to found a new publication. A second meeting of the Russian Social-Democratic Labor Party had been proposed for May, 1900. Lenin and several other associated revolutionists were to be nominated as the editorial board which would manage *Rabochaya Gazeta.* Out of this came a statement of purpose for what eventually was known as *Iskra,* a celebrated underground newspaper in Russian revolutionary history. It would be a national newspaper, drawing together diverse Marxist organizations, Lenin said. There was one obvious problem. While Lenin was in exile, a number of local Social-Democratic committees or groups had emerged, some with their own newspapers. They were not likely to merge into a central organization that promised suppression of their views. Lenin tactfully proposed that local newspapers could usefully publicize differing opinions among party workers, while the central newspaper would be responsible for broad theory and practice.[8] The problem of divergent opinions within the party always threatened. Before the first issue of *Iskra* appeared, its statement of purpose had been changed, partly under pressure of old-guard Russian Marxists with whom Lenin was allied for a time. The revision came out: "We do not intend to make our organ an ordinary storehouse of diverse views. We will conduct it, on the contrary, in a spirit of a strict, definite school of thought. This school can be expressed in a word: Marxism."[9]

By this time, Lenin had returned from exile, made contact with local Social-Democratic organizations, and settled in Europe. It was there that *Iskra* was printed and then smuggled by ingenious means into Russia. Writing as an *Iskra* editor, Lenin insisted that the newspaper could transform the "several local movements into a single national movement." It should be a political publication, through which all dissatisfaction and protest could be concentrated. It could nurture the revolutionary movement. The laboring class, Lenin said, was prepared to accept and support the struggle, "and we have an obligation to create a forum to publicly unmask the czarist government; . . . through the proletariat, the newspaper will penetrate ranks of the urban middle class, the rural craftsmen and peasants and will become an authentic national, political newspaper."[10] Borrowing a thought from the German Marxist Wilhelm Liebknecht, Lenin argued that a newspaper not only was a propagandist and agitator, but a collective organizer.[11] Moreover, there had to be a guaranteed flow of information about the revolutionary movement to the center, and a reliable means to deliver the party newspaper. These requirements, Lenin said, compelled "creation of a network of local agents of a single party, agents actively in touch with one another, aware of the general situation, accustomed to systematically executing minute functions of national political work."[12] These agents would form the "skeleton" of the party organization. There would be sufficient numbers to cover the country. They would be resourceful, capable of acting independently when necessary, but they also would accept iron discipline. Lenin's ideas were by no means unanimously accepted. He defended them at length in a monograph, *Chto Delat?* (*What To Do?*) published in 1902, in which he pressed for creation of a national revolutionary organization centered in a newspaper staff.

The root issue was Lenin's demand for centralization of both political activity and doctrinal interpretation. His own rigidity and determination led eventually to a split in the Social-Democratic Party, at its second congress in 1903. Differences erupted over the formation of *Iskra*'s editorial board, and over party organization and tactics. Lenin championed an elite, centralized party. When the congress was concluded, the party was divided, Lenin leading the majority, the Bolsheviks, against the minority, the Mensheviks.[13] Not long afterwards, the Mensheviks gained control of *Iskra* and Lenin subsequently established another newspaper, *Vpered,* to combat the Mensheviks and promote his own strategy for revolution. He was to be editor and/or contributor for dozens of other newspapers after that.[14] These newspapers, it should be noted, ordinarily were modest in size. Many of the legal and underground publications, of the Bolsheviks and other political organizations, were short-lived. *Vpered* lasted five months; only 18 issues were put out. Then, under another name, *Proletarii*, it was made the official newspaper of the Social-Democrats, and continued publication in Geneva until November, 1905. Typically, the newspaper's editorial staff was composed of leading party members, as was the case with *Vpered* and *Iskra*. The party press was a fact of life in Russia, whatever one's politics. If a newspaper was not clearly associated with a political party, it ordinarily had clear political leanings.

By the end of 1905, Russia was in the midst of radical reform. Russia's defeat by Japan in 1904 had created great discontent. New political parties were forming. One, the Socialist Revolutionary Party, advocated adoption of agrarian socialism. Another, the Constitutional Democratic Party, pressed for parliamentary government. In January, 1905, czarist troops at the Winter Palace fired on a crowd of petitioners led by Father Gapon. The incident became known as "Bloody Sunday." In

October, 1905, strikes spread across Russia. The nation was almost paralyzed. Nicholas II issued a manifesto making Russia a constitutional monarchy, and promising greater authority for the state duma, or parliament. A liberal program of reform was begun, extending to civil rights. Freedom of the press was broadened, though many restrictions remained. There were penalties, for example, for disseminating untrue reports about government agencies and officials.[15]

Lenin returned to Russia from Europe in November, 1905, and helped establish a legal Bolshevik newspaper, *Novaya Zhizn*, which lasted about a month. With relaxation of government press controls, Lenin more forcefully advocated the unity of Bolshevik publishing activities. "All party literature, local as well as central, must without questions be subordinated to the party congress and the corresponding central or local party organization," he demanded. "The existence of party literature not connected . . . with the party is impermissible."[16] A few months earlier, he had chastised Moscow Bolsheviks for making insufficient use of the then official Bolshevik newspaper, *Proletarii*, in their own publication. He wanted local newspapers to reprint slogans and articles from *Proletarii* and to create the attitude among workers that it was "their own ideological center."[17]

By this time, Lenin's views on the press were set. He was engrossed with forming and developing a tightly knit, highly disciplined political party. There were hard reversals. Lenin compromised when he thought it tactically necessary. The Bolshevik-Menshevik warring went on, newspapers being a prime weapon. Various Social-Democratic newspapers were begun. Some lasted a few months, others managed to stay alive for several years. *Sotsial-Demokrat*, one of many central organs of the Russian Social-Democratic Labor Party, survived from 1908 to 1917. *Pravda*, the predecessor of today's official Soviet Communist Party newspaper, first appeared in May, 1912. Joseph Stalin, still relatively undistinguished and unknown, was among *Pravda*'s organizers. *Pravda* published for two years, and was revived in 1917.[18] Leon Trotsky, who later battled with Stalin, produced his own *Pravda* in Geneva from 1908 to 1912. Mensheviks, Socialist Revolutionaries, Constitutional Democrats, among others, all had their publications. And they were all centers of political advocacy and organization. Contests were waged over editorial control of newspapers because among the revolutionary parties they were virtually synonymous with the party itself.

The feverish political and journalistic activity reflected mounting discontent in Russia, the increase in literacy, and an industrial development which swelled worker ranks. Russia's entry into World War I in 1914 diverted the nation temporarily, and the people united under the czar. But by 1916, the toll of lives, economic strains of the war, and lack of fundamental political reform conspired to weaken Russia's monarchy. In March, 1917, the czarist government collapsed, Nicholas II abdicated, and a provisional government came to power. Over the following eight months, until the Bolshevik seizure of power, the government attempted to fight the war, and institute wide-scale social reforms. Russia was declared a republic, and a constituent assembly was to be selected to formulate a new political structure. Meanwhile, the provisional government struggled for support among impossibly diverse political factions. The Soviet of Workers' and Soldiers' Deputies in Petrograd (the new name of Russia's capital) had gained authority with the March Revolution. An unwieldy conglomeration of professional revolutionists and workers, it had been formed in 1905. In 1917, it functioned almost as a second government, such was its power and such the instability of the provisional government. In July, a brief but serious uprising occurred in Petrograd. The cry was all power to the Soviets, whose leadership was at that time dominated by Mensheviks. The uprising was put down, but dissatisfaction grew throughout Russia. The nation was war weary. Economic conditions worsened. Revolutionary parties vied for control of the government, or agitated for a new, socialist government.

In these circumstances, Bolsheviks gained control of the Petrograd Soviet, With a majority on the executive committee and with Trotsky as chairman of its policy-making presidium, the Bolsheviks withdrew support from the provisional government. Plans were made for an armed revolution. It came swiftly and with little bloodshed in Petrograd on the night of November 6–7. A congress of Soviets established a new executive agency, the Council of People's Commissars. Lenin was chairman. Trotsky was named commissar for foreign affairs, and Stalin, commissar for nationalities. The Bolsheviks' next order of business was to consolidate power, and the press was to be one means to that end.

By 1917, Lenin had formed clear views on the press. They derived as much from practice as from theory. In Lenin's political career and writings, the press was never considered an independent institution. Lenin's first experience with a newspaper, in St. Petersburg with the abortive *Rabocheye Delo*, suggested that it was an instrument and expression of a political organization. Its function was to consolidate a political movement. In this, however, the press served a dual role. First, it was an organization center for professional party members. Without a newspaper, there was no party machinery. In Lenin's mind, the newspaper and the party were one and the same. Second, the newspaper rallied mass support for political action. It was to connect the proletariat to the center. Lenin envisioned the newspaper simultaneously as a corporate institution and a medium of communication.

In both roles the newspaper informed and educated. It was to supply reports of current events interpreted from a distinct ideological viewpoint. The mass political newspaper thereby would form a united movement with common outlooks and objectives. Lenin's attitude was that a newspaper gave its readers what they should know, for their own salvation. What a newspaper printed therefore was selected with a preconceived end in mind. Facts and opinion were measured against their relevance to an ultimate goal.

"Freedom of the press," in the sense of absence of government restrictions and guarantees for dissenting opinion, was subordinate in Lenin's view to the political movement. Lenin approved of discussion, but not of fundamental dissent from Marxist theory, or for that matter, from Bolshevik strategy in the critical moments. Lenin's political experience showed him that a newspaper represented a faction; his Marxist outlook led him to believe that the press served a particular social class. Lenin's call on the eve of revolution was therefore for nationalization of printing plants and newsprint in the interests of the workers' state and the proletariat. The latter was to be led by a select political apparatus possessing scientific knowledge of laws of social development—that is, the Bolshevik Party. The "people's press" would be the servant of mass society. Such was Lenin's vision. Yet, Lenin's political instinct was to gain monopoly control of the press first.

A Bolshevik Press: Formative Years

The Bolshevik Party seized power in Russia on November 7, 1917. The next day, acting without any elective authority, the Military Revolutionary Committee, which had been set up on the eve of the Bolshevik Revolution to command the uprising, closed a number of Petrograd newspapers from which immediate opposition was anticipated.[19] Two days later, on November 10, the Bolshevik-controlled Council of People's Commissars issued a brief but sweeping decree that authorized the council to suppress temporarily or permanently any newspapers urging "open resistance or insubordination to the workers' and peasants' government," creating confusion by "means of clearly slanderous distortion of facts," or advocating criminal acts. This decree was to be rescinded when "normal conditions" prevailed once more.[20] To extend its authority over the press further in these first hectic, postrevolutionary days, the Council of People's Commissars then declared on December 1 that all advertising was a state monopoly, an action that attempted to carry out Lenin's demand made in the early fall of 1917. The decree was a thorough and, as it turned out, overambitious effort to deprive all newspapers except those selected by the Bolshevik Party of any financial support. Newspaper publishers or businesses dealing with advertising were instructed, under threat of confiscation of property and prison sentences, to divert all announcements and income from them to the government. The decree was effective as of December 5. That same day, when it was apparent that few if any conformed to the order, the council instructed the Commissariat for Press Affairs vigorously to enforce the decree, and all newspapers illegally containing advertising on December 5 were ordered closed.[21]

Seizure of printing plants was made legal on February 18, 1918, when a Revolutionary Tribunal of the Press was established and given broad authority over all publishing activity. Composed of three persons, the tribunal had power to investigate "crimes and misdemeanors by use of the press." Included under this general category were "communications with untrue or distorted information on public affairs, so far as they are an encroachment on the rights and interests of the revolutionary people, as well as violations of laws on the press published by the Soviet state." Decisions by the press tribunal were not subject to review by higher authority. The tribunal was not supposed to punish individuals, only publications. But the interpretation given to its activity by the Council of People's Commissars included the right to subject to arrest or exile persons who had written "counterrevolutionary" articles. The three-man agency also had power to levy fines, order the retraction of newspaper reports it considered objectionable, close publications temporarily or permanently, and confiscate equipment.[22] Somewhat later, on August 20, 1918, a general decree prohibited private ownership of land, and in cities of buildings above a certain value as fixed by local authorities. The decree thus provided for confiscation of publishing plants over and above previous directives.[23]

These immediate attempts to superimpose Bolshevik authority over the existing Russian press sytem were, like most actions those early months after the revolution, born of pragmatism and baptized by theory. The objective was simply to get things under control. The actions were not entirely on paper. Some newspapers were closed at once, and others not in full sympathy with Bolshevik forces were published under the constant threat of suppression. Even before the special Revolutionary Tribunal on the Press was created, its parent agency, the Military Revolutionary Committee, conducted investigations of newspapers that printed articles considered hostile to the Soviet state.[24] In the spring of 1918, several Moscow newspapers were closed by the city government and Commissariat for Press Affairs for opposing the peace treaty with Germany that took Russia out of World War I.[25]

But subjugation of the opposition press was not achieved as easily as a description of decrees might indicate, nor were decrees as effective as Lenin hoped. Several years later, at a Moscow party meeting in October, 1921, he acknowledged with characteristic candor that the decree declaring advertising a state monopoly "remained empty paper" and that the directive was "naive and in a certain sense mistaken," although he conceded that it conformed with overall efforts to establish a socialist state.[26]

Of greater significance were protests from other political factions and within the Bolshevik Party itself against the decree on the press which authorized closure of newspapers. Published in *Pravda* and *Izvestia*, the decree was written and signed by Lenin, who defended it as a temporary and extraordinary measure in the interests of the people against the "bourgeois" enemy.

"Everyone knows that the bourgeois press is one of the most powerful weapons of the bourgeoisie," Lenin wrote in the preface to the decree. "Especially at this critical moment, when the new state, the state of workers and peasants is consolidating itself, it is entirely impossible to leave this weapon in the hands of the enemy, at a time when it is no less dangerous than bombs and machine guns."[27]

But to many, suppression of newspapers the day after the revolution and then the decree on the press giving such actions state authority were not only a threat to publications—of Mensheviks and Socialist Revolutionaries, as well as conservative forces—but contradicted the concept of freedom of the press based on public ownership that had been described by Lenin himself. Protests resulted in a meeting on November 17, 1917, of the Bolshevik-dominated Central Executive Committee, the de facto government, to discuss press freedom and the decree in particular. Dissenters, including Yuri Larin, a former Menshevik, proposed that the suppressed newspapers be permitted to publish. Their demand was beaten down. A resolution adopted by a 34 to 24 vote reaffirmed the necessity to close hostile newspapers. Several members of the Council of People's Commissars resigned in protest. Defending the decree on the press, Lenin argued that "we declared earlier that we would close bourgeois newspapers if we took power. To tolerate the existence of these newspapers means to cease being a socialist."[28] The essence of the resolution approved by the Central Executive Committee was similar to Lenin's remarks contained in the press decree itself. Views hostile to the new Soviet government had to be restricted for the sake of survival. It further urged "confiscation of printing plants and paper supplies . . . in order that the party and groups may use the technical means of printing in accordance with their own actual ideological strength, that is, in proportion to the number of their own supporters."[29]

It is worth noting that Lenin had written a draft of this resolution which placed considerable emphasis on a publicly managed press system. The statement, somewhat different than the one finally adopted, and not published until 1932, defined freedom of the press as freedom from "oppression of capital, the transfer of paper factories and printing plants to state ownership and assignment to every group of citizens obtaining a certain membership (e.g., 10,000) equal right to use a corresponding share of paper supplies and a corresponding amount of labor for printing."[30] This concept of a publicly owned press was subsequently embodied in the first Russian constitution, approved in July, 1918. The press clause of that document read:

> In order to guarantee workers genuine freedom to express their opinions, the Russian Socialist Federated Soviet Republic abolishes dependence of the press on capital and assigns to the labor class and poor peasants all technical and material means for publishing newspapers, brochures, books and any other productions of the press and guarantees their freedom of distribution throughout the country.[31]

The circumstances in which the Bolshevik Party found itself, however, were not conducive to a publicly owned and operated press system. It was a critical time for the Bolsheviks. Not only was the country in desperate economic trouble as a result of World War I and revolution. Beginning in 1918, the fledgling government had to contend with civil war, which pitted Bolshevik forces against an array of contenders for power, some of them aided by foreign troops. Domestically, the main problems consisted in finding support for the government and bringing stability to the country. The press was considered one means to these ends, no less than it had been an instrument to achieve organization of the Bolshevik Party and stimulate opposition to the czarist and provisional governments. Thus, rather than a press under public management, Lenin emphasized the obligation of the press to help manage the public, to give wide publicity to such practical matters as labor discipline and, broadly, to devote itself to the "economic reeducation of the masses."[32] In the fall of 1918, as the civil war progressed to serious proportions, Lenin published an article on this theme in *Pravda*, then as now the party's official newspaper. He criticized Bolshevik newspapers for printing so much "political trivia," for bombast, lofty intellectual discussions, and unnecessary repetition of worn-out themes. What Lenin wanted at this time was a functional press in the sense of a vocational school for building a new society. Its primary purpose was therefore that of telling the masses of Russian workers and peasants how to run their factories and farms, what mistakes were being made, and where the most critical problems lay. Whereas before the Bolshevik seizure of power, newspapers under party control were mainly concerned with arousing hostility to the government, the Bolshevik press in 1918 was cast in the role of defending the new government and helping it supervise the state. Political matters became much less important than bringing order and stability to the economy and fighting the White armies.

"A little more economics," Lenin urged, "but economics not in the sense of 'general' discussions, scholarly reviews, intellectual plans and like trash, which unfortunately too often is only trash. No, we need economics in the sense of a collection, a careful checking and study of facts in the actual construction of a new life. Are there in fact successes in large factories, agricultural communes, committees of the poor, local economic organizations in the building of a new economy? What sort of successes are they exactly? Have they been proven? . . . How are these successes achieved?"[33]

The generally poor performance of the press as a means of public control was reiterated in March, 1919, when a congress of the renamed Communist Party (Bolsheviks) convened to adopt a new program. In the process, it surveyed the state of the press and subsequently issued a resolution, the first since the 1917 Revolution to enumerate general policy and specific instructions for the press. The newspapers under Bolshevik control already suffered from bureaucratic conformity. They published long, dull government decrees and involved articles that hardly appealed to the rank and file of workers or peasants, many of whom were illiterate and had to be read to. The goal was to bring the press under central control and deprive oppositional factions of the means to influence public opinion. Thus, in April, 1918, the government had ordered all newspapers to print on their front pages directives and instructions of the Central Executive Committee, as well as decrees of local Soviets.[34] Such acts, essential from the party's point of view to communicate its policies, worked for an uninspiring press. They also reflected Lenin's fundamental view that the press was an instrument to mobilize public opinion. For all Lenin or the Russian constitution had to say about assigning printing facilities and newspapers to political parties and groups of ordinary citizens, there were actually no steps taken to put this system into practice. Existing conditions made the ideal impractical. There was barely enough equipment and paper stock to sustain the government's press, which was of paramount political importance and took precedence over other demands. And, in its effort to consolidate power, the Bolshevik Party recoiled from diversity of opinion, which would only encourage divisions that the Bolsheviks sought to eliminate.

The important 1919 Party Congress resolution on the press was critical of newspapers on a number of counts. It emphasized that the "press is a powerful instrument of propaganda, agitation and organization."[35] Editors of party and government newspapers were instructed to staff their publications with "more responsible, more experienced party workers," and local party committees were commanded to give editorial staffs "general political directives and instructions." *Pravda* specifically was ordered to "direct the provincial press" and to give full support to party policies. Such direct party management of the press was a heritage of the Russian Social-Democratic

Labor Party's 3rd Congress in 1905, when the party newspaper was made subordinate to the Central Committee. The 8th Party Congress significantly enlarged the scope of direction, and in December, 1919, new rules gave lower party organizations explicit authority to appoint editors and direct press activities.[36] As general goals, the 8th Congress urged newspaper editors to search out instances of criminal activity in the country, to expose and criticize inefficiency in party and government organizations. Persons or institutions that came under press assaults were required to refute the criticism or explain what had been done to correct alleged errors, under threat of investigation by the Revolutionary Tribunal. The local press was reminded that to reach its mass audience it should be "lively and popular." Its content should appeal to workers, peasants, Red Army troops, women, and youth. This section of the press resolution in particular reflected the fact that the rural newspapers had become dry and dull, and were having far less effect on mass public opinion than was desired.

But there was little prospect of improving the press, chiefly because the material was not at hand. Most of the capable men who had edited or worked for Bolshevik newspapers before the revolution had been drawn into other party, government, or military duties. Newspapers were left in the hands of persons with little or no journalistic experience, often of little education and sometimes with little sympathy for Bolshevik policies. Not only journalists, but printing equipment and paper were scarce. Some newspapers had to print on wrapping paper. *Pravda* itself was cut from four to two pages during the civil war years.[37] Besides, the Bolshevik Party was not fully in command of the country and did not yet have a reliable mechanism by which to manage the press. Except for the central newspapers published by the Bolshevik Party or the Central Executive Committee in Moscow, the new capital, there was virtually no control over the existing press network beyond decrees and instructions. These were issued by various agencies, including the Commissariat on Press Affairs, the Council of People's Commissariats, the Central Executive Committee, and occasionally the Commissariat for Education, which later supervised press censorship. The Revolutionary Tribunal, which in May, 1918, absorbed its offspring—the Revolutionary Tribunal on the Press—remained in existence as a government watchdog over the press. Except for outstanding cases of anti-Bolshevik activity in the press, however, there was little that the party could do to tighten up control of newspapers. Faced with a desperate struggle for survival against hostile forces, the party was not able to extend its authority very significantly into the countryside. At best, it could try to silence the big opposition newspapers in the cities and encourage local Soviets to publish newspapers helpful to the government, but it could not very effectively enforce its desires.

In 1918, there were 884 newspapers published in Russia. Average individual circulation was 3,100 copies, and total press run was 2.7 million or about 18 newspapers per 1,000 people. By contrast, in 1913, there were 1,055 newspapers, with a total circulation of 3.3 million issues, or approximately 21 per 1,000. There were 1,472 magazines and journals published in 1913, compared with 743 in 1918.[38] These figures say nothing of course about the type, stability, or quality of publications. During Russia's civil war from 1918 through 1920, a good many were directly concerned with military matters, and they came and went with no fanfare. By the end of 1918, there were more than 90 military newspapers and magazines, and within a year that number increased to 170. On the eastern front alone, 25 military newspapers with a circulation of 250,000 were being published in October, 1919. The newly created Russian Telegraph Agency sent out teams which, operating from special boats along rivers or from "agitation trains," published small newspapers for troops.[39]

The civil war years saw the beginning of the later developed and refined press structure devised to reach particular segments of the population with special newspapers. *Pravda* was the chief publication of the country and of primary importance in party matters. Hampered by newsprint shortages, *Pravda's* circulation was erratic, From 200,000 in 1917, it plummeted to 58,000 in 1918, then rose to 238,000 two years later.[40] Besides general information, government decrees, and instructions for party members, *Pravda* had special sections for women, Red Army troops, and youths. Other central newspapers were *Izvestia*, official publication of the government, and *Bednota*, party Central Committee publication; the last was established in March, 1918, with the merger of three other newspapers, and was directed toward the peasantry. Reflecting the importance the government attached to winning peasant support and extending its authority into the countryside, *Bednota's* daily circulation was nearly 100,000 in 1918, greater than *Pravda's*.[41] There was also a special newspaper, *Zhizn Natsionalnostei*, for the non-Russian peoples of the country, and one called *Ekonomicheskaya Zhizn*, published by the Supreme Council of the National Economy and the People's Commissariat of Finance to transmit information on trade, finance, and economics. Beyond these major Bolshevik publications, there were several hundred local newspapers published by governments in provinces (*guberniya*) and districts (*uezd*), administrative regions inherited from czarist Russia. According to incomplete figures for 1920, there were 246 provincial newspapers and 334 district. In addition, the so-called "wall newspaper" made its first appearance during the civil war years. Later developed into a large network of publications, these wall newspapers were little more than bulletin boards displaying handwritten announcements, slogans, and political appeals. They were compiled in both Red Army units and industrial enterprises under the direction of party organizers.[42]

As a means of controlling information available to the press, the Bolshevik government was quick to recognize the value of news gathering agencies. By decree of September, 1918, it created the Russian Telegraph Agency, which operated under the direct supervision of the Central Executive Committee.[43] ROSTA, as it was known in the Russian abbreviation, replaced two other news agencies and was accorded a monopoly for gathering national and international information. One organization eliminated was the Petrograd Telegraph Agency, which evolved from the Russian Ministry of Finance information service set up in 1902. Subsequently renamed the St. Petersburg Telegraph Agency (and changed once more in 1914 when the Russian capital was renamed Petrograd), it was made an official government service in 1909, operating under the Russian Council of Ministers until 1917. The Bolshevik Central Executive Committee also had created an information gathering agency, called the Press Bureau, which was merged into ROSTA. The new agency was given control over all existing Russian news bureaus abroad and within the country. As for distribution of newspapers, the Bolshevik government in November, 1918, assigned the existing postal-telegraph department the responsibility of selling all party or government publications beginning December 1, 1918. And by January of the following year, it was to assume the entire job of selling subscriptions and delivering newspapers and magazines.[44]

Despite these first steps at organization, the press remained a haphazard structure. When the civil war ceased and the

Bolshevik government turned to economic recovery and political consolidation, the press system underwent radical changes.

Stalin and the Company Press

The 1920's in the Soviet Union were years of political conflict and social experimentation. Lenin's New Economic Policy —NEP—adopted in 1921 ushered in a period of economic recovery after years of foreign war, revolution, and then civil war. Lenin's death three years later intensified a succession struggle among political factions. Ultimately, the Georgian revolutionary, Joseph Stalin, was the victor, and with his full conquest of power about 1927, the Soviet Union's human and natural resources were bent to rapid industrialization. During the 1920's, the Soviet press progressed from a disorganized array of publications to a structured network of newspapers and magazines designed to reach all elements of Soviet society. Radio broadcasting began, though it remained primitive and unexploited as a means of communication and persuasion until after World War II. In broad terms, press development during the 1920's mirrored political and economic events. The party and government attempted to set up the new machinery of a socialist system, while in practice during the NEP years they were mostly working with the old. The party, divided within, struggled to gain control of the Soviet state.

As to the press specifically, political leaders were concerned with three objectives—increasing the number and circulation of newspapers, extending their influence in the provinces, and bringing the press under direct supervision of the party at the central and local levels. These aims were in harmony with general policies on economic recovery and political consolidation, and they faced the same desperate problems. The years of fighting had left Russia weary and drained. Cities and villages had been damaged. Factory production and transportation were running at slack pace. Added to this, a terrible famine struck in 1921 during which at least 5 million people perished. Though civil war had ceased, armed bands roamed the countryside. Peasant uprisings were common, and in March, 1921, Russia's new political leaders were shaken by a rebellion at the Kronstadt naval base. Armed force was required to quell the revolt. Besides direct threats to Bolshevik power, factions maneuvered within the Communist Party, and there were still remnants of other revolutionary parties to deal with.

In these conditions, creation of a "people's press" and press freedom were farthest from Lenin's thoughts. Yet they were current topics. A free press was one demand of the Kronstadt sailors. Some people recalled that the 1917 decree on the press had pledged to remove restrictions when normal times again prevailed. Of course, one could argue, as Lenin did, that these were not normal times. "We have begun to make newspapers tools for educating the masses and for teaching them how to live and how to build their own economy without landowners and capitalists," Lenin wrote in February, 1921. "Less political trivia in the press, less general discussion and abstract slogans by which the inexperienced are charmed. More propaganda for production, but most of all, more businesslike, skillful recounting of practical experience fitted to the level of development of the masses."[45] As immediately after the Bolshevik Revolution, Lenin clearly was thinking of the practical functions the press could perform in stabilizing the economy. "General discussion" was superfluous. Yet there was growing opinion among some that press freedom should be expanded, now that civil war and direct threats to Soviet power had receded. As one Soviet historian of the press has expressed it: "People were found in the party who began talking about the need of freedom of the press for all. . . . The critical statements of bourgeois newspapers, they said, would be useful to Soviet power."[46] One such was Alexander Myasnikov, a young Bolshevik rebel, who became a deputy chairman of the Caucasus Federation's Council of People's Commissars and editor of *Zarya Vostoka*. In both a report to the Communist Party Central Committee and published articles, Myasnikov argued for loyal opposition opinions in the Soviet press. His statements stirred Lenin, in August, 1921, to defend press restrictions, and to recall some of his earlier thoughts on politics and the press:

> Freedom of the press in the RSFSR, surrounded by bourgeois enemies of the whole world, is freedom of *political organization* of the bourgeoisie and its loyal servants, the Mensheviks and SR's [Socialist Revolutionaries]. . . . The bourgeoisie (the world over) is still many times stronger than we. To give it still the weapon of freedom of political organization (freedom of the press, since the press is the center and foundation of political organization) means to ease the enemy's cause, to help the class enemy. We do not desire to end in suicide and so we will not do this.[47]

Despite Lenin's adamant views, debate on press freedom lingered in the 1920's, and was not resolved finally until Stalin achieved political power. There were two main reasons. First, until Stalin eliminated his political opposition, splinter groups used newspapers to propound their views, not only on politics, but on economic development, legal theory, policy toward the peasantry, and the function of arts in a socialist society. In Leningrad, where Grigorii Zinoviev controlled the party organization, the newspaper *Leningradskaya Pravda* for a while opposed Stalin's steady ascendancy. In turn, *Pravda*, the party's official central newspaper under Stalin's influence, began an energetic campaign in 1924 in his behalf. Subsequently, in December, 1925, the Communist Party's 14th Congress gave full blessing to Stalin on several key issues, and ordered the Central Committee to "change and improve the *Leningradskaya Pravda* editorial staff."[48] Later, Trotsky, trying to repair his crumbling authority, used the press to criticize Stalin. Trotsky's opposition was ineffective. But it did give Stalin the opportunity to denounce the use of the press for dissent. In the fall and winter of 1927, he berated the operation of "illegal" printing plants and any definition of internal party democracy that would allow "freedom for a couple of intellectuals split from the revolution to talk endlessly, and to have their own printed organs."[49]

A second reason for lingering debate on press freedom stemmed from NEP. To encourage agricultural and industrial growth, a certain amount of private enterprise was generated in Russia after 1921. Concurrently, various concessions were granted to persons considered "bourgeois" or otherwise alien to socialist principles. Relaxations stimulated broad discussions in the press on important issues of the day. Within a year after NEP began, the 11th Party Congress expressed concern in the spring of 1922 about "bourgeois" influence in literature and culture. And the problem persisted. Of 678 printing plants existing in mid-1923, for example, 233 were privately owned.[50] The Russian newspaper press was a bewildering mixture of urban and provincial publications, managed by diverse organizations, and leaning in all directions. Central party control of the press was weak. This allowed for a range of opinion, even though the large, conservative prerevolutionary newspapers had been closed and publications opposed to general government policy functioned under duress. Pitched political battles and controversy over economic and cultural institutions spilled into newspapers.

Unquestionably, the trend in Russia in the early 1920's was

toward a one-party press. However, until the one party was firmly entrenched, the press remained no more or no less independent than other Russian institutions. Like all major industry in the 1920's, the press was broadly subordinate to the political order. This association implied two things: first, political convulsions affected the press, as they did Russia's whole social structure. Had factions and dissension been tolerated within the political system, the Soviet press would have developed in a radically different direction than it did. Second, the press was an object of utilitarian value. It was a means of instituting change. He who dominated the press could likewise influence what twists history would make. Thus, as Stalin captured the political machinery and therefore national purpose, the press was enlisted in his causes. And to the extent that all Soviet institutions were rigidly channeled, so the press fell victim to centralized control.

Stalin's personal views on the press derived almost entirely from politics. Intellectually inferior to Lenin, Trotsky, and other Bolshevik revolutionaries, Stalin excelled in political tactics and organization rather than in sweeping essays on social movements. His attitude toward the press was that of a battlefield commander's toward his communications and intelligence networks. The press was a weapon of struggle, a means of surveillance and information contributing to ultimate victory. Stalin's concept of the press was scarcely novel, but it was distinctive for its narrowness. One searches in vain in Stalin's writings for any suggestion that the press had a loftier function than a telegraph system. "The press," Stalin said in 1923, "is the most powerful instrument with which the party daily, hourly speaks with the laboring class in its own vital language. There exists . . . no other such flexible apparatus."[51] Stalin's thinking was further revealed in an exchange in 1923 with Sergei Ingulov, a well-known Bolshevik journalist. Editor of *Zhurnalist,* a press periodical, Ingulov contended that the press should lead public opinion and function as a watchdog for the state, exposing corruption and inefficiency. He challenged use of the press as a political control device. Stalin attacked these views. He charged that Ingulov misinterpreted Lenin's express conviction that the press was an organizational force. "It is not only that the press agitates and criticizes," Stalin declared, "but above all that it has a large network of workers, agents and correspondents throughout the country, in all industrial and agricultural areas, in all districts and villages, so that the thread from the party, through the newspaper, extends to all worker and peasant districts without exception, so that the interaction of the party and state, on the one hand, and industrial and peasant districts, on the other, is complete."[52]

As the institution of worker-peasant correspondents developed in the 1920's, Stalin characteristically looked on these amateur journalists not simply as critics, but "commanders of proletarian public opinion" in alliance with the party.[53] They were not only drawn into campaigns, but functioned as local reporters and agitators, very much as the field staff of an American political candidate. Stalin's inherent disposition to manage the press and his essentially totalitarian nature allowed for little dissension. He disciplined himself severely, and was merciless with those who opposed him. The press structure, as Stalin conceived of it, was no less immune from discipline than the party. Nor should either permit conflicting opinion to detract from overriding national goals. Stalin's fierce struggle with Trotsky, after Lenin's death in 1924, revolved on the question of who would determine these objectives. In this, Stalin's authoritarian streak and immense ego led him quite naturally to deny means of mass persuasion to any but himself and political allies. Hence, in 1927, as Trotsky's star dimmed, Stalin observed acidly that if Trotsky could use the press to promote his views, "It means the existence of several centers in the party, each having its own programs. . . . What is there left then of the iron discipline in our party?"[54]

On a broader scale, Stalin assigned the press exclusively to the "proletariat," in the traditional Marxist interpretation that he who controls a society's economic structure dominates its other institutions. In a marathon interview with foreign journalists in 1927, Stalin argued that since printing plants, newsprint enterprises, and newspaper buildings had been nationalized, the masses enjoyed freedom of the press. "We do not have freedom of the press for the bourgeoisie," Stalin said. "We do not have freedom of the press for Mensheviks and SR's, who represent here the interests of the beaten and overthrown bourgeoisie." Indeed, Stalin wondered, since the laboring class had seized power how could one "demand from the proletarian dictatorship freedom of the press for the bourgeoisie?"[55] Here Stalin put emphasis on access to the physical plant of newspaper publishing as a measure of press freedom. But that being part of an economic structure in which politics were pervasive, Stalin likewise did not imagine that press content would be unrestricted. It, too, should be planned, purposeful, and instrumental in "building socialism." The more Russia under Stalin was harnessed to that goal—which translated to mean making Russia an industrial and military world power—the more the press was construed as a means to unite Russia's various nationalities, to give the mass population a sense of common purpose, to reshape the habits and values of a largely agrarian society, and to reinforce the Communist Party and especially Stalin as the legitimate political authority.

The initiative in forming the press structure during the 1920's came directly from the party, or indirectly from the government. Parallel organizations evolved. The party's chief agency was the Central Committee, which theoretically administered the party apparatus. In 1919, however, three other agencies were formed. One was the political bureau—politburo—which became the party's policy-making center. The second was an organizational bureau—orgburo—which dealt with internal party administration. And the third was the secretariat, whose duties were at first vague, but which eventually supplanted the orgburo as manager of internal party matters.[56] Stalin served on both the politburo and orgburo, and was named party general secretary in 1922. From these bases of power, he ultimately commanded the whole party apparatus, including the secretariat. The party agencies went through numerous reorganizations in years afterward, but the Central Committee, politburo, and secretariat survived in one form or another. Many of the early directives on the press originated in the orgburo. Departments of the secretariat handled ideological and operational guidance.

The government apparatus was similar in design to the party's. The 1918 constitution provided for a national Congress of Soviets, the supreme legislative body. When it was not in session, a Central Executive Committee exercised power, and it was authorized to appoint a Council of People's Commissars. The last, composed originally of 18 commissariats, administered various branches of government. The 1924 Soviet constitution retained this structure, but as well declared the Union of Soviet Socialist Republics. By the middle of the 1920's, the various nationalities of czarist Russia had been brought or forced into a federation. Major nationalities like the Ukrainians and Byelorussians were accorded republics; others were assigned autonomous regions within republics. In sum, a nation of republics was formed under a parliamentary government. This was dominated by the party apparatus, and Soviet power thus rested with the party agencies. However, government agencies became responsible for many administrative functions. As these concerned the press, the government formally was in charge of physical plant for newspapers and magazines, and maintained press censorship. In both the party and government apparatuses, a hierarchic administration was established. At the top, of course, were the central agencies; below them the republic, then regional, district, city, and village. These were revised off and on, but the general scheme persisted.

As we have noted, the thrust of the post-civil-war years was toward a strong political center which could command not only the cities, but the Russian countryside. The press felt the impact of political consolidation. A department of agitation and propaganda, known better as *Agitprop,* was established in the party Central Committee in 1920, and in local party organizations. Its duties broadly were promotion of political themes, as well as cultural and educational programs, in both the party and government systems.[57] In November, 1921, a "special apparatus" specifically to direct and guide the press was created in *Agitprop.* Simultaneously, provincial (*guberniya*) and district (*uezd*) party committees were instructed to "take political direction" of their own newspapers and, through *Agitprop* departments, to guide the press of lower party organizations.[58] The *Agitprop* subdepartments for the press were transformed in February, 1924, into full departments in their own right under the Central Committee secretariat. This change also affected some republic and some provincial party committees,[59] and reflected a concurrent campaign to extend party control over the local press especially.

Suggesting the extent to which the Communist Party was assuming vast authority over the entire press network, the press departments were assigned full ideological supervision of newspapers and magazines in August, 1926. Specific authority ranged from recruitment of staff to checking of content to distribution. Press departments not only were to stimulate the press in actively implementing party decisions, but to maintain close surveillance of press performance. The departments also were to assess current public opinion, and when they found ignorance of party policies or special problems concerning policy implementation, they were to instruct the press accordingly. Training and appointment of journalists fell under press department authority. So did supervision of the expanding worker-peasant correspondent network. The departments were responsible for compiling party directives on press operation, subject to approval of the central press department in Moscow.[60] Thus, by 1926, the press departments had developed into the prime mechanism of party direction of the press.

In addition to the press department of the Central Committee secretariat, an information department was created in 1924. Its job broadly was to maintain control over the flow of intraparty documents, reports, decrees, and the like. It also was a source of information supplied to the press about internal party affairs. The information department published its own periodical, *Izvestia TsK RKP (b)* (*Izvestia* of the Central Committee, not to be confused with the government's newspaper by the same name). It was issued weekly, beginning in 1924, for distribution to party members. The department additionally supplied articles to *Pravda* on a fairly regular basis.[61]

That the press departments especially were not as efficient as the political hierarchy desired is evident in repeated commands from Moscow to local party committees to improve press content and make the press a more influential channel of persuasion. To the extent that local party committees were well staffed and loyal to Moscow, the press was an extension of central authorities. Yet, however well organized the control system on paper, and however energetically party members sought to put that system into practice, there were obstacles to perfection. To mention them briefly here, all through the 1920's (and after), the press suffered from a lack of experienced journalists, shortage of equipment and newsprint, and frustrating circulation problems caused by insufficient transportation and steadily mounting bureaucracy. Hence, in the 1920's no less than during later years, the party's influence on the press performance was in part real, but in part also mere declaration of intent.

Besides the party press departments, another supervisory agency emerged in the 1920's. This was *Glavlit*—the chief administration for literary and publishing affairs, an old czarist institution. Re-created by decree of the Council of People's Commissars in June, 1922, and placed under the Commissariat for Education (*Narkompros*), *Glavlit* became the chief censorship agency.[62] Exempted at first from *Glavlit* surveillance were all publications of the Comintern (established in 1919, with headquarters in Moscow), central and regional party organizations, the government newspaper *Izvestia*, state publishing house works, and those of the Academy of Sciences. Beyond these limitations, *Glavlit* could halt publication of any newspapers and periodicals (and books, maps, pictures, and drawings) which contained "anti-Soviet" statements, military secrets, pornography, or "false information" that aroused public opinion or inflamed "nationalistic and religious fanaticism." According to the 1922 *Glavlit* statute, local bureaus were to be established in all major cities. They were to censor and issue clearance—called the *Glavlit* visa—to publications. *Glavlit* worked in conjunction with the state political administration, known by its Russian initials, GPU, then the OGPU, the internal security police. The latter was responsible for combating underground publications, confiscating those prohibited by *Glavlit,* and some supervising of printing plants. Unlike its predecessor, the Cheka, the newly named GPU (1922) did not directly handle censorship.[63]

Essentially, *Glavlit* was concerned with keeping certain information out of the press. It thus complemented the party press departments, whose job was to inject particular information into the press. Because the party press and other publications were exempted from *Glavlit* censorship, the agency was at first of no consequence for a good share of the press network. Gradually, however, *Glavlit*'s authority grew, and by the mid-1930's almost all printed matter passed before the censor's eye. In conjunction with the GPU, the agency initially was an instrument by which the central authorities could suppress opposition opinion. There was no recourse to courts or appeal of any sort against *Glavlit* decisions. Its ties with the internal security police, which were virtually law unto themselves, gave *Glavlit* a particularly extensive power. It thus became the screening center not only for military secrets, but for economic and political information, and broadly speaking for the moral content of the press. It was perhaps *Glavlit,* with the inherent dullness of a bureaucracy and with suspicion of a counter-intelligence agency, that more than any other Soviet organization turned the press into a gray, monotone voice for the party and Stalin.

Among other government agencies was a Committee on the Press. Originally under the trade commissariat, it was placed in August, 1926, directly beneath the Council of People's Commissars. The press committee regulated all production, printing, and financial activities of newspapers and journals (and books), whether private or state owned. It served therefore as

management for the physical plant of the press.[64] Further, in
the realm of government, there were laws concerning press
content. The RSFSR criminal code of 1926 prohibited "propaganda or agitation inciting the overthrow, subversion or
weakening of Soviet power or the perpetration of various
counter-revolutionary crimes." The penalty was six months.
Such activity conducted on a mass scale, or playing on "religious
or nationalistic prejudices," was punishable by death.[65] Insult-
ing remarks or drawings in the press could bring six months at
forced labor or a fine up to 300 rubles. Slander—"the deliberate
distribution of falsehoods or defaming fabrications"—in the
press carried a penalty of six months hard labor and a fine of up
to 1,000 rubles. It is worth noting that the 1924 constitution,
supreme law of the newly created Soviet Union, contained no
press freedom clause (nor any other civil liberties guarantees)
as did the 1918 document. The concept of a "people's press,"
about which Lenin and even Stalin spoke, was given lip service
in various statements. But events were coursing in another
direction.

Along with party press departments and the government's
Glavlit, another mechanism for shaping press content was
the news agency. Until 1925, ROSTA—the Russian Telegraph
Agency—had been primarily responsible for supplying international and national information to the central and local press.
However, in the early 1920's, the Russian state had expanded
its boundaries from the narrow confines of civil war years. By
1924, the newly constituted Soviet Union consisted of the Russian, Ukrainian, Byelorussian, Georgian, Azerbaidzhan, and
Armenian republics, the Turkmen and Uzbek republics being
added in 1925. In line with the new structure, ROSTA was
made the Russian republic's news agency, and the Telegraph
Agency of the Union of Soviet Socialist Republics—known as
TASS—was established in July, 1925. TASS had exclusive right
to distribute information nationally in the Soviet Union, whether
it originated abroad or within the country. Republic news agencies could transmit within their own republics, but for all practical purposes they were subsidiaries of TASS. Under the 1925
statute, TASS could open foreign or domestic bureaus, and was
responsible for supplying information abroad about the Soviet
Union. TASS operated as an arm of the government, under the
Council of People's Commissars, which appointed the TASS
nine-man board of directors.[66] Indicative of the importance of
news agencies, only ROSTA issued information about the Rus-

sian republic government to the press. Since this republic was the dominant power of the Soviet Union, it meant that ROSTA in conjunction with TASS was the press spokesman for the whole Soviet government.

The press network over which these various party and government agencies exerted control gradually broadened in the 1920's. Even then, the number of newspapers was modest and remained so until a very rapid expansion around 1930, with the forced merger of private farms into large collectives and with industrialization. The newspaper press had contracted sharply during civil war years, partly as a result of government suppression of some publications, partly because of equipment and newsprint shortages. Then in January, 1922, the press was struck a financial blow. State-owned newspapers and magazines, which had been issued free until that time, were required to be economically self-sufficient. Of 803 newspapers published that January, only 313 survived into July. Circulation fell from around 2.5 million to a low of about 1 million when, as Stalin reported to the 12th Party Congress the following year, the "press had to stand on its own feet." The party tried to cushion the blow. In the spring of 1922, the 11th Party Congress granted new state subsidies for the press, and obligated all party members, individually or collectively, to subscribe to at least one party newspaper. Within a year, the situation had improved somewhat. The number of newspapers had increased to 528, and circulation had risen to about 2 million. Still, state subsidies were necessary, especially for the non-Russian, peasant, and Red Army press, which was of special concern to the central party as it sought to unify the country. Approximately 70 per cent of non-Russian and 23 per cent of peasant newspapers were wholly subsidized by the central party press department, for example. By 1925, with government support, the newspaper network had expanded slightly to 589 publications.[67]

During these years, the Communist Party and government were engaged in a three-pronged drive to develop the press system. First, they were concerned with gaining editorial control of newspapers and magazines, primarily through party channels and especially in the countryside and non-Russian areas. Second, the party worked out a press structure that conformed both to political divisions and segments of the population—peasants, workers, youth, and so on. Third, there was a concerted effort to mold content of the press so that it echoed central party and government policies. Simultaneously, argument over press freedom receded. It was a live issue as long as power within the party was dissipated. After Lenin died in 1924, Stalin moved adroitly against other contenders for power. In that year, sweeping directives on the press were issued by the central party apparatus and by national party meetings, both of which were increasingly under Stalin's control. The press more and more reflected Stalin's views in the savage debates over foreign and domestic policies. The question of whether the press should be a forum of discussion was not so much answered. It simply became academic. The few voices for diversity in the press were pitifully weak; the clash of political struggle drowned them out. The operative principle in that battle was to deny the press to one's enemies.

The press structure itself evolved from given circumstances. The country was part urban and worker, mostly rural and peasant. Russians dominated, but other nationalities were being wooed and coerced into a unified state. There were party agencies and the government apparatus. These contained central, republic (after 1924), provincial (*guberniya*), regional (*oblast*), and district (*uezd*) organizations. Further, there were trade unions, youth groups, and the military, each with special interests. The task therefore was to devise a mass media system to reach these various groups, with particular information, in an appropriate form, language, and style. Given the rapid and continuous change in Russia during the early 1920's, the system was built by trial and error, some of it forever remaining on paper.

Beginning in 1921-22, the newspaper press was reorganized broadly for two groups of readers—worker and peasant. Simultaneously, the central and local press was oriented toward both mass and specialized audiences. New large circulation newspapers joined the familiar *Pravda*. In 1923, *Krestyanskaya Gazeta*—another large farm newspaper—was established. By 1925, its circulation was 1 million, larger than any Soviet newspaper's. *Rabochaya Gazeta,* for workers, first appeared in 1922. In addition to these mass circulation newspapers, there were new ones for narrower categories of readers. *Trud*, the trade union publication, began publishing in 1921; *Gudok*, for railroad workers, in 1920; *Komsomolskaya Pravda* and *Pionerskaya Pravda*, for Soviet youth organizations, in 1925; *Krasnaya Zvezda*, the Red Army paper, in 1924. In the countryside, according to the 1921-22 press reorganization, provincial (*guberniya*) newspapers generally were to be for workers, unless the territory contained a large peasant population. The small district (*uezd*) papers were almost entirely farm publications. Each province was to have one mass circulation daily, and a weekly or twice weekly newspaper directed to party and government officials. In regions (*oblasts*) the party-government newspaper was to be a daily. District newspapers generally were weeklies.[68]

In predominantly non-Russian areas of the Russian republic, newspapers or sections of them were to be published in native languages. In the Ukraine, Byelorussia, and other areas where a national language press was as common as in Russia, native language newspapers continued to publish. Both the national and rural press received inordinate attention from Moscow. Thus, of the 589 state-owned newspapers published in 1925, 141 were classified as peasant publications, and 153 were national language newspapers. By contrast, there were 76 labor newspapers.[69] However, development of all but the central press was slow. Local newspapers were tabloid size, of poor quality, and with small circulation. *Pravda* and *Krestyanskaya Gazeta* had 20 per cent of the 7.5 million circulation in 1925. The central press carried much of the responsibility for publicizing and promoting party-government policies, which were being spawned at a dazzling rate.

In 1924, a stream of new directives, orders, and regulations came from Moscow, some from the 13th Party Congress of May, many from the Central Committee secretariat or the orgburo. Generally, they tinkered with and adjusted the press system devised the previous three or four years. What ultimately was formed, as outlined in a party decree of April, 1926, was a structure divided first horizontally—the central or national press, the republic, regional, district, and lower. Vertically, one found ten divisions—the party-government press, general circulation labor newspapers, and the trade union, military, farm cooperative, peasant, women's, economic, youth, and native language press.[70] Generally, these divisions were represented at the central and republic levels. Below these, newspapers were predominantly party-government, worker, or peasant oriented. This structure was created and implanted in an incredibly short time. But, while it conformed roughly to the country's ethnic and occupation profile, it was considerably artificial (hence the need for state subsidies in the 1920's, when newspapers tried to survive in a market economy). This was, however, of secondary consequence. The first task was to form a mass media network capable of serving national economic development and political unification.

Quite naturally then, press content drew the lion's share of attention. After the civil war, many newspapers were, as the party Central Committee bluntly said in 1921, "beneath any criticism." [71] Moreover, many were in the hands of politically unreliable editors, in Bolshevik eyes. As late as 1925, an estimated 38 per cent of editors and assistant editors had been recruited from the Menshevik, Socialist Revolutionary, and other political parties. Not a single editor of the politically sensitive national language papers had been in the Bolshevik Party more than seven years. [72] Thus, the central party apparatus was faced with restaffing the press and upgrading content. As we have seen, the mechanism—party press departments and *Glavlit*—to accomplish these goals also had to be built. In 1921, local party committees were told to establish the "closest contact" with newspaper editorial staffs. [73] This was a recurrent theme in party directives. Time after time during the 1920's (and thereafter for that matter), the central party lamented inept management of the press. In 1924, the 13th Party Congress demanded that local party groups "must become more involved in deciding all basic questions of press direction." In 1927, "party committees must consistently instruct the press in conducting the most important campaigns." [74]

Meanwhile, detailed instructions on editorial content were being dispatched. Particularly important were newspapers' departments of party affairs. They were to be staffed by experienced journalist party members, who as assistant editors also were to participate in party bureau meetings. These instructions in 1924 came from the central party orgburo, [75] of which Stalin was a member. Clearly, Stalin was constructing his own network of press publicists to echo his views. Beyond the personal politicking involved, there was a general effort to define press content. This stemmed partly from the central government's desire to use the press, and partly from a need to instruct the many amateur journalists in basic newspaper editing. In 1922, for example, *Agitprop* issued what amounted to a journalism primer for provincial newspapers. It proposed dividing newspaper staffs into various departments (local development, foreign affairs, agriculture, military, party activities, industry, etc.), a standard arrangement before 1917. The primer also suggested how much page space each department should have and what

each should cover. For example, the foreign affairs department:
"Only past events. The struggle of labor with capital. Revolutionary movement. All events and facts having an immediate
connection with the Soviet republic. Normal space, 80–100
lines." Or the department of industry: "The situation and work
of local industry. The effect of NEP on it. Private industry.
Facts and figures, livelily presented and explained. Space, from
100 to 150 lines." [76] Similarly, specific guidelines for the whole
labor and peasant newspaper network went out from the party
orgburo in 1924. Labor newspapers, for instance, were to deal
with production increases, work of factory party organizations,
conditions in the countryside, and party programs for the
peasants. [77]

Of the general tone and bias of the press in these years, we
can get some idea from the pacesetting *Pravda*. Articles proclaimed: "Opening of the Kashira State Electric Station," "First
Woman Doctor in Kirgizia," "From the Workers' Diary of the
Moscow Factory 'Hammer and Sickle,' " "2,000 Workers Join
the Party," "England Gives de Jure Recognition to the USSR,"
"The General Line of Our Development." The press made each
event an accomplishment, each fact a lesson, each experience
a general education. The press cajoled, urged, and agitated. It
trumpeted advance, and turned adversity into cause for greater
sacrifice and work. It portrayed a vast society in vast and hope-
filled revolution. It proclaimed a nation moving forward, unified,
inspired, in control of its own destiny.

Clearly, for all of this to have effect, the press had to speak
in a popular language. It was said that the average worker or
peasant, if he could read at all, had a 2,000-word vocabulary. [78]
The local press, because it circulated among the most uneducated, was to keep in mind that the masses "almost everywhere are barely literate and even illiterate. . . . Articles and
news items must be short, written clearly and accurately. . . .
Editors must be certain that every printed line, every word in
the newspaper neither is incomprehensible nor bewildering in
the most distant, most remote village." [79] Such appeals for
clarity and simplicity became commonplace.

Also during the 1920's, the party began training journalists
and shifting party members with newspaper experience back to
editorial staffs. Journalism education had been disrupted, of
course, by the revolution and civil war. It revived feebly in
1919, when ROSTA organized a short course, primarily to train
journalists for Red Army newspapers and so-called "agitation

centers."[80] In 1921, a Moscow Institute of Journalism was established, at first to produce worker-peasant correspondents; but then in 1923 it was reorganized into a college offering a three year course. At the same time, Moscow University began training students in editing, publishing, and literary criticism, and graduated about 420 young journalists between 1922 and 1929. Odds and ends of journalism courses and lectures were begun at provincial universities, on newspapers, and in journalists' organizations. Various publications were issued for journalists, among them *Zhurnalist, Krasnaya Pechat, Krasnoarmeiskaya Pechat, Rabochii Korrespondent*, and a bulletin, *Agent-ROSTA*.

Much of this training and guidance was short on journalism and long on politics. "It is essential," said a party resolution in 1924, "that party organizations give the most serious attention to party-political education of press workers." The ideal accordingly was the politically partisan journalist who thought in unison with the party; in short, a skilled public relations man. To this must be added Russia's traditional association of literature and the popular press. Both literary monthlies, the "thick journals," and newspapers published quality essays and fiction. In the Soviet period such famed authors as Maxim Gorky, Mikhail Sholokhov, and Ilya Ehrenburg wrote for the mass press. And even as professional journalism took hold in latter years, the Soviet press retained a literary tone. Essays, literary criticism, poetry, and fiction were side by side with strident party proclamations, harvest reports, and industrial production statistics. Certainly the second group came to dominate the press, reflecting the supremacy of technicians over philosophers in Soviet society.

With development of the mass press in the 1920's came the phenomenon of the worker-peasant correspondent—*rabselkor*—and the pervasive wall newspaper. Both contained seeds of a popular press at the grass roots. But what began more or less spontaneously turned into an institution of a spongy state bureaucracy. The *rabselkor* was an outgrowth of Lenin's scheme for a newspaper with a network of correspondents, and combined several roles. As an amateur journalist, the worker or peasant contributed items to newspapers. He was particularly valuable as a critic and muckraker in his own small bailiwick. Better than the local regional or district newspaper, short of staff as it was, the factory worker knew what was amiss in his plant, the peasant what was wrong in his village. From the central party's vantage point, the *rabselkor* was a means of drawing tens of thousands of people into the job of reform and development: he could be the link between the great masses and the press. A newspaper written by the common man, the argument went, would be read by the common man. Beginning about 1921, the local press was encouraged to form networks of worker or peasant correspondents. Without "vibrant connections with readers," the party declared, "the newspaper will not successfully fulfill its job, and subsequently the most important means of influencing the masses—the newspaper—will remain unexploited."[81] Gradually during the 1920's the *rabselkor* institution drew from the broad rank and file, whether worker, peasant, soldier, or student. Groups of *rabkor*—worker correspondents—were formed in factories, and *selkor*—peasants —in villages (where they also had the job of reading to illiterates). Small at first, the *rabselkor* network had 100,000 correspondents in 1924, but within a year counted 216,000, and thereafter grew rapidly.

As a sweeping June, 1925, directive stated, the party was to guide the *rabselkor* but in no way exercise "petty tutelage" over correspondents, censor their news items, or interfere with their job of exposing wrongs. The *rabselkor* was seen as a popular mass movement to be delicately influenced, lest it be deadened. Slowly the *rabselkor* was infiltrated by a large state agency called the Worker-Peasant Inspection, a sort of mass public surveillance over bureaucracy. Simultaneously, correspondents were used more and more as informers and agitators by the party apparatus, and as amateur sleuths by the police. These activities hardly won the *rabselkor* popularity. Correspondents were derided and assaulted. A series of confidential government circulars between 1924 and 1928 emphasized the "significant number of cases of murder of rural and worker correspondents." Attacks on correspondents were regarded both as criminal and political matters, and newspapers gave full

GROWTH OF *RABSELKOR* AND WALL NEWSPAPER NETWORKS: 1924–1930

Rabselkor		Wall Newspapers	
Year	Number	Year	Number
1924	100,000	1924	3,000
1925	216,000	1925	40,000
1926	250,000	1928	60,000
1927	300,000	1929	50,000
1928	500,000	1930	200,000

SOURCE: *Sovetskaya Pechat,* No. 6 (June, 1957), pp. 27–29, 30–31; No.7 (July, 1957), p. 33.

play to prosecution of persons charged with assault and murder of correspondents.[82]

Like the *rabselkor*, wall newspapers were a spontaneous development of the early postrevolution years. They first appeared during the civil war in factories and Red Army units, and were nothing more really than handwritten announcements and news notes. Gradually they were named, illustrated, and given a more orderly appearance. Still they were wholly unprofessional, and were gotten up at will. In 1924, there were only 3,000 wall newspapers in the whole country, but a year later the estimate was 40,000.[83] As with the *rabselkor*, the central party soon recognized the value of wall newspapers as the last, small extending veins of the press network. Their very simplicity and popular origin made them potential channels of mass persuasion and a means to help rally and mobilize millions of people. Hence, in a 1924 directive, local Communist Party and Komsomol organizations were told to take hold of both factory and village wall newspapers. Their informal and untrained editorial boards were to work with local party members, and draw on the assistance of worker and peasant correspondents. The wall newspapers contained personal, detailed information about the work and activities of a single factory shop, Red Army unit, or a small village. This was the place where individuals were praised or criticized, where minute problems could be pinpointed, new production methods proposed, announcements made, and the like. Inevitably, this mass of illustrated bulletin boards had a homemade look. Presumably their manufacture by the hands of co-workers gave them an appeal that the conventional press could not duplicate. But one can reasonably question their actual influence. Constant commands from the center to improve wall newspapers, as well as the *rabselkor,* were one measure of their imperfection from the party's vantage point. Regardless of the faults, this entire array of amateur journalism was tied into the press system and political structure, and its spontaneity was thereby diminished. This probably was not the intention. But to the central party it was preferable to have less spontaneity and more supervision than the reverse at the grass roots.

The periodical press of the early 1920's followed similar lines of development to those of the newspaper. All party press department directives and party congress resolutions applied equally, of course, to magazines. Magazine editing and production were under the same supervision of *Glavlit* and economic agencies, and editors of periodicals increasingly were drawn from and approved by party committees. In sheer numbers, magazines surpassed newspapers in the 1920's. From 856 periodicals in 1921, the network expanded to 1,749 by 1925, and annual circulation climbed from less than 16 million to about 156 million copies.[84] Many of these publications were simply bulletins, government documents, guidebooks for party members, and similar recipe lists. But among them also were the stimulating literary monthlies, such as *Novy Mir, Oktyabr, Pechat i Revolyutsiya,* and *Znamya,* all of which were established in the early 1920's. Two central journals, *Revolyutsiya i Tserkov* and *Ateist,* conducted intense propaganda against religious beliefs. The Central Committee issued special periodicals dealing with political theory and policy, including *Bolshevik, Kommunisticheskaya Revolyutsiya,* and *Pod Znamenem Marksizma.* And a number of large newspapers contained magazine supplements. *Krokodil* was published as part of *Krestyankaya Gazeta,* the farm newspaper. *Pravda*'s supplement was *Prozhektor,* and *Izvestia*'s, *Krasnaya Niva.* As mentioned earlier, there were various periodicals for the press itself, ranging from *Zhurnalist,* which conducted probing discussions into the form and purpose of the press, to *Krasnaya Pechat,* a party Central Committee publication containing stodgy instructions and guidelines for journalists.[85]

Although there were several popular mass circulation magazines begun in the 1920's, the periodical press was never looked upon as a means of mass persuasion equal to newspapers—an attitude one can trace to Lenin and prerevolution habits. Many periodicals were edited for relatively narrow readership and carried specialized information. Whereas the party's theoretical journals, for example, published weighty articles on Marxism, the popular newspaper press tended to reduce theory to slogans for general consumption. By their nature, periodicals were unsuited for the job of transmitting government policies across the land quickly and, just as necessary, frequently. Thus, the party devoted more funds and energy to newspapers and the companion wire services as the vehicles of mass persuasion. The periodical press remained of secondary importance in this respect, though in terms of solid information and thought-provoking essays it probably ranked above newspapers.

Radio broadcasting, too, lagged behind the newspaper as a channel of political communication with the masses. The reason was not radio's unsuitability for the job, or a lack of understanding among political authorities of radio's potential. In a country where 45 per cent of the population under fifty officially was illiterate as late as 1926 (and perhaps 25 per cent more just barely able to read), radio was an invaluable educator and advertiser. In 1920, when radio broadcasting everywhere was in its infancy, Lenin envisioned the day when "we will have hundreds of radio receivers, and all of Russia will be able to listen to a newspaper read in Moscow."[86] Yet radio developed slowly. Broadcasting technology was new. Electricity had yet to serve the countryside. Moreover, the cost of loudspeakers for a mass network was prohibitive. Hence, even on the eve of World War II, Soviet broadcasting was largely confined to cities and reached less than a third of the population. This same pattern of development can be seen in American radio broadcasting. It, too, had to wait for electrification of rural areas before the radio became a household item everywhere. American broadcasting far outpaced Soviet advances, however, mainly because of the financial incentives of advertising and radio receiver manufacture and a greater concentration of population in the cities. Russia of the 1920's lacked a built-in economic motivation. And political leaders, choosing among many critical needs, gave radio a relatively low priority.

During the early 1920's there was sporadic experimental broadcasting, either over telephone line loudspeaker systems or the airways. In September, 1922, the central radio-telephone station transmitted the first concert, and in January, 1924, ROSTA began transmission of information, at dictation speed, to the local newspaper press. The first regular broadcasting for the public was not begun until October, 1924, when the Moscow trade union's Sokolnicheskaya station went on the air. Broadcasts beyond Moscow started two years later, and were carried by telephone lines to several major cities.[87] The radio audience was extremely small. Even by 1928, there were only 70,000 radio receivers in the Soviet Union, and 22,000 loudspeakers (connected to sending stations by telephone lines), and all of these were in large cities.[88] The same year, 23 stations with a total power of 141 kilowatts were operating.

Administration and technical development of radio broadcasting was under the People's Commissariat for Postal Services and Telegraph. Then, in 1933, the commissariat's National Committee for Radio Broadcasting, which had been created two years before, was placed directly under the Council of People's Commissars. The government agencies for radio (and later television) dealt mainly with construction of stations, manufacture of radio receivers and loudspeakers, and the like. Through *Glavlit*, the government also censored radio programming. Within the party apparatus, *Agitprop* was assigned ideological direction of radio news broadcasts, lectures, and concerts in February, 1925. As far as management of radio broadcasting was concerned, what emerged then was a duplicate of the system overseeing the printed press.

By the mid-1920's, therefore, parallel with the development of central and local political agencies the Soviet mass media network had become a government-financed and managed enterprise. Unquestionably it was at a primitive, disorganized stage, as was the country generally. One cannot imagine—given the radical social reforms, the controversy over NEP, the artistic experimentation, and the political struggle—that the press was the pedestrian huckster it later became. The 1920's was a period of popular excitement. The 1917 Revolution could still invoke enthusiasm for remaking the old order into a society dedicated to the welfare of all men. It was also a time of disillusionment among Communist idealists who feared a backsliding into bourgeois ways, the result of NEP concessions to private entrepreneurs and capital. The 1920's, in retrospect, were a breathing spell between the fighting and sacrifices of revolution and civil war, and the enormous new hardships and terror that were to come under Stalin's regime in the 1930's. The instruments of government, the lines of power, and plan of national purpose were in their early, testing stages. And so the press system, while looking relatively structured in the party and government directives, was in actuality a half-built edifice.

What was of paramount importance, of course, was the mass media's wedding to the political system. During the 1920's and thereafter, this connection meant that the values, attitudes, opinions, and facts disseminated by the mass media proceeded more from an expectation of the future than an acceptance of the present reality. Essentially the press, in the Stalin years, was devoted to inspiring hope and belief in communism, in the Soviet industrial state, in progress, in Stalin—and to concealing and minimizing the means by which the ends were sought. The mass media abandoned any commitment to subjective recording of history and turned instead to gross fabrication and adulation of a great society of tomorrow. This made for a dreary history of the Soviet press during Stalin's rule.

The 1930's: Years of Growth

The mechanism of controls had been roughed out by 1927, when Stalin engineered Trotsky's expulsion from the party Central Committee, ending a crucial political struggle. Trotsky subsequently was exiled from the Soviet Union in 1929, and during the following decade, Stalin proceeded to purge the party, the military, and the rank and file of real and supposed enemies. With equal ruthlessness and determination, Stalin began collectivization of some 25 million peasant households. By 1935, more than 80 per cent had been merged into large, state-managed collective farms, and millions of peasants who had resisted had been killed or herded into forced labor camps. Simultaneously, in 1928–29, the first five year economic plan heralded rapid industrialization. "We are 50 or 100 years behind the advanced countries," Stalin declared in 1931. "We must make good this distance in 10 years. Either we do, or we shall be crushed." Under Stalin's dictate, the country was mobilized as if for war, and with it came the paradoxical mixture of enthusiasm and terror, of hope and tyranny. The cataclysmic changes during these years are much too complex to deal with here except to note that the press, along with all other institutions, was harnessed to modernization, and to the modeling of Stalin into a "beloved leader" and a "great genius."

Thus, the mass media were brought under stifling censorship and supervision. Simultaneously, the press network expanded rapidly. Large state sums poured into newspapers, magazines, and radio, accurately reflecting Stalin's belief that the mass media could mobilize the masses and shape their desires and values. The number of newspapers increased from about 1,200 in 1928 to 7,536 in 1932, reaching a record total of 10,668 in 1934. Total circulation (dailies and weeklies combined) rose sharply from 9.4 million to 34.7 million during the same period.[89] Much of the newspaper increase can be traced to an abrupt enlargement of the local press network, including small factory and farm weeklies or bi-weeklies. By 1932, about 1,000 new factory newspapers were being published. And in 1933, there were 2,150 small newspapers (average circulation of each was 900 copies; size was about 8 x 10 inches) being issued by political departments of the so-called machine-tractor stations, and about 700 on state farms.[90] Until World War II the newspaper network fluctuated between about 8,500 and 10,000 newspapers, including all the small local tabloids, and then it contracted sharply.

Circulation stayed between 36 and 38 million, and average individual press run totaled about 4,500.

SOVIET NEWSPAPER PRESS: 1913–1953

Year	Number of Newspapers	Circulation (millions)	Average Circulation (thousands)
1913	1,005	3.3	3.3
1918	889	1.7	3.1
1919	1,000	....	....
1920–21	.....	....	....
1922	803	2.5	3.2
	(313)*	(1.0)	(3.0)
1923	528	2.2	2.6
1924	.....	....	....
1925	589	....	....
1926–27	.....	....	....
1928	1,197	9.4	7.9
1929–31	.....	....	....
1932	7,536	35.5	4.7
1933	8,319	35.7	4.3
1934	10,668	34.7	3.3
1935	9,990	35.7	3.6
1936	9,250	38.0	4.1
1937	8,521	36.2	4.2
1938	8,550	37.5	4.4
1939	8,780	38.0	4.3
1940	8,806	38.4	4.4
1941–44	.....	....	....
1945	6,455	23.2	3.6
1946	7,039	29.6	4.2
1947	7,163	31.1	4.3
1948	7,178	31.6	4.4
1949	7,211	33.5	4.6
1950	7,831	36.0	4.6
1951	8,195	39.8	4.9
1952	8,299	41.7	5.0
1953	7,754	44.2	5.7

SOURCES: *Pechat SSSR za sorok let*, p. 123; *Pechat SSSR za 50 let*, p. 132.

*In 1922, Soviet newspapers were required to be financially self-sufficient. The number of newspapers declined to 313 by mid-1922.

The periodical press showed less radical change in terms of size. The number of magazines, journals, and bulletins averaged about 2,000 all through the prewar years. Annual circulation changed erratically, amounting to 303 million in 1928, rising to 418 million three years later, and then leveling off at about 250 million in the mid-1930's.[91]

SOVIET PERIODICAL PRESS: 1918-1953

Year	Number of Periodicals*	Annual Circulation (millions)
1918	753	-----
1920	596	-----
1921	856	-----
1925	1,749	156.1
1930	2,226	340.2
1935	2,101	202.4
1940	1,822	245.4
1945	657	72.8
1950	1,408	181.3
1953	1,614	267.1

SOURCE: *Pechat za sorok let*, pp. 107–108.

*Figures include magazines, bulletins, scholarly journals, and statistical, technical, and other references or collections of information issued periodically. The share of magazines in the total has been on the order of one fourth to one third. In 1940, for example, 681 magazines were published; in 1950, 430.

Radio broadcasting made fair progress, indicating the expansion both of the Soviet electrification program and of industry. At the end of 1933, there were 60 operating radio stations, and about 1.3 million government-registered receivers and wired speakers. By 1940, 30 more transmitting stations had been constructed, and receivers and speakers totaled nearly 7 million (of which, however, only 1.6 million were in rural localities). Television was also in the experimental stage by 1940, and 400 sets had been manufactured.[92]

With this expansion of the mass media, various party-government control devices were refined and made far more effective than they had been during the 1920's. Industrialization provided the rationale and excuse for overbearing central direc-

tion of the press. And Stalin's inherent suspicion, which pervaded all of Soviet society, generated an oppressive censorship,
ostensibly to guard state secrets from the bourgeois enemy. In
practice, of course, censorship also prevented information of a
pessimistic, defeatist, or politically scandalous nature from
reaching the Soviet public. The censor thus helped form an
atmosphere of unanimity, accomplishment, and of trust in the
political leadership.

Glavlit, the government censorship agency, was given new
powers and enlarged as the first five year plan progressed.
According to a 1931 regulation, *Glavlit* was assigned "pre- and
post-control over literary publications, whether from a political-
ideological view, or military and economic, as well as over radio
broadcasting, lectures and exhibits." *Glavlit* agents were assigned
to printing plants, editorial offices, broadcasting studios, telegraph agencies, border posts, and post offices. Publications of
central and local Communist Party organizations, the Academy
of Sciences, and the government Central Executive Committee
were checked for military, but not political information. All
printed matter subject to *Glavlit* surveillance had to carry the
censor's visa, which consisted of a letter and several digits,
such as G5438. Still functioning in the 1930's under the Commissariat for Education (*Narkompros*), *Glavlit* was organized
according to political administrations. Thus, there was the central *Glavlit* in Moscow, then republic agencies, regional (*oblit*),
district (*railit*), and city (*gorlit*) offices.[93]

Glavlit censors supplemented by staffs of the OVT, the organs
of military censorship, were guided by the *perechen,* the list of
prohibited information.[94] This was a most detailed explanation
of what could and what could not be published, and was compiled by both *Glavlit* and military censoring organs. Exacting
instructions covered mention of defense installations, weapons,
and maneuvers. Harvest figures could not be used in the press
until they had appeared in *Pravda* or *Izvestia*. Unflattering
photographs of Lenin or Stalin were not to be published. Any
events that suggested unrest or instability—such as murder of
officials or popular disorders—were not to be reported. As Merle
Fainsod has noted in his summary of Soviet documents on
censorship in the 1930's, what was demanded of the censor was
not always the practice. Some censors performed their duties in
mechanical fashion. Lack of trained personnel made censorship
on local levels haphazard and crude. Moreover, newspaper editors were not entirely cooperative with censors, who as before

worked in conjunction with the secret police. Instances were documented in the 1930's of local authorities using censorship to conceal their own mistakes and ineptness, and this conflicted with editors' duties of exposing inefficiency. And we can imagine that some editors and journalists, even in the 1930's, were dedicated to the ideals of a popular press expressing the people's aspirations. These notions were hardly compatible with functions of the censor. Censorship also suffered from bureaucracy's inborn malady, the conflict between close supervision and personal initiative. Although censors were guided by precise regulations, they were expected to exercise reasonable judgment. But given a choice, censors tended to err on the safe side, chopping out any debatable fact or opinion.

During the 1930's, the Soviet mass media also were subject to rigorous economic and planning controls. In 1931, the old Committee on the Press was abolished, at the national level, and its responsibilities were turned over to *Gosplan*, the central state planning agency. On lower levels, press committees survived until 1933, when their duties were split among several agencies. In general, government controls included long-range financial planning for the press, auditing, supply of newsprint, printing equipment, and facilities.[95] In 1930, a special committee was created under the Commissariat for Postal Services and Telegraph to supervise all newspaper and magazine distribution. The effect of these steps was to divorce editorial staffs from the physical plant, each being supervised by different government and party agencies.

In the Communist Party apparatus, there was equal shuffling of press agencies. The party secretariat's press sections had been absorbed by the agitation and propaganda department in 1928. That in turn was split in 1930, and a department of culture and propaganda—*Kultprop*—became responsible for ideological orientation of the press. In 1934, *Kultprop* itself was divided into five sections, one of which took charge of press and publishing in all aspects.[96] Then in 1938, departments of agitation and propaganda, including press sections, were resurrected on central and local levels.[97] These agencies assumed broad political direction of the mass media. They proceeded from the fact that editors of newspapers and magazines, and directors of radio programming, were appointed by the party at various levels and in most cases were members of party executive committees. Thus, the problem was not so much how to coerce basically hostile journalists to support the mass campaigns and government policies, but rather how to manage a conglomeration of experienced and inexperienced party publicists, keeping alive some spark of initiative and creativity without permitting them independent opinion. Thus, for example, in 1931, the party press sections supplemented two TASS publications (*Vestnik* and *Byulleten*) with their own thrice monthly instructions, model articles, and criticism of press performance. Party staff instructors were to tour *raion* newspapers and discuss current work. In general, the press sections used published reviews, conferences of editors, appointive powers, journalism education, and confidential instructions to shape mass media content.

Staffing of the press was perhaps the key problem. If editors and the central party apparatus were like-thinking, the press would tend to move in unison with the party's decisions. But the few journalism institutions were not producing many graduates in the 1930's. And few had any desire to work in the backward provinces, which was exactly where journalists were most needed. One result was that local party committees edited and published newspapers as a sort of sideline, and the products were never very satisfactory. Staffing, let alone financing and supply of the press, was all the more critical in the 1930's as the mass media network expanded. In 1930, coincident with a political administration reorganization, development of a large network of *raion* newspapers was started. By 1932, about 2,300 of the small weekly or twice weekly papers were operating. For staff (there being few trained journalists), these were to draw on worker-peasant correspondents, as well as local officials and specialists who contributed essays and polemics. The performance of these *raion* newspapers can be glimpsed in a 1931 decree of the Urals *oblast* party committee, which complained of "evident undervaluation of the role of the press and in some instances a direct distortion of the party line and control of the press."[98] One reaction of the central party was to promote journalism education, which often meant quick courses, and to assign party members with press experience to newspapers. New journalism departments also were set up, and training of local editors instituted, all under the party's agitation and propaganda department.

The 1930's also saw a striking growth in the worker-peasant correspondent corps, and diligent efforts to draw the masses into the press. One source reports more than 3 million correspondents working by about 1930.[99] Wall newspapers numbered about 200,000 that year, compared with 60,000 in 1928. A series of party resolutions organized the *rabselkor* into an assault force against bureaucracy, inefficiency, and law violations. The "shock correspondent," analogous to the Stakhanovite in factories, was born. "Raids" were organized, whereby huge teams of worker-peasant correspondents conducted minute investigations of a given factory or collective farm and reported whatever flaws they unearthed.

As before, the mass local press played a dual role. From one view, it was in fact an independent check on party policies, on economic performance, and management. The local press also brought hundreds of thousands of people into campaigns for overfulfilling production targets, for spring sowing, overtime work, mass education, improved farm management, factory construction, and dozens of other goals.

The central press was, of course, the pacesetter. Large newspapers like *Pravda* and *Izvestia* proclaimed the mass campaigns and surveyed performance of the lower press. *Pravda* began the first "review of the press" in October, 1929, under the headline: "The proletarian press must relentlessly and consistently fight for the party line." Circulation of the central press increased, and new papers were added. By 1940, there were 46 national or all-union newspapers, accounting for about one fifth of total newspaper circulation. Many of these were specialized publications, for the state labor union, peasants, teachers, and Communist youth movements. Also, by 1940, about a fourth of the total of 8,806 newspapers was published in non-Russian languages, reflecting the continuing drive to unify the multinational Soviet state.

On the eve of the Soviet Union's entry into World War II, the central party had erected a formidable mass media system. The quandary is in judging how well it worked, given its structure and its goals. We can make allowance at once for human imperfection, and for the general backwardness of the Soviet Union, which pervaded performance of all institutions. The Soviet mass media of the 1930's had little in common with a sophisticated, white-collar public relations staff. The dominant technique of persuasion and public opinion formation meant the heavyfooted repetition of slogans. The press—newspapers, magazines, radio—saturated its audience with standard messages. It presented no real alternative views, and no exact detailed information on the political system. The mass arrests, trials, and executions of the 1930's, for example, were distorted by the press as victories over enemies of the state.

The mass media were bound to lack some credence among the

Soviet masses. Perhaps the best glimpse of audience reaction comes from an extensive interviewing after World War II of Soviet émigrés on attitudes toward the press. As reported by Alex Inkeles and Raymond A. Bauer, a surprising 80 per cent of the intelligentsia interviewed granted that some or most information in the Soviet press was reliable.[100] Among white-collar workers, the figure was 70 per cent; common workers, 42 per cent; and peasants, 36 per cent. That is, the better educated Soviet citizens put more faith in the official mass media than the less schooled. At the same time, because of the general awareness that the press contained distortions, other sources of information—rumors, conversations with friends, official lectures—were widely used as checks on what the mass media presented. Generally, Inkeles and Bauer found that newspapers were more frequently used as sources by the intelligentsia and white-collar employees than by workers and peasants. The latter two groups relied considerably on word of mouth for information. Still another revealing pattern emerged: the more ambitious for a career he was, the more a person was likely to keep up with events in the mass media, so his exposure to official views was greater than that of less motivated persons. All groups of Soviet citizens seemed to have developed a skill at reading between lines. They became adept at catching a new phrase or different use of a word, as the Soviet mass media became standardized and conformist.

Whether they believed what they read and/or inferred is difficult to assess. Attitudes and thought patterns present in the Soviet press during Stalin's years were reflected in individuals, and possibly most clearly among the intelligentsia. Moreover, there probably was an inclination to accept as more or less true the mass media's image of the world beyond Soviet borders. Domestic information, by contrast, could be more readily cross checked by an individual's own experiences and observations and those of personal informants. And it would seem true, following further along this line, that local information was held in most skepticism of all. However, Soviet citizens' reactions to the mass media of the 1930's must remain speculative. No large, scientifically based opinion samples were made. And allowing for prejudices and faulty memories, the recollections of Soviet émigrés provide only a rough framework of some audience reactions.

If the Soviet mass media did not wholly shape a popular opinion, they did it seems clear serve other purposes with some efficiency. For one, the press focused predominant attention on the policies and goals of the party and of Stalin. The press simply excluded information detracting from national objectives. For example, there was no independent discussion in the Soviet press of the wisdom of further collectivization after the initial disastrous experience in 1929 and 1930. By contrast, the contemporary Soviet press has been immersed in debate over the extension and direction of economic reform. This tells as much about Soviet politics, of course, as it does about the press itself. Stalin's mass media system was anything but a forum of discussion. It fulfilled the functions of informer, detective, cheerleader, critic, and sentry. The press essentially was a oneway channel of communication, from the center to the provinces. Stalin's press went through the motions of allowing popular expression, but Stalin did not himself value the wisdom of mass opinion. Thus the concept of the people's press, which fired some imaginations in 1917 and before, turned into clay. It was kept in view, to be sure, in the Stalin constitution of 1936, a document which proclaimed a parliamentary government and extensive civil rights. Article 125 declared:

> In conformity with the interests of the workers and for the purposes of strengthening the socialist system, citizens of the USSR are guaranteed by law: (a) freedom of speech, (b) freedom of press, (c) freedom of assembly and meetings, (d) freedom of street processions and demonstrations. These citizen rights are ensured by placing at the disposal of the workers and their organizations printing presses, supplies of paper, public buildings, the streets, communications facilities and other material needs for the exercise of these rights.[101]

These freedoms remained fictions during Stalin's lifetime. If one accepts that the 1930's were not unlike wartime, it is easy to see how civil liberties were abrogated. In the most democratic societies, civil rights are trimmed during time of national crisis. The Soviet Union not only went through multiple crises during the 1930's, but a political dictatorship could exaggerate the threats from without and within to explain and justify the harshest suppression of individual liberty. And that is what happened.

During World War II, the Soviet mass media rallied the nation for battle, rather than for industrialization. The press was filled with glossed-over accounts of defeats and excited portrayals of victories. The number of newspapers and magazines was drastically reduced. Central national newspapers had their circulations cut back. *Pravda*'s fell from 2 million in 1940 to half that in 1944. Republic and *oblast* newspapers went to two pages, five days a week. *Raion* papers switched to weekly publication.[102] Meanwhile, resources were diverted to the military press. By 1944, 4 newspapers and 18 journals were being published in Moscow for the armed forces. In addition, 800 newspapers with a total circulation of 3 million were being published by units of the army and navy, and about 270 partisan and underground publications had been established.[103] By 1945, total newspaper circulation had slumped to 23 million. It did not reach the prewar level of 38 million until six years after the war.

Magazine publishing was even more curtailed during World War II. Only a third of the 1,800 journals published in 1940 survived to 1945. Annual circulation plummeted from 245 million to 73. Similarly, radio broadcasting was converted to wartime needs. Manufacture of civilian radio receivers was halted, and by 1945 there were fewer than 500,000 operating in the whole country, though the number of wire loudspeakers remained constant at about 5.6 million.

Thus, for several years after the war, the main task was simply to reconstruct the mass media's physical plant and reorganize editorial staffs. The revived civilian press was little different than what existed in the 1930's. Postwar reconstruction presented domestic crises as formidable as those of the 1930's. Added to these were new international problems with former wartime allies, chiefly the United States. Therefore, the mass media were engrossed in bolstering morale at home, urging greater reconstruction efforts, and increasingly in presenting the West as an aggressive military bloc. The truly creative and spontaneous war reporting, which enlisted such writers as Ilya Ehrenburg, gave way once more to bureaucratic grayness as Stalin reestablished harsh political suppression. His death in March, 1953, created a power vacuum, and presaged enormous changes in Soviet society, the mass media included.

Khrushchev: The "Thaw Press"

Nikita Khrushchev presided over a social revolution in the Soviet Union. The years between 1953 and 1964, when Khrushchev fell from power, witnessed a political and cultural evolution in the Soviet society as dazzling as the economic revolution under Stalin. It became apparent after Stalin's death that no one could replace him, either in the exercise of near absolute power or as the object of a mystical, often fearful reverence among the masses. The press had complicated the political succession problem. As an extension of Stalin's enormous ego, it had created a mythical leader. The mortal Stalin could not have succeeded himself. On December 21, 1949, when Stalin was seventy years old, *Pravda* had published a 12-page edition, rare at that time, of congratulatory messages. They continued to appear in *Pravda* for nearly two years. Khrushchev himself, adding to official greetings from lesser political figures, exclaimed in the newspaper: "Glory to our dear father, wise teacher, the genius leading the party, the Soviet people and the working people of the whole world, Comrade Stalin!" And suddenly Stalin was gone. His death was a tragic shock to millions in the Soviet Union. Many millions of others quietly rejoiced. The emotions were intertwined; it would be difficult to say which predominated.

The problems facing Stalin's political survivors were first to assure stability in the country, and second to apportion power among themselves. The mass media promptly generated a mood of calm and directed the nation to mourn over Stalin. After some initial maneuvering in the Communist Party presidium (the former politburo), Khrushchev was made party first secretary, and Georgi Malenkov, once Stalin's heir apparent, became Soviet premier. Collective leadership was the theme in the press. But over the next few years, an acute observer and practiced reader of the Soviet press could begin to pick out variances among the political leaders. Controversy centered on priority of heavy industry versus consumer goods production, and on agriculture, a chronic illness of the Soviet economy. As after Lenin's death, individuals vied for power in the context of domestic and international policy decisions. In these circumstances, the mass media began to reflect divisions within the political structure. At the same time, carried by momentum of habit, the press continued to trumpet clichés and energetically to propagate policies of the collective leadership. Given its origin in political revolution, and conversion by Stalin into a mass mobilizer, the press had no tradition of independent existence to recall. What lay before it was the adjustment to a new political climate, and to an altered role in a reformist-minded Soviet society. The impulses came from above, but partly in reaction to what was sensed below. The Soviet leadership evolved new assessments of Soviet domestic needs, and of its country's place in the world. These yielded, toward the end of the 1950's, a relaxation of political controls at home, and a more conciliatory policy toward the West.

The watershed event was Khrushchev's "secret speech" on Stalin to the Communist Party's 20th Congress in February, 1956—a document never published in the Soviet press. In detailed, astounding disclosures, Khrushchev described Stalin's crimes against the Soviet people—the mass arrests, secret police torture, star chamber trials, and terror on a grand scale. There is much debate on why Khrushchev denounced Stalin. In part, his report was a political move. In part, it was a daring effort to reject a way of life that no longer served national needs. The event had unimaginable consequences. From 1956 onward, Soviet relations with both Communist and non-Communist countries underwent startling changes. Khrushchev's de-Stalinization campaign caused the first crack in the Soviet-Chinese fissure. East European nations, swept into the Soviet sphere after World War II, later dared defiance of Moscow.

Within the Soviet Union, denunciation of Stalinism reverberated through the social structure. Stalinism and Soviet society had become almost synonymous. Try as Khrushchev did to separate the two, it was impossible. And though the old forms of rule persisted, the practice and content of politics were increasingly characterized by persuasion instead of coercion. In a broad shift of the national mentality, individual liberties and human dignity acquired value once more. First literature, then segments of the mass media, began to speak of the Stalinist terror. In the Soviet legal system, a sham under Stalin, a spirit of justice slowly emerged. Reforms did not come all at once. The left and right contended. Conservatives, fearful of a popular awakening, longing perhaps for a seemingly simpler day when power, discipline, and order seemed secure, resisted reform. Liberals, always in the minority, and with no real political power, battled not just against slothful bureaucracy, but mostly against the Stalinist psychology. The cutting edges were such writers as Ilya Ehrenburg (*The Thaw*), Boris Pasternak (*Doctor Zhivago*, a work never published in the Soviet Union), Alexander Solzhenitsyn (*One Day in the Life of Ivan Denisovich*), and Yevgeny Yevtushenko (the poems "Babi Yar" and "Stalin's Heirs," among others). These and others of the liberal camp were repeatedly attacked for their essays into delicate social themes and the political past. The battle continued through the late 1950's and the 1960's.

The mass media in these years responded to several forces. One was Khrushchev himself. Another was the growing corps of academically trained journalists, who had at least equally as much journalistic as political education. A third was the rising educational level of the Soviet population, particularly in urban areas. And a fourth was the new orientation of the press in a political system relying more on manipulation and persuasion than on massive brute force.

Although Khrushchev was a product of and participant in Stalin's regime, his attitude toward the press was not as one-sided as Stalin's. The explanation lies in Khrushchev's own conflicting traits. Edward Crankshaw has written that because Khrushchev was a "peasant, a ward politician, a powerseeker on a grand and ruthless scale, as well as a dreamer and, towards the end, a statesman, he was incapable of an all-embracing and coherent design."[104] That was perhaps the mass media's gain. For without an iron-willed, singleminded Stalin reigning over it, the press showed a spark of individuality. It underwent its own partial rehabilitation. If the press was servile in Stalin's time, it became more of a servant in Khrushchev's. The distinction may seem minor. But the transition was made in a remarkably few years, and it seemed irreversible.

Khrushchev's outlook on the mass media was closer to Lenin's than Stalin's, though Khrushchev lacked the intellectual depth of Lenin. He had a romantic's notion of the publicly owned press championing the people's cause. If the Soviet press fell short of this lofty ideal, it was because Khrushchev was too much the politician, and caught up in maintaining his own power and the party's in perilous times. Yet, the old Marxist critique of the private versus government press survived in Khrushchev's mind. "Controlling the means of production," he lectured foreign journalists in 1963, "the class of exploiters [capitalists] control as well the radio, press and television. That is, it controls the means of mass persuasion and attempts to form a particular public opinion, a frame of mind advantageous to itself. . . . This is why it is particularly important for the workers, the people, fighting for their independence to have their own press, radio and television through which they can wage a struggle against imperialism and colonialism."[105]

To the guest journalists, most of them from Africa, Asia, and Latin America, these words may not have sounded as alien as they must to Americans. But the core thought was perhaps no different than a militant American labor unionist might have uttered in the 1930's. He too would have argued for a labor press, from the class point of view. Khrushchev went further. The old alliance with the political hierarchy remained.

"As an army cannot fight without weapons," Khrushchev said in 1957, "so the party cannot successfully carry on its ideological work without this sharp and militant weapon, the press." The mass media, as he never failed to remind journalists, were allies of the party, the "transmission belt" between the party and the masses.[106] No less than authoritarian politicians of any nation, Khrushchev was fundamentally distrustful of an unmanaged press, and of spontaneous popular opinion expressed in the mass media. It was beyond his beliefs and politics to consider the press otherwise than as part of a vast social machinery which despite breakdowns was within man's capacity to control. And it was inconceivable to him that the press, in the Soviet scheme of things, could do otherwise than champion national goals conceived by the Communist Party. Yet, mixed with these views, and reflecting his own flamboyance, Khrushchev abhorred a dull press. He prodded journalists to write in lively, picturesque style. They should, he said, be skillful enough to describe complicated subjects so that the nonspecialist could understand them. Khrushchev chided editors for monotonous, unappealing formats. While deploring flashiness and sensation, he understood that the form as well as the content of the mass media affected audience reaction.[107]

With the lingering idea of a people's press, Khrushchev scoffed at the western concept of press freedom. "Everyone is free to write what he wants," he said in 1963, but "If a publisher finds that the writing does not help strengthen the capitalist system, he rejects it, he does not print it, and it turns out to be written not for people, but for mice." [108] The Soviet press, he argued, must be a "true people's forum," aiding the party and the masses in the creation of a Communist society. This was, of course, no more than had been said for nearly half a century in the Soviet Union. But circumstances had changed. By Khrushchev's twilight years, the Soviet mass media had become a giant industry. True, letters to the editor were counted as evidence of a people's press. So were articles in local and central newspapers by factory foremen, peasant milkmaids, or young Komsomols. But these were mechanical gestures to an ideal that had ossified. The press by the 1960's not only was entrenched in the party bureaucracy, but was in the hands of professional political journalists. Like their foreign colleagues, they were not inclined to draw the unskilled masses into editorial work. That wispy vision of little knots of common men producing their own newspapers had been made obsolete by industrialization if nothing else. The Soviet mass media's tendency was toward size and professional management. Ignoring for a moment political obstacles, the ordinary Soviet citizen had no more chance of swaying *Pravda* or *Sovetskaya Sibir* than the American of influencing *The New York Times* or the Chicago *Tribune*. True, Khrushchev pushed editors to establish councils of specialists, nonstaff writers' groups, and to bring worker-peasant correspondents into closer contact with newspapers and broadcasting. But the best writing and reporting, the more important social commentary in the Soviet mass media was produced by the intelligentsia, by the skilled specialists, professional writers, government and party officials, and trained journalists. The Soviet factory worker or the collective farmer could turn to the big newspapers for an ally against bureaucracy, to voice complaints or to suggest new techniques. And he had his small factory or farm tabloid and the bulletin board wall newspapers, though these were in the hands of generally uncreative party apparatchiks. The mass audience had become the object of the press, rather than the press having become an amplifier of the masses. As a whole, the mass media had grown into a mammoth institution with its own ethics and habits. A heritage of Stalin's years, it was fearful of innovation, apprehensive of saying what had not been said at the top, unsure of making individual judgments. The press had become a series of dull news releases. Most Soviet journalists were easy prey for surviving Stalinists. The spirit of the mass press had been broken, along with that of many millions of Soviet citizens. The mass media's quandary in the Khrushchev years and after was not how to transform themselves into a magical "people's forum"; Soviet society was too stratified, too authoritarian, and too urbanized for that sort of populist dream. The quandary rather was in how forcefully and truthfully the press could focus on the moral, political, and economic problems of Soviet society and help solve them, when many of these problems went to the heart of the Soviet system.

Khrushchev's prime legacy to the contemporary Soviet press was flexibility and experimentation. Under his prodding, the face of Soviet printed media was redone. Newspapers and magazines, which for long had reflected Stalin's conservative tastes, became more attractive and eye-catching. Writing was brighter. Large photographs and illustrations appeared on front pages. The changes were gradual. To westerners, accustomed to super-charged journalism, the Soviet press even into the 1960's was a model of Victorian moderation. Splashy, fast-moving journalism went against Soviet political and cultural norms. Thus, in 1958 for example, the party Central Committee pompously criticized several large newspapers for spreading large photographs across their pages and displaying the "harmful influence of the western bourgeois press." [109] Against such bromides, reformists argued that the press essentially had lost its influence and its integrity under Stalinist controls. Perhaps, during industrialization and the war, the mass media served well as the great mobilizer of the masses. But, the reformists' brief went, the press in post-Stalin times had to become a creative, stern critic of society. If it were to be an effective ally of the party, the press had to be informative, interesting, and truthful.

A pacesetter in the mass media's change was a young activist, Alexei Adzhubei, a 1953 graduate of Moscow University's School of Journalism, and also Khrushchev's son-in-law. Nepotism in this instance benefited the press. Talented in his own right, Adzhubei moved rapidly upward. Named editor of the major youth newspaper, *Komsomolskaya Pravda,* in the late 1950's, Adzhubei remade the publication. Compared with other newspapers, its pages sparkled with snappy headlines, pictures, well-written human interest features, and news stories. In 1959, Adzhubei took over editorship of the dull government newspaper, *Izvestia.* Under his imaginative management, *Izvestia's* circulation, along with *Komsomolskaya Pravda's,* swiftly increased. Moreover, Adzhubei was a prime mover in the formation of Press Agency Novosti in 1961, and was a force in the Union of Journalists, created in 1956-57. Both worked to draw the mass media out of their worst lethargy and conformity.[110]

Adzhubei symbolized a new generation of Soviet journalists. They were less given to banal slogans, and more concerned with authentic reporting and interpreting of social change. That clichés and stereotypes all too often characterized the Soviet press in the late 1950's and during the 1960's was as much testament to force of habit as to necessity. The limits of the permissible had moved out, farther at times than journalists were psychologically prepared to explore. The poets and novelists were more courageous and determined to test the boundaries of acceptable thought. And in some areas, political restrictions on the press were unquestioned. The mass media did not intrude during Khrushchev's years as critic of Soviet foreign policy, nor do more than laud the sacrosanct Soviet military machine. The press glorified political victors and vilified the fallen as the moment demanded. But in other spheres, the Soviet press raised doubts, asked questions, challenged old ideas. It discussed and debated farm issues, industrial management, education, economic planning, and problems of morality and culture, particularly in relation to the young postwar generation. The press conducted a continuing campaign to inculcate a new political-social ethic, in place of Stalinism.

The touchstone was Khrushchev's grandiose Communist Party Program of 1961, an attempt to stir the nation once again with the dream of a great new society. It was not notably successful. The nation had grown weary of large promises. It had become jaded by descriptions of a future paradise. To Soviet youth especially, the present counted for more. Some Soviet journalists recognized the changing mood. But the press as an institution had its vested interests in the political structure; for most editors, their base of power was in the party, not the mass audience. So even the reform-minded journalists moved cautiously and warily. The traditionalists performed as docile press agents. Only toward the end of Khrushchev's years did a few journalism educators and editors begin to argue convincingly that the press had lagged behind changes elsewhere in Soviet society, and that for all the furor over "moving closer to the masses," the press was out of step with its audience. Thus arose the new interest, coincident with the revival of Soviet sociology, with audience tastes and attitudes.

Khrushchev was deposed with stunning swiftness in October, 1964. The press underwent no radical alterations as a result. Like other Soviet institutions the press had been conceived largely by Lenin, structured by Stalin, and shaken to its roots by Khrushchev. The contemporary Soviet press is not wholly of another, post-Khrushchev era. Rather, in its content and operation, it reflects an era in which Khrushchev was a dominant figure.

CHAPTER 3

WRITTEN AND UNWRITTEN RULES

No society allows its mass media to roam at will, entirely free to disseminate to a mass audience all events and thoughts they choose. Freedom of the press, like good and evil, always falls short of the absolute. And, the reverse, no system of mass communications, regardless of political or economic affiliations in its society, is ever perfectly managed. Rather, societies chart out areas in which the press operates with little hindrance and often much encouragement. Obviously, some societies are more permissive than others with the mass media. The American press is granted wide latitude to probe the faults and virtues of society, to record its change and conflicts. By comparison, the Soviet mass media operates within narrow confines.

The difference is not so much freedom versus nonfreedom of the press. That dichotomy assumes a common definition of "freedom" by which the mass media's status in a society can be gauged. What is press freedom in France may be obscenity in the United States. What is the mass media's right to fair comment in the United States is antistate propaganda in the Soviet Union. Any one society's description of press freedom reflects its own cultural and moral content, and ultimately its concept of the nature of man and his relation to society. The University of Missouri's School of Journalism has tried to measure press freedom in most of the world's nations according to 23 criteria. Reflecting the American emphasis on independent, private management of the mass media, 11 of the 23 criteria deal directly with government control or regulation of the press. Only 2 relate to purely economic—private or public—restrictions.[1] In this measurement, the more government involvement, the less free the mass media. Applied to the world's press, the privately owned media automatically have the edge on the freedom scale, and the state- or publicly owned press rates low. Leaving aside any propensity to wage ideological war, were Moscow University's School of Journalism to draw up criteria of a free press, it unquestionably would include more items on economic or financial management of mass media. The more the press was tied to a nation's private economic structure, the less its freedom. The point here is not to argue the proper criteria of a free press, but that any criteria are drawn from the standards of a given society, and in particular from the purposes and roles historically assigned to the mass media.

Whether in the United States, the Soviet Union, or any other nation, these are established vaguely by tradition, custom, current social mores, and "good taste." More precisely, boundaries for the mass media are drawn by regulations, laws, court decisions, or political decrees. When the mass media move beyond these limitations, they meet progressively stiffer resistance in disseminating information and attitudes. Most simply, it may be opposition from a segment of readers or listeners who sense that a belief or moral value is threatened. Many American newspaper readers objected, for example, to publicity given early opponents of the Vietnam war because, as letters to editors implied, news of protests held patriotism in question. The Soviet press met resistance after Khrushchev's fall from power in 1964 in continuing its criticism of the "cult of the individual" —Stalinism. In this case, opposition came from a segment of the political bureaucracy. It argued that the Khrushchev-initiated campaign against Stalinism detracted from Soviet accomplishments during Stalin's rule, and defamed the nation. Subsequently, the phrase "cult of the individual" was largely banned from the Soviet press.[2]

The mass media also encounter trouble when information seems to betray or harm the national interest. In the United States, the crunch often comes in time of war or an international diplomatic crisis that threatens war; but in domestic crisis, too. The Kerner Commission on Civil Disorders severely chastised the American mass media for exaggerating the violence that erupted in cities during 1967, and thereby doing a disservice to national tranquility.[3] In the Soviet Union, where there is prior censorship of the press, like conflicts are resolved most often privately, among editors, censors, or Communist Party officials. However, given the imperfection of man's institutions, disputes inevitably surface. In 1966, during the 23rd Communist Party Congress, the popular literary journals *Novy Mir* and *Yunost* came under attack for persistently publishing fiction that, to high-ranking party critics, presented a pessimistic, inaccurate view of Soviet society, and thus distorted public attitudes, particularly among the young.

In a more complex process, the mass media may be encouraged generally to move beyond accepted thought and opinion, only to be discouraged or rebuffed when they do. In the United States, there are "controversial" television documentaries or reports. They are controversial precisely because they portray something about or for one element in society that another would prefer not to have popularized. Mass media discussions of birth control were, and perhaps still are, controversial because of conflict within the United States over the morality, among other questions, of preventing conception artificially. In the Soviet Union, initial reports of "concrete sociological research" were controversial partly because the Soviet press was promoting empirical investigations of Soviet society against an entrenched opinion that such research was unscientific and "western."

One cannot find exact parallels in the Soviet Union and the United States for every instance of the mass media exceeding what is commonly and vaguely thought their proper domain. And even where similarities exist, there are large differences of degree. However, the point is that the mass media functioning in their own society are influenced not simply by the written law or decree, but by unwritten restraints that are as much a part of the journalists' mental makeup as the mass audience's. In the United States, these restraints tend to be the product of public consensus. In the Soviet Union, they are formed more frequently by a small political bureaucracy. Thus, the private lives of political leaders are not considered proper topics for the Soviet mass media as they are by the American press. Even when the Soviet press has assaulted the fallen, such as Stalin, Malenkov, and Khrushchev, it has not attempted to discredit them with scandalous revelations of personal failings or idiosyncracies. The private lives of Soviet citizens are likewise not for publication, with the exception of persons accused of crimes, especially political crimes. By contrast, diplomats, correspondents, and other foreigners are at times subjected to vicious attacks on their character. These press traits are not a matter of Soviet law, but of political custom and official attitude toward the mass media's rightful place.

At this point, it may be useful to suggest a context in which general and specific restrictions on the Soviet press exist. Just as in the United States, the mass media in the Soviet Union derive many of their characteristics from basic social concepts. As an institution of people, as well as things, the press is shaded by traditional prejudices and mores, and by theories on the nature of man and society.

The American Model

The American press is heavily imbued with the idea of the rational individual.[4] Influenced by thinking of the seventeenth and eighteenth centuries, the press for long assumed that it addressed men who, given information about their government and other social institutions, could rule themselves. Consistent with this, the press was to operate as a check on government, which in American history has been generally suspect. By the same token, it was imperative that the press be free of government restraints. The American press allied with other privately managed institutions, the better to perform its role as watchdog against government infringements on individual rights.

This, the libertarian theory of the press, posited a clash of differing ideas. Some would be sound, some irrelevant, absurd, unorthodox, or demonstrably false. But from the conflict and intermingling of ideas, truth—fully recognizable by reasonable men—would emerge. Thus, the American press implicitly was encouraged to present not only a critique of government, but a range of opinion. Its own responsibility stopped short of managing society. It was enough that the press acted as a marketplace of ideas. Since this activity had to be paid for by someone, and since the government was ruled out as a benefactor, the American press developed as a business institution. But, unlike manufacturers of shoes or steel, American political doctrine attached special importance to the press as a social agency. It thus shared the commercial inclinations of industry, but was assured protection in the constitution against government regulation.

It should be obvious that the libertarian theory of the press did not spring full grown. Nor did theory ever coincide precisely with reality. American attitudes toward the role of the press in society evolved gradually. Barriers, in the form of laws on libel, obscenity, and sedition, were erected around the press by a society that was not fully trustful of unfettered opinion. And the press, while theoretically addressing itself to the rational man, also appealed to man's emotions. Information of a sensational nature sold newspapers in the mass market, while reasoned essays satisfied the demand only of an educated elite. The concept of the rational individual, weighing and judging diverse opinion to arrive at a moment of truth, was more the visionary model than the flesh-and-blood man.

The libertarian theory remains an underpinning of contemporary American mass media; but the idea of social responsibility competes strongly with it today. The latter emerged with the American technological and industrial revolution. Along with other business enterprises, the American press in this century has tended to a large corporate institution.

And it has been argued that the mass media have responsibilities for serving public goals, beyond merchandising information. The swing from the notion of the press as an entrepreneur of news to the concept of mass media as partners in social development has been slow. But the tendency is to regard the press more as a public utility, albeit with distinctive characteristics that separate the mass media from electrical power or telephone companies. But a utility in the sense that its first responsibility is public service, rather than profitable operation, and preferably functions with the least government regulation.

The mass media's social responsibility role has grown with, for one thing, a better educated corps of journalists and, for another, with the rise of social welfare concepts generally in the United States. Where the traditional libertarian sanctified the individual, in both political and economic spheres of society, and emphasized the individual's superiority in the social scheme, the social responsibility theory focuses on collective action, arising from highly interdependent institutions in society. The theory moves newspapers, magazines, television, and radio somewhat toward an alliance with government, insofar as all levels of government are the devices for dealing with major social problems. James Reston suggests: "Most of the time, contrary to official mythology, the people who write the news are not the enemies but the allies of [government] officials. They are usually delivering the news as the post office delivers the mail, and when officials and reporters perform this cooperative service, which is what they do most of the time, they are undoubtedly an influential combination."[5]

The American press still of course performs as the critic of political authority, out of tradition and out of its contemporary understanding that government power unmonitored can become excessive. But the mass media also support and promote welfare for the mass population, which is considerably different from sanctification of the individual. And while the American press jealously guards its independence from government restrictions, so as to offer opinion and news free of vested interest, it recognizes that mass welfare is a government function as much as a private. This implies a constructive criticism of government, rather than a persistent battle against it, for the good of society as a whole.

The major crises posed in the press—urban congestion, poverty, air and water pollution, and racism—are beyond the individual's scope. Their resolution requires mobilization of most of the population to save itself and its society. The American press, often in cooperation with government agencies, has become one of the mobilizers. This is not to imply an ominous trend toward government control of the press. Rather it is to suggest that social changes have dictated a different role for both the press and government. Whatever community of interests they have arises not from conscious decision, but from cumulative responses to daily needs and problems. Thus, the American press now is receptive to discussions of a federally guaranteed income for every American family, of government economic planning, and of publicly financed medical care for all. Half a century ago, when the idea of individual accomplishment and self-reliance stood stronger in the national mentality, these ideas would have sounded as alien in the press as do today occasional advocates of repeal of all welfare programs.

Similarly, the American mass media include or exclude information and attitudes on a variety of other topics because of broad changes in common thought. Sex is treated more openly now than two or three generations ago, reflecting a rise of the national educational level and a decline of traditional, religious moral strictures. Government officials are far less the target of scurrilous, vicious press attacks than in the past. This is perhaps the result of a more sophisticated thinking among journalists, more capable federal and state officials, and a greater sympathy and understanding on the part of journalists for the problems of government. Frequent presentation of Negroes in a favorable context is characteristic of American mass media today because a large segment of American thinking has changed, partly because of the press itself.

As these examples suggest, the American mass media, though operating in a pluralistic society with great latitude for dissenting and varied opinion, conform to broad trends of thought. Even beyond relatively precise written rules, such as laws on libel or pornography, the press is censored by constantly changing social attitudes, and indeed censors itself out of a sense of social responsibility.

The Russian Mind

The Soviet mass media also perform within a framework of thought and social restrictions that ultimately reflects interpretations of man and society. Soviet circumstances are perhaps more complex than the American. For the Soviet national mentality is part artificial, in that official political doctrine proposes one concept, while there exist also traditional Russian attitudes that influence the functioning of the press.

In sharp contrast to the American mass media's heritage, Russia's tradition has lacked adulation of the individual man's capacity. In a country where the nobility and Church were the dominant propertyholders, the small landowner, with whom American individualism is inextricably linked, failed to emerge as a dominant social force. Rather, the commune, the village, was the molding influence of vast millions of Russian peasants. Even as Russia began to build its industrial cities in the late nineteenth century, the entrepreneur middle class remained miniscule. The notion of hard labor, thriftiness, individual accomplishment, and personal gain, all of which propelled Americans at the same period in history, were largely absent from Russian society. They were not the values of the old nobility, nor the intelligentsia. And the mentality of the masses of peasants derived from centuries of serfdom and the estates of the privileged. The Russian philosopher Nicolas Berdyaev proposes:

> The ethical ideas of the Russians are very different from the ethical ideas of western peoples, and they are more Christian ideas. Russia's moral values are defined by an attitude towards man, and not towards abstract principles of property or of the state nor towards good in the abstract. The Russians adopt a different attitude towards sin and crime; there is pity for the fallen and debased; nor is there any love for grandeur. The Russians have less of the sense of family than western peoples, but immeasurably more of the community spirit; they are seeking not so much organized society as the sense and experience of community, and they are less academic. The Russian paradox is summed up in this, that the Russian people are much less socialized than the peoples of the west, but also much more community conscious, more ready for the life in common.[6]

On the same theme Wright W. Miller observes:

> . . . While Russian history has been strong in forces tending to preserve the traditional collective life, it has always been weak in forces which could develop the status and rights of the individual. And these forces have not merely been weak because collective forces were strong; they have simply been lacking or almost lacking.[7]

The pervasive nature of the commune in Russian history is glimpsed in the fact that the Russian word *"mir"* simultaneously means commune, the world, and peace. It was the refuge of the devout, God- and czar-fearing peasant, as the individual homestead was the source of the life and attitudes of the early God-fearing American pioneer. Beyond the commune, Russian Orthodoxy has eminently shaped the Russian tradition. Divorced from the mainstream of western culture, notably the Reformation and the scientific revolution, the Russian was not part of that intellectual movement that spawned free inquiry, individual pursuit of truth, skepticism, and doubt. Strong and unchallenged, Russian Orthodoxy promulgated belief in the will of God and the authority of the czar. Fate and destiny were not, as they were in the West, challenged by belief in man's ability to control his life, at least not until the arrival of Marxism in Russia, and particularly not until the Soviet social system was implanted in Russia after 1917.

The Russian was therefore a different soul than the American of the industrial revolution. The Russian was persuaded to believe in Orthodoxy, autocracy, and nationality. His personal initiative was discouraged. His individual rights were of little concern to czars and officials who believed that they were vested with the right and responsibility for commanding the Russian empire.

True, in the twilight years of Russian autocracy, before the cataclysm of World War I, reforms were attempted; central European concepts of human rights and democratic government had entered the Russian intellectual stream. But coming from an essentially conservative system, the reforms were half measures, and the assorted western ideals merged with Russian thought as antagonists and revolutionaries against the old order.

The Russian press, of course, mirrored the structure of society. It was largely directed toward the nobility, government bureaucracy, and the intelligentsia. These being the educated, literate segments of the population, they were naturally the prime audience. But it was a minority. The 1897 census showed that only 21 per cent of the Russian population could read and write, and of 104,321 persons with a higher education, 73 percent were children of nobles or government officials.[8] The Russian press therefore developed differently than in the United States, where editors were engrossed with a mass audience rather than an intellectual elite. Russian newspapers and "thick" journals took on a literary tone from the frequent publication of leading writers of the day for the relatively sophisticated reader. And though the popular press slowly developed in Russia during the second half of the nineteenth century, it was conservative in form and content. Large, bold headlines and huge illustrations, which in the United States were devices to compete for the attention of a relatively unsophisticated audience, were viewed as sensational journalism in Russia. [9]

Implicit in the Russian press system was the vast cleavage between a small governing privileged class and the mass of peasants and workers. The press lacked a tradition of popular democracy and the idea of the rational individual capable of governing himself. No political philosophy spurred Russian newspapers to criticize the czarist government. The czar, after all, took his power from God, and was the protector and defender of the masses. True, as the revolutionary organizations began to form in Russia, there were newspapers and periodicals that challenged, however obliquely, the presumptions of monarchy. But the powerful press was allied with monarchy and on the whole was not an obstacle to state power.

One reason was the integration of economic and political institutions. Russian economic development was much more a state-motivated process in Russia than in the United States. Thornton Anderson notes:

> While the entrepreneurs of the west, armed with the laissez faire doctrine of Adam Smith, were freeing themselves from government controls and increasing the momentum of the industrial revolution, those of Russia remained, on into the 20th century, largely dependent upon, and subservient to, the government.[10]

Similarly, Hugh Seton-Watson concludes of the Russian economy of the late nineteenth century:

Russian business and Russian government used and profited from each other, but on balance it was the government which gained the most, and the government which kept the direction of the economy. There was a much closer correlation between the industries which developed most and the industries required for state interests than was the case in countries in which the industrial revolution was a spontaneous process initiated by private invention and private profit-seeking.[11]

This government-business relationship was reflected by the press. Russian newspapers and periodicals, though privately owned, did not function in an intellectual atmosphere in which the government was considered the chief enemy of private enterprise. Clearly, Russian political philosophy was changing at the turn of the century under the pounding of revolutionary thought. But there was no ingrained principle compelling the press to oppose the state as there was in the American tradition. Further, the state presumed to control the press, as it presumed to direct the economy. Government abolition of censorship in 1905, after popular uprisings, was among reforms designed to blunt revolution, rather than to open the floodgates of free expression.

The Bolshevik Revolution predicated an entirely different concept of man and society. An offshoot of Marxism, the Bolsheviks shared a utopian streak with other advocates of a new order—socialists, populists, anarchists. The Bolsheviks invested the mass man with a theoretical capacity to take active part in the collective management of his society. Lenin was certain that any ordinary worker could run the machinery of government. The Bolsheviks assumed that, given control of their own lives and destinies, the masses would respond out of a spirit of brotherhood and common purpose. The self-interest and personal gain that powered the gears of capitalist societies, and that to the Marxists stimulated the crass instincts of men, would be exorcised from human society. By communal action, man would be liberated to pursue the noble goals of truth and beauty. "Man" meant the common man—the victimized humanity of the capitalist industrial revolution that worked the machines and harvested the fields. These in any event were the lofty ideals. They corresponded to existing possibilities about as much as peasant Russia conformed to the Marxist condition for violent transition from advanced capitalism to beginning socialism.

But they accounted for that glimmer of a "people's press." We have already seen how that idea was shunted aside by the exigencies of achieving and maintaining political power. Though unrealized, the idea of the mass people's press survived in official Soviet attitudes; so too have other of the revolutionary ideals. As social values with political sanction, they form a Soviet society which reflects reality to the extent that perhaps the total product of American advertising does.

In one instance, then, the Soviet mass media function in a somewhat artificial world. They perpetuate codes of behavior, social mores, and Marxist-Leninist thought that have been superimposed in a remarkably short time over a Russian culture. Soviet values are those of a society still undergoing modernization under strong central leadership. Hard work, frugality, unity of purpose, discipline, obedience, rewards for efficient production, trust in the leadership, and faith in the future are among the values appearing constantly in the Soviet press. They are not wholly alien to old Russian culture, and where the Soviet model of society does not conflict with the prerevolutionary Russian, the values remain intact. But where they do, the old have assumed an underground existence so far as the mass media are concerned. Thus, the infinite Russian optimism permeates the Soviet press, while equally boundless melancholy rarely is transmitted. The first has been coopted into official mores. In a modernizing nation, where sacrifice and deprivation are demanded, optimism is a potent and essential force. Melancholy, sadness, and pessimism, by contrast, are minimized in the Soviet press precisely because they discourage progress and accomplishment. In the United States, somewhat the same result occurred during World War II. The government and the press, though not in tight coordination, generated a spirit of optimism by disseminating hopeful information when possible, and in other cases, the most favorable interpretation of the worst.

Despite the concerted attempt to create new values and mores, purely Russian tradition survives. The notion of community, which has been institutionalized in the Soviet Union as the factory and farm collective, bulks large in the Soviet mentality. Personal sincerity, honesty, integrity, and truthfulness are repeatedly the subjects of exemplary articles in the Soviet press. Traditional Russian suspicion and distrust of authority is diverted, in the mass media, to criticism of bureaucracy. Insofar as it is popularly directed toward the central leadership or vaguely toward the system—"they"—it is almost concealed, and exists in a second, subsurface Soviet society.

It is in this society that the unthinkable is spoken and myths give way to realities. The division between *should be* and *is* is narrower now than under Stalin. In one sense, "liberalization" of Soviet society has been concerned precisely with the existing duality. Often enough, what attracts the foreign eye in the Soviet press is information commonly known in the underground society but not admitted in the official, public world. Most Soviet citizens knew that many people were sent to labor camps during Stalin's years. The public admission of Stalin's injustices was sensational partly because it was *public*. Thereafter what was said and known privately could, in large measure, be said publicly, too. Similarly, candid acknowledgments in the press of rural poverty and backwardness, of slow economic growth, and of nihilism and disenchantment among youth have narrowed the gap between theory and reality.

What is apparent is that the framework of thought in which the press operates constantly alters. But there does exist some framework, which even without censorship and political controls, influences mass media form and content. Proceeding from a general view of man and society, a mixture of the Russian heritage and Soviet concepts, there are the vagaries of good taste, popular morals, and acceptable behavior. These find reflection in the press, partly because they are imposed by the official morality, and partly because they are indeed the nature of Soviet mass society; or both. Patriotism is an official virtue, and also an authentic emotion among the bulk of the Soviet population. No law exists prohibiting well-intentioned and constructive criticism of the Soviet state (though "anti-Soviet" agitation and propaganda are illegal); but both official and popular opinion still is disinclined to accept much of it in the mass media (or in literature).

Even if the Soviet journalist were moved to exceed the accepted limitations, he would find both official and popular resistance. But the Soviet journalist, being a product of Soviet education, culture, and politics, works mostly within boundaries —for two reasons. First, there are official pressures put on him. And, second, somewhat like his American counterpart, his own thoughts are influenced by subtle or direct social pressures. The Soviet press still deals with sex with Victorian shyness, equating it with romantic love of the old Hollywood B movie variety and reflecting the puritan quality of Soviet society. The Soviet press is cautious in reporting political news, not only because of official restrictions, but because tradition is against a press standing with the rank and file against state power. Though Soviet

Marxist thought turns on the common man, he is seen as part of a mass, homogeneous society in which leaders and led share like values. The attitude is not conducive to the press playing the political critic (leaving aside for the moment the fact that the political establishment actively discourages this function). To understand the Soviet press in this respect, one may reflect on the American mass media's treatment of racial problems before the 1954 Supreme Court decision on school segregation. The American setting was such that journalists did not write of racial inequality in the condemning tone common today. The information on black poverty and prejudice was not available, nor was there popular encouragement and reception of it. Similarly, the Soviet journalist works in a system that is not structured to provide full and frank details on political activities: he is not directed from any quarter to seek the information. The sort of political commentary and reporting common in the United States is as implausible to the Soviet journalist as, for example, an aggressive probing into the personal activities and and qualifications of religious leaders is to American journalists.

Taboos of the Soviet mass media encompass more than politics. "Sensational" journalism is deplored, very much as it was in the late nineteenth century. Although Khrushchev himself was an unrelenting advocate of attractive formats and lively writing, the Russian tradition combined with a quarter century of Stalin's conservative tastes have built formidable psychological barriers to change. Only in the past decade, as younger, professionally trained men and women have entered journalism, has the Soviet press begun to abandon its reserved appearance and prosaic style. Even so, it has been an uphill fight. The Communist Party newspaper *Pravda*, a pacesetter in lifeless journalism, scolded after Khrushchev's fall: "The tone of the press must be calm and businesslike. It cannot be considered normal that some newspapers and magazines (this applies equally to radio and television) try to please low tastes, at times chase after cheap sensationalism and loudness and sometimes descend to saccharine sentimentality." [12] Just what defines sensationalism in the Soviet press is not quite clear, least of all to Soviet journalists. The "sob story" certainly falls into that category. On the other hand, after about 1965, for reasons of politics and prestige, true life spy thrillers tending to glamorize the state security committee (the Soviet intelligence and investigative agency) were acceptable. Natural catastrophe, murder, bizarre behavior, plane crashes—all that Americans are accustomed to learning about daily from their mass media—are understated in the Soviet press, if reported at all. This has been the Soviet way, partly because unpleasant information was considered negative propaganda for an avowedly superior (to capitalism) form of society. And although the press is slowly discarding the conceit, custom exercises a force.

In sum, there are imprecise areas of the acceptable and impermissible so far as the performance of the Soviet mass media goes. Certain paths have been established for disseminating news and attitudes. The Soviet journalist moves along these as unchallenged as American journalists reporting Fourth of July oratory. When he breaks from the norm—and, as in the United States, only a minority of imaginative iconoclasts attempt to do so—he can expect reaction, first among his professional peers and superiors; second, from his audience, particularly the political bureaucracy; and third, from the formal state and Communist Party machinery which maintains precise limitations on the press.

The State: Laws and Censorship

Like the American mass media, the Soviet press is subject to laws against libel, slander, and pornography. But in addition, the Soviet press labors under government censorship, which American media have not experienced since World War II— and never as severely as Soviet publications and broadcasting. Further, in the realm of Soviet government restrictions, there exists a catch-all prohibition against "anti-Soviet propaganda and agitation." In vagueness, it approaches the sedition laws of earlier times in the United States. In recent years, it has been a device for intimidating and persecuting Soviet writers. But there is no evidence that professional journalists have been prosecuted under the anti-Soviet law. Beyond these restrictions, there are the Committee on the Press, the Committee on Radio Broadcasting and Television, *Soyuzpechat*—which manages all circulation for printed media—and finally state economic agencies, all of which exercise varying degrees of control over the press.

The total result of laws, regulations, and institutions dealing with the press is, on paper, state conformity of all information. In practice, there is more margin for varied opinion and thought than would be supposed from a clinical description of press management devices. This is explained partly by the fact that human imperfection sabotages even perfect intent. And despite unpredictable cycles of thaw and freeze in cultural-literary policies, the trend since Stalin's death has been toward freer expression. But the institutions for control of the mass media persist, and it is undisputable that even with some emphasis on self-regulation by the press, they act as final checkpoints of information and ideas.

Glavlit

Censorship is one of those phenomena known to everyone in the Soviet Union, but upon which no one elaborates for the public record. Consequently, we have only a few pieces of the puzzle, and some are very old at that. As we have seen, however, censorship of the press was as much a czarist Russian as it has been a Soviet predilection. After the interlude of the 1918–20 civil war, the regrouping Soviet government simply renewed the czarist censorship agency, in 1922, and it has existed ever since. Its responsibilities are no more original than they were under the czar, but they are far more sweeping and better executed than before the Bolshevik Revolution.

Russian censorship over books was established by Czar Fëdor II, during his brief reign from 1676 to 1682.[13] Censorship depended on the particular likes of officials until 1804, when a censorship law was adopted. This was revised and expanded in 1826, with a new regulation of 230 articles. Still another censorship law was adopted in 1865.[14] Generally, the laws provided for preliminary censorship, fines, seizure of publications, and licenses, although specifics changed with various laws and the application depended on the individual czar's attitudes.

The Soviet censorship agency gradually adopted the most extensive and restrictive of censorship devices. By the 1930's, *Glavlit*—the Chief Administration for Literary and Publishing Affairs—had grown into a pervasive network of government censors. Typical of its powers are those described in a 1931 statute, when *Glavlit* was being expanded coincident with enlargement of the press network. "*Glavlit* may prohibit the printing, publication and distribution of works: a) containing agitation and propaganda against Soviet authority and the dictatorship of the proletariat; b) revealing state secrets; c) arousing nationalistic or religious fanaticism; d) of a true pornographic character." [15] All printed matter—from newspapers to magazines to sketches—was subject to *Glavlit*'s and military agen-

SOVIET GOVERNMENT AGENCIES FOR THE MASS MEDIA

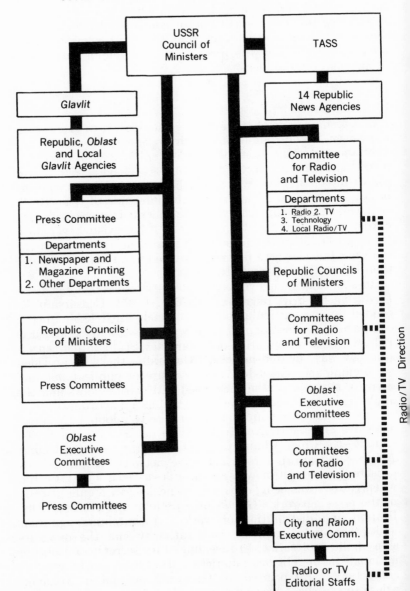

cies' surveillance for military secrets. But Communist Party publications, works of the Academy of Sciences, and the government newspaper *Izvestia* were exempted from political-ideological screening. The last published statute on *Glavlit* is dated 1936. It required all printed matter to carry the *Glavlit* stamp—a letter and several digits—unless it was "secret" or "absolutely secret." There was a two-step process to publication. The content of some publications needed *Glavlit* approval before it was sent to the typesetter. Established newspapers and magazines, such as the party press, had general permission to forward material directly to the printer. In both instances, however, *Glavlit* approved publications before printing, and only after an ostensibly exacting check. The *Glavlit* agent assigned to a given printing plant was first to read page proofs and enter his corrections. These were to be made, and a second proof pulled and read again by the *Glavlit* representative. If he was satisfied, he signed each page proof; the publication was then cleared for printing. No corrections could be made thereafter by editors, unless *Glavlit* once more approved.[16]

At least in the 1930's, *Glavlit*'s powers were immense. In addition to precensorship, the *Glavlit* network maintained surveillance over newspapers and periodicals after publication. *Glavlit* agents were assigned not only to printing plants, but to editorial offices, radio broadcasting stations, post offices, telegraph agencies, and border points. The agency was authorized to suppress publications, and to halt import and export of literature which, in *Glavlit*'s opinion, violated any of numerous restrictions. Further, in issuing "permission visas" for publication, *Glavlit* dictated that circulation and size of newspapers and periodicals must conform precisely to existing limitations.[17] Any organizations engaged in printing of any sort had to account to *Glavlit* for their consumption of paper and lead.[18] The end result was that *Glavlit* theoretically acted as the clearinghouse for the entire Soviet mass media in all aspects. Its objective was not only to screen approved publications and radio broadcasting for political, economic, and military information, but to deprive any but approved organizations of access to the press. With *Glavlit*'s overseeing of paper and lead use, it obviously was impossible for any organizations to establish their own publications without conforming to *Glavlit*'s norms or else violating the law.

As to the latter, *Glavlit* was its own judge and jury. None of the statutes on *Glavlit* in the 1920's and 1930's provided for appeal to courts of *Glavlit*'s decisions. Further, *Glavlit* worked in conjunction with the Soviet internal security police in rooting out ostensibly subversive literature. By this association, *Glavlit* also took on the character of an extralegal authority responsible only to political agencies.

From the mid-1930's to the present, we are forced to assemble scraps of information in order to see how *Glavlit* developed. Published Soviet regulations stop at 1936; obviously, censorship did not. The *Glavlit* visa continued to appear on back pages of newspapers and periodicals. A few years after Stalin's death in 1953, the name *Glavlit* was changed to Chief Administration for the Protection of Military and State Secrets in the Press, and sometime before 1966 the "military" was dropped,[19] for reasons unknown. *Glavlit*, in any case, surveys nearly all Soviet mass media for prohibited political, economic, or cultural information.* Its work is supplemented by censorship departments of the Soviet military, the KGB (state security committee) and the atomic and space agencies.[20]

Divulging of state secrets, military or economic, is punishable under Article 75 of the Russian republic criminal code by from two to eight years imprisonment, depending on circumstances.[21] According to a 1956 decree of the Soviet government, state secrets include: mobilization plans, storage sites, and stockpiling of reserves, operational plans, data on strength and location of troops, plans of military installations, information on war industries' production and fulfillment of plans, data on precious and rare metals, discoveries and inventions of major military importance, state currency reserves, and "other data" that the Council of Ministers determines are state secrets.[22] *Glavlit*, of course, is chiefly responsible for assuring that proscribed information of this type is not published or broadcast. But it has not abandoned surveillance of political or ideological content.

During the 1966 trial of the writers Andrei Sinyavsky and Yuli Daniel, on charges of engaging in anti-Soviet propaganda and agitation, testimony and cross examination revealed that *Glavlit* had prepared a report on the authors' works published abroad. Obviously supporting the state's prosecution of the case, *Glavlit* found a strong "anti-Soviet" tone in the literature.[23] In a private letter to members of the Soviet Union's Union of

---

*Although the agency's title was changed, the original Russian abbreviation—*Glavlit*—is used throughout this book for ease of identification.

Writers, in the spring of 1967, Alexander Solzhenitsyn, author of the celebrated *One Day in the Life of Ivan Denisovich*, denounced *Glavlit*'s censorship of literature along purely ideological lines.[24] Scarce as it is, there nonetheless is evidence that *Glavlit* has not relinquished its authority over political views. Nor, as the Sinyavsky-Daniel trial and Solzhenitsyn's letter indicate, is it divorced from the Soviet security police, the KGB. The two agencies seem to cooperate out of a dual responsibility for blocking publication of politically subversive material.

Several refinements must be noted. First, precensorship by *Glavlit* is most rigorously applied, as far as we can learn, to literature, rather than to journalism. The logical and apparent reason is that a number of Soviet writers have, since the mid-1950's, been the most outspoken critics of Soviet society, particularly on civil rights. The Soviet mass media have been less volatile as a rule. There are exceptions, accounted for by the fact that literature and journalism in the Soviet Union are not so sharply divided as, for example, in the United States. The Soviet literary journal *Novy Mir*, one of the most popular periodicals in the country (which publishes essays on many topics other than literary themes, and in addition to fiction), also has had conspicuous difficulties with censorship.[25] Other periodicals and newspapers are apt to be censored more for their literary works than their journalism.

This leads to a second point. The working Soviet journalist, by his professional training, by his integration in an editorial staff, and by the nature of his job, is less the iconoclast than the Soviet writer. Moreover, with few exceptions, Soviet editors have obtained and held their positions because they have been reliable spokesmen for the political bureaucracy. Consequently, the Soviet journalists' corps engages in self-censorship out of several vested interests. This is not to imply that the Soviet press is monolithic and unchanging. It is to suggest that the duties of *Glavlit* censors, who still are posted in printing plants and who still issue "visas," have been preempted increasingly by journalists themselves. Editors and correspondents have developed a sense of what is wholly acceptable, what is questionable, and what is proscribed material. No Soviet editor would try to publish the location of Soviet missile sites, even if he had the information. But he will confidently print an exposé of waste or corruption in a local factory. When he moves from the customarily acceptable information to the questionable, however, the existence of *Glavlit* (and political agencies) influences if not dictates his decisions.

Third, precensorship of the Soviet mass media by *Glavlit* has never been a developed art. In the 1930's, censorship was more the hacking of a butcher than the precision cutting of a surgeon. Most often, censors sliced out objectionable material, but sometimes they missed. Although they received lists of information that was not to appear in the press, censors could be inefficient, lackadaisical, and inept in their jobs. Merle Fainsod notes in his study of the Smolensk *oblast* Communist Party archives: "The operations of censorship were seriously handicapped by a lack of trained, politically reliable cadres and the indifference of lower party organizations to the need for this type of activity." [26] The picture we get from the Smolensk documents is of a rather haphazard censorship system, involving not only *Glavlit* but security police, the military, and local Communist Party leaders, that succeeded imperfectly. After the early 1930's, when censorship was being expanded, *Glavlit* became more efficient. Certainly during World War II censorship tightened, and by the time of Stalin's death, the Soviet mass media reflected, in their almost absolute conformity, the expertise of *Glavlit* as well as the submission of journalism to Stalinism.

How effective and significant is *Glavlit* as a censor of the contemporary Soviet press? We know that *Glavlit* representatives approve all newspapers and periodicals before they go to press, from the smallest weekly on up to *Pravda* and *Izvestia*. It is evident that much information regularly issued by American mass media (even on the Soviet Union) does not appear in the Soviet press. Some of it—on military matters, for instance—is simply not available to Soviet journalists. Some is known, but not published or broadcast until it has approval of the central political bureaucracy. Still other information is withheld because editors think its publication would be controversial. And finally, there is *Glavlit* as another, but not necessarily the final arbiter. According to one Soviet journalist: "*Glavlit* tries sometimes to interfere with our work. Mainly *Glavlit* checks on military secrets. If we publish a picture of a tank or plane, we have to have the *Glavlit* stamp on it. But then sometimes *Glavlit* tries to tell us this or that is wrong and should be taken out. Then it depends on the editor. If he says, 'Fine, please, I agree,' that's one thing. But if you say, 'No, I don't agree,' then you have a discussion. *Glavlit* calls the Ministry of Culture, then we call some [Communist] party officials. It is all decided by higher authorities." [27]

On the work of the *Glavlit* censor, the editor of an Irkutsk *oblast* newspaper explained: "He checks for facts—like military information—that are prohibited. But he has no say over general content. Our job is to write. His is to see if the facts are prohibited."[28] In the same vein, one editor of a Leningrad newspaper commented on censorship: "Call it comradely control. Earlier, *Glavlit* censored, but not now. He [the censor] is concerned mainly with military information. We understand each other. We know what statistics we can publish and which ones we can't in the national interest. Maybe we would ask him if this [pointing to a picture of an armored troop carrier to be used for a Red Army day issue] is new and he [the censor] says no. If he objects to some political article, we tell him to go to the devil." [29]

What these comments suggest is that prior censorship of the Soviet press concentrates on military and state secrets, while ideological or political matters are open to some bargaining. This interpretation is reinforced by the fact that articles in the Soviet press generate controversy over their ideological correctness. Clearly, this form of postcensorship—in the sense that journalists are pressured not to maintain a certain view—is unnecessary if there is rigorous precensorship of political content.

Censorship by Law

Glavlit operates according to statutes ostensibly approved by the Supreme Soviet, the Soviet parliament. But *Glavlit*'s censorship is extralegal in the sense that it is not subject to court review. By contrast, there are published laws in the Soviet Union that do involve the press. The most controversial is Article 70 of the Russian republic's criminal code concerning anti-Soviet propaganda and agitation. It outlaws: "Agitation or propaganda conducted for the purpose of subverting or weakening Soviet power or for the purpose of committing particularly dangerous state crimes; dissemination, for the same purpose, of slanderous fabrications that discredit the Soviet state and social system; as well as dissemination or preparation or possession for the same purposes of literature with a like content." [30] The penalty is imprisonment for six months to seven years, or exile to Soviet provinces for two to five years, or both. The same crime, in connection with a state offense, such as treason, is punishable by up to ten years imprisonment.

Article 70, like *Glavlit* censorship, has been used to intimidate

Soviet writers. Sinyavsky and Daniel were tried under the provision, and in January, 1968, four Soviet citizens involved in publication of an underground literary journal, *Phoenix 66*, and distribution of foreign propaganda were convicted under Article 70.[31] There is no record of established, working journalists being prosecuted under Article 70 (although some may have been in secret trials). The pattern to date suggests that its practical use, from the standpoint of political authorities, is against the illegal press, or against writers who do not publish through the standard Soviet channels.

In spirit, Article 70 is similar to the 1798 Sedition Act in the United States. The latter, contrived to silence press criticism of the Federalists, outlawed "any false, scandalous and malicious writing . . . against the government of the United States, or either house of the congress . . . or the said president . . . or to excite against them the hatred of the good people of the United States." [32] The American 1918 Sedition Act, adopted during World War I, was in the same vein. It prohibited writing or publishing "any disloyal, profane, scurrilous or abusive language about the form of government of the United States or the Constitution, military or naval forces, flag or the uniform." [33]

Like these laws, the Soviet Article 70 is so imprecise as to be applicable to almost any statements critical of the government, depending on interpretations made by police and judges. Particularly in political cases, Soviet courts have been instruments of the Communist Party. The consequence is that Article 70 provides a legal ruse by which minor and major dissenters can be brought into court and conviction assured. And while the law has not been applied to the state-owned press, it is a convenient device to stop individual internal publications—mimeographed or typewritten—that are overtly critical of Soviet society, and that do not pass through the usual channels, where official censorship and editors' self-censorship may check them.

A second and related Soviet law, Article 71 of the Russian republic criminal code, prohibits "war propaganda" and carries a punishment of from three to five years imprisonment, and two to five years in exile in the provinces.[34] Article 228 outlaws the dissemination of printed works of a "pornographic character" and provides a prison sentence of up to three years, and a fine of up to 100 rubles ($111 at the official exchange rate).[35] Article 71 seems academic as far as the Soviet mass media are

concerned. War is discussed in two contexts—either wholly negatively, or as the focus of military strategy in the event of foreign aggression or threatened attack. The source of the latter
is the Soviet military, whose press is unlikely to be prosecuted
for conducting "war propaganda." Article 228, on pornography,
is operative, but not in the realm of the mass state press, which
is overreserved in its treatment of sex. It is applied, however,
to clandestinely produced pornography. In one case, for example,
"ham" radio operators, transmitting without required amateur
licenses, were tried for broadcasting information of a pornographic character.[36]

In somewhat the same category as Article 70 is a 1963 Soviet
supreme court decision on broadcasting, largely by amateurs.
The court ordered punishment under Article 206 of the Russian
republic criminal code for persons who broadcast "mischievous"
information, or who showed disrespect for society, interfered
with regular programming, or disrupted public order.[37] This
decision seemed to be sufficiently broad to cover a multitude
of sins. Either this law or the one on pornography may have
been applied to a case in Belaya Tserkov where 200 "radio
pirates" were tried for interfering with airwaves and giving
sexually suggestive talks on the air.[38]

Soviet laws on libel (*kleveta*) and insult (*oskorblenive*) have
also become of some importance to the Soviet mass media. As
a reaction to the Stalinist years, when tens of thousands of
persons were unjustly accused of disloyalty, there has been
some caution in the Soviet press in discrediting or defaming
individuals. This does not extend to clearly political matters,
such as some of the recent writers' trials, or to muckraking,
such as campaigns against hooliganism. But in its daily work
of criticizing factory and farm, the press has been urged by
political authorities to show "seriousness, tact, conscientious-
ness, and respect for human dignity."[39] Journalists show some
sensitivity to the problem of libel and insult. Libel is defined
in Article 130 of the criminal code simply as the "dissemination
wittingly of lies defaming another person."[40] Libel in the press
carries a prison sentence of up to three years, or work at an
assigned place for up to a year. Insult carries the latter or a
fine of up to 100 rubles. It is defined in Article 131 as the "in-
tentional abasement of an individual's honor and dignity, expressed in a crude form."[41]

The practice of the Soviet press, like the American, is to
avoid legal action for alleged libel or insult. But rather than

publish or broadcast a retraction of a possibly libelous item, Soviet editors prefer to publish a favorable item about the injured person. The rationale, according to some editors, is that a second item retracting the first only repeats the controversial remarks and further injures the person.[42] It also calls attention to the fallibility of the press. However, retractions do appear. A senior editor of an Azerbaidzhan state publishing house complained to *Izvestia* that a review of a book he edited distorted the text, and that comments on a short story he had translated attributed words to him that he had not used. In a correction, *Izvestia* agreed that the editor was "unreasonably and unfairly insulted as an editor and translator. The criticism of his work was quite biased and unsubstantiated."[43]

Libel cases do sometimes end up in court. In one instance, a district hospital director was accused by the national newspaper *Meditsinskaya Gazeta* of libeling two young doctors in a series of letters written to local Communist Party committees and newspaper editors. The hospital director sued, asking for a retraction by the newspaper, and his suit was rejected by a local Moscow court.[44] In an aborted case, the mother of one of four persons convicted of anti-Soviet propaganda and agitation threatened publicly to sue *Komsomolskaya Pravda*, chief newspaper of the Soviet youth organization, the Komsomol. She claimed that the newspaper libeled her son by describing him as a paid agent of a foreign anti-Soviet organization.[45]

The most celebrated case in recent years concerned several jurists and two major Soviet newspapers, *Izvestia* and *Literaturnaya Gazeta*. In one of a series of articles over the question of when an accused is considered guilty, an assistant prosecutor's views were linked to the Stalinist years. For this attack, both the author and *Izvestia* were sued under the Soviet criminal code article on insult (rather than on libel). A court rejected the assistant prosecutor's suit, on the basis that his own position on guilt and the accused was erroneous. He was admonished by both the court and *Izvestia* for his attitude.[46]

There are several observations worth making on libel and insult cases. First, they do not occur very often, or they are not reported in the press very often. Second, it is probably very difficult for a Soviet citizen successfully to bring a libel suit against a Soviet newspaper. Editors prefer to settle disputes quietly, without publicly acknowledging libel or insult. And, third, the laws on libel and insult do seem to be operative. Although they are seldom brought into play, they act as some check on the mass media against abusing private citizens.

Compared with American libel law and its application, Soviet statutes are underdeveloped. There are no provisions for collecting monetary damages under Soviet law, and judging from publicly reported cases, there is no developed body of judicial opinion on what constitutes libel and insult, beyond definitions contained in the statutes themselves. By the same token, the idea of truth as a defense in libel suits has not been elaborated upon in the Soviet Union and it is unclear whether this would constitute the sole defense or whether other factors would enter in.

As a practical matter, an ordinary Soviet citizen faces imposing power in bringing a libel suit against a Soviet newspaper. The same can be said for the American citizen, but for a different reason. The Soviet citizen would not have to be concerned about huge court costs because of state-provided legal services, but he would be opposing a very influential political organization. In an American context, a libel suit brought by a factory worker against his company's house publication would more nearly approximate the Soviet citizen's action. The ordinary American citizen does, however, face a wealthy organization in bringing suit against a major newspaper or magazine. And since few libel cases are clear cut, and can be appealed to successive courts, legal expenses become a deterrent to initiating action. At the same time, most American printed and broadcast media are extremely cautious with statements that may even border on the libelous. This must be attributed to the operative strength of American libel law.

As a general body of law, Soviet statutes defining rights and restrictions for the press occupy sort of second-class citizenship. Party management of the mass media and censorship, especially by *Glavlit*, mocks attempts to put press operation within a legal framework. That essentially was the criticism of a Soviet author and military correspondent in early 1967, when he encouraged adoption in the Soviet Union of a comprehensive press law. The recently instituted (October, 1966) press law in Czechoslovakia was held up as a model and the target of criticism was quite obviously *Glavlit*, though censorship was not mentioned. The proposal evidently found much support among journalists. In response to many inquiries, *Zhurnalist* published a translation in June, 1967, of large portions of the Czechoslovak law. However, there was no subsequent discussion of the topic and evidently there were political objections to the press law scheme.[47]

The Government Bureaucracy

A number of other government agencies and institutions beyond those already mentioned perform as control devices on the Soviet mass media. The most indirect, but among the most influential, is journalism education, which will be dealt with in the next chapter. In general, Soviet schools of journalism instruct not only in professional skills, but in political attitudes, as does the entire Soviet educational system. This does not ensure the production of intellectual robots—and indeed that is not the goal of Soviet education—but journalism schools continue a process of weaving a particular world outlook into the mental fabric of Soviet youth. Whereas the aspiring American journalist receives an apolitical education in the sense that inquiry, skepticism, and doubt are the underpinnings of his instruction, the Soviet student is heavily impressed with a faith and trust in the Soviet order and the existing political system. The Soviet graduate of a journalism school is therefore more nearly a product of a corporate structure than the American. He is trained in a broad sense by the organization he is expected to serve, somewhat analogous, for example, to West Point's or Annapolis's education of future officers.

Of the government agencies, the Committee on the Press and the Committee on Radio Broadcasting and Television, both subordinated to the Soviet Council of Ministers, exercise direct responsibilities and controls over the mass media. The press committee, originally formed in the 1920's and then disbanded in 1931–33, reappeared in August, 1963, at both the national and republic levels. It was to supervise newspaper and magazine publishing plants, the Soviet printing equipment industry, and the country's entire book publishing enterprise. As lord of the publishers, the committee continues to screen books to "guarantee a high ideological-theoretical level." From 1963 through 1965, *Glavlit* also functioned under the press committee, as indicated by the career of Pavel Romanov. A Central Committee staff member concerned with press affairs since 1945, Romanov was appointed head of *Glavlit* in 1957. Then in 1963, he was promoted to director of the press committee, which simultaneously incorporated *Glavlit* as a subdepartment. Two years later, after Khrushchev's fall from power, a former Minister of Culture, Nikolai Mikhailov, replaced Romanov; and shortly thereafter (apparently in early 1966), Romanov was made chief of *Glav-*

lit once more and the agency was again made an independent organization attached to the Council of Ministers.[48]

The Committee on Radio Broadcasting and Television, in contrast to the press committee, is the government's management for the broadcasting industry. Its authority is far greater than the United States Federal Communications Commission, which concerns itself with broadcasting content more as a public critic (former FCC chairman Newton Minow's celebrated "vast wasteland" judgment of television being an example) and licensee rather than as an editor. The Soviet commission is editorial supervisor for the entire broadcasting network. Its origins go back to 1924, when Soviet radio broadcasting was first being developed. By 1928, broadcasting had been placed under the supervision of the People's Commissariat for Postal Services and Telegraph, and then in 1933 a special committee was established for the radio network alone. In 1953, a chief administration for radio information was created in the Ministry of Culture, and finally in 1957 the present state Committee on Radio Broadcasting and Television came into being under the Council of Ministers.[49] The committee is divided into four chief sections—foreign radio broadcasting, domestic radio, domestic television, and material-technological supply. The functions of these will be dealt with in Chapter 6 on radio and television. Suffice to say at this point that the committee is to Soviet broadcasting what a board of directors is to an American radio-television network. It should be recalled also that *Glavlit* censored radio scripts in earlier years, and there is no reason to doubt that it continues to check scripts today.

The Soviet printed press, unlike the American, is not its own distributor. This job is handled by the Ministry of Communications' chief administration for distribution of the press—commonly called, in the Russian abbreviation, *Soyuzpechat.* The state-owned press distribution system originated in 1918. The significant date after that is 1930, when subscription and retail sales were merged into one organization.[50] At present, *Soyuzpechat* is a large government business with representatives in the more than 67,000 post offices and telegraph offices. It manages 215 stores and more than 21,000 newsstands. In 1966, its income from retail sales and subscriptions amounted to 125 million rubles ($138.7 million).[51]

Soyuzpechat's job is twofold—to conduct an annual mass subscription campaign for all Soviet newspapers and periodicals;

and to see that printed publications get to readers, either by mail or via newsstands. On the average, 80 per cent of newspaper and magazine sales are by subscription, although in large cities newsstand sales account for as much as 35–40 per cent of circulation. For its services, *Soyuzpechat* charges percentage fees. To circulate subscription copies of national newspapers published in the *Pravda* and *Izvestia* plants (each of which prints several newspapers), *Soyuzpechat* receives 6.5 per cent of subscription income; for magazines printed in the same plants, 13 per cent. Other national newspapers and periodicals pay *Soyuzpechat* up to 17 per cent of subscription income; republic and *oblast* newspapers, 7.5 per cent, and magazines, 15 per cent. Local newspapers pay 6.4 per cent. The *Soyuzpechat* fee for newsstand distribution is 7.5 per cent and 13 per cent of sales income for newspapers, depending on category, and 19 or 26 per cent for magazines. Newspapers and magazines also must

The Milwaukee Journal.

A typical newsstand of the Soviet press distribution agency *Soyuzpechat,* in the Soviet Siberian city of Irkutsk.

pay the Soviet post office set rates for delivery service.[52]

The whole distribution process is a business operation from which *Soyuzpechat* is expected to, and does, show a profit. For the first half of 1967, for example, the agency had a profit of 22.2 million rubles ($24.6 million) from income of 67 million ($74.4 million).[53] Newspapers and magazines similarly are on the system of *khozrashchet,* or financial self-sufficiency, and thus enter into agreements with *Soyuzpechat* on distribution at their expense. The arrangement is no different than that in the United States where some magazines buy the services of a subscription agency or regional newsstand distributor, except that in the Soviet Union there is but one distribution organization.

Soyuzpechat conducts vigorous advertising campaigns in the fall of each year to increase press circulation. These have steadily expanded since about 1960, when rather elementary advertising in several regions was found to contribute to circulation gains.[54] Partly because of *Soyuzpechat's* efforts and partly because of population increase and improved newspapers and magazines, circulations have mounted, and with them *Soyuzpechat's* workload. Between 1956 and 1966, for example, one issue newspaper circulation almost doubled, going from 53.5 million to 102 million. In the same period, annual magazine circulation rose from 326.6 million to 1.4 billion.[55]

As a large bureaucracy, in which more than 85 per cent of the paperwork involved in subscriptions and newsstand sales is done by hand rather than calculating machine and computer,[56] *Soyuzpechat* suffers standard inefficiency. Complaints are frequent enough of newspapers and magazines never reaching subscribers, or arriving days and weeks late. The problem is most acute in the smaller cities and in villages, and is the product not only of *Soyuzpechat's* deficiencies, but of post office mishandling and the fact that newspapers do not always come out on time, thus disrupting delivery schedules.

Soyuzpechat also has been the victim of political policies. Over the years, the practice had been to maintain quotas for newspapers and magazines. The effect was to maintain huge circulations of such politically favored newspapers as *Pravda*, though they were not as popular as other publications. Thus, *Soyuzpechat* had to merchandise what to customers were not always attractive goods. This led to "tie-in" sales, whereby a Soviet subscriber had to buy a slow-selling newspaper or periodical in order to get the one publication he actually wanted. At times, he could not get it at all, if the subscription quota was exhausted. There also existed "institution-budgeted" subscriptions. Government and party offices not only could obtain subscriptions to publications with limited quotas; under the guise of needing certain newspapers and periodicals for their daily operations, the state bureaucracy was also purchasing with Soviet taxpayers' money unessential but entertaining publications. Most of this was prohibited in October, 1964, when the quota system was abolished for national newspapers and magazines, and in 1966, when it was ended for the local press.[57]

No less than the American, the Soviet printed media strive for circulation. But there are differences of motivation. As business concerns, the American newspapers and magazines are preoccupied with income-producing sales. And their content, particularly that of the competitive publications, is fashioned to attract regional mass audiences, or specific segments of national readership. American editorial staffs are not much involved in circulation problems; but newspaper and magazine managements are, and they are therefore acutely sensitive to reader likes and fancies. This sensitivity to some extent infiltrates editorial offices. Consider, by contrast, the Soviet system. Newspaper and magazine editors traditionally have given subordinate attention to mass readership (not circulation) because their prime audience was a select political bureaucracy that willingly subsidized unprofitable publications to promote its point of view. *Soyuzpechat,* working independently of editorial staffs, thus was given publications to merchandise. Only with the revival of Soviet sociology and opinion studies have the printed (and broadcast) media begun to orient themselves toward authentic tastes of their audiences. This development, combined with abolition of the circulation quota system, has bred a somewhat competitive spirit in the Soviet mass media.

A moderating or retarding force, however, is state management of the economy. Newsprint and printing equipment are rationed out in the compilation of five year and annual economic plans. Hence, politically favored publications are produced in abundance. It is rare in the Soviet Union for copies of the day's *Pravda* or *Izvestia* not to be available on newsstands. But popular newspapers like *Vechernyaya Moskva* (Moscow's local evening newspaper), *Sovetskii Sport,* or *Nedelya* (*Izvestia*'s weekly supplement) sell out rapidly. Although editors have a vested interest in building circulations, they must depend both on *Soyuzpechat*'s circulation campaign fervor and, for newsprint and printing, on decisions of economic planners. The result is a ponderous bureaucracy, which responds slowly to circulation and readership problems, even when it wants to. By and large, the will is there. Soviet political authorities, because they have a message to tell, are as conscious as American publishers that a newspaper or magazine not sold or not delivered might as well not have been printed. And they are beginning to realize that a newspaper not read might as well not have been produced, either.

The Party Machinery

If there is a single policy-making management for the Soviet mass media, it is the Communist Party apparatus. The formal structural relationship of the press and party is obvious enough from accumulated documents concerning both the party organization and its controls over the press. Indeed, many of the government regulations and institutions just discussed are the administrative expressions of the party's extralegal management of the mass media, and derive from the integration of party and government in Soviet society. For its part, the Communist Party apparatus is primarily concerned with ideological and information content of the mass media. But necessarily it deals with the nuts and bolts of the press, both as a publisher and as political-economic manager of Soviet social institutions.

The elementary party-press union rests on two traditional practices. First, nearly all Soviet newspapers are co-published by the party and government, with the party having the decisive voice in management. For example, the Volgograd *oblast* newspaper is, typically, the organ of the *oblast* Communist Party committee and the soviet (council) of workers' deputies—the *oblast* government. This arrangement goes back to the first years of Bolshevik power and assures Communist Party authority over the newspaper industry to the extent that newspapers are realistically considered party publications, regardless of the government co-publisher. At the national level, newspapers are organs of particular organizations, such as the Central Committee, the Council of Ministers, or the Ministry of Defense. As a second aspect of the party-press union, editors and subeditors of these as well as all other newspapers are approved by the central or lower party apparatuses. The practical consequence is that editors not only are party members, but also hold posts on the appropriate party committees. Party appointment of editors originated with the 1905 Congress of the Social-Democratic Party. After the Bolshevik seizure of power, as party control over the press expanded, the appointments did too. By 1934, for example, party rules provided for "naming the editorial staff of the central organs working under its [the party's] control, and confirmation of editors of party organs of large local organizations." [58] Today, the Communist Party Central Committee's apparatus for the press names the editor in chief, deputy editors, managing editor, and department editors of central party newspapers and magazines. [59] Lower party organizations likewise appoint editorial management, subject to confirmation in Moscow.

Soviet periodicals are, like most national newspapers, the publications of various organizations. On paper, most are independent of party authority; in practice, the organizations themselves are directed by party appointees and through this interlocking arrangement, the periodical press is tied to the party. The same is true of radio and television broadcasting. The state management committee for broadcasting falls under the government's Council of Ministers. However, the "nomenclature" system, by which the central party apparatus appoints all important administrators and managers, covers the radio and TV committee along with such other state enterprises as factories or scientific research institutes.

If specifics are mostly concealed in party archives, there is nothing secretive about the party mass media coordination in general. Party committees at each level of the political hierarchy are supposed to work closely with editorial staffs. The general principle was laid down at the 8th Party Congress in 1919. After that—in haphazard form, judging from numerous admonitions and demands of the central party apparatus—the party organizations became in effect publishers with all the prerogatives. In the Smolensk party archives, for example, there is an *oblast* party directive to *raion* party organizations reading: "On December 1st [1935] you shall place in all *raion* newspapers articles devoted to the life and work of Kirov. In these articles . . . you will present Kirov's role as that of one of the greatest leaders of the party, the party's forum, beloved by all toilers, fiery fighter for the party of Lenin-Stalin against the ignoble Zinovievite-Trotskyite opposition of right wing opportunists." [60] In 1945, to cite another example of the party's scope, a Central Committee resolution advised provincial party agencies to "give daily help to newspapers, to review plans of newspaper work and to give direction to coverage of the most important problems. . . ." [61] This sort of counseling and guidance remains an obligation of all party organizations today. Ideally, from the political management's standpoint, editors should be in constant communication with party secretaries, much as an American press spokesman should be with his policy-making executives. Through this personal contact and cross fertilization of attitudes, the Soviet organizational chart implies, the mass media should effectively transmit national policy, disseminate necessary information, and put a proper interpretation on events of the day.

The specific party organizations are dominated by the department of propaganda, whose origin and evolution has already been discussed. Since the 1930's, following a decade of finding its place in the Soviet political bureaucracy, *Agitprop* has had a relatively stable history.* The exception was a brief period under Khrushchev. In November, 1962, as Khrushchev began to clamp down on literary unorthodoxy loosed by de-Stalinization, an ideological commission was established in *Agitprop*'s place. Under Leonid Ilichev, former deputy editor of *Pravda* and *Agitprop* chief (from 1958 to 1961), the commission seems, by its title, only to have reflected the attempt to modernize Marxist-Leninist propaganda for the 1960's. A year before the commission was born, Khrushchev had unveiled his "new program" for the future. De-Stalinization had generated cynicism and disenchantment. There was a void, particularly in the younger ranks, of ideological or spiritual commitment, and the increasingly outspoken "liberal" writers were filling it with imaginative commentary on man and society. The "new program" was Khrushchev's counterthrust against an ideological malaise, and Ilichev's commission was a new initiative in propagating the Marxist-Leninist world view.

After the party presidium and Central Committee felled Khrushchev in October, 1964, two things happened. Under the new party first secretary, Leonid Brezhnev, the ideological commission went through a thorough shaking up, from top to bottom. And its name changed again, to department of propaganda and agitation. The purge was the more important of the two events. Ilichev was replaced in May, 1965, by Vladimir Stepakov, a professional ideologist who had directed the Russian republic's ideological commission under Khrushchev, and who edited *Izvestia* for a few months after Khrushchev was replaced.

*_Agitprop_ is no longer the proper abbreviation for the department of propaganda, but it is arbitrarily used throughout the present study for sake of continuity.

During 1965 and the early part of 1966, a new deputy to Stepakov
was appointed, along with chiefs of at least three sections in
the department. The Russian republic's propaganda and agitation department likewise was restaffed, with a new chief in
February, 1965, and at least three other officials later the same
year. In the remaining 14 Soviet republics, new directors or
deputies were installed in 9 departments of propaganda and
agitation during 1965 and early 1966.[62]

In roughly the same period there was a shakeup on editorial
staffs of leading newspapers. Stepakov immediately replaced
Khrushchev's son-in-law, Alexei Adzhubei, as editor of *Izvestia*.[63]
And the next year, in September, 1965, after Stepakov was
shifted to the party Central Committee's propaganda and agitation department, Lev Tolkunov became *Izvestia*'s editor.

Pravda's editor since 1956, Pavel Satuykov, also promptly
lost his job—in November, 1964—and was replaced temporarily
by Alexei Rumyantsev, a political economist and former editor
of the party's chief ideological journal, *Kommunist*.[64] Rumyantsev, considered something of a "liberal," lasted less than
a year; in September, 1965, Mikhail Zimyanin became editor
of *Pravda*.[65] The post-Khrushchev shakeup in the mass media
extended also to the Committee for Radio Broadcasting and
Television. Its director, Mikhail Kharlamov, was replaced by
Nikolai Mesyatsev in October, 1964.[66]

The restaffing of *Agitprop*, leading newspapers, and the radio-
TV committee was significant on two counts. First, it was clear
that the post-Khrushchev leadership of Brezhnev and Premier
Alexei Kosygin had no abiding trust in the party public relations staff that Khrushchev had assembled. Adzhubei obviously
was considered still loyal to Khrushchev and so *Izvestia* could
not be left in his hands. The *Agitprop* apparatus similarly must
have been suspect as a reliable spokesman for the new leadership, and it too had to be reorganized. Second, political align-
ment became especially critical in the fall of 1965, after a more
conservative cultural policy had begun to emerge.[67] The change
in *Pravda* and *Izvestia* editorships, along with continuing restaffing of *Agitprop*, reflected the party leadership's uncertainty
over its ideological apparatus as the new policy took effect. The
question is why this should be, if the Soviet mass media is so
effectively and continuously under party guidance? The answer,
judging from available evidence, is that the apparatus on paper
does not accurately describe its operation in practice. There
should be no need for staff purges in *Agitprop* with a new leader-

ship, unless authentic conflicts of view are anticipated and the leadership expects that its policies will be distorted or sabotaged in transmission. This is not to say that *Agitprop* is an autonomous empire, for the central party apparatus can restaff it at will. But it is to point out that even the party's mechanisms for managing the mass media are susceptible to political infighting.

By title, Khrushchev's ideological commission was twice changed after October, 1964. Sometime in the spring of 1965, probably when Stepakov replaced Ilichev, it reverted to department of propaganda and agitation.[68] Then, sometime in the summer of 1966, the agency was once more renamed, department of propaganda.[69] The change suggests that oral agitation was transferred to or made into another Central Committee department at the national level, leaving the printed and broadcast media under a single party agency. But this cannot be documented.

The department of propaganda is one of more than 20 agencies of the Communist Party Central Committee's secretariat. It is through the secretariat that the Soviet political leadership manages the party apparatus, and therefore Soviet institutions. The propaganda department is, in turn, subdivided into sectors, each responsible for a specific area of the mass media. In late 1966, five of these sectors were identified—sector for newspapers, for magazines, for radio and television, for publishing and distribution, and for printing plants.[70] There may be others, although these five could reasonably cover the entire mass media network and operations.

Below the national level, in the 14 republic party organizations (the RSFSR being administered by the national Central Committee), there are departments of propaganda and agitation, which are of a size to have sectors also. On the next level downward, in the *oblast*, *raion*, and city party organizations, there are single sectors for the press, radio, and television combined.[71] It should be noted also that the Komsomol, the national youth organization, contains a department of propaganda and agitation in its Central Committee. A press section exists as well in the Ministry of Defense's main political administration of the Soviet army and navy. The Komsomol's *Agitprop* and military's press section are responsible respectively for the ideological content of Komsomol and military newspapers and magazines, but subject to the Communist Party's authority.

The party's departments and sectors provide the chief daily, working contact with the mass media. It is through the propaganda department apparatus, for one, that editors can be briefed on national policies, in private or public. After the 23rd Congress of the Communist Party, a national conference of newspaper, magazine, radio, and television staffs was held in Moscow in October, 1966, on themes and goals of the mass media. Among the speakers was a deputy chief of the central department of propaganda. Such briefings, at national and local levels, are common after Central Committee meetings, as well as congresses, where major policies are formally approved.

The propaganda department also maintains a critical surveillance over the press in three forms. Its staffs constantly check content of printed and broadcast media and, again either publicly or privately, issue critiques of performance. At the national level, these appear as directives from the Central Committee that both single out faults and indicate proper remedies. The Turkmen republic's mass media, for example, were called to account for a number of weaknesses—not giving sufficient emphasis to internationalism, failing to encourage readers' letters, devoting too little attention in radio and TV broadcasts to social and political themes, and lagging in the battle against "feudal" attitudes toward women in the central Asian republic. Party Central Committee recommendations were of a general nature so as to apply, along with the criticisms, to the entire Soviet mass media.[72]

A second form of guidance is investigation by a propaganda department "instructor." The Latvian republic newspaper *Sovetskaya Latviya* recently underwent a thorough content study by a department instructor, who subsequently reported his findings in the Soviet journalists' professional magazine, *Zhurnalist.*[73] Finally, there is the device of official reports by editors at department of propaganda offices. For example, excerpts of one such meeting noted: "A. Subbotin, editor in chief of *Trud*, advised [the propaganda department] how the problem of the five-day work week was being covered in the newspaper's pages. . . . A number of critical articles in the newspaper have not contained thorough analysis of mistakes in the transition of this or that factory to the new work system; particular problems of the five-day week still have not been reflected in *Trud.*"[74]

These direct, personal contacts between party propaganda department officials and editors are supplemented by two other arrangements. One is the "review of the press," conducted ac-

COMMUNIST PARTY AGENCIES FOR THE MASS MEDIA

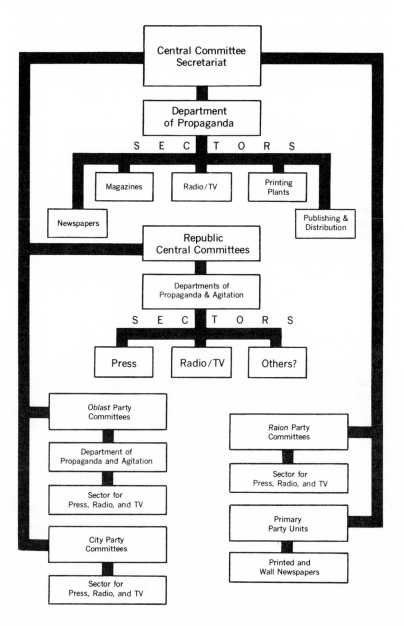

cording to clear pecking order from the top to the bottom. That is, *Pravda* publishes critiques of the whole mass media network or any part of it. The republic press casts its analytical eye to newspapers or radio and TV broadcasting in republics, *oblasts*, cities, and *raions*. And so on down. These reviews, which began in the late 1920's, have come to be rather pedestrian, unimaginative commentary. Consider statements from a typical *Pravda* editorial on the press: "Our press, radio and television must do much to spread the initiative of Muscovites, who pledged to complete the five year plan in volume of production by November 7, 1970. . . . The press, radio and television have begun to give more attention to the propaganda of the revolutionary battle and labor traditions of our people."[75]

The second and more influential supplemental channel for guiding the press is the central distribution of national and international news and commentary. Virtually all information in these two categories is supplied by TASS (the central news agency), Press Agency Novosti, and the *Pravda* and *Izvestia* news bureaus. Headquartered in Moscow, these organizations are gatekeepers for the most important political and economic news, foreign and domestic. They also edit and disseminate regional news, all of them having correspondents posted around the country. They are roughly analogous to the large news agencies in the United States, such as the Associated Press, or the New York Times news service, in the sense that both the latter, too, largely determine the news of the day by what they do and do not disseminate to subscribers. But there are large differences of intent and purpose between Soviet and American information distributors. And the fact of close management of central Soviet news organizations by the political management, as contrasted to considerable autonomy among the American, should be clear from what has been said to this point about the Soviet mass media.

Myths and Realities

It is easy to suppose from a bald description of written and unwritten rules, of government agencies, and of the party machinery concerned with the Soviet press that such a press can scarcely utter a word without approval of the state. But Soviet society, because of human flaw if nothing else, is not so perfectly regimented. Nor, in fact, is absolute conformity of the mass media the ideal objective of political authority. The conformist press of the Stalinist years was, one can argue, useful in focusing national energies on priority tasks. But regimentation led to a dull product. As educational levels rose in the Soviet Union, the press increasingly lost its ability to attract an audience, at least for political messages. A poll of more than 1,600 television viewers in Leningrad revealed that 84 per cent enjoyed sports programs, but only 16.4 per cent liked broadcasts on social and political topics.[76] Of about 26,000 *Izvestia* readers sampled for attitudes, 75 per cent "systematically" read articles on social themes, while only 18 per cent regularly turned to political essays.[77] Even before such elementary statistics were collected, it was obvious that the Soviet press was not effectively reaching its audience. "There still is much that is gray in our newspapers," Khrushchev lectured journalists in 1959. "You can pick up a newspaper any time, read it and put it aside. And afterward you don't remember what was in the paper."[78] If Khrushchev did not have data to support his claim, his political instincts led him—not to mention the more imaginative Soviet journalists—to veer from a disciplined, one-voice press.

While all the Stalinist institutions for rigorous management of the mass media remain, they operate differently than in earlier years. It is perhaps more a matter of "style" of politics and Soviet society than substantial change in legality, though the second is a factor. A libel suit against a Soviet newspaper was not characteristic of Stalin's years. Yet *Glavlit* survives with broad powers of precensorship, powers that have not been tested against the Soviet constitution guaranteeing freedom of press. That *Glavlit* is no longer as heavyfooted nor as narrowly exacting in its work is apparent from a cursory reading of Soviet newspapers today compared with 20 years ago. But why *Glavlit* is less suppressive can only be explained by reference to nebulous changes of the Soviet political atmosphere, to what is generally called the "liberalization" of Soviet society. The United States experienced such a metamorphosis of national political climate in emerging from McCarthyism in the 1950's. The change was not a matter of legal reform, but of public attitudes. In the Soviet Union, management of the press has been altered less by legislation than by a difference of political style, primarily in the Communist Party apparatus. The party and government bureaucracies possess most of the same devices of the Stalinist years for directing the press, but the application differs.

Indeed, it is inaccurate to counterpose the party-state bureaucracies to the press. Since they are intertwined, there necessarily is interaction. The Soviet newspaper editor who simultaneously is a member of a city party bureau or of a city mayor's staff does not stand in opposition to the political structure. His relationship is that of, for example, the director of the United States Information Agency to the Secretary of State. This being the case, the Soviet mass media's operation depends on two factors: (1) general policy guidelines as established in formal law and in Communist Party decrees and resolutions on the press, which have the force of law; and (2) personal relationships in the whole mass media network.

What mitigates minute, word-by-word management of the press, even if this were the objective, is the human factor. At one extreme was the situation in which *Glavlit* censors sympathized with and aided some of the more unorthodox Soviet writers in the early 1960's, thus neutralizing a system of independent checks on the press.[79] What makes such bizarre occurrences possible is, for one thing, the immensity of the Soviet political bureaucracy and the mass media network. Beginning at the center, there are the national party and government apparatuses, and the national printed media and radio and television broadcasting networks. Subordinate to the central authorities are party and state bureaucracies of 15 republics, 135 *oblasts*, 16 territories (*krais* and *okrugs*), 747 cities, 417 city *raions*, and 2,746 rural *raions*, most of which are involved with the mass media. And this is not to mention the thousands of small party units in factory shops, department stores, libraries, offices, and so on, which produce wall newspapers.

Given the regimented nature of the party, the channel of command and directive is open from top to bottom. But given the human nature of bureaucracy—whether of a military or civilian organization—the opportunities for distortion, inefficiency, error, empire building, personal favoritism, and policy sabotage exist to a considerable extent. Thus, *Pravda* can expose a case in which the Communist Party Central Committee instructed the Kaluga *oblast* party agency to hear reports from local newspaper editors at least twice a year. But, *Pravda* said, *oblast* officials had not done so for more than three years.[80] Similarly, the local Smolensk newspaper *Rabochii Put* was berated for "dry and dull reports," and party officials were criticized for being wholly indifferent to content plans and progress reports of editors.[81]

In the Perm *oblast*, the party organization was criticized, not for failing to supervise the mass media, but for doing so perfunctorily. The party committee regularly issued instructions that began: "It is suggested that editors of the *oblast* newspapers *Zvezda* and *Molodaya Gvardiya*, and of the territorial, city and *raion* newspapers, that the Committee on Radio Broadcasting and Television systematically cover . . ." followed then by the subject of interest, all in a lackluster tone.[82]

By contrast, there are instances of local party officials working closely with editorial staffs. A Ukrainian *raion* party official was lauded because he attended critiques of the *raion* newspaper, encouraged his staff members to write for the newspaper, and issued continuous criticism and advice on newspaper content.[83]

These examples indicate that, within a framework of party admonitions and policies, there is fair room for varied relationships, depending on the quality of party-government and editorial staffs. That there is a framework is clear. At some points, it is quite definitive: no confusion or doubt exists, for example, as to who hires editors and by what authority a newspaper speaks. At other points, the framework is plastic. What precisely constitutes "dry and dull reports," for example? At what point, in *Pravda*'s assessment, does a newspaper become lively and interesting? Obviously, the answers to these questions must be subjective and abstract. The party-government bureaucracies easily enough determine gross output of steel in measurable quantities. However, by their nature, the mass media are not subject to precision management. In their daily performance, much of what they do seems to rest on human trial and error, though within the permissible boundaries determined by society and its institutions.

CHAPTER 4

JOURNALISTS AND POLITICIANS

In 1959, at a Kremlin reception, Nikita Khrushchev patronizingly lectured Soviet journalists: "You are not only the true aides of the [Communist] party, but literally the apprentices of the party, the active fighters for its great cause."[1] Such a simplistic subordination of Soviet journalists to the party's political management was moving from reality to desire even in 1959. Professional training, expansion of the Soviet press, and the "liberalization" of Soviet society after Stalin's death were all contributing to an erosion of the Communist Party's rigid presumption to dictate confidently to the Soviet mass media. A decade later, the party apparatus's stereotyped directives to journalists—to help mold the Soviet man, to inculcate youth with a spirit of Marxism-Leninism, to recall the Bolshevik revolutionary tradition—seem all the more obsolete. True, journalists give the political management its puffs and praise. Newspapers, as one journalist put it half cynically, half jokingly, are "all for Soviet power." The conformists and careerists among the some 60,000 Soviet journalists[2] glibly produce exuberant reaffirmation of the existing order, in the tone and style of American press tributes to the Fourth of July, Memorial Day, and the American way of life. As one Soviet critic wrote of the ritualistic treatment of proscribed themes: "The article begins with a lengthy introduction. Then you get a well-known history of the problem and the significance of the topic today in one or two paragraphs in general terms. . . . It is no wonder that people say about these articles that you get used to them. Like the rumble of train wheels, you stop paying attention to them."[3]

An awareness among Soviet journalists of press agentry journalism during the Stalin era stems from several causes. Some among the political bureaucracy itself, in the Khrushchev years and after, began to realize how antiquated such journalism was in a nation that required as much factual information and discussion in the mass media as ideological sermons and incantations of optimism. Thus *Pravda* editorialized: "Publicity and information are invariable prerequisites for the development of criticism and self-criticism as a means of enhancing the responsibility of officials to the people and of improving the activities of all echelons of administration."[4] Further, the "liberalization" of Soviet society since Stalin's death has given Soviet journalists greater opportunity to travel abroad and to read the foreign press. The late Ilya Ehrenburg noted: "I read *Le Monde* about half an hour. It is rare that I spend that much time reading our newspapers. This is not because it is more interesting to me to find out events and news in *Monde*. . . . Many things occur in our country, but not all of them by far find expression in the newspapers."[5] This is not to suggest that Soviet journalists wholeheartedly admire the western European or American press, but that they have become more conscious of and to some extent influenced by foreign styles of journalism. Finally, professional journalism education in the Soviet Union— particularly that of the postwar generations of journalists who escaped apprenticeship in the mass media of Stalin's times— has left its mark on the contemporary Soviet press.

Symbolic of the difference perhaps are the attitudes of two generations of Soviet editors. Representative of the older, Pavel Satyukov, who entered the Communist Party in 1939 and became *Pravda* editor in 1956 (replaced in 1964), proclaimed at a national conference of journalists: "It is our sacred duty to defend the purity of Marxism-Leninism not only in the struggle against our outright class enemies and against imperialists of all stripes . . . but [against those] who in fact vulgarize Marxism-Leninism."[6] At the same conference in 1964, Alexei Adzhubei, then editor of *Izvestia,* and representative of a younger generation of journalism school trained newsmen, commented: "When our reporting is honest, frank, bold and dramatic, when it portrays life truthfully and summons people forward, the Soviet reader accepts it. He is strict and exacting. He will not tolerate literary embellishments."[7]

If both attitudes survive today in some unmeasurable ratio, the latter is more frequently heard than a decade ago. The contemporary Soviet journalist is less the political revolutionist of the breed who wrote and edited Bolshevik papers, or who succumbed to Stalinism, than—at least in the large urban press—the professional publicist. His position in Soviet society

is secure, his rewards are substantial. The press itself has burgeoned into a powerful institution in its own right. If it fails
to delve into root issues of Soviet political power, that is mainly
because journalists are vested members of the political establishment. It is in that sense that they can be equated with
American corporate public relations executives or government
public affairs spokesmen. But they draw also from principles and
a tradition of journalism which transforms them into professional journalists. They may simultaneously be propagandists
insofar as they willingly distort or fabricate information. But
that is a compromise for career advancement. A Soviet journalist, as a Soviet writer, can be committed to an honest and realistic portrayal of his own society, though he is pressured often
enough to be otherwise and the consequences of ignoring the
pressures may be severe. However, like the editor of an American
labor newspaper or of a magazine with a recognizable bias
(e.g. the *New Republic* on the political left, the *National Review*
on the right), he can stand for a cause and still produce
good journalism.

Journalism Institutions

Much depends on the Soviet journalist's education and his
concept of the mass media in his society. Among Soviet journalism
educators and practicing journalists themselves, there has been
a running discussion over journalism training. What should
the future journalist study? Should he be the specialist first,
and journalist second, or vice versa? What is his role in Soviet
society? Some Soviet journalism educators lean to a general
education for aspiring journalists, granting to the working
press the responsibility of specialized training in economics,
politics, and cultural affairs.[8] A leading Soviet journalism educator, the late Yevgeny L. Khudyakov, described the journalist
as "above all a political, social activist, a man with a lively
mind, a bright personality, with a highly developed sense of
what is new and, at the same time, a master of words, knowing
how to transmit his thoughts and impressions in a lucid,
talented way."[9] A Soviet editor suggested that a journalist combines three things: "Specialization in any one branch of
economics, science or culture, . . . a knowledge of Marxist-
Leninist philosophy and history, psychology and pedagogy
which would establish a basis of independent thought . . . and,
finally, mastery of techniques of literary creation and the art

of words."[10] That is to say, within the journalist's general ideological commitment to the Soviet social system, he is considered variously as a transmitter of information, a political activist, and something of an intellectual.

Traditionally, Soviet journalism education favored political over professional qualifications. This was the case after the Bolshevik Revolution on through the 1920's and into the 1930's. The problem was a shortage of talented administrators in all fields. Experienced journalists were siphoned off into other work, chiefly political. Those who staffed the press were assessed more in terms of political loyalties than journalistic abilities. From 1919, when the Russian Telegraph Agency (ROSTA) began conducting short courses in journalism, until the early 1930's, journalism instruction remained a rather low priority discipline.[11] Various institutes and technical schools of journalism were established in the 1920's, but a gauge of their size is the fact that the main one, at Moscow University, graduated only 350 students from 1925 to 1929.

In 1930, in coordination with newspaper expansion, the central political apparatus undertook an ambitious improvement of journalism education across the nation.[12] Much of this training was assigned to newspapers whose editorial staffs were to run courses in journalism. But an odd mixture of institutions —the Communist Academy, the Higher School of the Trade Union Movement, the Communist Institute of Journalism, as well as local technical schools—also were instructed to establish courses not only for young students, but for working journalists. The directive creating the Communist Institute of Journalism in 1934 suggests that predominant attention was given to journalists in charge of newspaper political departments.[13] Institute courses ran from as little as two months to as much as three years. Correspondence instructions in journalism were offered as well, covering such topics as Lenin and Stalin on the press, the press as an instrument of socialist building and newspaper writing, with emphasis on the newspaper "as a political organ, subordinated to the party committee."[14] Organized hurriedly and haphazardly, in the midst of the industrialization drive, the institutes of journalism in such places as Moscow, Leningrad, and Sverdlovsk evidently faded out before or during World War II.[15]

In the postwar years, journalism departments were reestablished, first in Leningrad and Sverdlovsk, then in Alma-Ata, Minsk, Kharkov, and, in 1947, at Moscow University. Moscow's department was raised—the first to be so—to the status of a faculty (or school) of journalism in 1952. Subsequently, other journalism departments—usually attached to faculties of philology—were made into separate schools of journalism. By 1967, six university schools of journalism—in Moscow, Leningrad, Kiev, Lvov, Sverdlovsk, and Alma-Ata—and fifteen departments of journalism, about half of them night schools, were offering the five year course of instruction.[16]

Supplementing these is a network of Communist Party schools which train full-time party staff, including journalists. The first and still dominant of these, the Higher Party School in Moscow, was established in 1946.[17] It offered two study programs, one of three years and a second of nine months, the latter for "retraining" of republic and *oblast* party workers. As the programs concerned journalists, they were to draw editors and deputy editors of the provincial press. The three year course was limited to 300 journalists, and the refresher program to 600. Party membership, a minimum of a high school education, and an age of under forty were among admission requirements. The study plan for all enrollees, journalists or not, included history of the Soviet Union and Communist Party, international relations, foreign policy, economics, literature, language, and, for editors, journalism. In addition to the Higher Party School, branch schools were planned in 50 Soviet cities, 15 of which were to include journalism departments. They offered two year programs, plus short refresher courses for editors of small city and rural newspapers.

In the mid-1950's, the party school network was reorganized, the Moscow school program was reduced to two years, and regional schools programs were increased to four. Enrollments in the journalism departments evidently are quite limited. In 1964, the Higher Party School in Moscow graduated only 100 persons from its press, radio, and television section.[18] The Leningrad Higher Party School, one of the largest in the country outside Moscow, graduated between 100 and 200 journalists annually from 1958 to 1965, chiefly for the *raion* and small city newspaper press. However, with a reorganization in 1962 of the *raion* press, the Leningrad Higher Party School journalism department contracted. From 1965 to 1968, it had not graduated a single journalist from its four year course, and only in 1965 had it received permission to enroll one group of 24 trainees.[19]

There seems to be little difference between journalism instruction in party schools and that in universities. However, the former train party members who have had some years of experience in administration and possibly journalism, and their course work is reasonably at a more advanced level. Further, the party schools seem to lay somewhat more stress on Marxism-Leninism and economic matters than the university schools of journalism.

Additional journalism instruction and guidance is provided by the Union of Journalists. One of many quasi-official Soviet public organizations (of writers, architects, engineers, artists, and teachers, for example), the Union of Journalists was established in 1956–57 and subsequently organized branch divisions in the 15 Soviet republics, in large cities, and in *oblasts*. By 1959, when the union held its first national congress, it had 23,000 members.[20] At the time of the second and most recent national congress in 1966, there were more than 43,000 members.[21] Somewhat like American editors' and publishers' organizations, the union is concerned with journalistic standards and practices, and with the education of journalists. It publishes its own magazine, *Zhurnalist*, dealing with the mass media, and the weekly *Za Rubezhom,* which prints translations of articles from the foreign press. The union also conducts seminars and conferences on topics of special interest to Soviet journalists, and maintains contacts with foreign journalists. In more formal or structured journalism education, the union and its local branches conduct lecture courses and seminars for both professional journalists and amateurs—the *rabselkor*. For example, the Leningrad Union of Journalists in 1967 had a two year "university of journalists" with an enrollment of 250. It also sponsored a three month refresher course and ran lecture series for journalists dealing with sociology, social psychology, and political economics.[22]

Of the Soviet university programs, Moscow University's School of Journalism remains the largest, and probably the most influential. Scheduled to have an enrollment of 125 students its first year—75 in the newspaper department, and 50 in the editing-publishing department[23]—the Moscow school in 1964 had about 800 full-time students enrolled, 600 night students and 1,000 correspondence students, representing approximately 40 per cent of students in the then five schools (not departments) of journalism. In addition, it had 30 resident graduate students, and 30 others taking graduate work by correspondence (which in the Soviet Union involves periodic visits to a university for testing). Its teaching staff numbered about 70.[24] Most recently, the Moscow School of Journalism has been graduating about 350 students annually, of all categories. In 1966–67, the 21 Soviet schools and departments of journalism enrolled 2,100 first year students, more than half, however, for correspondence study.[25]

Forming the Journalist

From the first, curriculum has been an issue. When Moscow's School of Journalism was established in 1952, there were essentially three proposals—to train specialists, in economics or agriculture, for example; to educate types of journalists, such as satirists, commentators, or essayists; or, finally, to offer essentially a liberal arts education. The last won out, though controversy went on.[26] In 1965, as the dean of Leningrad University's School of Journalism noted, there were new proposals for specialization.[27] And, in fact, journalism schools had established special seminars and courses in economics, science, culture, and politics.[28] But the weight of opinion still favors the broadly educated man of letters, in the Russian tradition of writer-journalist, and the committed, activist journalist, in the Soviet tradition of political publicist.

Along with discussion over curriculum, Soviet journalism educators have expressed continuous concern over the quality of students in schools. They have been required to give preference to youths with military service or two years of work after high school, a policy adopted in 1957. Since 1965, admission has been restricted to those who have published in newspapers or magazines, or written for radio or television.[29] The theory is that those with a journalistic flair would first try their talents and then, presumably more mature, would return to universities for formal education. But this theory does not seem to have wholly proven out. For one thing, Soviet schools of journalism have difficulty attracting students. In the 1966–67 school year, the Moscow School of Journalism, along with the law school, had the least number of applicants per opening of all departments in the university. In the Kazakhstan University School of Journalism there were only 5 applicants for 75 openings in the first year class.[30] As for attracting youths with demonstrated interest in journalism, a check of 231 Leningrad University journalism students with work experience revealed that only 29 had been on newspapers.[31] In sum, the journalism schools have not attracted either the quality or quantity of students they would like.

During his five year education (six years for correspondence students), the Soviet student divides his time among journalism courses, subjects in other fields, and practice work. Moscow University's study plan for 1957 totaled 3,866 hours of instruction, of which 1,236 were journalism courses and the remainder language, literature, history of the Communist Party, Marxism-Leninism, and the like. He also had 24 weeks of practice work on newspapers, or at broadcasting stations, now raised to 36.[32] Currently, the Moscow School of Journalism offers four specialties—newspaper and magazine journalism, editing-publishing, radio broadcasting, and television.[33] Students in each specialty take several mandatory courses. For example, in the newspaper-magazine cycle, studies include the theory and practice of the Soviet periodical press, production and layout of publications, and photojournalism. Editing-publishing students take basics of editing, book production, economics of publishing, and history of publishing. Radio and television broadcasting students take speech training, radio or television technology, and radio or television journalism. In the second year, all students begin five one-semester special courses from among eight categories—theory and practice of the party-Soviet press; history of the Soviet press; radio broadcasting; television; history of Russian journalism and literature; editing and publishing; writing and linguistics; and mechanics of journalism (makeup, editorial staff organization, etc.)

In addition to his journalism subjects, the student has mandatory courses in Marxist-Leninist philosophy, history of the Communist Party, Russian and foreign languages, literature, economics, atheism, science, law, art, typing, and shorthand. He spends much of his time every week in the classroom. The 1957 study plan required 28 to 32 hours of classwork weekly during the first four years.

Soviet journalism education is heavily oriented toward ideology and politics. Basic reading lists are compiled chiefly of Marx's and Lenin's writings on the press, Communist Party and government directives and regulations, formal reports delivered at Communist Party congresses and, finally, Soviet books and monographs on the press, which are drawn in good share from official documents.[34] The touchstone of the journalist's education then is Soviet Marxism-Leninism, in a broad sense to include the philosophical content of Soviet society,

the Soviet Union's history, and its goals. Soviet journalism
education is predicted on the idea that the press reflects its
society and, indeed, is obligated to help achieve society's objectives. That these objectives are primarily defined by a small
political bureaucracy, holding intensely to a particular social
doctrine, accounts as well for the concentrated formal education
of journalists in Soviet political philosophy.

The aspiring Soviet journalist also is imbued with "class
consciousness." He is instructed to interpret events from a
socialist point of view, somewhat in the sense that the American
labor press assesses information from labor's vantage point.
But for the Soviet journalist, this means that "truth" has no
objective quality. Rather, since each man in Marxist-Leninist
philosophy is part of his society and reflects his class, the
Soviet journalist is led to understand "truth" in a subjective
manner. Not that individual facts may not be true in themselves
to all men. If a government changes leadership, if a nation under-
goes a revolution, or if a war breaks out, these are "true" events
that can be dated and titled. But the significance of these
events, and therefore the information that a journalist transmits about them, derives from a class consciousness. And so the
essential "truth" of any phenomenon for a Soviet journalist corresponds to a particular philosophy—Marxism-Leninism—of
what forces move and change society. Even subtracting for deliberate propaganda, Soviet "class journalism" leads then to wholly
different interpretations than those in the American press of
the same events.

If the Soviet journalist at the end of his five years' training
has been immersed in Marxism-Leninism, he also comes equipped
with professional skills. They differ somewhat from those
taught in American schools of journalism, which offer a heavy
dose of reporting and editing. Soviet journalists place as much
or more emphasis on the style of reports as on the technique of
collecting and transmitting information. Except for TASS dispatches and occasional local reports, which are written in a
style familiar to American newspaper readers, the Soviet press
devotes its space to editorials, news reviews, interpretive and
background reports, opinion and advice columns, interviews,
humorous and satiric essays, book, film, and theater reviews,
and discussion articles. Soviet journalists therefore are familiar-
ized in universities with various forms of journalism, reporting
being only one of a half dozen or so.[35]

The result is that the Soviet journalists tend to a literary rather than a staccato news style, to opinion and interpretation rather than dispassionate transmission of facts, and to discussion of trends and processes rather than description of individual, isolated events. Counterposed to this traditional Soviet, and indeed Russian journalism, is an increasing emphasis on factual information rapidly transmitted and on *reportazh*—best defined as "personalized journalism." The motivation for the former is mostly political. Soviet authorities have been impressed with the speed by which foreign journalists collect and report information, and disturbed by how quickly foreign communications agencies disseminate it in the Soviet Union. Dmitri Goryunov, director of TASS until 1967, told a national conference of journalists:

> Powerful apparatuses of bourgeois propaganda such as the Voice of America and BBC and tens of other radio stations literally rake whole countries and continents with pernicious shots, poisoning the minds of people with misinformation. . . . We should remember, literally every hour, that one of the major conditions in today's ideological battle is maximum speed, the rapidity of disseminating our information, commentary and reporting. Being late with dispatches, we as much as give odds to our ideological opponents, and sometimes create for ourselves the need to eliminate doubt in the minds of people infected by harmful propaganda.[36]

With this cold war view of journalism, the Soviet mass media have been pressed to report and react rapidly to international events, and to Soviet domestic occurrences that gain international attention. Changes in this direction have not been swift, nor very noticeable. The Soviet press, like the American, is essentially a conservative bureaucracy which while urging change and innovation upon other institutions adapts new techniques only gradually. Its old forms and entrenched attitudes have a momentum of their own. And because the Soviet mass media are so dominated by the central press, politically and professionally, innovation must be accepted there generally before it affects the lower echelons. That is also where innovation emerges because the most talented, imaginative Soviet journalists are found in the national press.

The Journalist in Society

No more than American journalists do Soviet journalists fit into any single category. At one extreme are the influential, practiced editors and correspondents of the national mass media; at the other are the part-time editors of tens of thousands of wall newspapers. Ranging between these are the mass of journalists who produce the republic, *oblast,* city, and *raion* newspapers, and who staff the local radio and television stations and the regional periodicals.

The majority of Soviet editors and correspondents lack formal journalistic education, although they may have taken night or correspondence courses to supplement practical experience. In 1959, there were only 5,200 students enrolled in all of the Soviet Union's schools and departments of journalism, and Moscow University's school had graduated fewer than 1,000 students in its then seven years of operation.[37] Between 1959 and the end of 1966, only 10,000 journalists were graduated nationwide.[38] The consequence is an acknowledged shortage of trained journalists to staff the Soviet mass media. In 1966, for example, only one out of five managing editors of the Soviet Union's 2,500 *raion* newspapers—4-page publications issued three times a week and averaging a circulation of 4,500—[39] had a journalism education. A survey in 1965 of 372 managing editors of *raion* newspapers (which then employed about 15,000 journalists), revealed that 38 per cent had a higher education of any kind, 20 per cent had some advanced schooling, 40 per cent were high school graduates, and 2 per cent had not completed high school.[40]

Of course, given a choice and opportunity to do otherwise, Soviet journalists with higher education, like most Soviet citizens with university degrees, prefer the urban centers to the economically depressed and unsophisticated countryside. Theoretically, journalism students like those of other disciplines can be required to spend two years at assigned places of work. For most journalism graduates, this could mean editing a small-town newspaper or reporting for a regional broadcasting station. In at least one city, Leningrad, the pattern has been different. A check showed that between 1963 and 1966 the city's two major newspapers lost 22 staff members to larger and more prestigious publications, but drew only 3 replacements from smaller newspapers in the Leningrad area. That is, relatively few journalism school graduates seemed to be available from the *raion* weeklies.[41] The Soviet periodical for journalists, *Zhurnalist,* has since January, 1967, published lists of vacancies on newspapers, nearly all of them on *raion* publications, and most frequently in Soviet Siberia, the far east, or central Asia. Typical Help Wanted notices read:

"In Tselinograd region of the Kazakh SSSR: writer on the *raion* newspaper *Prostor*; city of Atbasar. . . .

"In the Amur *oblast*: assistant editor in chief and editor of the industry department on the *raion* newspaper *Vpered*; village of Tygda. . . .

"In the Murmansk *oblast*: managing editor for the *oblast* youth newspaper *Komsomolets Zapolyarya*: city of Murmansk. Monthly pay, 125 rubles [$138.75], plus a 40% zone differential; 10% increase every two years, two months pay for moving expenses, apartment guaranteed. . . .

"In the Krasnoyarsk territory: chief director and chief editor of public affairs programming for the Krasnoyarsk television station; city of Krasnoyarsk. . . ."[42]

What all this suggests is that, given the demand of the larger newspapers, periodicals, and broadcasting stations for journalism school graduates, it is difficult to staff the local press (which, like the American weeklies and small-town dailies most desperately needs talented, energetic journalists). The advantages of the urban mass media are apparent enough to young and old journalists alike. A job on a Moscow or Leningrad newspaper, for example, assures one a residency permit, which is difficult to get in these and other large Soviet cities attempting to control population expansion. Moreover, except for isolated regions of the Soviet Union where salaries include a 10 to 40 per cent hardship bonus, the best paid journalism is in the large cities, where the major publications and broadcasting stations are located.

Correspondents of *Pravda* average salaries of 270 to 300 rubles a month ($300 to $333), including bonuses for major articles. *Izvestia*'s reporters earn between 300 and 350 rubles ($333 to $388) on the average.[43] By contrast, the editor in chief of a small local newspaper may earn only 150 rubles a month ($166), and of a city paper (except for those in Moscow, Leningrad, and other major centers) about 200 rubles ($222).[44] While these salaries are above average—in 1968, the average factory and office wage in the Soviet Union was 115 rubles (about $127)—the major newspapers demonstrably offer a more comfortable life, both in terms of wages and urban surroundings.

Beyond that, the journalist's work in the major Soviet mass media carries more prestige, offers greater challenge and opportunity for travel, for promotion, and for associating with the important and influential in Soviet society. Honors and medals come to the most successful Soviet journalists. They receive the customary rewards of middle and high officials in Soviet Communist Party, government, military, scientific, and academic circles. These include comfortable apartments, automobiles, summer homes, access to foreign and domestic information unavailable generally (foreign publications, for example), the scarcer consumer goods, and, as important as any of these, position. Whether they abuse their status or not, leading Soviet editors and journalists—no less than their American equivalents, and probably more—enjoy influence. On a base level, they can get their sons and daughters into universities through personal contacts. Their books and monographs can easily be published, adding substantially to their incomes. Permission for travel to non-Communist countries is easier for them to obtain. In other words, they move, as do important American publishers, editors, and journalists, in the elite community.

For that, their careers are stimulating, they are nurtured with a heady sense of controlling their own and others' destinies, and they can privately boast to themselves of having the confidence and perhaps admiration of others. In short, they are successful. Yet, like American executives, their responsibilities and pressures are great. They work hard and long. As they rise up the success ladder, their jobs become increasingly less concerned with journalism per se, and increasingly caught up in politics and power.

Soviet journalists move to high positions essentially by two routes—the political apparatus or the mass media. There are Soviet equivalents of American political party and government press secretaries, who combine political life and journalism. There also are counterparts of leading American commentators, who begin their careers in obscure regional newspapers and, both talented and ambitious, rise to national prominence. Something must be said of the differences. Ranking Soviet journalists, although their bylines are known to many readers, do not enjoy the popular prestige that American commentators do. One does not hear references in the Soviet Union to Yuri Zhukov's articles in *Pravda* or to those of Vladimir Kudryavtsev in *Izvestia*, although both are byline writers with considerable official standing. The fact that they are official spokesmen, somewhat comparable to a presidential press secretary, lends authority to their essays. But among the Soviet population they are not looked upon as independent observers of world affairs. If the Voice of America broadcasts are accepted by Soviet listeners as Washington's views, Zhukov's articles in *Pravda* represent Moscow's. The Zhukovs, however, are atypical of Soviet journalists, as prominent columnists are of American. Most remain anonymous to the Soviet audience. Their careers are neither so unusual nor so accomplished as to attract public attention, as for example Alexei Adzhubei's was. We can glimpse some of the various and standard careers of Soviet journalists from the following notices of promotions published in *Zhurnalist*:

Victor Yakovlevich Pushkarev, named a deputy editor of the newspaper *Sovetskaya Rossiya*. He was born in 1924, and graduated from the Moscow *oblast* Pedagogical Institute. From 1948 to 1951 he was first secretary of the Serebrynye Prudy *raion* committee of the Moscow *oblast* Komsomol. Following that he edited the *raion* newspaper *Kolkhoznaya Stroika* and worked as a staff correspondent for the Moscow *oblast* newspaper

Staff members of Izvestia's department of industry and construction discuss a forthcoming article.

Leninskoye Znamya. From 1960 to 1962 he was editor of the agricultural department of that newspaper. And from 1964 to 1967 he did staff work in the apparatus of the CC CPSU [the Communist Party Central Committee].[45]

Mikhail Stepanovich Penkin, approved as a member of the editorial board and as editor for the department of literature and art of *Izvestia.* He was born in 1910 and graduated from Moscow's Lenin Pedagogical Institute. From 1950 to 1954 he was chief of the Soviet literature editorial staff in the publishing house Khudozhestvennaya Literatura, and then for 10 years he worked as a deputy editor of the literature and art department on the journal *Kommunist.* For the past three years, he has been a member of the press committee of the USSR's Council of Ministers and editor in chief of its editorial staff for literature.[46]

Georgi Ivanovich Kunitsyn, named a member of the editorial board and editor of the department of literature and art of *Pravda.* He was born in 1922 and graduated from the Pedagogical Institute and from the Academy of Sciences of the CC CPSU. He is a candidate of philosophy. He edited the Tambov newspaper *Komsomolskoye Znamya* and from 1948, after demobilization from the army, he did party staff work. Beginning in 1950, he published articles in the national press on literature and esthetics. He has published in the journals *Kommunist* and *Voprosy Literatury*, and in *Iskusstvo Kino* and *Literaturnaya Gazeta.* He is the author of the book, *On Class and Party Literature.*[47]

Nikolai Nikolaevich Chigir, named TASS commentator for international affairs. He was born in 1929, and worked for TASS before graduating from the Institute for International Relations. He was a [TASS] correspondent in Moscow, editor of the press bureau and editor of the department for American countries. From 1959 to 1963, he was chief of the TASS bureau in Havana, and from 1964 to 1966 he was the TASS correspondent in Chile.[48]

Mikhail Iosifovich Stepichev, named editor of *Pravda*'s department of culture and life. He was born in 1921 and has a higher education. From 1947 to 1952, he worked on a Ukrainian republic Komsomol newspaper, and then for three years was a departmental editor on the republic newspaper *Pravda Ukrainy.* After graduation in 1957 from the Higher Party School of the CC CPSU, he worked for *Pravda* as a special correspondent of the party affairs department and as deputy editor of that department.[49]

While these brief biographies by no means represent all journalistic careers in the Soviet Union, they suggest profiles of journalists who are more or less successful. Several characteristics stand out from these and other sketches. One, a Higher Party School diploma and/or staff work in the central party apparatus—probably the press sections—are fairly common among journalists chosen for responsible positions. Second, relatively few have professional journalism education. The generation of journalists moving into higher editorial jobs in the 1960's was schooled in the 1930's and 1940's when journalism training was undeveloped. But many have formal education of some kind and in a number of instances hold advanced degrees. Third, successful journalists commonly have begun their careers in the provincial press. Few went directly to large newspapers or journals after graduation from school (whereas some younger Soviet journalism graduates do so today).

The pattern is not strikingly different among those who reach executive positions or who, like Zhukov, become star commentators. Zhukov, of Khrushchev's generation, was born in 1908, received a "higher education" in truck design and engineering, and turned to journalism in the 1930's. His essays and features on industrial development during the first five year plan, and on the far east construction projects of the 1930's, and his war reporting were published by *Komsomolskaya Pravda*. After World War II, he moved over to *Pravda* as its chief commentator on international affairs.[50] Sergei Lapin, appointed director of TASS in 1967, is an example of a Soviet mass communications executive who merged government work and journalism. Born in 1912 in Leningrad, where he graduated from Leningrad University's philological faculty in the mid-1930's, he worked on newspapers and radio stations, apparently during World War II and after. In 1953, however, he moved over to the foreign ministry and served as Soviet Ambassador to Austria from 1956 to 1960. Then after several years as a deputy foreign minister in Moscow, he was assigned in 1965 as Ambassador to Peking, but was withdrawn a year later when Soviet-Chinese relations deteriorated.[51]

Indicative of the stature of communications executives like Lapin, he was made a member of the Communist Party Central Committee in 1966 at the 23rd Party Congress. Among the delegates to that congress were Boris Burkov, chairman of Press Agency Novosti; Mikhail Zimyanin, editor in chief of *Pravda*; Nikolai Mesyatsev, chairman of the state Committee for Radio Broadcasting and Television; Nikolai Mikhailov, chairman of the state press committee; and Dmitri Goryunov, then director of TASS. All of these men also were deputies at the time to the Supreme Soviet, the Soviet parliament.[52]

Even these brief biographical facts indicate what is conventional wisdom in the Soviet Union—that the mass communicators are simultaneously enmeshed in the party-government bureaucracy. Yet, it would be wrong to conclude that they therefore unanimously and consistently defend and protect the political bureaucracy. What seems to exist in the Soviet mass media is a conflict of loyalties and attitudes. The editors of *Oktyabr*, "conservative" literary monthly, and of *Novy Mir*, the "liberal" journal, quite obviously do not share the same opinions on literature and its role in Soviet society. And those of the Soviet political bureaucracy who deal with the mass media and ideological education do not agree particularly with *Novy Mir*. Alexei Rumyantsev was removed from the *Pravda* editorship in 1965 probably because his thinking did not coincide with some element in the party apparatus. There also appears to be conflict among segments of the press whereby, as Sidney Ploss has documented in his study of press treatment of Khrushchev's agricultural policies, national newspapers take sides in a dispute.[53] That is, Soviet editors and journalists, confronted with dissension among policymakers in the party and government bureaucracies, tend to align themselves with one or another faction. As well, they find themselves in conflicting roles. They are charged with publicizing and promoting acceptance of national policies and administration of the Communist Party. Simultaneously, journalists are encouraged to criticize social institutions and to defend the public against bureaucratic injustice and blundering. Much of the time these tasks can be carried out in harmony, or one subordinated to the other, depending on the issue. But some of the time, critical and muckraking journalism reflects on the policies themselves, however obliquely, or on their administration.

We should consider first what the Soviet mass media deal with. What makes "news" in the Soviet Union? What are journalists writing about and what are editors publishing? As a general view, there is the often quoted definition of Nikolai Palgunov, former director of TASS: "News is agitation by facts."[54] More than a decade later—the statement was written in 1955—Palgunov's view still enjoys official popularity. One can choose at random in Soviet literature on the press and find such old saws as: "Soviet news . . . puts before itself the task of education, the task of practical help in the cause of building communism."[55] By comparison, *Pravda* suggested, "The chief function of news is, in addition to reporting verified facts and events to the world's public, to discover the interrelationship and mutual influence of phenomena and to show their essence. . . ."[56] A theme in Soviet statements on "news" is the purposefulness of what is reported. Variously, it is to help the Communist Party in its work, to build a better society, to reveal flaws in industry or agriculture, to wage an ideological battle on behalf of the Marxist-Leninist world view, to counter "bourgeois propaganda," and to form the morals of youth.

These goals, however, are germane to Soviet mass media only to the extent that American journalism's functions—for example, to provide the citizenry with information about government and society—bear on the mass media's daily work. The Soviet journalist is not told what makes one event significant and worth reporting, and not another. American research on the subject of what is and is not news suggests that journalists decide often enough according to prevailing attitudes of their newspapers. They learn from the editing of their writing, from reprimands, and from the expressed opinions of their editors what the "news" is. Their own attitudes and opinions tend to be formed by what one writer calls the "news gathering bureaucracy." And although they envision themselves as participants in a democratic society, in which their duty is to inform the public, their reporting and writing defers to their colleagues in the newsroom.[57] This seems very much what happens in Soviet editorial offices. The young Soviet journalist forms his judgment of what is necessary and publishable information from his understanding of accepted and encouraged practices. If he has had formal journalism training, he has been impressed with these principles: the Soviet press serves society led by the Communist Party; it is a "people's press"; the journalist must help develop society, but he also must be truthful in his writing. He also has read Soviet newspapers and periodicals, he has listened to the radio and watched television. He tends reasonably to recognize, from his own experience at least, that some things consistently go unreported in the Soviet mass media. As he acquires experience in the editorial offices, he learns a routine, the pattern of Soviet journalism. He may not agree with it. He may envision different ways of informing the public. *Zhurnalist*, in fact, regularly publishes articles on what is wrong with the

Soviet press. However, the average Soviet journalist, confronted with large mass media and with the political bureaucracy, is not apt to feel that he can revolutionize Soviet journalism. One Soviet TASS correspondent, asked why the news agency writers consistently reported official visits of foreign dignitaries in the same form, responded: "TASS has five or six styles for items like that. That's how they're written. On other subjects, you can write in whatever style you want."[58] To challenge such trivial conformity is possibly to damage one's career. Soviet journalists tend, it seems, to go along with the norm. They are encouraged to do so by promise of advancement, by praise and criticism from superiors, and by established practice.

One must differentiate among journalists. Take, for example, the editor or correspondent in a small Soviet town working on a thrice weekly newspaper with a circulation of perhaps 12,000. If he is middle aged, he has little expectation of advancing to more rewarding and challenging work. He has little incentive to buck city hall. In fact, because his newspaper is an official publication of city hall—the local Communist Party committee—his interests generally coincide with the local political bureaucracy. If the journalist is young, with his future before him, he is not apt to improve it by being unorthodox or aggressive. The Voronezh *oblast* newspaper *Kommuna* showed initiative by publishing a column, "Our Everyday Life," containing routine household hints on clothing and food preparation. *Pravda* promptly criticized the feature as being insipid and suggested that *Kommuna* instead devote its efforts to checking on the work of tailoring and repair shops in Voronezh.[59] A writer on a small *raion* newspaper, *Novy Put*, produced a satiric article on corruption in the district's road department. When there was no reaction from local party officials, the writer and his editor attended a party meeting. According to a *Pravda* correspondent who wrote about it later, this was the scene:

"You think you're smarter than everyone else!" the first secretary of the *raion* party committee began, addressing the author of the article. "We'll fire you now, and no one will give you work. I mean it! And you" (to Comrade Makarov, editor of the newspaper), "remember this: Communists, especially the *raion* officials, are not to be criticized without the knowledge of the *raion* committee. Is that clear?" Later, the party secretary complained to the *Pravda* correspondent: "The newspaper does no good with its articles. It only undermines authority of officials." [60] This may not be the unanimous attitude of Soviet political officials, but it reasonably represents a majority. The press as critic has few friends in state bureaucracies anywhere. In the Soviet Union, a directive of 1939 explicitly prohibited newspapers from publicly opposing actions of Communist Party committees,[61] and practice over the years has impressed on editors an obligation to coordinate their work with the party-government decisions.

Among provincial publications, in the rural villages and towns, journalists find themselves somewhat in the position of American rural editors. Where the American weekly newspaper survives because of its support and encouragement of local busi-

The editorial board of the *oblast* newspaper *Priokskaya Pravda,* published in Ryazan about 115 miles southeast of Moscow.

ness, the Soviet small-town newspapers must cater to the political community. Editors establish close personal relations with community leaders. Although they may perform worthwhile services to their communities, they are not likely to challenge the local power establishment. On the contrary, they tend to think of themselves as part of that group, sharing its interests, values, and opinions.

As the Soviet journalist moves to progressively larger publications, his position and range of opportunities changes. The editorial managements of republic and large *oblast* newspapers function amid more complex bureaucratic structures. In large cities, there are several layers of party and government organizations somewhat equivalent to city, county, and state networks in an American urban area. The Soviet journalist's personal contacts may reach into any one of these. His editors are members of various party and government executive committees. While there is unanimity concerning the immediate needs and goals of the newspaper's area—industrial development, housing construction, consumer services, and the like—the journalists deal with many party-state agencies, each with its particular responsibilities and demands. In these circumstances, editors easily become involved in local power struggles and interagency jealousies. *Pravda* recounted the travails of a Lithuanian republic youth magazine which, in investigating management of a collective farm, antagonized a local party secretary. In an attempt to suppress an article about the farm, the party secretary contacted acquaintances in the republic party organization's agriculture department. It in turn arranged with the local party committee where the magazine's managing editor was registered as a party member to put pressure on him. The harassment, including a personal telephone call from the agriculture department's director, continued for two months, when finally the managing editor wrote to *Pravda* recounting the incident.[62]

Soviet journalists working in the large national mass media are likely to be more involved in the political infighting. Their own stature and authority is greater than that of provincial editors. Their publications tend more to align themselves with particular interest groups and factions of opinion. Subject to the broad unanimity of purpose imposed by the party bureaucracy, the national press is drawn into current controversies by its own inclinations and by the appeals and demands of other organizations to which it is allied. At times, the mass media rather mechanically present various views on an officially approved topic of discussion. There have been national discussions on reform of the Russian language, on marriage and divorce legislation, and on the progress of Soviet economic reorganization. In other instances where substantial policy decisions are involved, the national press becomes involved in sniping attacks among various elements. The post-Khrushchev handling of the Stalin issue falls into this category. Such questions of national policy are debated in obscure Aesopian language, clear to the initiated, but sufficiently modulated not to excite public controversy.[63]

In these conflicts, Soviet editors must sense which way the wind is blowing, or they must be assured of support in some segment of the party-state bureaucracies. The press sections of the party Central Committee do not examine the contents of every publication before it appears. Editorial boards must decide on the publication and editing of most individual articles. Editors know that one does not print articles unfavorable to the security police, the defense budget, or space exploration. However, in other areas, the guidelines are broad. Criticism of government ministries, of depressed agriculture, of cultural programs for youth, of lagging housing construction, of air and water pollution, and of excessive labor mobility is acceptable. The question then is how biting, penetrating, and revealing should criticism be? Provincial editors are prone to take their cues from articles and press reviews in *Pravda*, *Izvestia*, and perhaps *Komsomolskaya Pravda*. Editors of other national publications and the larger *oblast* press perforce must deal with information for which there are no specific guidelines. Their primary reference logically is national policy, but their second is apt to be their own circle of friends and contacts, in and out of the mass media, and their own notion of what their publications should be doing. In this, their attitudes tend to coincide more with select circles rather than mass attitudes.

Journalists' attitudes further are influenced by their continuous, close contact with the political bureaucracy. As we saw earlier, the party press sections function as critics and advisers of the journalist corps. Conferences with party officials, and with government bureaucrats, to discuss general policies and press coverage of specific themes take up much of a Soviet editor's time at the provincial and national level. Since editors are chiefly beholden to the political bureaucracies, their views are more apt to correspond than diverge. At the same time, Soviet journalists have a stated loyalty or commitment to the mass audience—the common workingman and the farm peasant who lacks influence, power, or prestige. Thus, they must constantly rationalize and justify their activities.

What may very well happen most of the time is that the Soviet journalist accepts the bureaucracy's administration and decisions as being largely in the best interests of the masses. Analogously, editors of large American newspapers support many official programs more from the point of view of government bureaucracies and community elites than from that of the common citizen. Simultaneously, they cast their endorsements in terms of general welfare. Thus, American editors give wide publicity to campaigns against poverty, for urban renewal, for car safety legislation, natural resources conservation, expanded education, improved health services, and charity drives. Most of these programs originate with government and academic groups and may well benefit the citizenry; but, while editors have a vague notion of what their audiences want, they tend to form their attitudes in concert with a small segment of the community. Their outlook is apt to be one of critical cooperation with the major public and private institutions concerned with the common welfare. Editors tend to feel that they must lead and promote innovation against unenlightened, conservative opinion.

Soviet editors are under considerably more pressure than American to march in step with official policy, whether it seems wise or not. Yet, being privy to much of the internal discussion, aware of limited alternatives, and conscious that they are on the management side of the line, Soviet editors approach their responsibilities as leaders and organizers of the community. Where existing conditions or policies conflict with their own attitudes or conscience, they have a choice. They either rationalize (live today to fight tomorrow), or attempt some degree of opposition, in private discussions or in publications supported by some element in the party-state bureaucracies.

However, much of what Soviet journalists deal with does not raise insoluble moral dilemmas or challenge the stated principles of Soviet journalism. Relatively few journalists are involved in writing on national and international issues, where bias and distortion are most commonly called for, and where independent assessment may conflict with established attitudes. Most Soviet editors and writers process and transmit prepared information supplied to them from the central press, information agencies, outside experts, or the political bureaucracy. A directive of the Communist Party Central Committee is published with no more question than American editors reserve for standard advertisements in their newspapers. Editors simultaneously know of information that is not published, or views that are not represented in the mass media. The more audacious, imaginative, and idealistic may attempt to fill the void, although they more likely receive criticism than praise for the initiative. Thus, editors tend along general themes, as formulated by their major sources, that is, the party-government agencies, TASS, and the more explicit party directives.

A meeting of Izvestia's editorial board.

The Journalist's Product

We might best deal with general content of the Soviet mass media by categories and themes. As in the American press, certain groupings of information are standard in Soviet newspapers, magazines, and on television and radio. They reflect the judgments of editors and writing journalists, as well as the party-government agencies that manage the press. In each category, one can find changes of specific information and attitudes. But the Soviet citizen, in his daily reading, listening, and viewing of the mass media, is exposed to the following areas of information:[64]

THE PARTY—Official directives of the Communist Party Central Committee, published verbatim in large newspapers, often in magazines, and in TASS summary in smaller publications. Official appearances of national party leaders: speeches of party authorities at conferences and national congresses, also frequently verbatim. Methods and examples of party leadership, role of the party member in society. Sketchy reports of routine party meetings, ordinarily mentioning only the topic of discussion and names of participants. Occasional notices of reassignment, censure, or other discipline of party members. Overall theme: the party as the leading force in Soviet society, guided by the doctrine of Marxism-Leninism and composed of principled, dedicated individuals.

MARXISM-LENINISM—Essays applying Marxism-Leninism to current and broad issues of Soviet society and the world, such as Soviet economic development, ideological pronouncements of Communist China, progress of underdeveloped societies, and trends in capitalist countries. Usually abstract in the style of an academic treatise, and often appearing in scholarly journals, but also in major newspapers. Essays and instructive articles based on Lenin's writings applied to current problems, and to justify particular policies or programs.

THE REVOLUTION—The meaning of the 1917 Bolshevik Revolution for the Soviet Union, and for international communism. Reminiscences and recapitulations of events leading up to and during the revolution. Theme: a cataclysmic event leading to formation of a social order unprecedented in world history.

THE NATION—Articles and reports extolling past national accomplishments—e.g., industrial development, expansion of welfare services. Instances of cooperation and harmony among Soviet nationalities and progress of national republics under Soviet socialism. Criticism of internal nationalistic tendencies in art, literature, or custom, but excluding folklore as historical fact or national cultures as subordinate to Soviet nationhood. Some discussion in scholarly journals on nationalism, national characteristics, and assimilation of nationalities. Articles on the "Soviet man" as a unique product of a socialist society.

SOVIET ALLIES—Communist nations allied to the Soviet Union through military, economic, trade, and cultural agreements. Communist parties of other nations, focusing on their advances among the masses and their persecution by the existing government. Practical experience and methods in other Communist countries. Direct editorial criticism or critical tone in articles concerning developments in these countries displeasing to the Soviet government.

SOVIET ENEMIES—Essays, editorials, and articles on international imperialism, developments in capitalist countries, predominantly the United States and nations of western Europe. Particular stress on West German military strength as a threat to peace, and on American global military and economic interests as confirmation of inherent imperialism of capitalist countries. Instances of cooperation between the Soviet Union and capitalist countries as evidence of validity of peaceful coexistence. Caution on contact with foreigners, need for security.

OTHER NATIONS—Developments in Latin America, Africa, Asia, the Middle East, generally cast in terms of national liberation wars, of rejection of colonialism and imperialism, of independence of nonwhite peoples, of progress toward socialism. Articles on foreign policy toward the Soviet Union and other nations, and items on Soviet economic (sometimes military) assistance, and on commercial ties.

DIPLOMACY AND FOREIGN RELATIONS—Official statements, often via TASS, of Soviet government positions. Essays and articles on goals and aspirations of the Soviet state, usually in generalities. Analyses and editorials on diplomatic relations with and foreign policies of other nations, often well documented from articles in the foreign press, though reaching conclusions in harmony with Soviet foreign policy (e.g., rising militarism in West Germany, failure of American policy in Vietnam, improved relations with Middle East nations, deterioration of NATO). Exclusively laudatory tone in articles dealing with Soviet foreign policy.

SOVIET GOVERNMENT—Decisions of the Council of Ministers, sessions of the Supreme Soviet, national and local elections, speeches by government leaders. Articles discussing roles of local and national government, of mass participation in administration of government. Individual examples of problems of local governments, how the problems were resolved. Responsibilities of elected representatives to electors. Discussion of roles of Communist Party organizations and local government.

DEFENSE, WAR, AND PEACE—In the popular press, articles reaffirming Soviet military strength, need for a strong military as a deterrent to nuclear war and protector of interests of other nations. Speeches by military leaders, praise of Soviet servicemen, particularly on official days such as Soviet Artillerymen's and Rocket Troops' Day, Soviet Border Guards' Day. Military strategy and tactics in the military press, such as *Krasnaya Zvezda*, newspaper of the Ministry of Defense. Formulas for world peace, disarmament and nonaggression pacts. Reminiscences of World War II.

ECONOMIC ACTIVITY— Industrial production, statistical reports, industrial construction and expansion, factory management, banking, national budgets, long-range economic plans, financial relations among state institutions. Consumer services and goods. Wages and cost of living, prices, taxes. Transportation, railroads, shipping, automobiles, civilian aviation.

AGRICULTURE—Production statistics, innovations in agricultural equipment and practices, farm administration, experiments in farm management, sowing and harvesting reports, conservation of soil and water, farm prices and wages, marketing of produce to the state and in peasant farm markets, rural life and culture, rural industry and trades, farm labor problems, capital investments and financing of agriculture, mechanization of farming.

LAW AND COURTS—Function of law in Soviet society, changes in Soviet statutes (usually in specialized journals or, sketchily, in conjunction with reports on Supreme Soviet sessions). Criminal and civil cases, usually intended to be instructive and educational about the workings of Soviet law and to show punishments for criminal activity. Legal reforms, advice on legal questions of interest to most citizens (e.g., legal requirements to exchange apartments), discussion of rights of citizens, of duties of Soviet lawyers and state legal authorities and courts.

CRIME—Reasons for major and minor crime, juvenile delinquency, occasional general and isolated statistics on crime, citizen participation in maintaining law and order, role of security police and uniformed militia in preventing various types of crime (including foreign espionage).

ACCIDENTS AND DISASTERS—Occasional and brief reports of floods, fires, earthquakes, plane crashes, ship sinkings, and automobile accidents (when a well-known person is killed).

HEALTH AND WELFARE—Benefits to the masses of the socialist system. Pensions, medical care, medical research, personal hygiene, child-care centers, rest and vacation centers for adults, government welfare and health agencies.

EDUCATION—Role of education in Soviet society, discussions of universities, technical institutes, secondary schools, curriculum and reforms, expansion of education.

SCIENCE AND INVENTION—Reports on research and technology, peaceful use of atomic power, organization of research, space exploration. Machinery, equipment, and consumer products as benefits of science. Theory of science. Rare and sketchy reports on military science and invention. Weather, including weather forecasts.

ATHEISM AND RELIGION—Scientific atheism, evolution, philosophic materialism. Combating religion, motivations and psychology of religious believers, religious customs as vestiges of the past, education of youth in atheism.

YOUTH—Rearing of youth in Soviet Marxism-Leninism; attitudes of youth, differences between generations, work training and formal education, articles on exemplary youths, criticism of unorthodox behavior.

PEOPLE—Exploits and accomplishments of common men, tributes to the strength of the masses, exemplary workers in factories, offices, and on farms. Aspirations and goals of the masses. Personal ordeals and tragedies. Tributes to the famous and prominent on birthdays. Obituaries of leaders in party, government, science, etc.

FAMILY AND SEX—Family relations, marriage in Soviet society, reasons for divorce. Infrequent discussions of sex and sexual relations, usually in clinical tone.

LITERATURE, ARTS, AND CULTURE—Place of literature and arts in society, critical reviews of books, theater, painting, sculpture in terms of socialist realism. Mass culture, including films, museums, television, architecture. In both the popular press and journals, poetry, fiction, art.

A summary of Soviet categories of information in the mass media cannot very well supply the tone and style of writing. These vary with the writer and form. A *Pravda* editorial on Marxist-Leninist thought differs considerably from one written by a university scholar. It is not enough to say that one or both are propaganda. The word "propaganda" has several meanings. It is often used in the Soviet Union, among the rank and file, to describe tendentious information, whether in *Pravda*, broadcasts from Communist China, or the Voice of America. A more formal or official meaning equates propaganda with the propagation of a point of view or a body of knowledge. In that sense, the word lacks the connotations of deceit, untruth, and distortion. The Soviet political bureaucracy enjoins journalists to improve "propaganda" of party affairs or the Soviet moral code. The result is sermonizing, laudatory press agentry.

In contrast to political indoctrination, the mass media conduct propaganda in the sense of publicity. Press articles and television or radio broadcasts disseminate information on health care, work techniques, management methods, and what can be broadly called a life style. These too are "propaganda," but differ little from instructive and informational articles in the American press.

What perhaps gives the Soviet mass media distinguishing characteristics are the omissions. Every subject, attitude, and style of writing in the Soviet mass media has its equivalents in the American press, but the reverse is not true. The conscious purposefulness of information eliminates facts and opinion that, while trivial, could lend depth to an individual's awareness of the world around him. Information unfavorable to the Soviet state seldom reaches the Soviet public, or does so in diluted form. This sort of bias is particularly conspicuous in mass media coverage of foreign affairs. Soviet foreign policy ranks with military affairs as a sacrosanct topic. Regardless of indisputable facts, the Soviet press inclines toward an optimistic, favorable presentation of events in much of its information, a heritage of earlier years when the mass media were mobilizing for gargantuan tasks.

The noticeable trend, however, is toward increasingly critical, realistic writing. That is, if the countryside is depressed, which it is, the press describes it so, and does not stretch for the flower among weeds. However, opposing forces work on journalists. The political bureaucracy, with its concern for maintaining its power and authority and accomplishing particular objectives, insists as any bureaucracy does on a cooperative press. Thus on May 5, 1968, Press Day in the Soviet Union, *Pravda* proclaimed:

> The ideological work of the press has to be more closely connected with the tasks of further increasing the labor and social activity of the masses and with the tasks of successfully completing the five year plan. . . . It is the most important duty of our press to wage an offensive struggle against bourgeois ideology and to actively oppose the efforts of certain literary, artistic and other works to intrude with views alien to the socialist ideology of Soviet society. . . . The education of the younger generation in the glorious revolutionary, militant and labor traditions of the people must be the subject of constant concern for the press. . . ."

Such broad obligations turn Soviet editors along identical paths. *All* Soviet newspapers began publishing discussions and reports of the transition from a six- to a five-day work week in the course of 1967, as the five-day week became a general condition. Since, however, the five-day week is a formally decreed change, Soviet journalists with this and other official acts are psychologically oriented to documenting and promoting its ultimate success.

This sort of news management has its critics. In discussing Soviet newspapers' publicity on the fiftieth anniversary of the Bolshevik Revolution, Lev Tolkunov, editor of *Izvestia*, wrote: "In a number of instances, this work is purposeless, inconsequential, superficial and, finally, simply dull. Page through newspapers and you see a large headline on the jubilee, and under this a hope-filled, ringing subheadline. And under the headline, ordinary, gray, incidental items." [65]

Yet, there is a difference in the word and the deed. *Izvestia's* coverage of the Bolshevik Revolution produced no pathbreaking journalism. With the rest of the press, it was able to publish column after column on a half century of Soviet history without once mentioning Joseph Stalin or Nikita Khrushchev, who between them dominated the Soviet state for forty of its fifty years. The equivalent would be a review of American history since 1930 without reference to Franklin Delano Roosevelt.

The political reasons for omissions in the Soviet mass media are apparent enough. The point is, however, that such political editing cumulatively forms a picture of Soviet society lacking major elements. Living in the Soviet Union, reading its press and watching its television, one comes to forget that day in and day out people are murdered, airplanes crash, trucks run off the highway, executives are fired, politicians argue, people are sent to prison, men and women commit suicide, young men are drafted, university students criticize the Communist Party, bureaucrats take bribes, or that government agencies are deciding innumerable questions of public importance. Unless one witnesses these occurrences in the Soviet Union, they have no reality. One can argue that some are not significant. But at the least they create in their repetition an awareness of what is happening, and at the most, they alert the public to unfavorable conditions. Absence of such information in the Soviet press creates a different picture of society, generally of one that is tranquil and stable. Change, as the Soviet mass media present it, tends to be controlled and manageable. Social problems are seldom if ever beyond solution. Uncertainty, despair, and doubt are neither characteristic of the political leadership, nor of the official national mood.

In presenting such a society, Soviet journalists perpetuate a credibility gap. Often what they write does not correspond to reality as their audience understands it. Precisely this has been debated and discussed among Soviet journalists. A Soviet correspondent, describing the inclination of officials and some journalists to minimize the Tashkent earthquake of 1966, concluded: "Obviously to some, it still seems as if earthquakes can be everywhere, but not here [in the Soviet Union]. Others suggest that one must write 'not about destruction, but about creation.' Still others do not want to 'arouse emotions. . . .' And the reason for all of this, apparently, is distrust of the reader." [66] Another Soviet journalist noted: "Letters continue to reach editors in which readers complain that they have to get much of their news from neighbors, not from the papers." [67] Of about 1,200 readers queried on newspaper readership in a small Soviet city, 26 per cent said their opinions disagreed with views of the press. One reader responded: "They [journalists] know what it's all about, but just the same, they write it wrong. Much embellishing." [68]

Such views from journalists and readers alike constitute a force for more dispassionate, disinterested writing in the Soviet press. This is not the same as "objectivity," which Soviet journalism rejects outright. Rather what concerns some Soviet journalists is the common practice of finding facts in order to reach conclusions that are predetermined by a combination of the political bureaucracy, prejudices, and such other intangibles as the "national interest" or tradition. It is obvious that the party-state administrative agencies lean to this practice because of their interest in successfully implementing policies and programs.

However, the mass media become dysfunctional when they so overwhelmingly concentrate on portraying success, progress, and accomplishment, and thereby ignore evidence to the contrary. In a changing industrial society like the Soviet Union, the need for an independent statement of conditions increases rather than decreases. Partly this is because expanding education works against government press agentry. It becomes less and less believable, and people turn to other sources of information. This accounts, for example, for the popularity of foreign

broadcasts in the Soviet Union, and for the political bureaucracy's attempt to counter them.

Further, as Soviet society becomes more complex, and as the
mass population is drawn into administration, the decision-
making process requires widespread dissemination of factual,
hard information. In a small American company, only a few
people need to know the actual condition of its finances, and
its production, labor, and marketing problems. But in a giant
corporation, many more people must have this information or
parts of it, in order to make daily decisions in harmony with
the corporation's best interests. In Soviet society, where there
is an attempt to involve the rank and file in the administration of institutions, the mass media increasingly perform an
educational and problem-solving role, along with their function
of mobilizing human resources. For this reason, Soviet journalists and editors have tended in recent years to emphasize
a more realistic appraisal of society. It is somewhat comparable,
to mention a specific example, to the expanded attention currently being given by the American mass media to the problems
of Negro ghettos and cities. That is, the urban crisis is recognized as a national problem, requiring efforts on the part of the
majority of the population to solve it. Consequently, there must
be general education in the urban problem and its possible
solutions. On a broader scale, encompassing many social problems, the Soviet mass media gradually are adopting a similar
attitude.

CHAPTER 5

THE PRINTED WORD

IT IS RISKY to generalize about the Soviet press. Like the American, Soviet newspapers range from professionally edited and written publications such as *Pravda* and *Literaturnaya Gazeta* to the slipshod, small-town papers hardly worth reading. Within a broad conformity, measured for example by simultaneous publication in all Soviet newspapers, and in many magazines, of Communist Party decrees, there is considerable diversity. The Soviet political bureaucracy establishes general goals and functions for the press. How well individual newspapers and magazines measure up, however, depends chiefly on their editorial and Communist Party apparatus. The whole is perhaps analogous to an American newspaper chain in which, despite a central management, the weak links are tangled with the strong.

The American printed press is structured by the demands of the marketplace, the Soviet by decision of a political bureaucracy. Overall, the results are quite similar. The newspaper and magazine industries of both countries are dominated by relatively few national publications, which command authority and influence because of their close association with political and/or economic power. *Pravda* is to Soviet society roughly what *The New York Times* is to American. Not in purpose, of course, but in the sense that both are sources of authoritative government opinion, and both set the standard for their respective national newspaper networks. Of less influence and usually, but not necessarily, of inferior quality in both countries are the large area publications, then the regional, city, neighborhood or surburban, and small-town newspapers. Finally, in both countries there is a potpourri of university, factory, office, and village publications. The newspaper industries in both countries also are categorized by audiences, although the Soviet press is more deliberately and consciously structured according to age, nationality, and social class or careers of readers than the American.

The most common type of newspaper in the United States and in the Soviet Union is edited for the mass audience. But both countries also have printed media for special interest groups and ethnic minorities. Obviously, the original motivation for the development of press networks differed. For example, the early Soviet government spent a good deal of money and effort constructing a rural press, when in fact a majority of peasants could not read. But the anticipated political return seemed to justify the investment. In the American experience, the press followed market demand. It expanded outwardly from the cities into the countryside as public and business needs could be translated into financially profitable newspaper operations. The Soviet ethnic language press grew at a rate that exceeded natural demand, particularly in central Asian regions where educational levels were low. But once again politics took precedence over economics. The American nationalities press came with the great immigrations of the nineteenth century, and declined as successive generations were assimilated into American twentieth-century society and no longer presented a large, distinct newspaper market.

What the final press systems suggest is that common characteristics of industrial societies—literate populations, varied by occupation, education, and social status, but needing large quantities of specialized and general information—force themselves onto the structure of the mass media. Whereas these characteristics operated on the American press from the ground up, so to speak, they were impressed on the Soviet mass media from the top down. Thus, in the United States, public demand in conjunction with private enterprise, which sought commercial markets for information and publicizing of products and services, determined the form of the printed press network. In the Soviet Union, the political bureaucracy, seeking to reach the rank-and-file reader, so structured the press as thoroughly to disseminate information and attitudes. However, both American entrepreneurs and Soviet politicians were led to much the same ends in the organization of the printed press.

All this is not to ignore the differences between the American and Soviet press. The Soviet structure—excluding for a moment content—has more an organizational chart quality. As in the military, where each base has its newspaper, each division its publication, so in the Soviet Union, each *oblast* methodically is furnished its major newspaper, each *raion* its weekly. The American press structure is more haphazard. Newspapers survive or perish according to the flow of population and economic changes. They are tied closely to whims of the marketplace, whereas Soviet newspapers respond to decisions of a general staff.

The Soviet press operates somewhat as a subsidiary of a single, mammoth corporation. Like other Soviet enterprises, newspapers and magazines are on the system of *khozrashchet*, or economic accounting. They have annual budgets, incorporated in a series of steps in the the national government, the party or Komsomol budgets, and are expected to show a profit; and many do. Sales of Communist Party publications, such as *Pravda*, the theoretical journal *Kommunist*, and *Ekonomicheskaya Gazeta*, produce about 35 per cent of total party income.[1] *Izvestia*, the national government newspaper, is said to yield a profit of 12 per cent, with 30 per cent of its income spent for newsprint, 25 per cent for circulation costs, 30 per cent for mechanical expenses, and 3 per cent for editorial and management.[2] *Leningradskaya Pravda*, the major party newspaper in the industrial Soviet city of Leningrad, produced a handsome annual profit of about 500,000 rubles ($555,000) a few years ago. Unlike some Soviet newspapers, it carries no advertising. Hence, its income is wholly from sales. Circulating 352,000 copies in 1964, at 2 kopecks a copy (a little over 2¢), *Leningradskaya Pravda*'s annual income came to about 2.2 million rubles ($2.44 million).[3] By comparison, another Leningrad paper, the Komsomol publication *Smena*, circulating 105,000 in 1964, had an annual profit of about 200,000 rubles ($223,000) from an income estimated at 650,000 rubles ($721,000).[4]

A financially independent press has been more the exception than the rule in Soviet history. After the NEP years, when the press network was expanded to spur industrialization, state subsidies of newspapers were commonplace. In 1959, however, a Communist Party directive zeroed in on financially ailing newspapers.[5] It revealed such cases as these: the evening newspaper in Baku, with a press run of 20,000 copies in 1959, had a planned subsidy of 10,400 rubles ($11,540). The Vilnius evening paper was losing 45,000 rubles ($50,000) a year; a Kishinev paper, 59,000 rubles ($65,000). A Byelorussian paper dealing with literature and arts sold for 4 kopecks (4.4¢), but cost 13 kopecks (14.4¢) to produce. Many of the small factory, farm, and office weekly or monthly tabloids were being subsidized as well to pay writers and editorial staff.

In another specific case, a Moscow periodical dealing with housing construction and architecture was being kept alive in 1962 almost entirely by subsidies. Although it had only 2,300 subscribers, its press run was 6,000 copies. Its direct state subsidy was 39,000 rubles ($43,300), and if government organization subscriptions—paid for with public funds—were added, the subsidy came to 60,000 rubles ($66,600).[6]

The huge network of *raion* newspapers survived with government subsidy at least through 1968. In September of that year, however, the party Central Committee issued a decree designed drastically to reduce state support of the local press. Editors were instead to look to advertising revenue of Soviet businesses, industries, and private individuals as a major source of income in addition to subscriptions. The Committee on the Press was given the job of working out advertising rates for what was a significant shift of the newspaper press toward advertising revenue.[7]

The major national Soviet newspapers and periodicals, and at least the larger provincial publications, are probably financially self-sufficient. Profitability of a newspaper remains a different matter in the Soviet Union, however, than in the United States. Given the decision of the political bureaucracy to maintain a newspaper or magazine for a particular purpose, it will survive regardless of its financial situation. Television and radio broadcasting are almost wholly funded from government monies (which derive from various public taxes and from profits of industry). In a socialized economy, it is really just a matter of bookkeeping as to whether a given newspaper exists from sales income or on government subsidies. Ultimately, the public pays through subscription fees or taxes.

What profit does in the Soviet Union, however, is measure the economic rationale of an individual newspaper or magazine. That is, given state-established wage scales, newsprint and printing costs, and sales price (kept at 2 to 3 kopecks—a little over 2¢ to 3¢—for most of the newspaper press), does a newspaper pay its way? And if it does not, is it worthwhile for other reasons to sustain it? Government encouragement of editorial managements to keep their publications profitable also injects an incentive to make newspapers and magazines appealing to readers. After all, the best gauge of any publication, be it Soviet or American, is whether people want it enough to buy it. This is not an immutable principle in the Soviet Union, and probably not in the United States either. Soviet citizens buy publications because they feel they should or must (many Communist Party members subscribe to *Pravda* for this reason), rather than because the newspapers or magazines are indispensable to their lives. Then, too, the cost of most papers and periodicals is low enough that, pressed by annual *Soyuz-pechat* circulation campaigns, some Soviet citizens subscribe for the convenience of occasional reading. But profit, as reflected by sales of newspapers and magazines in the Soviet Union, remains a better gauge of popularity and effectiveness than press runs, which can be maintained at artificially high levels by state subsidy. When they are, of course, they reflect a "popularity" among the political bureaucracy.

The Advertising Business

After decades of neglect, advertising is gradually emerging in the Soviet Union both as a source of revenue for the newspaper press and for radio and TV broadcasting, and as a device to publicize and merchandise goods. The fact of a seller's market in the country for most of the past half century inveighed against advertising. So did Soviet ideology. Advertising, to the Soviet political mind, symbolized the big, private capital press. As we have seen, advertising was declared a state monopoly almost immediately after the revolution. More importantly, a mass press heavily dependent on advertising revenue, even of state industry, could not be structured and manipulated as easily as a state-subsidized system. The press network built up in the late 1920's and early 1930's, especially in rural areas and among minority nationalities, could not have emerged if newspaper editors had had to rely on advertising income. Instead, the press was government supported and therefore could be organized when and where Soviet political leaders thought necessary.

The advertising that did survive in the Soviet Union was of the American institutional type. It pleaded for special causes rather than merchandised goods. The present-day American "commercials" on harmful effects of smoking or on pollution of air and water correspond more in spirit and tone to the poster advertising that has been practiced in the Soviet Union. Further, the Soviet press turned, in a sense, to mass political advertising. If advertising is designed to introduce and win popular acceptance of an object, there is nothing inherently different between a full-page advertisement for an American political candidate or for a citizens' lobby cause and Soviet press publicity for the nation's goals and its leaders. The form differs. Soviet mass political advertising, using easily understood slogans and repetition of ideas, has been in the "news columns" rather than in identifiable advertising space of a newspaper.

Commercial advertising as it is known in the United States and as it was practiced in prerevolutionary Russia reappeared haltingly in the Soviet Union after World War II. Radio Moscow began accepting paid announcements from business and educational institutions in May, 1947.[8] And gradually in the 1950's, display advertising began to appear in the newspaper press. It was and remains rather primitive, unimaginative, and low key. Most of what appears in the printed press is less advertising than announcements. Soviet newspapers publish unillustrated listings of radio and television programs, current films, and theater productions. Until recently, divorce announcements were by law printed in newspapers, at the personal expense of those getting a divorce. Provincial, but ordinarily not national, newspapers also carry what is essentially classified advertising. One type announces dissertation defenses and examinations for various civil service jobs, ordinarily with universities and institutes, or with industrial enterprises, at the management level. A second type, inserted by industries, advertises for skilled labor. Industries further sell surplus equipment and materials through classified ads.

Many Soviet newspapers also advertise the various kinds of income-producing lotteries in the Soviet Union. These are either sponsored by the government, or a particular organization, the Union of Writers or the Union of Journalists, for example. Lottery advertising generally is illustrated, with a sketch of an automobile, motorcycle, television set, and other prizes to be given away. *Soyuzpechat* is one of the most consistent advertisers, although its subscription campaigns are conducted in cooperation with individual publications which use simple display advertising to promote their own sales.

Finally, there is a small amount of product advertising in Soviet newspapers. Until recently, this was prosaic, declaratory merchandising. A representative advertisement in a Leningrad city newspaper read: "At All Food Stores of the Administration of Retail Food Trade. Grapes and Plums for Sale." Then after two paragraphs on the nutritional value of fruit, the advertisement continued: "Grapes and Plums—the Best Dessert. Buy Grapes and Plums!"[9] An advertisement in the national trade union newspaper *Sovetskaya Torgovlya*, directed to state retail and wholesale organizations, promoted black shoe polish with the words: "Careful Attention to Shoes Preserves Their Outward Appearance and Prolongs the Life of Socks."[10] An innovation in 1968 was an 8-page weekly advertising supplement to the Moscow evening paper, *Vechernaya Moskva*. The first issue, illustrated and printed in black and red ink, publicized color television, dry cleaning, baby foods, summer cruises on the Black Sea, and tours of east European countries.[11]

Soviet economic development, resulting in greater foreign trade with non-Communist countries and in a greater variety of both consumer and industrial goods within the Soviet Union, has spurred advertising. Having to compete abroad for sales, Soviet trade organizations advertise in foreign language publications sold abroad. For example, an issue of *Moscow News*, a weekly English language tabloid, recently advertised farm tractors—"These machines are of excellent quality, effective in use, highly productive and most profitable."[12] Within the Soviet Union, advertising serves about the same purposes as in the United States. It educates people in new products, and helps in distribution of merchandise by telling people what is available and where. One Soviet economist argued that with the growing diversity of Soviet products the "job of advertising [is] to bring goods to the consumer's attention. By acquainting customers with goods and by sparking a demand for them, advertising thereby promotes the growth of merchandise turnover."[13]

To develop commercial advertising, two organizations were established in 1965—a National Association for Commercial Advertising, and a Chief Commercial Advertising Administration, the first under the Council of Ministers, the second within the Soviet consumers' cooperative agency. Wide-scale advertising has been hampered, however, by a shortage of experienced and talented copywriters and business executives, the more so because the advertising departments of Soviet enterprises or government organizations are not the well-financed, glamorous agencies that they are in the United States. In 1965, retail trade organizations of the Russian republic, which includes the large cities like Moscow and Leningrad, spent only 0.02 per cent of their income on advertising.[14] Soviet editors and businessmen gradually seem to be accepting the uses of advertising, however. In 1966, for example, Moscow trade officials found themselves with warehouses of canned fruit juice. The city newspaper *Vechernyaya Moskva* worked up an advertising campaign that extolled the good taste and health-giving qualities of fruit juice. The warehouses were soon cleaned out.[15]

Radio advertising approximates that found in the printed press. That is, it consists mostly of announcements about jobs, films, lotteries, and products, the last in the form of matter-of-fact instructions as to where they can be bought with perhaps a word of encouragement to buy them. A small amount of product advertising has begun to appear on television. And there is some talk of expanding the commercial basis of broadcasting. A writer for *Zhurnalist* recently described a radio station in the Crimea, which had paid expenses from advertising revenue until the local Communist Party committee learned of the arrangement and censured the station manager, a Communist Party member. The journalist, in commenting, suggested that commercial advertising could be developed gradually, and that radio stations, and perhaps television, could finance themselves.[16]

Advertising, both in the printed press and on radio and television, seems likely to develop more quickly in the next few years than it has done over the past 30 or 40. There is some economic motivation for advertising—to move merchandise and to educate—although illustrated feature articles in the press do the same. But as the consumer goods sector enlarges, and as Soviet industrial enterprises gain more responsibility for selling their products—one of the goals of the economic reform begun in 1965—advertising probably will expand. Working against it is an unfavorable Soviet opinion of advertising in the West, insofar as it is considered deceptive, sensational, and a means of developing demand for unessential goods. Further, unless the government decides to finance expansion of the mass media primarily with advertising revenue, newspapers, magazines and radio and television broadcasting have no great incentive to develop advertising staffs and skills. Soviet mass media have been almost wholly oriented toward the government and/or the public in their attitude to finances, just as American educational television operates with government and foundation money. To change from that to, for example, an American newspaper's or television station's business practices would require considerable education and psychological adjustment.

The Newspaper Press

The Soviet newspaper industry, as a nationally planned and directed enterprise, divides into six segments. The most important, as in the United States, is the national newspaper group. The structure then breaks down, corresponding to political administration areas, into the republic, *oblast,* city, *raion,* and, finally, the "lower" and *kolkhoz* (collective farm) newspaper group.

In all, in 1968, there were 8,754 newspapers being published in the Soviet Union with a total single press run of 126.5 million copies, or about 50 for every 100 Soviet citizens.[17] The figure for newspapers includes, however, about 4,800 in the category of the lower and *kolkhoz* press. Though the average circulation of these newspapers ranges from 1,900 (for the lower press) to 700 (*kolkhoz*)—equal to those of some American rural weeklies—they are generally of tabloid size or smaller, and of only two or four pages. Most of the lower newspapers—those published in Soviet offices, factories, and universities—are published once or twice a week. The majority of *kolkhoz* newspapers are issued one to three times a month.

Thus, in any comparisons with the American newspaper industry, the Soviet lower and *kolkhoz* press should probably be subtracted, or the thousands of American university, religious, agricultural, and labor newspapers should be added to standard American statistics on the daily and weekly press.

Taking the former approach, the Soviet Union in 1968 had just under 4,000 newspapers with a circulation of 118. 9 million. The United States in the same year published 11,212 daily and weekly newspapers, the 1,749 dailies alone circulating 61.6 million.[18] In the Soviet system, there were 177 daily newspapers (publishing six days a week, except for *Pravda*) in 1968, with a circulation of 60 million, and 222 five-day a week papers, circulating almost 10 million copies.

Two other caveats are in order. The Soviet *raion* press, which encompassed approximately 2,800 newspapers and accounted for 13.4 million circulation in 1968, is generally small and primitive. Most *raion* newspapers would most accurately compare with a tabloid-size American college paper, rather than an American small-town weekly. Thus, it is not imprecise, when speaking of the Soviet and American newspaper industries together, to subtract even the Soviet *raion* press. This would mean a total of 1,165 Soviet newspapers of a substantial size.

SOVIET NEWSPAPER PRESS: 1954–1968

Year	Number of Newspapers*	Circulation (millions)	Average Circulation (thousands)
1954	7,108	46.9	6.6
1955	7,246	48.7	6.7
1956	7,537	53.5	7.1
1957	7,951	56.7	7.1
1958	7,686	57.7	7.5
1959	7,585	60.4	8.0
1960	6,804	66.7	9.8
1961	6,692	70.7	10.6
1962	4,771	76.9	16.1
1963	5,167	83.0	16.1
1964	5,067	88.0	17.4
1965	6,253	102.0	16.3
1966	6,528	109.4	16.8
1967	7,087	119.9	16.9
1968	7,307	125.5	17.2

KOLKHOZ PRESS**

Year	Number of Newspapers	Circulation (millions)	Average Circulation
1957	1,985	1.1	.550
1960	2,740	1.9	.700
1963	1,624	1.1	.700
1965	1,434	1.0	.700
1968	1,447	1.0	.700

SOURCES: *Pechat za sorok let,* p. 123; *Pechat SSSR v 1968 godu,* p. 66; also for 1967, p. 66; for 1966, p. 67; for 1964, p. 75; for 1962, p. 63; and for 1960, p. 153.

* Totals include some newspapers published in two languages and counted as two newspapers.

** The *kolkhoz*—collective farm—newspapers were established in late 1956. Through the year 1963, the total includes some *sovkhoz*—state farm—newspapers.

·It should also be kept in mind that even a large Soviet newspaper such as the government's *Izvestia* is not strictly comparable to a major American paper, on two counts. First, the Soviet newspaper ordinarily is 6 pages, with little or no advertising, while the American metropolitan daily runs to 50 to 100 pages or more, with advertising. Second, the Soviet national paper has an enormous circulation—*Izvestia*'s was 7.7 million at the beginning of 1968.[19] An American newspaper is considered large when it is in the 250,000 and up circulation range. So what the Soviet national daily lacks is page size—and since it has no advertising, a 6-page paper would be equivalent to about 24-page American daily—it makes up in circulation.

FREQUENCY OF NEWSPAPER PUBLICATION: 1968

Type of Newspaper	Daily	5 Days a Week	4 Days a Week	3 Days a Week	Twice Weekly	Weekly
National	9	---	---	6	4	7
Republic	38	17	1	32	28	38
Oblast, krai, okrug	73	104	2	90	14	6
Autonomous oblasts and republics	26	22	---	36	11	1
City	31	78	216	271	1	---
Raion	---	1	2	2,741	47	2
Totals	177	222	221	3,176	105	54

SOURCE: *Pechat SSSR v 1968 godu,* p. 67.

Note: Figures do not include lower and *kolkhoz* newspapers. The majority of the 3,349 lower newspapers (65%, comprising 62% of the 6.5 million circulation) are published once a week, and 14% are issued twice weekly. The remaining are published one to three times a week. As well, the majority of 1,497 *kolkhoz* newspapers published one to three times a month in 1967.

Soviet national newspapers such as *Pravda* and *Izvestia* dominate the whole industry to a striking degree. Of the 4,000 newspapers, the 9 national Soviet dailies account for about one third of the total circulation. Another notable characteristic is that nearly three out of four Soviet newspapers are published in the Russian language and account for 77 per cent of total circulation. Ukrainians, the second largest nationality in the Soviet Union, have 897 Ukrainian language newspapers, with a circulation of only 12 million; the Byelorussians, 130 newspapers, with a circulation of 1.4 million; the Uzbeks, 135 papers, circulating 2.4 million; and so on, through the remainder of 58 national language newspaper groupings.

What the figures suggest is a considerable disproportion in the nationalities press. Russian, being the official Soviet language, pervades newspapers. Among minority nationalities, newspapers in the native language vary widely in circulation per capita. Taking statistics for 1959, the year for which we have figures on language distribution in the Soviet Union, such differences as the following emerge: there were 40 daily and weekly newspapers printed per 100 Russians (i.e., persons who said their native language was Russian); 17 per 100 Ukrainians; 14 per 100 Byelorussians; 6 per 100 Uzbeks; 30 per 100 Georgians; 18 per 100 Kazakhs; and 35 per 100 Lithuanians.[20] Politics partly explains the differences. Since the Soviet newspaper press is subject to central management, the political bureaucracy can open and close national language newspapers at its pleasure. But public demand may also have an effect. One study of the Byelorussian press indicates that several Byelorussian language newspapers closed down in 1962 apparently for lack of readership[21] (although it is true that deliberate government reduction of circulation can make it appear that a newspaper enjoys no reader demand).

Beyond the nationalities press, there are seven categories of Soviet specialized publications. For example, 129 newspapers were published in 1967 for members of the Young Communist League—the Komsomol. The largest of these is *Komsomolskaya Pravda*, whose circulation in 1968 was 6.7 million. The Pioneers, a youth organization for grade school children, had 27 newspapers, the dominant one being *Pionerskaya Pravda* with a circulation of 9.2 million, the largest distribution of any newspaper in the Soviet Union. In addition to the youth press, other specialized newspapers exist for industry and construction, transport, agriculture, literature and art, education, and sports. It is not clear from Soviet sources whether all military newspapers are included in statistical surveys of the press. *Krasnaya Zvezda* (circulation 2.4 million in 1968), official newspaper of the Ministry of Defense, is counted among national daily newspapers. There are also military district newspapers and these may not be incorporated into newspaper totals.

The Soviet Union also publishes 18 newspapers in eight foreign languages, primarily English and German. Papers in those two languages account for more than two thirds of the 617,000 circulation. Being for foreign readers, these 18 newspapers are in a special category so far as content goes. Their conspicuous effort to project a favorable image abroad of the Soviet Union makes them less representative of the Soviet press than newspapers published for the Soviet population.

The National Newspapers

Like such American papers as *The New York Times, Christian Science Monitor*, and the Washington *Post*, the Soviet national newspapers overshadow the whole press network. The

SPECIALIZED NEWSPAPERS: 1950, 1960, 1967

Type of Newspaper	Year	Number of Newspapers	Circulation (thousands)
Komsomol	1950	72	2,628
	1960	117	7,718
	1967	129	13,175
Pioneer	1950	21	2,154
	1960	23	7,494
	1967	27	17,118
Industry, construction	1950	2	50
	1960	6	605
	1967	5	1,102
Transportation	1950	105	377
	1960	71	952
	1967	34	887
Agriculture	1950	8	836
	1960	7	1,153
	1967	6	7,723
Literature, art, culture	1950	11	652
	1960	16	1,242
	1967	17	1,479
Teaching	1950	10	399
	1960	15	1,081
	1967	15	1,819
Sports and physical culture	1950	5	180
	1960	12	1,101
	1967	14	3,326

SOURCES: *Pechat SSSR za sorok let,* p. 125; *Pechat SSSR v 1960 godu,* p. 166, and for 1967, p. 70.

main ones—*Pravda*, official publication of the Communist Party Central Committee; *Izvestia*, newspaper of the Council of Ministers; and *Komsomolskaya Pravda*—are well enough known in the world. In addition, among the 26 national papers published in 1968, were *Krasnaya Zvezda; Trud,* national labor union paper; *Literaturnaya Gazeta*, the literary and cultural weekly; *Ekonomicheskaya Gazeta*, the economics tabloid weekly; *Selskaya Zhizn*, a farm daily; *Sovetskii Sport*, a sports daily; *Uchitelskaya Gazeta*, a bi-weekly for educators.

The national newspapers have fluctuated in number. There were 46 in 1940, but after World War II some of the newspapers that had been shut down were never revived and in 1950, only 23 national newspapers were published. By 1955, the number was down to 18.[22] Then, in the late 1950's, several new national newspapers were established—among them *Selskaya Zhizn, Sovetskaya Aviatsiya,* and *Sovetskii Patriot*—

Two of the Soviet Union's major national daily newspapers, *Krasnaya Zvezda* (top), the ranking newspaper of the Ministry of Defense, and *Selskaya Zhizn,* a Communist Party central committee daily that focuses on agriculture.

A front page of *Ekonomicheskaya Gazeta,* a newspaper of the Communist Party central committee. Published weekly in tabloid size, it deals with economic and financial information and news.

bringing the total in 1968 to 26. A recent addition was *Sovet-skaya Rossiya,* formerly a Russian republic daily, transferred to national status in 1966. Press runs of national newspapers were substantially increased during and after the Khrushchev years. In 1955, the average circulation of a national paper was 855,000.[23] By 1968 it was 2 million.

Each of the national newspapers is designed for a specific audience market, with the exception of *Pravda* and *Izvestia*, and perhaps *Komsomolskaya Pravda*. Though content varies somewhat from one to another, these three are general mass circulation newspapers. By contrast, *Ekonomicheskaya Gazeta* focuses narrowly on economics, finance, and industry. Typical of the way in which Soviet newspapers are established and oriented, *Ekonomicheskaya Gazeta* was formally created in 1960 by decree of the Communist Party Central Committee.[24] The decree stipulated a 4-page newspaper the size of *Pravda*, published six times a week (it was later made a weekly), with a circulation of 500,000 and price of 20 kopecks (reduced to 2 kopecks—a little over 2¢—after the 1961 currency devaluation). The paper, an official Central Committee publication, was to publicize the Communist Party and discuss such matters as investment, use of productive forces, and economic plans. It was to draw on the best Soviet scholars, engineers, industrial managers, and agricultural specialists for interesting material. Overall, it was to cover the developments of communism, and the peaceful competition between socialism and capitalism.

Similarly, other national newspapers have their particular bailiwicks which make them sources of rather specialized information. *Krasnaya Zvezda* speaks for the military, for example; *Literaturnaya Gazeta*, for the Union of Writers; and *Sovetskaya Kultura*, for the Ministry of Culture.

The Republic Press

The 157 republic newspapers (in 1968) are official publications of the combined republic party organization and government, with the party being the preponderant voice in management. Since World War II, their numbers have fluctuated between, for example, 137 in 1950 and 180 in 1960. At the same time, press runs have marched ahead, in pace with the general newspaper circulation growth in the Soviet Union. Where the average republic newspaper had a 35,000 circulation in 1950, it was 134,400 in 1968.

About one third of the 157 republic papers are published five to six times a week, and the remainder three times or less weekly (one fourth are weeklies, for example). They are rather evenly apportioned among 14 of the 15 Soviet republics (the large Russian republic having no exclusively republic papers).

NEWSPAPERS BY LANGUAGES AND REPUBLICS: 1967

Republics and Languages	Number of Newspapers	Circulation (thousands)
RSFSR		
Russian	3,997	80,547
Other	274	1,481
Ukraine		
Ukrainian	890	11,168
Russian	384	4,751
Byelorussia		
Byelorussian	130	1,358
Russian	43	2,039
Uzbekistan		
Uzbek	121	2,067
Russian	72	689
Kazakhstan		
Kazakh	123	1,217
Russian	208	2,230
Georgia		
Georgian	104	1,785
Russian	11	262
Azerbaidzhan		
Azerbaidzhani	91	1,109
Russian	13	244
Lithuania		
Lithuanian	68	1,624
Russian	12	143
Moldavia		
Moldavian	45	845
Russian	55	424
Latvia		
Latvian	55	863
Russian	30	297
Kirgizia		
Kirgiz	35	442
Russian	30	255
Tadzhizstan		
Tadzhik	50	487
Russian	6	132
Armenia		
Armenian	72	758
Russian	3	45
Turkmen		
Turkmen	33	416
Russian	12	140
Estonia		
Estonian	29	783
Russian	10	105

SOURCE: *Pechat SSSR v 1967 godu*, pp. 188–189.

The Ukraine republic, for instance, has 18 republic newspapers; the much smaller Uzbek republic, 12; Kazakh, 16; the Lithuanian, 15; and the Armenian, 13.

The republic newspapers vary considerably in format and size. About 95 per cent are four pages. Of these, two thirds are the size of a standard American newspaper, and the remainder are tabloids of four pages. That is, the republic newspapers range from large, 4-page dailies to tabloid-size weeklies, the latter being little more than one can find in an urban American high school, or indeed in an urban Soviet university. But the larger republic newspapers, such as *Pravda Ukrainy*, a major Ukrainian daily published in Kiev, correspond roughly in the Soviet newspaper hierarchy to large regional American newspapers like the Los Angeles *Times* or the Chicago *Daily News*. Their reading audience and their coverage are mainly within their own republics. But they dominate their areas, competing only with the best-known national newspapers.

City and Regional Newspapers

The Soviet provincial press is with insignificant exception published in only 5 of 15 republics—the Russian, Ukrainian, Byelorussian, Uzbek, and Kazakh. For purposes of political administration, these republics are divided into *oblasts*, so-called autonomous republics, and, in the Russian republic only, *krais* (territories). More than half—157—of the 289 *oblast* and *krai* newspapers in 1967 were published in the expansive, populous Russian republic. As well, 74 of 96 autonomous republic and autonomous *oblast* newspapers were located in the RSFSR. The latter had average press runs of 29,400 copies; equal to a small American city newspaper. But about half were published three times a week, while the rest were issued five or six times weekly. And about two thirds were four pages of large-sized format, the rest being 4-page tabloids.

The *oblast* and *krai* newspapers have much the same profile, except that their circulation is about double—56,400—on the average. Nearly all *oblast* papers are four pages. Half are full-page size, and the rest tabloid. Of the 289 newspapers, 177 are published five or six days a week, and most of the rest, three times weekly.

The Soviet *raion* newspapers are mostly rural publications, and are largely published in the Russian, Byelorussian, and Ukrainian republics, which in 1968 accounted for about 2,000

NEWSPAPERS BY TYPES: SELECTED YEARS, 1940–1968

Type of Newspaper	Year	Number of Newspapers	Circulation (thousands)	Average Circulation (thousands)
National	1940	46	8,769	191.3
	1950	23	9,423	408.6
	1960	25	23,524	941.0
	1962	23	31,075	1,351.1
	1964	23	36,821	1,600.9
	1967	26	54,894	2,111.2
	1968	26	55,977	2,153.0
Republic	1940	135	5,284	39.3
	1950	137	4,819	35.1
	1960	180	13,187	73.3
	1962	173	14,430	83.4
	1964	148	17,441	117.8
	1967	155	19,457	125.5
	1968	157	21,097	134.4
Oblast, krai, okrug	1940	321	6,978	21.7
	1950	310	7,349	23.7
	1960	305	11,380	37.3
	1962	307	12,032	39.2
	1964	256	12,535	49.0
	1967	281	15,350	55.0
	1968	289	16,295	56.4
Autonomous *oblast* and republic	1940	119	1,197	10.1
	1950	71	838	11.8
	1960	96	1,691	17.6
	1962	96	1,809	18.8
	1964	95	2,096	22.1
	1967	96	2,588	26.9
	1968	96	2,819	29.4
City	1940	251	1,802	7.2
	1950	346	1,493	4.3
	1960	449	3,576	8.0
	1962	490	3,818	7.8
	1964	252	4,387	17.4
	1967	591	8,754	14.8
	1968	597	9,329	15.6
Raion	1940	3,502	8,647	2.5
	1950	4,193	6,903	1.6
	1960	3,397	8,630	2.5
	1962	115	254	2.2
	1964	.....	.....	.....
	1967	2,769	12,835	4.6
	1968	2,793	13,417	4.8

Type of Newspaper	Year	Number of Newspapers	Circulation (thousands)	Average Circulation (thousands)
Kolkhoz-sovkhoz production administrations	1962*	11,089	9,221	8.4
	1964	1,666	10,119	6.1
Lower (newspapers of factories, offices, universities, etc.)	1940	4,432	5,678	1.2
	1950	2,751	5,139	1.8
	1960	2,352	4,691	2.0
	1962	2,469	4,291	1.7
	1964	2,627	4,622	1.8
	1967	3,169	6,013	1.8
	1968	3,349	6,519	1.9
Totals**	1940	8,806	38,355	4.4
	1950	7,831	35,964	4.6
	1960	6,804	66,679	9.8
	1962	4,771	76,930	10.6
	1964	5,067	88,021	17.4
	1967	7,087	119,891	16.9
	1968	7,307	125,449	17.2

SOURCES: *Pechat v SSSR v 1968 godu*, pp. 65–66; and issues for 1964, pp. 74–75, and 1962, pp. 62–63.

* *Kolkhoz-sovkhoz* production administrations were created in 1962. Their newspapers were mergers of several *raion* papers. After 1964, when the administrations were abolished, *raion* newspapers were reestablished.
** Totals do not include *kolkhoz* newspapers.

of the total of 2,793. All but a few published three times a week. About 70 per cent are 4-page tabloids, and most of the remainder, 2-page tabloids. The average circulation in 1968 was 4,800.

The *raion* newspapers were subject to one of Khrushchev's management reforms when, in 1962, the *raions* themselves were combined into *kolkhoz* and *sovkhoz* administrative regions. As a result, *raion* newspapers per se were abolished, and in place of 3,240 such publications with average circulations of 2,200, about 1,100 larger papers—average press run was 8,400 in 1962—were created. When Khrushchev was deposed in 1964, this particular management reform was rescinded and, in 1965, the *raions* along with their newspapers were reestablished. But in the process, about 700 *raion* papers quietly died, while circulations of the survivors about doubled compared with the pre-Khrushchev reform days.

Since the re-creation of *raion* newspapers, they have been extensively discussed by both journalists and politicians, mostly in terms of modernizing the local press. In September, 1968, the party Central Committee provided for increased staffs and salaries on *raion* newspapers. It further directed party organizations and various supply ministries to concentrate attention on the rapid improvement of these papers, which they sorely

City newspapers in the Soviet Union are on the whole 4-page tabloids published three or four days weekly. The average individual circulation of 597 city newspapers was only 15,600 in 1968. Thus with a few exceptions, they exist in the shadow of the *oblast* or even republic newspapers, which also are published in Soviet cities and circulate there as well as in surrounding areas. The exceptions are the Soviet evening newspapers. Something of an oddity in the Soviet press structure, these 16 city papers tend to the light side, verging on the sensational compared with such eminently responsible and serious publications as *Pravda*. They ordinarily are the first to be sold out on newsstands, and the nickname *"vecherki"*—Russian diminutive of the word "evenings"—for these few city newspapers suggests a popular following and acceptance that the more official-sounding newspaper press does not enjoy.

Editorial staffs of city and provincial newspapers vary in size, and are determined by the central party apparatus. A 1945 party decree, still in effect, established 10 editorial departments for republic newspapers and 7 for *oblast* and *krai* papers.[26] Departments have up to 10 correspondents each, plus an editor. The newspapers' editorial management includes an editor in chief, two assistants, and a managing editor and his staff. In addition, the republic newspapers, according to the 1945 decree, had two correspondents stationed in each *oblast*, and the *oblast* and *krai* papers had one correspondent for every two or three *raions* in their area.

City newspapers generally have 7 departments, each with an editor and up to 5 correspondents. *Raion* papers ordinarily have only 3 departments, each with an editor, plus an editor in chief and managing editor. Total staff size ranges from about 5 to 20, depending on frequency of publication.[27]

The Lower Press

The larger Soviet industrial plants, universities, offices, construction trusts, and state and collective farms publish their own small newspapers. They originated in the 1930's, with Soviet rapid industrialization, when hundreds of factory newspapers were set up almost overnight. As *mnogotirazhnyi*—literally meaning "multiple circulation," but best translated as "printed" newspapers—they are distributed internally in Soviet institutions, and like the American factory or office papers deal mostly with events and people of their organizations.

In 1968, there were 3,349 enterprise, university, state farm, and office newspapers, with an average circulation of 1,900. Two decrees of the Communist Party Central Committee— one in 1956, the second in 1959—on the *mnogotirazhnyi* are instructive for information on these particular newspapers, and also on the central planning of the Soviet newspaper network.[28] By these regulations, institutions—whether factories, state farms, etc.—with 2,000 to 5,000 employees were permitted a weekly tabloid-size newspaper of two pages managed by one paid editor. In institutions with 5,000 to 15,000 workers, the newspaper was to be issued twice a week, and the staff increased to two men. If more than 15,000 employees, the organizations could have a 4-page tabloid published two or three times weekly by a staff of five. As for circulation, there was to be one issue for every three to four workers. Currently, 65 per cent of lower newspapers, accounting for the same percentage of their total circulation, are weeklies; 15 per cent are issued twice weekly; and the remainder, one to three times a month.

Decisions to establish such newspapers were to be made locally, but approved by the central party apparatus. Sales at the equivalent of 1–2¢ a copy were supposed to cover production costs of these newspapers. Anticipating deficits, however, the party regulations provided that a given organization's trade union should pay 10 per cent of any loss, and the organization itself was to make up 90 per cent out of its budget.

Kolkhoz newspapers, of which there were 1,447 in 1968 (compared with 37,000 collective farms in all), had an average individual circulation of 700. Like the institutional papers, these are local-events publications, small and lacking a professional quality. A quarter the size of a standard newspaper, and published once or twice a week, but more often one to three times a month, they generally are written and edited as civic projects by unpaid editorial boards and peasant correspondents (*selkor*). Like all Soviet newspapers, they are attached to the local Communist Party organization and usually the person responsible for the newspaper is a party official.

The Wall Newspapers

At the most elementary level of the Soviet press organization are more than 500,000 wall newspapers, produced entirely by amateur journalists, including some 5 million worker-peasant correspondents.[29] As noted earlier, the wall newspapers are akin to bulletin boards. A typical wall newspaper is a yard square sheet of paper or several sheets pasted end to end, on which typed or handwritten announcements, essays, and reports are glued. Titles or headlines, as well as the masthead, are hand lettered. The more elaborate wall newspapers are illustrated with snapshots and original art. The whole is then mounted on a wall, sometimes in a glass-enclosed display case.[30]

Wall newspapers ordinarily are gotten up before Soviet holidays or other special events, and perhaps a dozen are produced each year. Thus, it is mandatory for a wall newspaper issue to be ready before November 7, the anniversary of the Bolshevik Revolution. Others are produced before Women's Day, New Year's, Red Army Day, and so forth. Here and there, weekly wall newspapers or wall newspapers in several copies are compiled, although these are rare.

The wall newspaper press is the most pervasive, albeit not the most influential, in the whole newspaper structure. The papers can be found in theaters, public bath houses, factory shops, libraries, student dormitories, university departments, department stores, secondary schools, research institutes, military units, and on farms. Consistent with other newspapers, they are official publications of a Communist Party or Komsomol unit, in conjunction with a workers' soviet, for example, or a student organization. Formally at least, the local party bureau is responsible for the guidance and content of its wall newspaper, and a member of the bureau often is the editor. He has a staff, the ideal number being five to seven,[31] and a content plan, which includes short news items, critical articles, essays promoting local implementation of current national policies, perhaps letters to the editor, and feature articles.

For example, a 1964 wall newspaper of Leningrad University's far east department, published in conjunction with the university's Communist Party, Komsomol, and trade union organizations, contained these items: "On Training Leningrad Cadres," a report of a Communist Party meeting in the faculty; "Our Guest from Japan," about a visiting professor; "A Meeting with Indians," describing a department meeting with students

Two examples of Soviet wall newspapers. At top is *Za Kachestvo (For Quality),* produced in one section of a large cellulose and cardboard manufacturing plant in the Siberian city of Bratsk. This issue, produced for the 50th anniversary of the Bolshevik revolution, contains a lead article on the event. The caricature at top criticizes drinking by workers. The lower cartoon is the editor's tongue in cheek plea for items from readers. Note that the whole issue is hand written. The second example of a wall newspaper is *Rabochii i Sluzhashchii (Factory and Office Worker)* published by one department of Leningrad University. Contents of this issue were devoted to the 46th anniversary of the Soviet army and navy.

from India. It also displayed a series of snapshots entitled "With Our Own Eyes," taken by a faculty member who had toured Morocco, Algeria, and Tunis the year before.

Another wall newspaper, the *Bibliotekar* (*Librarian*), produced by the staff of the Academy of Sciences library in Leningrad, focused on the twentieth anniversary of the lifting of the World War II Leningrad seige. It had several articles recalling library operations during the war taken from a history book; a poem on the war; reminiscences by staff members; reprints of wartime letters; and a list of staff members who died during the Leningrad blockade. It was illustrated with a hand-painted scene of Leningrad and a simplified map showing lines of battle around the city. The *Bibliotekar* was published by the local party bureau, *raion* soviet, and the library itself.[32]

Wall newspapers are particularly local and personal in nature, and probably come closest of all in the Soviet press structure to the American weekly newspapers' columns of "personals," and incidental news notes. Officially, wall newspapers are supposed to act as critic and educator, and should reflect the interests and grievances of their own small circle of readers in the factory shop, university, or office. Criticism of inept management or inefficient workers is an obligation, though it does not extend to the party itself. "The wall newspaper may not carry articles directed against decisions of the party bureau," one Soviet source notes. "The primary party organization directs the wall newspaper, the party bureau must direct and control it, and not the reverse. If the wall newspaper comes out against decisions of the party bureau, it contradicts the party bureau of which it is an organ, and subsequently violates statutes of the CPSU."[33] Explicitly enough, then, the wall newspaper, along with published newspapers, is a voice of management. If an editor disagrees with a party decision, his opposition is not expressed in his small, amateurish publication, but at a closed party meeting.

One can argue that wall newspapers—although obviously they are not newspapers in the common understanding of that word—draw a good many Soviet citizens into political activity. Assuming that 10 persons contribute to each issue of approximately 500,000 wall newspapers, about 5 million adults would be enlisted in ferreting out deficiencies, restating national policy, promoting increased production, and the like. They ostensibly would attend editorial board meetings at which party members would review goals of the party and encourage even greater collective effort.

All this does take place. But the performance and quality of wall newspapers varies enormously, depending much on the ability and enthusiasm of each editor. Thus, some wall newspapers are gotten out perfunctorily. One can be skeptical of the influence of a wall newspaper that displays a few snapshots of a North African trip, or an article with bland recitation of a local party meeting. On the other hand, the wall newspaper that caricatures and names individual workers who regularly show up drunk, or frequently miss work, or whose production is consistently lower than the average, probably has some bite and draws its readers' attention. By the same token, the wall newspaper editor with imagination and ambition can produce relatively well-written, informative, and entertaining articles.

On balance, it would seem that the wall newspaper network is something of an anachronism in contemporary Soviet society. One reason is that other segments of the Soviet mass media have expanded and improved, so that the wall newspapers merely duplicate, in more detail and in more personal terms, what is generally known.[34] As for affecting an organization's work, a wall newspaper may supplement management's activities, but one wonders whether the bulletin board is much more influential than its American counterparts—that is, the routine internal house organ, with its trivial news items, management reports, announcements of company policy, and so forth.

The Soviet wall newspapers deserve attention if only because a substantial number of people are drawn into their production. And perhaps those who do the actual work or writing and illustrating, which is probably only a percentage of a given staff, do have a sense of participating in a collective project. But this can be done in quite an apolitical way, without an individual feeling that he does much more than fulfill a chore expected of him as an employee. Certainly, the wall newspapers are not the voice of labor, or of the students, or of farmers. As party organs, they preempt and substitute for what originally, in the 1920's, were to be the common man's spontaneous outpourings. The Soviet political bureaucracy, no more perhaps than the American corporate management, does not want a truly independent employee publication, even one so seemingly innocuous as a decorated bulletin board, that could as well be a hindrance as a help.

Pravda

Going from the general newspaper structure to specific ex-

A representative front page of *Pravda,* chief spokesman among newspapers for the Communist Party central committee.

amples, we can begin with *Pravda*. It is not really typical of any segment of the Soviet newspaper network, any more than

The New York Times is typical of American newspapers. But *Pravda* is in some fashion a model, particularly for provincial newspapers whose editors are ever looking for guidance as to current Soviet journalistic standards in an ideological, if not in a professional sense. *Pravda* represents the establishment. As the primary official publication of the Communist Party Central Committee, it shares the position of chief spokesman for the Soviet state only with the news agency TASS and the government newspaper *Izvestia*.

Like *The New York Times* perhaps, *Pravda* is not only a newspaper but an institution. It radiates responsibility. Indicative of reader reaction, in 1966, after the quota subscription system for Soviet national newspapers was abolished, *Pravda's* circulation dropped from 7 million to under 6.6. It took a year to regain its losses; in early 1968, circulation moved up to 7.5 million. *Izvestia,* by comparison, had reached a circulation of 8.3 million in early 1965, mostly under Alexei Adzhubei's editorship. Its circulation was reported at 7.8 million in early 1966, at 8.4 million a year later, and 7.7 million in early 1968.[35]

Solidly official and ponderous as it is, *Pravda* remains *the* Soviet newspaper. It is read or skimmed by every party and government official in the Soviet Union, and by government staffs in most world capitals. Yet it is normally only 6 or 8 pages, expanding to 12 for special events, such as a congress of the Communist Party when 90 per cent of *Pravda's* space will be given over to reprints of official speeches.

Pravda's editorial offices are in a modernistic seven-story Moscow building of the Pravda Publishing Plant. In addition to *Pravda's* press run, the plant prints about 16 million copies of five other newspapers, including *Komsomolskaya Pravda,* and 42 million copies of 35 different magazines and journals, including *Kommunist*.[36] In 1967, when *Pravda's* daily circulation was 7 million, 5.8 million issues were sold by subscription and the remainder on newsstands. Only 30 per cent of the circulation was printed in Moscow, the rest being run off in 34 other printing plants around the country. About one third of these were supplied facsimiles of *Pravda* pages by electronic means and made printing plates from these copies. The other plants received matrices by plane. With this system of reproduction, about 75 per cent of *Pravda's* readers had the newspaper in their hands the same day as Moscow subscribers. In parts of Soviet Siberia, which is several hours ahead of Moscow time, subscribers receive *Pravda* before it appears in Moscow itself.

Soviet communications authorities are now looking to the day when *Pravda* and *all* other central newspapers will be published everywhere in the country on the same day as they are issued in Moscow. This will be done by photoelectric means, either via transmission lines or communications satellites. An experimental system was being set up in late 1967 to transmit photographs of central newspapers to 12 cities, including Leningrad, Kiev, and Novosibirsk. By 1970, the Soviet communications satellite system is expected to transmit central newspapers to the far east and other distant regions of the country.[37]

Pravda's editorial offices give the impression more of a hotel than a newspaper office, at least of the American type. Opening off a single main corridor, paved with a green and vermilion runner, are offices marked with the name of one or two staff members. The atmosphere is hushed, lacking the mingling noises of typewriters, telephones, and voices one finds in American newsrooms.

The daily *Pravda* usually has 48 or 64 columns of news space (the equivalent of a 24- or 48-page American newspaper), a good fifth of which is taken up by photographs, weather reports, TV and radio listings, and headlines. *Pravda's* home office editorial staff, which ranks among the best in Soviet journalism, numbers about 150. It also has more than 50 correspondents in bureaus around the country, and maintains bureaus of one or two correspondents in 35 countries of the world.[38] Starting salary is 160 rubles a month (about $177), compared with an average industrial and office wage in the Soviet Union of about 115 rubles. Experienced *Pravda* journalists earn 350 rubles, and the average salary is about 200 rubles. In addition, *Pravda* writers, as writers on all Soviet newspapers, receive bonuses (*gonorar*) for each article they write. On other Soviet newspapers, at least, these bonuses can range from 20 to 50 rubles.[39] Salary is not the sole, nor even the primary attraction to *Pravda*. Rather its prestige, the chance to be on the "inside" of Soviet developments, the opportunity for a few staff members to work abroad, and finally the chance to live in Moscow are all advantages afforded relatively few others in the Soviet Union.

While *Pravda* the newspaper is atypical in Soviet journalism, *Pravda* the editorial organization is standard for Soviet newspapers. The only difference between its internal structure and that of, say, an *oblast* newspaper is more news and information departments and a larger staff. The ranking person on *Pravda*

The main entrance to *Pravda*'s editorial offices in Moscow. The building also houses editorial offices of *Komsomolskaya Pravda, Selskaya Zhizn* and *Sovetskaya Rossiya,* all major Soviet national newspapers.

is, of course, the editor in chief. He directs the newspaper with the counsel and advice of an editorial collegium (*redkollegiya*), which consists besides himself of two deputy editors in chief, a managing editor, and a number of departmental editors (seven in 1964, but the collegium's makeup is subject to change).

The operations center of *Pravda,* as of other Soviet newspapers, is the secretariat under the managing editor (whose title, literally translated from the Russian, is "responsible secretary"). Directly subordinate to the managing editor within the secretariat are several noneditorial departments—proofreading, typing, reference library, archives, and dispatch (which keeps track of written copy).

News and information departments, each with its own editor, also are subordinate to the managing editor, with the exception of the foreign news department. Divided into four sections—for Europe; Asia and Africa; North and South America; and Communist countries—the foreign department is the responsibility of a deputy editor in chief. Other *Pravda* departments are: Communist Party affairs; propaganda of Marxist-Leninist theory; industry, transport, and commerce; agriculture; letters and civic projects; news and sports; literature and art; press; science; schools and higher education; military; local correspondents; criticism and bibliography; satiric articles. In addition, *Pravda* has an illustration department (four artists and five photographers); the *Pravda* news service; and a staff to publish *Raboche-Krestyanskii Korrespondent*, a magazine for worker-peasant correspondents.[40]

This basic newspaper structure—editor, assistant editors, editorial collegium, managing editor, and departments—evolved from past czarist Russian press practices. It was formally shaped by party Central Committee directives of 1945, which listed required departments on newspapers, and 1948, when editorial collegiums were established for the national, republic, and 25 large *oblast* newspapers.[41] Hence, to know one Soviet newspaper's editorial and news structure is largely to know them all. Other national newspapers modify the model organization depending on particular interests. *Komsomolskaya Pravda* has several editorial departments dealing with youth—students, workers, and the Komsomol organization itself. The labor newspaper *Trud* has departments of labor unions and workers' social security. *Selskaya Zhizn*, the daily farm newspaper, in addition to editorial departments for agriculture, has a staff that covers farm technology and innovation for four separate regions of the country.[42]

An *Oblast* Newspaper

More representative than *Pravda* of the Soviet Union newspaper is the *oblast* paper *Leningradskaya Pravda*, established in 1918. *Leningradskaya Pravda*'s editorial offices are in a new building along the Neva river. Typical of a trend for Soviet newspapers, the building combines the editorial staffs of several papers, all of which are printed in a separate publishing plant operated as an independent enterprise, with which the newspapers contract for printing services. Typically too, *Leningrad-*

ORGANIZATION OF A SOVIET NEWSPAPER

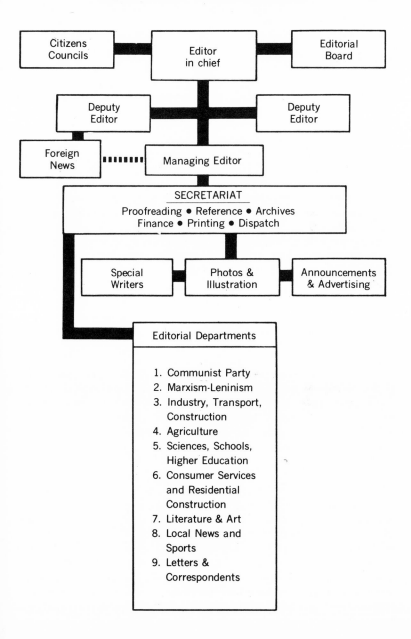

skaya Pravda's chief editors are simultaneously members of local Communist Party executive agencies.[43] For example, in 1964, the editor in chief was a member of the *oblast* Communist Party, and a deputy editor served on the Leningrad city party committee. The newspaper itself is the official publication of the Leningrad *oblast* and city Communist Party organizations and of the *oblast* and city governments.

Leningradskaya Pravda circulates chiefly in an area of 5 million people—the population of Leningrad *oblast*. About 3.6 million of these live in Leningrad itself. In 1964, the paper's circulation was 352,000, of which 18,000 were mailed outside the *oblast*, 284,000 were distributed within the city itself, and the remainder in Leningrad *oblast*. The bulk of sales—304,000—were by subscription, the rest being sold on newstands.

Leningradskaya Pravda has 10 editorial departments immediately subordinate to the managing editor, and ultimately to the editor in chief and two deputy editors. On the Leningrad paper, as other Soviet newspapers, the secretariat of the managing editor is the focal point of daily information processing. Editorial plans are first formulated by the managing editor. He coordinates work of department editors, compiles dummies of issues, and is responsible for the copy flow. Within the secretariat, under the managing editor's direction, are various essential sections—proofreading, reference bureau, illustrations, library and archives, and the typing bureau.[44] The last is worth comment. In Soviet editorial offices, typewriters still are scarce. Correspondents ordinarily write their reports in longhand, which are then given to typists to put into final form.

In 1964, *Leningradskaya Pravda* had an editorial staff of 86, including 43 writing journalists. Of these, 32 had university educations, but not necessarily in journalism. The starting pay on *Leningradskaya Pravda* was 70 rubles ($78) a month, supplemented by bonuses for major articles. An experienced writer earned 100 rubles, plus bonuses, and a few, 300 rubles and more. Editors of departments received a minimum wage of 150 rubles, and with their writing averaged about 300 rubles. The average of the whole editorial staff was about 240 rubles a month.

As a well-known *oblast* newspaper in a large city—comparable in the Soviet context to a Chicago newspaper—*Leningradskaya Pravda* has relatively little problem with staffing. The paper's editors maintain personal contacts with the staff of Leningrad

Editorial offices of *Leningradskaya Pravda* and several other local newspapers occupy this building along the Neva river in Leningrad.

University's School of Journalism, give lectures and conduct seminars there and in the process recruit new staff members from among promising students. Students also do practice work at *Leningradskaya Pravda* as part of their journalism training, and the best may be offered a job on graduation. Provincial publications also yield new staff members, young journalists who want to move up and to whom Leningrad offers a relatively comfortable life compared with rural towns of the Soviet Union.

Leningradskaya Pravda gets its information from a variety of sources—its own correspondents, from the information services TASS and Press Agency Novosti (APN), from its network of *rabkor* or worker correspondents, and from its readers *aktivs* or soviets. *Rabkor* correspond roughly to "stringers" or part-time correspondents of American newspapers. The *aktivs* are composed of specialists who both advise and write for the newspaper. Most Soviet newspapers make liberal use of outside writers, frequently Communist Party and government officials, but also academic specialists. In this respect, they differ noticeably from American newspapers, which only rarely draw on nonjournalists and then usually for columns of advice on medical and dental treatment and legal questions.

Leningradskaya Pravda's part-time reporters—the *rabkor*—numbered more than 1,000 in 1964. In addition to writing small news items, the *rabkor* alert the newspaper to stories and to situations that might deserve investigation, such as corruption or inefficiency in a particular factory or office, or the failure of a government agency to provide the services it is supposed to. Part-time correspondents also seem to be a prime source of letters to Soviet newspapers, though many come from readers unconnected with the papers. *Leningradskaya Pravda* was averaging 48,000 letters annually a few years back. Such an outpouring from readers is not untypical among Soviet newspapers. *Pravda* gets about 900 a day[45] and *Izvestia* upwards of 1,500.[46]

Being a morning newspaper—and all except *Izvestia* and the city evening papers are—*Leningradskaya Pravda* begins work about 10 A.M. six days a week. Sunday is the day off, there being no paper on Monday. The day ends about 7 P.M. and ordinarily only a night editor remains to check the next morning's newspaper before it goes to press. Much of *Leningradskaya Pravda*'s editorial work on a given issue is done several days or even weeks in advance. Unlike American daily newspapers, which receive, edit, and print much of their news content within 24-hour periods, Soviet papers concentrate less on immediate news and information. Rather, they tend more to operate as a magazine on a daily basis, planning much of their material in advance. The exceptions are national and international news items supplied by TASS or, in the case of the Soviet national newspapers, by their own national and foreign correspondents.

All Soviet newspapers are supposed to compile long-range editorial plans, covering perhaps three to six months, as well as monthly, weekly, and daily plans. The long-range plans probably are as much a mechanical gesture to general Soviet preoccupation with planning as operative and essential guides to newspaper production. For example, a long-range plan will include essays and articles on standard events, such as the annual celebration of the Bolshevik Revolution or of Red Army Day, or on current themes, such as a farm program or industrial management. A list of forthcoming articles is compiled, along with the writers, either staff or nonstaff, and the date due. Monthly plans are or should be more exact and detailed.

The following excerpts from a weekly plan of the national labor newspaper *Trud* provide a concrete example of a Soviet editorial plan: [47]

Article	Space (in lines)	Department Responsible
Page 1		
Lead editorial—"A million rubles to the fund of the Seven Year Plan" Dnepropetrovsk	140	Industry-economics
"Innovations—Under the control of the public" Riga	280	Industry-economics
"The city—To the country"		Industry-economics
Page 2		
"Is this an organized selection?"	280	
"Pearl of the south" Krasnodar	270	Labor protection
"Race of good work" Leningrad	210	
"Review of the press"	150	
Letter to the editor on lack of principle		
Page 3		
"Read these books"		Literature and Art
"14th anniversary of agreement with Korean People's Republic"	400	Foreign
Page 4		
"Sports Sunday at stadiums"		
"The *Trud* mailbox"		
Feuilleton		
News items		

A daily plan is essentially just a listing of the news, articles, and photographs scheduled for the next issue of the newspaper. This is made up at a *planyerka*—a planning session of the editor, or a deputy, the managing editor, and the editors of departments. On *Leningradskaya Pravda*, the *planyerka* is held at about 1 P.M. Comments and criticisms, if there are any, on that morning's paper come out, and the stories, articles, and artwork scheduled for each page of the next issue are discussed. Pages containing no "spot" news (and usually only one or two pages of a Soviet newspaper of four to six pages do so) ordinarily are in proof by that time. These are gone over, and last-minute decisions are made on material to fill space on uncompleted pages.

Unlike American newspapers, the front pages of Soviet papers mostly contain official information, such as government announcements, a stock photograph, and an editorial. News reports appear on an inside page. This page, as on *Leningradskaya Pravda,* is the last then to be made up. The Soviet process is similar to that on large American daily newspapers, although American editors are dealing mostly with the current day's news and there is more emphasis on late news. Long-range projects—those that would correspond to a Soviet newspaper's monthly editorial planning—also are planned on American newspapers, although this tends to be an increasingly informal and one- or two-man decision going from the larger to the smaller newspapers. American newspapers also have their equivalents of the Soviet advance pages. On American papers, these are whole sections containing "time" material or sometimes special advertising sections, also with "filler" articles.

Where practice diverges sharply is, first, in the deference Soviet editors, as those on *Leningradskaya Pravda,* give to official, ceremonial news, such as observance of a standard event (Navy Day, Women's Day, etc.) and government and Communist Party activities (a forthcoming party congress, for example), planning for which is more extensive than American editors would do. And second, related to this point, American newspapers are predominantly oriented toward current events, while Soviet editors focus much more on long-term topics and what are called, in American journalism, background, interpretive, and analytical articles.

Supplementing the *planyerka* on *Leningradskaya Pravda,* and other large Soviet newspapers, is the *letuchka,* a Russian word meaning a brief meeting, but also carrying the idea of swift, surging movement. The *letuchka* then is a staff meeting, held once a week, in which criticisms of individual departments, editors, writers, and articles are made. On large Soviet newspapers, the *letuchka* is a formally scheduled event. On the smaller papers, with a staff of half a dozen, the *letuchka* is an informal exchange of opinion, if such meetings are held at all.

As on the larger American newspapers, the staff meeting is simply designed to draw out current problems and grievances, directed toward improving the newspaper. And it also serves as a management device. Editors can keep their deputies abreast of the newspaper's immediate objectives, and call attention to policy failings.

FLOW OF INFORMATION ON A SOVIET NEWSPAPER

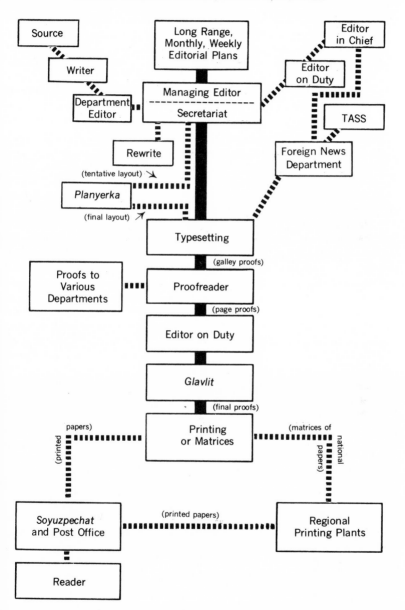

How the News Flows

Representative of most Soviet newspapers, *Leningradskaya Pravda* mixes local or regional information with national and international. Its handling of this information is perhaps more typical of Soviet newspapers than is *Pravda*'s or *Izventia*'s, which occupy privileged positions in the Soviet newspaper structure. On *Leningradskaya Pravda*, TASS dispatches are handled by the foreign and domestic department. Often enough on Soviet newspapers this is the job of a deputy editor in chief. The special attention indicates the importance and sensitivity accorded information on both Soviet national and foreign events. About 20 per cent of TASS material received by *Leningradskaya Pravda*—over three teletype machines linked with central TASS in Moscow, and one with the Leningrad TASS bureau (LenTASS)—is published. The remainder either is discarded entirely, or edited out of stories and articles.[48] Once edited, TASS stories are sent directly to the printing plant adjoining *Leningradskaya Pravda*'s offices.

Local material, whether from a staff or nonstaff writer, goes through a more time-consuming process. The article or news story is first read by the editor of whichever department originated it. If he is satisfied with the material, he passes it on to the managing editor. On some Soviet newspapers, such as *Leningradskaya Pravda*, the managing editor's secretariat has a staff man who rewrites particularly unsuitable or poorly styled material. All articles are then relayed to the editor on duty, who is usually one of the two deputy editors in chief having final responsibility for that day's issue. Particularly sensitive articles, those involving political matters, for example, may also go to the editor in chief himself.

Much of this material is set into type and proofs are drawn long before deadline for the current issue. Thus, when the *planyerka* is held at 1 P.M., departmental editors already have proofs of some articles and, as mentioned, some pages are already in proof form. The last page proof is drawn by about 8 P.M. All page proofs are read and initialed by the editor on duty. The editor in chief (or if he is not there, a deputy editor in chief) has, of course, seen most of the issue in page proof earlier in the day. The page proofs are then read and initialed by the *Glavlit* representative, the censor, in the printing plant. When all changes and corrections have been made—the editor on duty has authority to insert last-minute news and to change layout—

the pages are molded and the press run begins. As newspapers come off the press in the early morning, they then become the responsibility of *Soyuzpechat,* the distribution agency, and the post office, to deliver to readers' homes and to newsstands.

Leningradskaya Pravda's processing of information is, of course, not quite as mechanical and untroubled as a brief description suggests. Many small and large decisions must be be made: first, what events or topics will be written about; second, when articles will be published; third, what will be published and where. Soviet newspapers are plagued by a shortage of space, and—like American newspapers, actually—receive and produce far more information than they can print.

What do they print? Take the issue of *Leningradskaya Pravda* for February 20, 1964. Although this is several years old, we have some observations of the newspaper's editors as to why particular articles were used in that issue.[49] On Page 1, on the left-hand side, was the lead editorial—2 columns wide and three quarters of a page long. Headlined "Save Metal," it discussed the importance of conserving waste metal in Leningrad's many industrial plants. Next to it was a 6-inch TASS story from Moscow about a monument to be erected in honor of the Ukrainian poet Shevchenko and the visit of the then Premier Khrushchev to view a model of the monument. This article reflected the Soviet political leadership's concern with the nationalities problem, and in this case its attention to the Ukrainian republic. It also commanded publication, in the eyes of *Leningradskaya Pravda*'s editors, because Khrushchev was part of the story. Next to this item, on the upper right-hand side, was a 2-column photograph of a woman researcher at a laboratory working on vaccines against cattle disease. The overline was: "Decisions of the February Plenum of the CC CPSU in Action!" and a subheadline: "The City—To the Countryside." This photograph fitted in with a theme of Soviet industrial centers aiding agriculture. The major front-page article was headlined: "The First Step Is Important." Written by a state farm director, it discussed in detail the "intensification" of food growing on his farm. This was "leading experience," as the Soviet phrase goes, by which the most advanced techniques in industry and agriculture are publicized for others to emulate. This article occupied 3 columns for a total of 22 inches.

Below the fold on Page 1 were short TASS news items—three about a Bulgarian Communist Party delegation in Moscow, one about the forthcoming visit of the Danish prime minister, one recording the departure of American industrialist Cyrus Eaton from Moscow; another on Soviet-Finnish trade talks for 1966–70; one about a Yugoslav delegation in Leningrad to study local police administration; and finally, a 12-inch story about a Moscow reception for a Soviet Olympic team. These items appeared in *Leningradskaya Pravda* for two reasons. One, because *Leningradskaya Pravda,* like other Soviet newspapers, uses its front page for official information, which all of these items were. Second, articles mentioning the Bulgarian and Yugoslav delegations, Cyrus Eaton, and the Danish prime minister were as much intended for them—to show Soviet official receptivity—as for the reader, to indicate the same thing. The Olympic team reception story contained the names of the Soviet political leaders attending and was published as much for that as for readers' interest in the team.

Among articles on the two inside pages was one of a series under the general headline: "Each Enterprise—A Plan of Chemicalization." This series had a specific purpose. It was Soviet national policy in 1964 rapidly to expand the chemical industry. *Leningradskaya Pravda*, in unison with other Soviet newspapers, was instructed to promote this policy and, in fact, its editors being members of the Communist Party were obligated to do so. The article discussed use of chemical synthetics in shipbuilding, Leningrad being a major Soviet shipbuilding center. The article and others in the series were supposed to encourage factory and enterprise management to explore ways of applying the products of the expanding Soviet chemical industry. Competing for attention on Page 2 was a 3-column article—also one of a series, about Communist Party members in their daily work—dealing with the improvement of design organizations and the role of party members. It was written by two senior engineers of a local state architectural design institute. Page 2 also contained six letters from readers. One, for example, came from two factory workers who complained that their enterprise had been fined 800 rubles ($888) because management had not properly conserved metal.

Page 3 of *Leningradskaya Pravda* for February 20, 1964, was dominated by two articles on space flight, one written by an engineer, the second from notes of a lieutenant colonel who trained Soviet astronauts. The third major article, by an air force general, was a reminiscence about the World War II years. Page 4 contained the daily theater, film, radio, and television listings. There was also a book review. In addition to a few sports items and incidental news notes, about one fourth of the space was devoted to 10 short international news items under a standing headline: "TASS Transmits the Latest News." They occupied about 7 per cent of the total space. Among these items: "In the Spirit of Friendship," a Soviet-Finnish agreement over reconstruction of a canal; "Free the Fisherman," a New York dateline, demand by a New York attorney to free an arrested Cuban fisherman. "Barbaric Justice," Havana dateline, a Brazilian landowner shoots a peasant; "On Events in Gabon," Paris dateline, an uprising in the Former French colony of Gabon; "Cyprus Question Discussed," New York, the United Nations Security Council deals with the Cyprus dispute; "Expulsion of American and British Diplomats," New York, diplomats ordered out of Zanzibar; "New Greek Government," Athens, new cabinet in Greece; "Trial of Ruby," New York, start of Jack Ruby's trial in Dallas, Texas; "Catastrophe in the Atlantic," New York, a merchant ship sinks.

Except for the ship sinking, which had no political overtones, all the international news items conformed with then current Soviet policies and official attitudes. For example, the Soviet press generally gave thorough reporting to Jack Ruby's trial in the killing of Lee Harvey Oswald, building up the conclusion that President John F. Kennedy's assassination was an organized right-wing conspiracy. The Cuban fisherman story was support of Cuba. The item about the Brazilian landowner coincided with an official Soviet picture of the rich, corrupt Latin American oligarchs suppressing the peasant masses. The expulsion of diplomats from Zanzibar reinforced an official attitude that Africa was turning against the western imperialists. That is, the items themselves were factually accurate, but both the headlines and the selection of news revealed a bias.

The Weekly Newspapers

If *Leningradskaya Pravda*'s organization and operation is typical of most Soviet republic and regional newspapers, the small weekly newspaper *Ogni Angary*, published in the Siberian town of Bratsk, represents many of the small printed newspapers of Soviet enterprises, universities, and offices. *Ogni Angary*, a 4-page tabloid issued twice weekly, circulates 7,535[50] and is put out by the local Communist Party committee, a construction combine, and the Bratsk hydroelectric station administration. Most of its information, collected and edited by a staff of two editors and three writers, deals with the Bratsk station, construction, and related matters.

The issue of September 13, 1967, for example, devoted its front page to a photograph of the dam and an official announcement that the power station had been approved by a government inspection commission. Page 2 contained a picture of the dam under construction and an article by the chief construction combine that erected the dam. On Page 3 articles on a machinist who had moved from Leningrad to Siberia, to help build the Bratsk dam; another by a local Communist Party official on political education; a third by a trade union official concerning innovations adopted at a maintenance shop; and a fourth by the shop's director telling of its plan fulfillment. Page 4 carried an article about workers of a factory helping with the harvest; a picture and small item about a new movie; an article about a local bookstore; the weather forecast; television and film listings; and a Help Wanted advertisement.

In contrast to the national, republic, and *oblast* press, local papers such as *Ogni Angary* concentrate almost exclusively on their own communities. They publish little national or international information, since this is supplied by the large newspapers circulating in the same communities. Lacking talented journalists, relying on nonstaff writers, and being community boosters in the most undiscriminating way, the Soviet local newspapers emerge generally as amateur, bland journalism. One can reasonably question whether they are much read or bear at all on the opinions and attitudes of people in their communities.

The Periodical Press

The Soviet periodical network, like the newspaper system, is dominated by a relatively few national publications. It breaks down into two main categories—periodicals for a mass audience, and those for special interests, the majority falling into the latter group. For this reason, perhaps, Soviet periodicals stand second to newspapers both as a means of persuasion and of forming attitudes.

Although a total of 5,109 periodicals was published in the Soviet Union in 1968, fully three fourths of these were assorted bulletins (2,052), statistical and technical publications (1,846) or *Bloknot Agitatora* (76)—the last being a special type of peri-

Typical of the small format rural press in the Soviet Union is *Ogni Angary,* published in the Siberian town of Bratsk. Most *raion* and "lower" newspapers are of this size. Behind it is an *oblast* newspaper, *Vostochno-Sibirskaya Pravda,* official newspaper of the Irkutsk *oblast* party committee and *oblast* government.

odical for party propagandists.[51] Of 1,135 strictly magazines published in the Soviet Union in 1968, only 8 were weeklies and only 49 were issued more often than once a month. Almost three fourths were monthlies, and most of the remainder—253 publications—were issued six times a year. The single issue circulation was about 112 million copies, with the 752 monthlies accounting for 88 million of these.

Although Soviet magazines are published in 45 national languages (and 17 foreign languages), Russian dominates the periodical press as it does newspapers. About three fourths of the periodicals, with a one-issue circulation of 95 million, are in Russian. Magazines published in national languages number at most in the dozens—there are 53 Ukrainian language journals, for example—and mostly less than that. Their total single-issue circulations are in the 1 to 3 million range.

SOVIET PERIODICAL PRESS: 1955–1968*

Year	Number of Periodicals	Annual Circulation (millions)
1955	2,026	361.3
1958	3,824	637.4
1960	3,761	778.6
1963	3,912	1,066.8
1965	3,846	1,547.6
1967	4,704	2,295.7
1968	5,109	2,362.3

SOURCES: *Pechat SSSR za sorok let,* p. 107; *Pechat SSSR v 1968 godu,* p. 56; and issues for 1967, p. 56; 1962, p. 56; and 1964, p. 68.

*Statistics include magazines, scholarly journals, bulletins, and periodic collections of statistics, technical information, and the like. Magazines account for a fourth to a third of the total, judging from Soviet breakdowns for various years.

Of the 57 foreign language magazines, with a total circulation of 5.3 million, those in English lead with 23 publications, followed closely by journals in French, German, and Spanish. These are primarily propaganda magazines. Some, like *Soviet Life,* the slick English language monthly distributed in the United States, are wholly edited for a foreign audience. And although they portray a particularly optimistic, progressing, and harmonious Soviet society, such publications as *Soviet Life* rank

among the best of popular Soviet journalism. Others of the
foreign language journals, such as the illustrated monthlies
Sovetskii Soyuz (*Soviet Union*) and *Sovetskaya Zhenshchina*
(*Soviet Woman*), are published originally in Russian for internal distribution and then translated for foreign audiences.

As with the Soviet newspaper industry, the magazine network
has enlarged substantially since the mid-1950's, reflecting the
Soviet economy's postwar recovery. More funds were made
available for newsprint, and for editorial staffs. There were
only 547 magazines published in 1955, compared with more
than 1,135 today. Circulations have increased fivefold in the
same period.

SOVIET MAGAZINES: 1940–1968

Year	Number of Magazines	Annual Circulation (millions)	Average Circulation, Single Issue (thousands)
1940	673	190.2	26.1
1950	430	136.7	27.7
1960	923	576.9	57.3
1965	1,044	1,088.4	94.5
1967	1,115	1,664.0	135.9
1968	1,135	1,692.5	135.8

SOURCE: *Pechat SSSR v 1968 godu*, p. 56.

Somewhat as in the United States, the dominant Soviet
magazines are the popularly written, illustrated monthlies,
particularly those for women. *Rabotnitsa* (*Woman Worker*)
had a circulation of 10 million in 1968; *Krestyanka* (*Peasant
Woman*), 5.4 million. Among other leading magazines, *Zdorovye*
(*Health*) circulated 8 million; *Krokodil*, the thrice monthly
journal of satirical cartoons and articles, 4.6 million; *Nauka i
Zhizn* (*Science and Life*), 3.6 million; *Semya i Shkola* (*Family
and School*), 1.5 million; *Ogonyek* (*Little Flame*), 2 million;
Politicheskoye Samoobrazovaniye (*Political Self-Education*),
1.4 million; and *Za Rubezhom* (*Abroad*), 1.1 million.[52]
For the most part, such publications appeal to a cross section of readers. They publish articles, fiction, poetry, and news
items, and many are liberally illustrated with drawings and
photographs. They also have a deliberate political cast. The
purpose of *Rabotnitsa*, for example, has been described as the

"cultural and political education of working women and house-wives and their mobilization to fulfill the tasks established by the Communist Party."[53] But, of course, such official goals apply generally to the Soviet newspaper and magazine press, and account for publication even by the rough Soviet equivalents of *Good Housekeeping* or *Ladies' Home Journal* of whole de-crees of the Communist Party Central Committee.

Though political or social education is the thread that ties the printed press into one network, Soviet magazines vary substantially in content. Thus, in addition to mass audience publications, there are specialized journals dealing with military affairs, science, technology and industry, agriculture, commerce, medicine, physical culture and sports, language and literature,

FREQUENCY OF MAGAZINE PUBLICATION: 1968

Published	Number	Annual Circulation (millions)
Weekly	8	169.4
3 times a month	2	172.0
Twice monthly	47	271.0
Monthly	752	1.054.5
8–10 times a year	11	0.6
6 times a year	253	21.0
4 times a year	55	3.5
3 times a year	5	0.2
Twice yearly	2	0.5
Totals	1,135	1,692.5

SOURCE: *Pechat SSSR v 1968 godu,* p. 57.

art, atheism and religion, and more than 50 magazines for children and youth. Most of these are national publications, although circulations are at most in a few hundreds of thousands, or only a few tens of thousands. However, outside the RSFSR, each of the other 14 Soviet republics has local magazines, largely in the national languages. For example, the Ukrainian Komsomol organization publishes a monthly illustrated maga-zine in Ukrainian called *Ranok.* It circulates nearly 70,000 copies. Containing original art, poetry, fiction, and feature articles, as well as fashions and travel essays, it is edited chiefly for young adults.

Krokodil, published three times a month, carries satiric articles and cartoons. *Zhurnalist* is issued monthly specifically for journalists, but has a general readership also.

For every one issue of a local republic magazine, however, there are nearly four copies of national publications.[54] And with few exceptions, the national journals are the important ones, as they are in the United States. Moreover, with few exceptions, the large circulation magazines such as *Krestyanka* or *Krokodil,* while more widely read, are less significant than some of the smaller, specialized journals. *Kommunist,* official monthly journal of the Communist Party Central Committee, akin to American scholarly journals in format, carries authoritative political views. Its circulation was 720,000 in 1968. *Novy Mir,* the monthly literary magazine in the tradition of Russian "thick" journals, circulated 128,700 copies at the end of 1967, but because it prints some of the more unorthodox fiction, opinion essays, and poetry, its impact on Soviet society is greater proportionate to its circulation than the slick paper monthlies.

Za Rubezhom, publication of the Union of Journalists, begun in 1960, publishes edited translations from the foreign press, and because Soviet readers rarely have access to the originals of foreign newspapers and magazines, *Za Rubezhom* has enjoyed considerable success, as its 1.1 million circulation indicates. *Zhurnalist,* also a publication of the Union of Journalists, has gained instant popularity by revamping its format and publishing searching articles and research on mass media and Soviet society. Its circulation climbed from about 28,000 in 1966, to around 140,000 a year later, after its modernization.

Some of the most controversial and innovative opinion appears not in the mass circulation Soviet magazines, but the more scholarly journals. *Voprosy Ekonomika,* a monthly journal of economics, carries discussions of Soviet economic problems and proposals of national importance. The journal's circulation is small, about 33,000, and its style is weighty; but its contributors include the country's leading economic theorists. It is true of other specialized journals that the more experimental, unorthodox attitudes will appear in their pages long before they gain popular currency. One can find parallels in the American periodical press. *Foreign Affairs,* a monthly dealing with international relations, publishes interpretations and analyses by academic specialists and government officials whose views frequently enough later repeat in the popular press. The *Bulletin for Atomic Scientists, Science* magazine, and the *Literary Review* are other examples of American periodicals that carry essays of intellectual importance, but for select audiences.

However, unlike the large circulation Soviet periodicals, some popular national American magazines rank in the upper levels of original, imaginative journalism. *Harper's* magazine, *Atlantic, Esquire, Life, Fortune, Look* and, among the news journals, *Time* and *Newsweek,* outrank most American newspapers in thorough, well-written, and well-illustrated interpretations and analyses of topical events. The Soviet equivalents, and they do not come very close, such as *Novoye Vremya* (*New Times*), *Mezhdunarodnaya Zhizn* (*International Affairs*), and other national magazines already mentioned, tend to a prodigious repetition of stock attitudes and ideas, or to rather banal feature and travel articles, reminiscences, and uninspiring poetry and art.

One reason, perhaps, is that the Soviet political bureaucracy has never attached as much importance to the periodical press as to the newspaper network. If one surveys Communist Party decrees and regulations, Soviet literature on the press, and statements by Soviet leaders over the past half century, preponderant attention has been given to newspapers. The rationale, from the political point of view, is the relative influence of the newspaper press over the periodical. Soviet magazines tended to be edited for individual, specialized audiences, whereas the newspaper press was designed for the mass audience.

Certainly Soviet magazines have made rapid strides in recent years. *Rabotnitsa* circulated 1.7 million copies in 1957, compared with 10 million today; *Krestyanka,* to mention another popular magazine, has gone from 1.4 million to the present 5.4 million circulation.[55] Similar large circulation increases of other magazines gauge their mass appeal (and allocation of paper and funds by the government). And it is apparent that magazine editorial staffs are trying now to engage the interest of readers with well-designed pages and more stimulating articles. This does not apply as much to the scholarly and literary monthlies as to a few of the popular journals such as *Zhurnalist* or *Za Rubezhom.*

In many ways, the periodical press fulfills the same functions as the Soviet newspaper industry. It is a vehicle of political philosophy, of course, and also a means of innovation and channel of information. Women's magazines, for example, emphasize characteristics and habits of the model woman worker, housewife, or peasant farm woman. They transmit exemplary experience and codes of behavior, in somewhat the same way as American women's magazines cumulatively portray a model of the ideal American family and the woman's role. Similarly, the specialized journals for Soviet technicians, engineers, economists, Communist Party members, scientists, lawyers, historians, writers, artists, and Komsomol members and officials all reflect dominant ideas and innovations in particular fields.

Beyond this, the specialized journals, including the literary monthlies, perform as discussion clubs and testing grounds for controversial methods, views, raw information, and proposals. For example, *Voprosy Ekonomika* first published the results of a study that showed large unemployment, or at least under-employment, in the Siberian cities.[56] This was highly controversial, since a good deal of money and effort had been invested in attracting a labor force to growing Siberian industrial centers, and the mass Soviet press had been enlisted in promoting migration to the east. Moreover, "full employment" in the Soviet Union is held up for comparsion with unemployment in capitalist countries. In the American press, an equivalent documented criticism would be a major news story. In the Soviet Union is held up for comparison with unemployment in out-of-the-way academic or literary journal, and if it gains support, it then filters into the mass press. Even from the political management's vantage point, it is useful to have the rather exclusive discussion journals, where various experts can exchange information and thoughts without conforming to established and still desirable themes in the mass press. Trial balloons do not grow so large, rise so high, nor, if they finally explode, make so much commotion when they are floated in the academic journals.

Like American periodicals, Soviet magazines also deal with general and long-range issues, and usually in more depth than the daily newspaper press. There is probably less distinction in this respect between Soviet newspapers and magazines than American, because Soviet newspapers traditionally have published as much of what in the United States would be classified as essays and interpretive journalism as news and information. But infrequency of publication forces onto and encourages Soviet magazines, like American, to stand at some distance from a current issue. Moreover, the specialized periodicals can assume an audience initiated into the subject and therefore deal more thoroughly with a topic's complexities and subtleties. For example, *Partiinaya Zhizn* (*Party Affairs*), a periodical for Communist Party members, or *Sovetskoye Gosudarstvo i Pravo* (*Soviet State and Law*), a monthly publication of the Academy of Sciences Law Institute, have readers with an already substantial knowledge of the magazines' themes.

Four of the leading journals in the Soviet Union are (clockwise) *Novy Mir,* literary monthly; *Voprosy Ekonomiki,* a monthly dealing with economic issues; *Kommunist,* major theoretical journal of the Communist Party central committee published 18 times a year; and *Partiinya Zhizn,* thrice monthly journal of the central committee specifically for party members.

All this is to exclude ritualistic essays summarizing after the fashion of a *Pravda* editorial the most recent national policy adopted by the Communist Party, or the current government program that needs continuous advertising. These occupy a percentage of space in all Soviet magazines though they seem mostly to be unread except by those, such as local party and and government officials, whose jobs require a cursory knowledge of what is being published in political propaganda.

Finally, the Soviet periodical press is both critic and entertainer. These functions are combined in the satiric journals, of which *Krokodil* is the best known. With a circulation of 4.6 million, it has, one suspects, some impact on Soviet society. Its persistent targets are bureaucrats, drinking, politically wayward youth, poor housing construction, inefficient farm and factory production, low-quality consumer goods and services, and, in the foreign field, West German militarism, American imperialism, NATO, and United States racial discrimination. These themes change, of course, with the times, although Soviet bureaucratic bumbling and German militarism have been caricatured three times a month for more than a decade. *Krokodil* and local satiric journals such as the Ukrainian republic's *Perets* and the Uzbek republic's *Kulak* are also simply light entertainment, occasionally witty, sometimes funny.

Other periodicals function as critic, too. The literary journals are immediate examples, along with monthlies such as *Iskusstvo Kino* (*Art of the Cinema*) and *Teatr* (*Theater*), which by their nature are critics of the arts. But most every Soviet magazine, from the popular illustrated periodicals to the academic journals, is a critic of standard practices and attitudes, within prescribed limitations, if only by virtue of the criticism and self-criticism "principle" of the Soviet press system. In a broad sense, this is true of the bulk of American periodicals. Discussion and controversy on their pages are essentially directed against the status quo. What characterizes Soviet magazines more than the American is the propagation as well as criticism of the status quo. There is an obvious qualitative difference between an article that extolls the virtues of, for example, a Soviet government's farm program, drawing selectively on statistics to arrive at a predetermined conclusion, and an article that critically investigates Soviet rural poverty, allowing the data to give their own conclusion. The Soviet periodical press is inclined as much toward the former as the latter. And as such, it is both a mobilizer of public opinion in support of national goals and a mechanism for detecting and solving, or helping to solve, social problems. That it is frequently dull and ponderous is evident from a cursory reading of a few articles from, for instance, *Kommunist, Voprosy Istorii,* or *Zdorovye.* At the same time, the periodical press is informative, and as printing techniques and design improve and as young journalists enter magazine editorial staffs, the mass circulation magazines reveal a talent for popularizing ideas and events.

CHAPTER 6

RADIO MOSCOW AND THE BLUE SCREEN

SOVIET broadcasting fought with the printed media well into the 1960's for a place of influence and prestige. Perhaps because there was no commercial motivation as in the United States to analyze and dissect the psychological effects of radio and television, or perhaps because sociological studies were discouraged under Stalin or, finally, perhaps because political bureaucrats were slow to acknowledge the new electronic media—for one or a combination of these reasons, radio and television remained stepchildren among the mass media. A probing analysis in *Kommunist*, the Communist Party's leading theoretical journal, observed in 1965:

> There is an effort being made to discover the possibilities of home television, to establish its esthetic nature under socialism, to determine its role in society. On the one hand, there is the traditional hierarchic point of view which assigns home television a modest role among the means of propaganda. The press, film and radio have accumulated considerable experience and long ago became a part of everyday life. But the home television is a novelty. Thus an "inertia of attitudes" or a form of "table of ranks" interferes with giving television the role it ought to occupy. On the other hand, some conclude that television should replace all means of propaganda and even art.[1]

If this sort of dispute over television existed in the mid-1960's, recognition of the effects and impact of electronic media had not progressed very far in the Soviet Union. There had been a good deal of discussion and a good many assertions made about the extraordinary value of television and radio in political and cultural education; all of which may have been beside the point until radio and then gradually television broadcasting were formed into a national network reaching most or large segments

An announcer of Moscow Television just before broadcast.

of the Soviet population. But even in the mid-1960's, programming remained relatively lackluster.

The *Kommunist* critique discussed the faults of television. Programs lacked variety, announcers and commentators were mechanical in their presentations, television repeated what had already appeared in newspapers, major issues were treated superficially, far too few professionally trained and experienced television journalists were engaged in producing programs, television showed little talent as public critic. A Moscow television viewer, not untypical of the Soviet audience's reaction to television programming, had much the same attitude when a Soviet correspondent, disguised as a TV repairman, conducted an informal survey. "There are some shrewd people in television," the viewer noted. "If one channel's got a lecture, without fail the other one has a round-table discussion." [2] A Moscow scientist, in the same opinion survey, sympathized: "When the poor devil, the television viewer, gets through all the debris of form to the content, it turns out that all the while there was nothing there for him." [3]

Part of the complaint with television particularly, since it is the newest mass communications medium in the Soviet Union and arouses the most controversy, is that Soviet programming has adopted the content and style of the printed media. In this it has failed, the criticism goes, to develop its own character and, in what would seem the simplest of all, to entertain as well as inform. A TV critic writing in the national newspaper *Sovetskaya Kultura* quipped: "After studying television programs for the past few weeks and using fourth grade mathematics, we calculated the percentage of entertainment value of television broadcasts at 6% to 7%."[4]

The common theme, clearly, in judging Soviet broadcasting is its lack of imaginative, professional, and varied content. Criticisms may exaggerate to some degree, as blanket assessments often do. Relatively popular radio and television programs are aired in the Soviet Union. The Leningrad TV station inaugurated a series for young people that in *Pravda's* opinion was lively and stimulating and "does not shun acute and controversial problems."[5] Another Leningrad program called "In Our Circle" brought together a family (actors), who discussed domestic problems and issues of popular concern. In one of the first attempts to survey audience likes and dislikes, a sample of nearly 2,000 TV viewers gave high ratings to sports programs (such as broadcasts of soccer games), to concerts and variety programs, and such audience participation shows as KVN—the Club of Cheer and Wit, in which viewers and studio panels of university students engage in a test of knowledge.[6]

However, despite streaks of success, Soviet radio and television do not on the whole seem to earn praise from authorities, communicators, or audiences. That is not altogether an original state of affairs. In the United States, radio and television have equally harsh critics. The issue in each country is to some extent the same. Should broadcasting—especially television—educate and inform, or entertain? American television is predominantly an entertainment medium, although in very recent years both the large commercial broadcasting networks and educational television have produced public affairs, documentary, and investigative programs of high merit. Soviet radio throughout its history has been considerably devoted to purposeful entertainment. Readings of plays and broadcasts of concerts were to lift the cultural level of the population. A smaller portion of time was given over to dissemination of information. In the early 1960's, Radio Moscow's domestic programming of 545 hours broke down this way: 55 per cent of the time was allocated to music; 16 per cent to news; 10 per cent to social-political information; 9 per cent to literature and drama; about 7 per cent to programs for youth; and the rest a mixture.[7] Central Television similarly has leaned to entertainment, though not all of the light variety. In 1962 or so, when Central Television broadcast 64½ hours a week, 22 percent were taken up by films; 19 per cent, literature and drama; 18 per cent, music; 17 per cent, news; 14 per cent, programs for youth; 8 per cent, social and political information; and 2 per cent miscellaneous.[8]

A representative day of Radio Moscow—the listings for June 28, 1968—began at 8:45 A.M., with one of a series of talks on health, continued with a program on literature and then a talk by the first secretary of the Moscow City Communist Party organization. Other programs included a concert from Bucharest, Rumania, a report on the Supreme Soviet, a broadcast on "The Forest in Our Life," songs about Lenin, a program about high school graduates, sports news, commentary, and a review of international events. Programming ended after midnight with music. On the same day, Moscow television's Channel 1 (of four channels) began its broadcast schedule at 5 P.M. with a children's program, then offered a sports review, a concert from the Black Sea port of Odessa, and a soccer match. The broadcast day concluded at midnight with news and music. Channel 3—devoted largely to educational programs—offered during seven hours of programs, "Chemistry in the National Economy," a physics lecture for correspondence students, and German, English, and Russian lessons for high school students preparing for university entrance examinations.[9] Channels 2 and 4, broadcasting six hours each, from 6 P.M. to midnight, presented films, and a variety of discussions, interviews, and news programs.

There is no question that the educational potential of Soviet television is recognized. As in the United States, TV offers a means of mass instruction without the relatively expensive facilities of universities and institutes. On a practical level, television can be the channel for introducing technology, industrial production methods, farm skills and equipment, and construction techniques. It can partly shape a life style, by displaying fashions, work habits, architecture, and art, for example. And it can contribute to the formation of popular attitudes with films, dramas, discussion forums, lectures, and the like.

Soviet television has its political uses also. Khrushchev,

sensing the impact of the "blue screen"—the Soviet equivalent slang for "the tube" in the United States—spoke to the Soviet nation over television. Visiting dignitaries have been permitted to appear on Soviet television when such broadcasts contributed to Soviet foreign policy objectives. Local Communist Party and government officials have been encouraged to use television at regular intervals to report on current policies and problems, and to answer questions posed by the local citizenry.

The role of broadcasting, from the political bureaucracy's standpoint, is to encourage the acceptance of national goals and to help form a particular social culture. The unrefined interpretation of radio's and television's function corresponds then to the responsibilities of the printed media. In part, the lumping together of printed and electronic media is explained by the still elementary knowledge in the Soviet Union of how different communications media affect a mass audience. The Soviet mass media are consciously and rationally structured to encompass the Soviet audiences. But political authorities and journalists, too, have not until very recently wondered whether the large publishing and broadcasting structures were actually making contact with audiences, or influencing attitudes and habits. Such elementary matters as size of radio and television audiences, popular preferences as to form and content of programs, and correlations of television viewing with, for example, education have barely been touched. Soviet journalists are not certain whether an appearance on television by a local party official does more for his "image" or less, although they seem to suspect that television humanizes a bureaucrat who might otherwise be regarded distantly. When the Soviet Union celebrated its fiftieth anniversary in the fall of 1967, members of the Communist Party's politburo were televised at several official ceremonies. There was a rare scene—for Soviet politics—of Leonid Brezhnev, party general secretary, and Alexei Kosygin, Soviet premier, discussing something with obvious amusement, and then of Brezhnev turning away from a remark with a dismissing flip of the hand. Such brief and infrequent glimpses of Soviet leaders in unguarded moments must transmit a different impression than do the stock newspaper photographs of them ranged atop the Lenin Mausoleum reviewing a parade in Red Square. When Brezhnev spoke at the fiftieth anniversary, his soft, almost melodious Ukrainian accent must have contributed to a certain popular attitude toward the man, in the same way that American audiences associated certain characteristics with President John F. Kennedy's Boston cadence or President Lyndon B. Johnson's Texas drawl.

Soviet communicators have yet to explore, however, precisely what impression television appearances or radio addresses by political leaders make on a Soviet mass audience. Judging from Soviet literature on the subject, the Soviet political bureaucracy itself lacks a developed sense of television's potentialities in managing information and forming national opinion favorable to party-government policies. This is perhaps not surprising. American political organizations only gradually became aware of television's uses and began to tailor political campaigns, if not candidates, to the medium. Soviet television is young. To Soviet bureaucrats, it is an unfamiliar means of communication. Since they are not inclined to curry the favor of the citizenry (which can be a different matter than trying to shape mass opinion), it is easy for them to overlook techniques of television politics. Indeed, there is some question that they are aware of the most elementary techniques. Consider that an American President delivers a State of the Union Message in about half an hour, aware that a mass television audience soon becomes bored and inattentive. Brezhnev's televised address on the Soviet Union's fiftieth anniversary lasted four hours. One would like to know the audience rating of that production.

Various Soviet agencies are, however, beginning to appreciate both the positive uses and the disadvantages of television. One Soviet health institute is studying the effects of prolonged television viewing on children. Researchers grant TV's educational role, but they are concerned, no less than Americans, that children's minds are dulled by two to three hours (or more) of undiscriminating viewing daily.[10] Crime and violence are also topics of discussion. Violence of the American television variety occurs infrequently on Soviet screens. Soviet programming has its share of war films, World War II being the predominant theme, and of flashbacks into the revolutionary past, which contain a good deal of violence. But violence as a form of evening entertainment for the family is unknown on Soviet television. Soviet authorities, though they lack substantial data, suggest that the mass media can encourage crime and violence. The Soviet Ministry for Internal Affairs, which deals directly with crime, recently faulted the Soviet mass media for sensationalism in reporting crime, and television specifically for showing scenes of an American who shot several people.[11] It should not be imagined from such criticism that Soviet television programming is saturated with crime "news" or scenes of violence. To the contrary, there is none of the former on television and very little in the printed media, and that focuses on capitalist countries. What police authorities' comments indicate is a strong resistance to portraying even a minimum of violence. Both legal and police officials would prefer that the mass media minimize violence and emphasize a theme of law and order. This is not an unfamiliar refrain to Americans. A common criticism of television in the United States is that it creates an atmosphere in which violence is acceptable.

Soviet political officials and some journalists have been sensitive to this problem. They have, as well, been intent on the mass media picturing a tranquil, ordered society, regardless of existing conditions. Partly, they have wanted to portray a society superior to the capitalist. The objective, crudely put, is to show that Soviet socialist society is harmonious and does not stimulate crime and violence, while the reverse is true of capitalist societies. In addition to propaganda objectives, however, Soviet authorities consider that nonpurposeful fictional or documentary presentations of violence, crime, and civil strife by the mass media are inimical to society's interests. Much the same attitude has emerged in the United States, particularly in connection with civil rights. Some critics of the mass media advocate "positive" information about Negroes and minimum coverage—but not suppression of news—of civil disorders.[12]

As a channel of information and news, Soviet broadcasting generally is rated low. It was not until 1960 that radio was officially delegated the job of reporting information before Soviet newspapers and that the news agency TASS was instructed to transmit news promptly to central and local radio stations.[13] Radio still does not report major decisions until they appear in leading newspapers, chiefly *Pravda* and *Izvestia*. To American audiences, radio's advantage in disseminating news ahead of the printed media is daily knowledge. Soviet radio, however, suffered discrimination at the hands of political bureaucracy. Radio simply was not given priority over the printed press, for any purposes, until it was finally realized that broadcasting was grossly underused.

Even now, broadcasting has not quite supplanted the printed media in being first with information. Old prejudices and habits linger. The news director of the Estonian republic's major radio station, in Tallinn, complained that TASS frequently transmitted world news a whole day after events, lagging behind foreign broadcasts received in Estonia. Further, audience surveys revealed that 73 per cent of Tallinn radio's listeners considered radio late with the news. What Tallinn Radio did then was to tape record Radio Moscow news broadcasts and translate them from Russian into Estonian. Even this process was preferable, for airing timely news, to waiting for TASS.[14]

Perhaps the important point here is the increasing preoccupation of Soviet radio and television journalists with fresh and immediate information. The general criticism, as noted earlier, has been that the electronic media simply repeated what newspapers had printed. As this fact has been assimilated, Soviet broadcasting has improved somewhat. At least, Soviet research into mass communications now poses the problem of radio and television competition with the printed press. A study of *Trud*, the national labor newspaper, revealed that three fourths of its readers owned radios or television sets. The question therein was how *Trud* could retain the interest of an audience that already might have been informed by radio or television. Research indicated that people would turn to newspapers for interpretation of radio or television information, for additional facts, and for the newspaper's opinion.[15]

On balance, however, Soviet journalists remain unenthusiastic about radio and television programming. A panel of Soviet journalists and journalism educators brought together to assess *"Vremena"* ("The Times"), a revised version of central broadcasting's television news, noted the "lack of timeliness, the narrow-mindedness of information and the poverty of content" of television news broadcasts, and indeed of Soviet journalism generally.[16] Broadcasting is disdained not only for falling short of audience tastes and interests, but for being so ignorant of its audience as to schedule radio and television broadcasts specifically designed for workers during hours when most workers are on the job or shopping.

Regardless of their faults, Soviet radio and television—especially television—are of growing importance in Soviet society. One can see television antennas today in the smallest villages of the depressed Soviet countryside. We know generally the impact of American television, with its portrait of comfortable if not affluent middle-class life, on the emotions and expectations of America's poor, black and white. Soviet television, too, pictures a world that millions of Soviet peasants have neither experienced nor perhaps even knew existed. More than the printed press, the "information explosion" is sparked by television in the Soviet Union. This much the Soviet political bureaucracy recognizes. For documentation of the realization, we should turn to the development of Soviet radio and television networks.

Years of Development: Radio

"Our country," begins a Soviet chronological history of radio broadcasting, "is the mother of radio." [17] Without delving into rival claims for radio's invention, it is paradoxical that with the technical knowledge at hand broadcasting expanded as slowly as it did in the Soviet Union. Alexander Popov, the nineteenth-century Russian scientist whom Soviet historians credit with demonstrating the first crude radio receiver in 1895, the year that Guglielmo Marconi sent a brief message by wireless, was experimenting in radio two decades before the Bolshevik Revolution. Russia, like other industrializing nations of the time, was mastering wireless communications. The means of voice transmission was accessible shortly before World War I, although the first experimental voice broadcast was not made in Russia until 1920 and the first broadcasting station did not go into operation until 1922. [18] By the time the new Bolshevik government in Moscow was bringing civil war to a close in 1920 and turning its energies to political and economic reconstruction, American entrepreneurs were beginning to form the great empires that were to direct broacasts to nearly one out of every two American homes by 1930, and two of three of 1935.

In the Soviet Union, radio broadcasting did not reach the American level of 1930, in terms of total receivers, until the early 1950's. Yet, radio broadcasting was admirably suited to needs of the Soviet political bureaucracy. Its potential for disseminating information rapidly over large areas was hailed by Lenin in 1920. A Communist Party directive of 1925, in endorsing a national Society of the Friends of Radio, noted the "significant role which radio should play as a powerful means of agitation and propaganda."

However, two factors retarded radio broadcasting in the Soviet Union. One, implicit in Lenin's vision of all of Russia listening to a "newspaper read in Moscow," [19] was the equation of radio broadcasting with the printed word, rather than the recognition of radio as a fundamentally different medium of mass communications. This was not an uncommon attitude anywhere. After all, wireless transmission was originally used to relay dot-dash messages. In the Soviet Union, however, once the attitude became entrenched in the central bureaucracy, it was difficult to change. And although the potential of radio was exploited for cultural education—broadcasting of concerts, for example—radio tended to be viewed as a public address system for the printed word. So, even into the 1960's, the volume of radio broadcasting was frequently described in terms of newspaper pages.[20]

The second obstacle to radio's development was the large initial investment necessary to reach even the more populous western expanses of the Soviet state. Given at least a basis for a printed media network in the early 1920's, the new Bolshevik government easily leaned to expansion of that, devoting only secondary attention to radio. Indeed, there perhaps was no realistic choice from an economic standpoint. Radio required a developed electrical power system, which the Soviet Union lacked. Soviet electrical energy production in the mid-1920's was about a twentieth of American output. Radio demanded a whole new industry, from the ground up, to manufacture receivers and transmitting equipment, not to mention continuing large investment in research and development. It was still an experimental form of communications, and although its potential was recognized, its actual benefits and uses remained hazy. Moreover, in the war-ruined Soviet economy, there were more immediate needs than the wide-scale construction of a radio network.

What was lacking then was a motivation in the Soviet Union, equal in force to the commercial stimulus in the United States, to enter into extensive radio broadcasting. The fact that radio could, if developed, reach millions of illiterate people did not weigh heavily enough. First of all, illiteracy predominated in rural Russia among the peasants, and among national minorities in central Asia and the Caucasus. Although the central leadership was intent on establishing political management among these millions, as development of the printed media showed, the problem was absence of electrical power for radio precisely in regions where illiteracy was greatest. Second, the formation of corps of political agitators to deliver lectures and read newspapers aloud to the illiterate provided oral communications as effective perhaps as radio broadcasting.

In sum, radio was perhaps too young to draw the full support of the Soviet political leadership, the Soviet state too big and its population too dispersed in the provinces to make radio feasible and, finally, there were existing mass media alternatives to radio. The result was laggardly growth of the broadcasting industry, while newspapers were assigned the chief responsibility for educating, mobilizing, and informing the masses.

By 1928, there were only 92,000 receivers in the whole Soviet Union, and all of them in cities where only a sixth of the country's population lived.[21] The following decade witnessed a relatively spectacular advance, the number of operating receivers reaching nearly 7 million by 1940. Broadcasting stations, the first of which began transmitting in Moscow in 1922, numbered 23 in 1929 and increased to 60 by the end of 1932. Between then and 1937, during the second five year economic development plan, 30 more stations were built.[22]

From the very beginning, the Soviet broadcasting system used both standard radio receivers and diffusion networks by which broadcasts were carried over telephone lines to loudspeakers. Where communications lines already existed, it was much less expensive to install loudspeakers than radios. The result was that Soviet broadcasting was predominantly a loudspeaker network until the mid-1950's. By the same token, radio broadcasting was restricted mostly to cities, where both electrical power and communications lines were available. The vast Soviet rural regions barely knew radio until the early 1950's, and even after that there were areas without radio because they were without electricity. As late as 1967, the party Central Committee issued a special decree calling for a special effort to extend the wired loudspeaker system to *all* Soviet rural areas.[23] Lack of radios in the provinces has been chronic. Thus, for example, of the 7 million radios and loudspeakers in 1940, only 1.6 million were in the countryside. That meant 1 receiver for every 24 persons nationwide, and in the countryside where two thirds of the population lived, 1 for every 70. Most receivers—5.8 million out of the total—were loudspeakers hooked up in networks and frequently mounted in clubs, meeting halls, and along streets. Broadcasts thereby did reach a somewhat larger audience than ratios of receivers and population would indicate.

During World War II, many standard radio receivers were requisitioned by the government[24] and by 1945, there were only 473,000 sets operating out of the prewar total of 1.1 million, 80 per cent of them in cities.[25] By 1950, however, as postwar recovery advanced, the broadcasting network had been considerably enlarged. In that year, there were 11.4 million wired speakers and radio sets, still predominantly in urban areas, and by 1956 the total had reached nearly 30 million according to Soviet *estimates*. The most significant change in the early 1950's was a concerted effort to extend radio broadcasting to rural Soviet Union. Thus, of 22 million loudspeakers counted in 1956, almost half were in the villages, compared with about one fifth in 1950. The number of standard radio receivers also increased, from 1.7 million in 1950 to 7.4 million in 1956. However, reflecting the slow construction of transmitters and to some extent the economically depressed level of the countryside, most radio sets—5.5 million out of 7.4 million—were in cities. A disparity in Soviet statistics should be noted here. One source reports 19.5 million wired speakers and 13 million radio receivers in 1955, for a total of 32.5 million.[26] In any case, the pattern remains similar. That is, there was a sharp increase in the installation of loudspeakers, particularly in rural areas, in the early 1950's. This trend continued in the second half of the decade, so that by 1960 there were about 31 million wired speakers in the Soviet Union, 16 million located in villages, while the number of standard radio receivers had increased to 27 million.[27]

Also noticeable in the late 1950's and the early 1960's, the number of radios gradually exceeded loudspeakers. Thus by 1966, the loudspeaker network contained nearly 36 million units, while the number of radio sets had increased to 38 million.[28] But Soviet statistics must be accepted cautiously. In early 1968, *Pravda* reported 48 million radio receivers in the Soviet Union, and *Izvestia* gave a figure of 42 million "operating receivers."[29] These are large differences, and one must conclude that Soviet authorities do not know accurately how many radios or loudspeakers are actually in use.

In the early years, there was not much importance in statistics separating radio sets from loudspeakers. Central and local programming were picked up by both networks. In the 1950's however, as cold war intensified between the Soviet Union and the United States, radio receivers became objects of propaganda battles. With determination, the United States transmitted into the Soviet Union, and with equal determination, the Soviet government tried to jam broadcasts. The loudspeaker network was outside this conflict since obviously Voice of America and the BBC could not break into it. Soviet jamming of most foreign radio broadcasts ceased in 1963 (though it was resumed on a selective basis in 1968, after the Soviet-led invasion of Czechoslovakia). But both before and after that, production of standard radio receivers showed steady expansion. The proper question is why the Soviet government should deliberately reorient its broadcasting system more to radio receivers and away from loudspeakers, knowing full well that this simply compounded the problem of foreign ideological influence. The apparent reason, although it is not explicitly stated in Soviet sources on broadcasting, is that the economics of reaching a mass audience called for a radio receiver network. The revival and growth of Soviet communications industries after World War II meant cheaper and more reliable sets: the number of transmitters increased from 100 in 1950 to 407 in about 1962, and to "more than" 430 in 1968.[30] Not all of these were stations originating programs. In fact, the majority were relay stations for Moscow and regional broadcasting centers. Nevertheless, they provided the technical means for airing programs without stringing lines for loudspeakers.

SOVIET RADIOS AND SPEAKERS: 1928–1968

Year	Radios (millions)	Wired Speakers (millions)
1928	70 (thousand)	22 (thousand)
1940	1.1	5.8
1945	0.5	5.6
1950	1.7	9.7
1956	7.4	22.0
1958	21.7	27.1
1960	27.0	31.0
1962	30.5	32.2
1963	32.8	33.2
1964	35.2	34.6
1965	37.2	34.6
1966	38.1	35.7
1967	39.8	36.9
1968	42–48	39.0

SOURCES: *40 Years of Soviet Power*, p. 265; *Ezhegodnik bolshoi Sovetskoi entsiklopedii*, editions of 1962, p. 78; 1963, p. 78; 1964, p. 77; 1965, p. 79; 1966, p. 83; and 1967, p. 89. *Narodnoye khozyaistvo SSSR v 1966 godu*, p. 576; *Pravda*, May 7, 1968.

To summarize, the present-day Soviet radio system is made up of networks of an estimated 42 to 48 million radios and 39 million loudspeakers. They receive from more than 430 stations and relay transmitters, which broadcast a total of 1,200 hours daily (central and local) in Russian and national languages. Through one or the other, Central Radio in Moscow, broadcasting on long, medium, and shortwaves, reaches virtually the whole Soviet population.

In the countryside, where the loudspeaker system still predominates among about 45 per cent of the population, the government has almost a monopoly of broadcasting. In urban areas, however, where standard radio receivers are more plentiful, Soviet programming competes with stations broadcasting from other Communist countries and from non-Communist countries in western Europe, as well as from the United States.

Of the four Soviet programs (the equivalent of American stations), Programs 1 and 2 of Central Radio carry the major load of news and information. Program 3 is mainly music and literature, while Program 4 is edited for far eastern sections of the country.[31] In addition to the four central programs, local radio stations originate their own broadcasts to supplement central studios. Along with these broadcasts, received on standard radio receivers, the loudspeaker network is equipped to handle three programs in towns of 300,000 or more people, and either two or three in smaller communities.[32]

The actual listening audience, as contrasted to nearly 100 per cent availability of a receiver for Soviet citizens, is unknown to anyone, in or outside the Soviet Union. Registration of radio receivers at one time provided Soviet authorities with a fair count of potential listeners. When licensing of radio sets was abolished, evidently around 1960,[33] the only guides to the radio audience size were estimates of receivers which, as mentioned, have not been too reliable. Subscription fees—a form of registration—apparently are still paid for the use of loudspeakers and thereby provide a more accurate count of these facilities (and also defray costs of an otherwise state-subsidized broadcasting system). In any case, there remain the problems of measuring listening audiences at various times in various parts of the country.[34] So far, Soviet mass communications researchers have done little to measure radio audiences and listenership. All that Soviet authorities know is that the radio broadcasting network is technically capable of reaching all but a fraction of the Soviet population.

Years of Development: Television

The same imprecision applies to the Soviet television audience. At the beginning of 1966, when the Soviet Union counted nearly 16 million television sets, the potential audience was estimated at 50 million viewers,[35] or three viewers to the set. Thus, in early 1968, when there were 23 million television sets, the number of viewers was possibly 70 million. The television network was said to broadcast 900 hours daily (central and local) over an area containing 124 million of the 237 million population.[36]

Even if these estimates of viewers are only approximately correct, they symbolize the concerted growth of Soviet television in recent years. If the 1930's were Soviet radio's spawning period, the 1960's have been television's era of expansion. Before that, television was virtually unknown in the Soviet Union. This, too, is paradoxical. The first experimental television transmission was made in the Soviet Union in April, 1931, and "regular" TV broadcasting began on March 10, 1939, in Moscow, where 100 very small screen sets received a slow-motion 30-minute program.[37] By the beginning of 1941, 400 television sets had been produced and the Communist Party had ordered construction of television stations in major Soviet cities.

SOVIET TV STATIONS AND SETS: 1941-1968

Year*	Stations**	Relays	Sets (thousands)
1941	2	---	0.4
1945	---	---	0.2
1951	2	---	15.0
1956	18	---	1,324.0
1958	62	77	2,500.0
1961	100	175	4,800.0
1962	116	224	6,500.0
1963	130	231	8,300.0
1964	148	270	10,400.0
1965	168	334	12,900.0
1966	185	468	15,700.0
1967	125	607	19,000.0
1968	125	777	23,000.0

SOURCES: *40 Years of Soviet Power*, p. 265; *Ezhegodnik bolshoi Sovetskoi entsiklopedii*, editions of 1962, p. 78; 1963, p. 78; 1964, p. 77; 1965, p. 79; 1966, p. 83; 1967, p. 89; and 1968, p. 89. *Narodnoye khozyaistvo SSSR v 1960 godu*, p. 576.

*Numbers of stations are for beginning of year.
**"Stations" include large relay centers, as well as programming stations. In 1967, some "stations" were evidently reclassified as relays. This would account for the decrease of "stations" from 1966 to 1967.

World War II temporarily canceled these plans. At the war's end, the Soviet inventory of television sets was down to 200 and by the end of 1950 had reached only 15,000.[38] In the following decade, the pace of development gradually stepped up. At the start of 1956, there were about 1.3 million sets, and 4.8 million at the end of 1960.[39] Meanwhile, from the two television stations (in Moscow and Leningrad) of prewar years, the television broadcasting network grew to 18 stations at the close of 1955 and 275 in 1960, the latter figure including about 100 programming centers plus 175 relay facilities. The viewing audience by then was estimated at 20 million,[40] or about 10 per cent of the population.

One cannot say that postwar development of television was negligible. Yet it is evident that, despite its recognized effect in shaping attitudes and disseminating information, television had a low priority in Soviet planning. Had Soviet political authorities really been convinced of television's use and value, they could have directed a faster pace of growth. The technology was available. Research and development before World War II had given the Soviet Union a base on which to build. Investment funds, though acutely scarce in the 1950's, could have been taken from other sectors of the economy had Soviet leaders wanted to construct a TV network. However, the allocations were not made, and the conclusion must be that central planners simply did not believe television communications were sufficiently important when measured against the needs of heavy industry, the military, agriculture, and the like. And, too, the fact of an established and growing printed media and radio broadcasting weighed against making huge investments in television.

Around 1960, however, thinking began to change. A Communist Party directive of that year declared that "Television opens new and great opportunities for daily political, cultural and esthetic education of the population" but that "Soviet television is still far from fully used. . . ."[41] The directive went on to criticize the specific shortcomings of television, and to outline a plan for improvement, including better trained staff and more imaginative programming. With this political imprimatur, and with somewhat less strain in the economy, the central planners began a rapid expansion of television. Three years after the 1960 directive, the Soviet Union had double the number of television sets—10.4 million—produced in the whole fifteen postwar years up to 1960. Within five more years, the total was up to 23 million. Simultaneously, the transmitter

PRODUCTION OF RADIO AND TV SETS: 1932–1968

Year	Radios (thousands)	Television Sets (thousands)
1932	29	-------
1937	200	-------
1940	160	0.3
1945	14	-------
1950	1,072	12
1955	3,549	495
1958	3,902	979
1960	4,165	1,726
1961	4,228	1,949
1962	4,251	2,168
1963	3,500	2,147
1964	4,766	2,927
1965	5,160	3,655
1966	5,800	4,400
1967	6,400	5,000
1968	7,000	5,700

SOURCE: *Narodnoye khozyaistvo SSSR v 1965 godu,* pp. 138–139; and for 1962, p. 126; *Pravda,* January 26, 1969; January 25, 1968; January 29, 1967; January 24, 1964.

network was extensively added to. From the 100 TV stations in 1960, the system counted 125 programming centers in 1967.[42] The network of standard relay stations, to carry central programs nationwide, expanded from 175 to just under 780 at the start of 1968. With this growth, Soviet television broadcasts went to large rural areas in the western Soviet Union, and to the urban regions of Soviet central Asia, Siberia, and the far east.

Indeed, the most notable facts of Soviet television development have been the advances toward a national network, making use of cables, relay transmitters, and artificial earth satellites to reach distant points, and the construction of a major programming center in Moscow for the network. Initially, in the 1950's, programs of Central Television in Moscow were received directly only on sets within range of the Moscow transmitter, and indirectly by rebroadcasts of filmed programs over regional stations. By 1965, cables and relay stations linked most of the Soviet Union west of the Urals—that is, an area about the size of the United States—to Central Television. One coaxial cable extending nearly 2,000 miles from Moscow hooked up Simferopol in the Crimea, Sochi along the Black Sea, and the capitals of

Two young Russians survey a selection of phonographs, radios and television sets in a Khabarovsk department store in the Soviet far east. The set nearest them is priced at 240 rubles, or about $266. The short wave radio on the shelf between two television sets cost 139 rubles, equivalent to $154.

the Caucasus republics, Tbilisi, Yerevan, and Baku. By the end of 1967, large areas of the central Asian republics had been included in the national network. All of the expansive Kazakh republic was scheduled to receive Moscow television during 1968.[43]

These communications have been supplemented by a series of artificial earth satellites to relay television programs, telephone conversations, telegrams, and photographs from western regions to Soviet Siberia, the far east, and parts of central Asia. Between 1965 and the beginning of 1968, seven satellites of the *"Molniya"* (meaning "Lightning") series had been placed in orbit. As these trials were made, 20 ground stations were being constructed to receive central TV broadcasts bounced from the satellites. After some years of experimentation, the satellite relay and its *"Orbita"* system of ground stations began regular operations in the fall of 1967 and were said to transmit Moscow television programs to more than 20 million viewers.[44]

The programming center for the developing national TV network is in Moscow at the Ostankino station. It consists of a 1,750-foot tall tower rising over the Soviet capital and modern studios and equipment for both black and white and color television. Similar large complexes were scheduled to be built in Leningrad and Kiev in 1968. For the immediate future, Ostankino will be the prime developer of Soviet color television, which was inaugurated in October, 1967, in Moscow. One thousand color sets were produced for initial broadcasts. The Soviet television industry was scheduled to manufacture 15,000 more color sets in 1968, and move to an annual rate of 200,000 in 1970.[45] From this, it was apparent that color TV remained of secondary importance in the Soviet Union until at least the 1970's. Only Moscow, Kiev, and Leningrad, and gradually other major population centers—39 cities in all in 1970—were to get color broadcasts. Programming was scheduled to increase from 6 hours a week in 1968 to 20 hours in 1970.[46]

Of more significance has been the addition of channels to the Soviet TV network. Until 1964, there were two channels in large cities, and only one elsewhere. Central Television added a third in 1964, and a fourth in 1967; a fifth, the color channel, was established when the Ostankino station began broadcasting. With the new channels, Central Television was broadcasting 28 hours daily in 1968 and was supposed to increase to 50 hours in 1970.[47] By comparison, central programming totaled 8 hours daily in 1959, as Soviet authorities turned to more rapid development of television.[48]

The Broadcasting Network

Like many broadcasting systems in the world, the Soviet network is regulated and managed by the government. The early arrangement, for four years from 1924 to 1928 when radio was making its entry, was a so-called "joint stock company" of four agencies, including the Russian Telegraph Agency and the People's Commissariat for Postal Services and Telegraph.[49] In 1928, however, the post office and telegraph commissariat was given full management of radio broadcasting, and in 1953, the network was given over to the Ministry of Culture. Then, with the growth of television, the present Committee on Radio Broadcasting and Television was established in 1957 as one of numerous agencies in the Council of Ministers' apparatus.

The committee consists of four sections—editorial departments for radio, a separate editorial apparatus for television,

The Ostankino television tower, 1,750 feet tall including its antenna, is visible everywhere in Moscow. The tower contains three observation floors for tourists and a revolving restaurant. There are 21 studios of Central Television in buildings surrounding the tower. Broadcasts can be received up to 80 miles away.

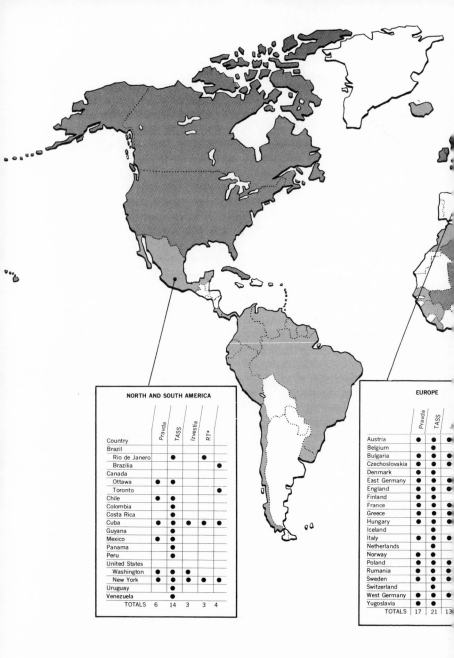

NORTH AND SOUTH AMERICA

Country	Pravda	TASS	Izvestia	RT*	
Brazil					
Rio de Janero		●		●	
Brazilia					●
Canada					
Ottawa	●	●			
Toronto					●
Chile	●	●			
Colombia		●			
Costa Rica		●			
Cuba	●	●	●	●	●
Guyana		●			
Mexico	●	●			
Panama		●			
Peru		●			
United States					
Washington	●	●	●		
New York	●	●	●	●	●
Uruguay		●			
Venezuela		●			
TOTALS	6	14	3	3	4

EUROPE

Country	Pravda	TASS	
Austria	●	●	●
Belgium		●	
Bulgaria	●	●	●
Czechoslovakia	●	●	●
Denmark	●	●	
East Germany	●	●	●
England	●	●	●
Finland	●	●	
France	●	●	●
Greece	●	●	
Hungary	●	●	●
Iceland		●	
Italy	●	●	●
Netherlands		●	
Norway	●	●	
Poland	●	●	●
Rumania	●	●	●
Sweden	●	●	●
Switzerland		●	
West Germany	●	●	●
Yugoslavia	●	●	
TOTALS	17	21	13

FOREIGN BUREAUS
OF SOVIET MASS MEDIA
1967

Key

■ Total of 1–2 Bureaus

■ Total of 3 or More Bureaus

*Committee for Radio Broadcasting and Television

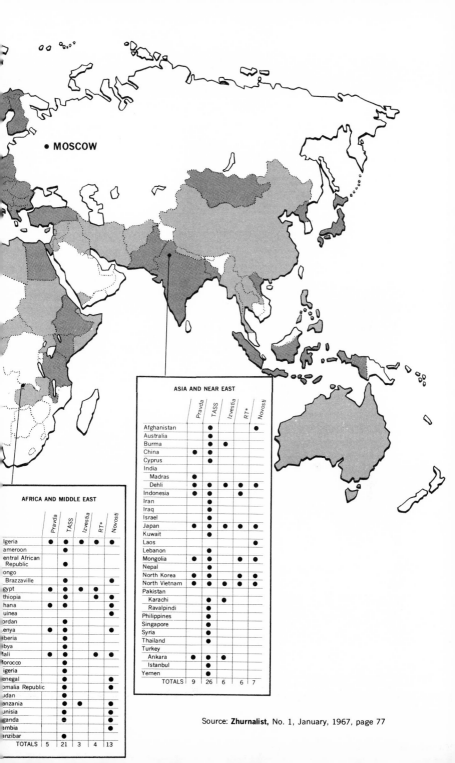

• MOSCOW

ASIA AND NEAR EAST

	Pravda	TASS	Izvestia	RT*	Novosti
Afghanistan		●			●
Australia		●			
Burma		●	●		
China	●	●			
Cyprus		●			
India					
Madras	●				
Dehli	●	●	●	●	●
Indonesia	●	●		●	
Iran		●			
Iraq		●			
Israel		●			
Japan	●	●	●	●	●
Kuwait		●			
Laos					●
Lebanon		●			
Mongolia	●	●		●	●
Nepal		●			
North Korea		●		●	●
North Vietnam	●	●	●	●	●
Pakistan					
Karachi		●	●		
Ravalpindi		●			
Philippines		●			
Singapore		●			
Syria		●			
Thailand		●			
Turkey					
Ankara	●	●	●		
Istanbul		●			
Yemen		●			
TOTALS	9	26	6	6	7

AFRICA AND MIDDLE EAST

	Pravda	TASS	Izvestia	RT*	Novosti
lgeria	●	●	●	●	●
ameroon		●			
entral African Republic		●			
ongo					
Brazzaville		●			●
gypt	●	●	●	●	
thiopia		●		●	●
hana	●	●			
uinea					●
ordan		●			
enya	●	●			●
iberia		●			
ibya		●			
lali	●	●		●	●
lorocco		●			
igeria		●			
enegal		●			●
omalia Republic		●			●
udan		●			
anzania		●	●		●
unisia		●			●
ganda		●			●
ambia		●			●
anzibar		●			
TOTALS	5	21	3	4	13

Source: **Zhurnalist,** No. 1, January, 1967, page 77

a combined editorial staff for local radio and television programming, and finally a conglomeration of departments, including reference libraries, correspondent networks, and technical services. As with Soviet newspapers, the main editorial departments are broken down into subsections, nine for the radio network and eight for television. And some of these in turn have various special departments. For example, the radio network's main editorial staff for political propaganda is made up of subdepartments for Marxist-Leninist propaganda; industry, transport, and construction; agriculture; youth broadcasts; and satire and humor. The equivalent section for television has subdepartments for economics, international affairs, culture and daily services, natural sciences and technology, sports, and the "latest news." Both radio and television also have separate departments for music programming, for literature and drama, programs for youth, and for Moscow City broadcasting.

There are slight differences of editorial structure for radio and television. The radio apparatus has a separate staff for the "latest news" department and another for exchange of programs with republic and *oblast* radio stations. Within each network, Moscow studios dominate the systems, somewhat as American broadcasting networks focus on New York offices and studios. While Central Television does much of its own programming for national distribution, the Moscow television center produces both programs for broadcast in the Moscow area and films and documentaries for reshowing in the provinces. For example, the national television network distributes up to 800 various types of programs a year to the 125 television centers, while the Moscow studios produce up to 1,500 for showing by local stations.

Subordinated to the state Committee for Radio Broadcasting and Television which manages the whole broadcasting network, are 157 republic and *oblast* committees attached to local government organizations, and about 2,500 city and *raion* radio editorial staffs. Local broadcast committees function as subsidiary management of a national network, rather than as supervisors of independent television and radio stations. Like the printed press, broadcasting editorial offices also are supervised by Communist Party organizations, which through their sectors for press, radio, and television counsel and instruct as to program content.

If we were to sketch the Soviet broadcasting network, we would find a central management overseeing program content of 157 subsidiaries (or local management), the whole network employing about 50,000 people. Editorial staffs of central broadcasting departments range from 30 to 150 persons each, including editors, correspondents, commentators, producers, and technical staffs. By contrast, a republic committee for radio and television numbers about 1,200 people in all, and an *oblast,* from 60 to 150.[50]

The amount of local radio broadcasting varies as does the size of the staff. In the Soviet republics, local stations air from 12 to 15 hours a day of local material, while in *oblasts,* they broadcast from 1 to 3 hours. For example, a recent annual programming of Leningrad's television studios included 4,330 hours of broadcasts, of which 1,620 were local programs, 1,610 were exchange and film programs, and 1,100 originated in Moscow and other cities. Or, to put the relation another way, in late 1964, when Moscow television was broadcasting 11 hours daily, the total volume nationwide of broadcasts was 850 hours daily. The 2,500 radio editorial staffs in cities and *raions,* using relay transmitters, broadcast from 20 to 30 minutes of locally originated programs up to three times a week. At other hours, Central Radio transmits through the local broadcasting facilities.

Most television programming seems to be concentrated in the large TV studios in Moscow, Leningrad, and capitals of the Soviet republics, although there are a total of 125 programming stations in the country.

In addition to domestic programming, Soviet radio and to some extent television engage in international broadcasting. Both the Central Radio and Central Television editorial organizations have separate departments to handle international broadcasts and exchange of programs. By and large, the exchange takes place between the Soviet Union and eastern European nations within the framework of the International Organization for Radio and Television Broadcasting (composed in 1966 of 24 nations), and of Intervision and Eurovision. However, the Soviet government judiciously limits exchange. And given the short broadcasting range of television, Soviet authorities have no great concern at the moment over unwanted foreign TV broadcasts as it has had with shortwave radio transmissions. When in 1963 Soviet television viewers saw the funeral of President John F. Kennedy in Washington via Telstar, for example, it was by consent of the Soviet government.

Soviet communicators envision the day, however, when satellites will relay TV programs directly to the home television set, bypassing existing ground stations which at present func-

SOVIET RADIO AND TV ADMINISTRATION

STATE COMMITTEE
FOR RADIO BROADCASTING
AND TELEVISION

CENTRAL TELEVISION
EDITORIAL STAFFS:

Social-Political

Departments

1. "Latest News"
2. Economics
3. Foreign Affairs
4. Public Affairs
5. Culture & Life
6. Natural Sciences
7. Sports

Music Programs

Departments

1. Symphony
2. Folk Music
3. Concerts
4. Arrangements
5. Developments in Music

DEPARTMENTS

1. Correspondents
2. Directors
3. Technology
4. Reference
5. Music Library

Combined Radio/TV
Editorial Staffs for
Local Programming

Local Radio/TV
Committees and
Editorial Staffs

CENTRAL RADIO
EDITORIAL STAFFS:

Political Propaganda

Departments

1. Marxism-Leninism
2. Industry, Transport,
   Construction
3. Agriculture
4. Youth 5. Satire

Natural Sciences

"Latest News"

Departments

1. National News
2. Press Review and News
   Summary 3. Sports

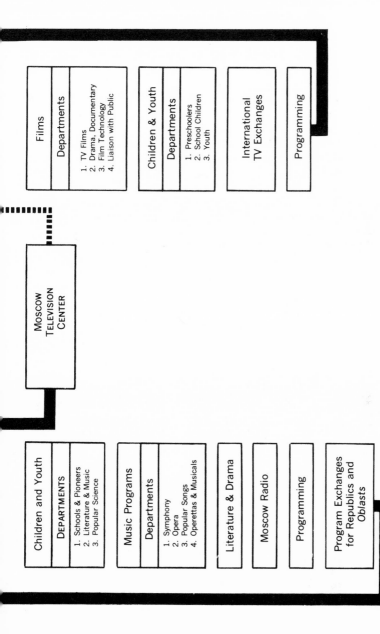

MOSCOW TELEVISION CENTER

Films
Departments
1. TV Films
2. Drama, Documentary
3. Film Technology
4. Liaison with Public

Children & Youth
Departments
1. Preschoolers
2. School Children
3. Youth

International TV Exchanges

Programming

Children and Youth
DEPARTMENTS
1. Schools & Pioneers
2. Literature & Music
3. Popular Science

Music Programs
Departments
1. Symphony
2. Opera
3. Popular Songs
4. Operettas & Musicals

Literature & Drama

Moscow Radio

Programming

Program Exchanges for Republics and Oblasts

tion as the "gatekeeper." In an interview early in 1968, for example, the Soviet Minister of Communications observed: "Quite probably in the future, television programs relayed by earth satellites will go directly to home television. Then we will be able to televise broadcasts in practically every place on our planet."[51] There are impressive technical obstacles in the way of worldwide television broadcasts via satellite from one nation to another, directly to the home sets. The political seem just as formidable. But Soviet communicators are beginning to think of the day when they can portray the Soviet Union to millions of people by television, and when foreign TV broadcasts may reach the masses of Soviet citizens. International Soviet radio broadcasts already have reached sizable proportions. In 1968, Radio Moscow was beaming 150 hours of programs abroad in 57 languages every 24 hours. These broadcasts are skillfully edited to appeal to specific audiences. Indeed, initial Soviet research in radio audience tastes was done by Radio Moscow with listeners in North America.[52]

An example of Soviet foreign broadcasting is Radio Peace and Progress, which began operating in 1964. It broadcasts a little over 15 hours a day, in eight languages, and mainly to western Europe, the United States, Communist China, and India. Although its staff of 60 uses Radio Moscow facilities, Radio Peace and Progress is ostensibly a "public organization" of the Union of Journalists, Press Agency Novosti, and other Soviet quasi-official agencies. As such, it does not speak authoritatively for the Soviet government as does, for example, TASS, although it de facto represents Soviet policies.[53] In return for the foreign broadcast activities, the Soviet government contends with the fact that both Russian and native language broadcasts of Communist China, the United States, Great Britain, Japan, west European and Scandinavian countries are received in the Soviet Union. International broadcasts by radio and conceivably in the future by television represent the most serious challenge to the Soviet political bureaucracy's monopoly of broadcast information within the country. In recent years, the Soviet mass media and political authorities have increasingly warned of the influence of foreign broadcasts on attitudes in the Soviet Union. The problem essentially was whether to prohibit foreign broadcasts by jamming networks, or to counter them. Especially since 1963, when most jamming ceased, the Soviet press has been directed to the second course. Thus, in 1965, as the post-Khrushchev Soviet leadership developed a noticeably

A staff meeting in an editorial office of Moscow Television.

"harder" cultural policy, the Communist Party's leading theoretical journal *Kommunist* warned of an extensive anti-Soviet
propaganda campaign engineered in western countries, chiefly
the United States:

> Bourgeois propagandists try to use the foreign radio, press and
> tourism as channels for injecting alien views into our midst. . . .
> It is essential to study the tactics of hostile propaganda and
> actively combat them. . . . But there is often little information,
> insufficient commentary and details in our newspapers and on
> radio to help understand current policies. In our time, when
> radio receivers are in almost every home, to ignore this or that
> event, to fail in pointing it out from the standpoint of socialist
> ideology means to give "freedom of action" to the falsifications
> of bourgeois propagandists. . . . More than that, it is important
> not only to correctly explain this or that fact, but it is essential
> to do it promptly. One must admit that bourgeois information
> agencies have achieved great efficiency, reacting quickly to every-
> thing occurring in the world, while we sometimes are late.[54]

One interesting effect of foreign broadcast competition seems to be a modification of Soviet communications behavior. When the Soviet government enjoyed a virtual monopoly of the airwaves, there was little motivation to program with the listener's tastes in mind. Indeed, Soviet broadcasting was considered essentially a medium of cultural education and entertainment. The attempted penetration of the Soviet Union by foreign broadcasts was temporarily deflected with massive jamming networks. Eventually this became politically untenable. How could the Soviet Union establish its place as a civilized, confident nation among nations, engaging in commerce, tourism, and political negotiations, and at the same time shielding its citizenry from the outside world? The two activities were incompatible. And, in effect, Soviet communicators were pressed to modernize the mass media to conform to the Soviet Union's international stature as a world power. About this same time, in the early 1960's, the reborn Soviet sociology was applied to mass media, among other areas, in an attempt to put Soviet communications planning on a more rational, scientific basis. This is not to say that foreign propaganda and news broadcasts were the primary motivation for reassessing and updating Soviet broadcasting. But they have been a strong stimulant, among several that would include a rising educational level, a conviction on the part of the political bureaucracy that the Soviet mass media were not reaching the public, and a better trained journalist corps that is also aware of foreign broadcast content and techniques. The total result was that Soviet television and radio underwent a process of expansion and improvement in the 1960's, in preparation for greater stature in the 1970's.

CHAPTER 7

NEWS OF THE WORLD: TASS AND NOVOSTI

$\mathbb{O}$F ALL the Soviet mass media, TASS is probably the single most important manager of the information that reaches the Soviet public. Virtually all that provincial newspapers and broadcasting stations disseminate on international events comes from TASS's Moscow offices. Even the major national newspapers and broadcasters rely heavily on TASS for foreign information, although some have their own overseas bureaus. The Telegraph Agency of the Soviet Union and 14 subordinate news agencies in each Soviet republic also are major sources of domestic information and commentary for the daily press.

In 1925, when TASS was established, it was given exclusive authority to distribute information about the Soviet government within the country and abroad. TASS no longer enjoys a firm monopoly. Both *Izvestia* and *Pravda* offer original reports of Soviet government and Communist Party affairs. And both of these national newspapers maintain press bureaus, somewhat like information syndicates, which feed the local press. Further, since 1961, Press Agency Novosti has supplemented TASS in distributing information about the Soviet Union to the foreign mass media and in covering international events.

However, TASS remains the acknowledged authoritative spokesman for the Soviet political bureaucracy in affairs of state, and with its bureaus in 94 foreign countries, it provides the Soviet people with the bulk of what they learn on a daily basis of the world about them.

It is because TASS is the channel for these two categories of information—about the Soviet state and international events —that it occupies a privileged position among the Soviet mass media. We know that all information in the Soviet press is managed to some degree by the political bureaucracy. However, the political apparatus is acutely sensitive to the form in which its decisions and attitudes are portrayed to the Soviet public and the world at large, and it therefore controls this information most carefully of all. Accordingly, TASS achieves its stature more by association with power and authority than by its own performance as a news agency. To put the point another way, it is questionable whether TASS would be ranked with the world's great news gathering agencies of the United States (Associated Press and United Press International), Great Britain (Reuters), and France (Agence France-Presse) if it were not part of the Soviet political apparatus. It is rare indeed when TASS excels other agencies in speed of news transmission, in thoroughness, and in dispassionate recording of international events, except when the Soviet government or the Communist Party is involved. As to the last, TASS of course has the advantage over all other mass media in being the major publicist for the Soviet leadership. TASS was the channel, for example, through which the replacement of Khrushchev was relayed to the world. It was a TASS announcement in *Pravda* that told the Soviet people that Soviet-led troops had invaded Czechoslovakia in August, 1968. TASS is the medium by which most major addresses of Soviet leaders and decrees of the Communist Party and Council of Ministers are distributed to both the foreign and the regional Soviet press. It is for this reason that foreign news reports quote TASS synonymously with the Soviet leadership. Indeed, TASS often enough is used directly as the spokesman for the Soviet government as other governments employ press offices or ministries of information to make official views known publicly.

The dual role of TASS complicates assessment of the organization as a news agency. TASS cannot be strictly compared with the Associated Press or Reuters, for example. For one thing, it is government operated, as an agency of the Soviet Council of Ministers, and it therefore has more than a normal inclination to weigh events from a nationalistic point of view. But neither can TASS be considered strictly a Ministry of Information for the government, in the way that the White House press office functions in the American government. TASS is simultaneously an information-gathering mechanism and a propagandist for the Soviet political apparatus.

Much the same can be said for Novosti, although that agency has a less defined position than TASS in the Soviet mass media structure. As a "public organization," it functions ostensibly as an independent agency. If that were truly its status, Novosti would be unique in Soviet society, and among the Soviet mass media. Suffice to say at this point that Novosti is entwined in the political bureaucracy but serves a somewhat different role than TASS as a distributor of information about the Soviet Union.

Possibly the closest analogous organization to TASS and Novosti in American society is the United States Information Agency, insofar as TASS and Novosti attempt to portray a favorable image abroad of the Soviet Union. Of the two, Novosti more accurately parallels USIA. Like USIA, for example, it publishes foreign language periodicals, issues various informational and reference works on the Soviet Union, and supplies the foreign press with photographs, commentary, and facts on the country. TASS, by contrast, issues the "hard" news to foreign subscribers, and in this sense operates in part as United Press International or Reuters. Within the Soviet Union, both TASS and Novosti service the Soviet mass media and therefore differ from USIA, which is prohibited by law from disseminating information in the United States.

TASS and Novosti share the central problem of any government agency. Their credibility is necessarily suspect, although they are not automatically guilty by association. When TASS transmits an explicitly authorized statement of the Soviet Council of Ministers, foreign governments attach very high credibility indeed to TASS. TASS dispatches from Peking in the mid-1960's, when Soviet-Chinese relations were strained, frequently were well-documented, factual accounts of what little could be learned by resident correspondents of Communist China's internal strife. TASS reports of nonpolitical events—a ship sinking, for example, or a natural catastrophe—are as unbiased and accurate as those of any world news agencies. But the bulk of TASS dispatches are of a political nature, in a broad sense to include governmental, economic, and cultural developments in various countries, as well as international relations. So, too, are reports of Novosti from its foreign correspondents. And ultimately, Soviet foreign policy interests thread through the operations of both agencies.

Managing Foreign News

All governments are concerned, of course, with the mass media's influence on foreign relations and opinion. All governments to one degree or another manage information to serve their international policies. Their success in this art depends partly on the institutional control they have over the mass media. It is relatively uncomplicated for the Soviet government to regulate or restrict official opinion, commentary, or facts that flow through its own media to the world at large. Comparatively, the American government—the executive branch along with the state and defense departments—works with an unpredictable mechanism in the American mass media, and where it cannot command a point of view, it must persuade or deceive the press in order to further particular foreign policy interests. But the relationship is not all combat. It is reasonable, as Bernard C. Cohen indicates, that American government officials are often suspicious and distrustful of the mass media's involvement in foreign affairs. However, as he also points out, the news media are consciously used to promote foreign policy, and indeed prominent commentators are frequently enough considered allies in explaining and publicizing government positions.[1] Further, the government bureaucracy actually deals with a relatively few writers of the wire services and the major newspapers, who largely shape the foreign affairs information emanating from Washington on any given day. Similarly, the Soviet government is concerned with a limited number of channels in disseminating international information. The essential difference is that American officials are not assured a favorable and monolithic presentation of their viewpoints, while the Soviet political bureaucracy has an unquestionable ally in TASS, Novosti, and the major newspapers.

Political practice bears also on the Soviet and American reporting of foreign information. In the United States, business, labor, and civic organizations as well as private individuals not only participate in international affairs, but indeed come very close at times to conducting American foreign policy. This is not so in the Soviet Union. Throughout the Soviet state's and Russia's history, foreign relations and any less formal matter touching on the country's interests abroad have been monopolized by the political apparatus. Thus, where the American mass media, along with other nongovernmental institutions, presume to propose and criticize foreign policy, the Soviet mass communications have never been cast in the role of critic of Soviet foreign policy, as they have been assigned to monitor internal policies.

However, the Soviet mass media, and most particularly TASS and Novosti, serve several other roles in international affairs. First, they contribute to formation of a world opinion whereby Soviet policies can be more easily implemented. Analogous to USIA, Novosti maintains foreign bureaus which distribute information about the Soviet Union and work with the foreign mass media to gain a "good press" for the Soviet government. TASS is the chief vehicle for raw fact and policy. With its own foreign policy objectives in mind, the political bureaucracy maintains constant themes in information oriented toward foreign audiences. In recent years, some dominant ones have been the growing militarism of West Germany, the aggressiveness of imperialism, the necessity of peaceful coexistence, the threat of NATO to world peace, the failure of American policy in southeast Asia, abandonment of Marxism-Leninism by Mao Tse-tung, unity of the Communist parties across the world, and the continuous ideological battle between capitalism and communism.

A study of the Soviet English language magazine *USSR*, edited by Novosti (and since January, 1967, titled *Soviet Life*), found special emphasis in the early 1960's on the Soviet Union as a peaceful, cultured, and dynamic nation, advanced in science and technology.[2] An investigation of the TASS international service dispatches for one week in 1959 revealed a very similar portrait of the Soviet Union.[3] In specific instances, the Soviet press is enlisted in concentrated efforts to implant a single idea. During and after the Arab-Israeli war in June, 1967, the Soviet mass media including TASS persistently labeled Israel as the "aggressor," aided by the United States, Great Britain, and West Germany.[4]

It is conventional wisdom that the formation of opinion is a complicated process and that mere repetition of an idea or slogan is no guarantee of its acceptance. The process is even more complex when one nation attempts to influence opinion in another, given differences of culture, political ideology, and language. One attempt to measure the influence of Radio Moscow's broadcasts to North America suggests some success. A group of 61 persons was divided into three sections, one of which listened to 25 hours of Radio Moscow broadcasts; a second heard 2 hours of programs; and the third, no broadcasts. The first section, of 34 persons, noted several changes of attitude after listening to Radio Moscow—a greater readiness to believe that the Soviet Union wanted understanding and

peace among nations, greater identity with Soviet citizens, a
heightened inclination to see the Soviet point of view, and a
questioning of American mass media information about the
Soviet Union.[5] Certainly, these results are only the barest
suggestion of what achievements the Soviet Union may hav
obtained in creating particular attitudes with mass med ..
No extensive research has been done on the effectiveness of
Soviet foreign information programs, least of all by Soviet
authorities themselves. We do know that the Soviet government spends a good deal of money to influence world opinion,[6]
and coordinates its mass media with foreign policy to the extent
that they are nearly synonymous. One cannot document a single instance where the Soviet press has been at variance with
current foreign policy, except perhaps by innuendo. Whereas
within the Soviet Union the press at times acts as critic of
policy implementation, beyond Soviet borders the mass media
are exclusively propagandists and transmitters of government
policy.

These functions go further than attempting to shape the
opinion of elites or masses of people toward the Soviet Union.
TASS, along with the major national newspapers, operates as
an extension of the Soviet foreign policy machinery in a dis-
tinctly diplomatic role. It is not uncommon for TASS to issue,
and the Soviet press to publish, formal government statements
which Soviet leaders obviously prefer to have internationally
publicized rather than transmitted privately through normal
diplomatic channels. TASS similarly transmits major political
documents—decrees of the party Central Committee and
speeches of Soviet leaders which concern foreign relations.
There is of course nothing unique in this practice. The point
is that TASS, like mass media the world over, acts as an inter-
mediary between governments, quite apart from a concurrent
effort to create favorable public opinion for the Soviet Union.
The Soviet political leadership knows that TASS is considered
everywhere an authorized spokesman, just as in a less formal
arrangement, American government officials know that *The
New York Times* is read in all foreign ministries for insight
into United States policy and opinion.

But TASS is all the same not quite the Soviet government.
Therefore what TASS issues (unless it is declared to be an
"authorized" statement) is not official Soviet policy. Thus, the
agency can be used for the trial balloon, as American mass
media are by the government. It can relay approval or disap-

proval of actions by the government, without the Soviet leadership committing itself to a course of action. It should be emphasized that TASS is not the only vehicle for informal international relations. Among the Soviet mass media, *Pravda* especially serves a like role.

Just how the political bureaucracy synchronizes the mass media and foreign policy is not precisely known. It is too easy to say that the Soviet foreign ministry supplies TASS or *Pravda* with official statements. Surely this is done, and TASS or *Pravda* or *Izvestia* simply is the mechanical means that the foreign ministry chooses at a particular moment to disseminate information. But much more information issued by TASS, Novosti, and the Soviet printed press originates with staff writers, either in Moscow or in foreign bureaus. We know that the Communist Party apparatus, through the department of propaganda, issues guidelines for the press that mesh with general policy. One Soviet journalist, describing fortnightly conferences of major Soviet editors with party officials, indicates that explicit instructions are issued concerning attitudes toward foreign political leaders, for example, or developments in other countries.[7] However, a margin for error and incompetence, insofar as the political leadership is concerned, must be allowed for. Guidelines cannot possibly be so precise as to encompass all contingencies. TASS editors and foreign correspondents necessarily assume responsibility for much of the detailed information processed every day on international developments. The Soviet foreign ministry and the central party apparatus, both large bureaucracies subject to the failings of all human institutions, can hardly sanction every TASS dispatch or every foreign affairs report in the press. The information managerial machinery is efficient, but imperfect.

This was illustrated in a recent case involving *Pravda* and the highly sensitive issue of negotiations on arms control between the Soviet Union and the United States. Referring to American discussion of antiballistic missile systems, a *Pravda* writer stated in February, 1967: "Speaking at a news conference in London, Premier Alexei N. Kosygin declared that the Soviet government was ready to discuss the problem of averting a new arms race, both in offensive and defensive weapons." Actually, during a state visit to Great Britain shortly before, Kosygin had been asked his view on a United States proposal to halt construction of antimissile networks. He replied: "I think that defense systems which deter an attack cannot be considered as the causes of arms races, but rather represent a factor preventing the annihilation of people."[8] The *Pravda* statement ultimately proved accurate as to Soviet intentions, but it distorted Kosygin's remarks. In response to an American government suggestion, the Soviet government was indeed willing to enter into broad discussions concerning both defensive and offensive weapons. However, this was not publicly confirmed until June, 1968, in a speech to the Supreme Soviet by Foreign Minister Andrei Gromyko.[9] Meanwhile, the original *Pravda* comment was privately refuted by the foreign ministry the day after it appeared.[10] Conceivably, *Pravda* editors misinterpreted Soviet policy at the time, although that is highly unlikely on the matter of nuclear weapons control. It is more reasonable to suppose that the leadership, or a faction of the leadership, was amenable to Soviet-American negotiations on arms limitations even in February, 1967, and that *Pravda* editors with the support of some political authorities so stated. That *Pravda*'s commentary was at once countermanded suggests confusion with the political apparatus on the issue.

In any event, the episode indicates that despite very close supervision of foreign affairs information, the mechanism is not foolproof. The political bureaucracy at any given time is concerned with a large number of international issues on which publicly and privately it formulates policy. The mass media hew to the policy generally, but the minutiae of foreign news and information certainly cannot be dictated. Rather, the task of assuring that foreign news dispatches conform to general policy must fall on editors, and ultimately on *Glavlit*.

The management of foreign information suggests another function of the Soviet mass media. The political leadership and the corps of analysts and diplomats dealing with foreign affairs must themselves be informed. Certainly, the bureaucrats have access to a wide variety of information other than that supplied by the Soviet mass media. Diplomatic and intelligence staff analyses and reports are the most obvious. However, Soviet foreign correspondents are an important supplement. TASS, Novosti, and the few Soviet newspapers that maintain foreign bureaus are in a sense intelligence collection organizations. In the past this has meant utilization of TASS by Soviet civilian and military espionage agencies, although one study has found no evidence in recent years that TASS correspondents have doubled as espionage agents.[11] Yet, the TASS organization, along with dozens of other Soviet agencies involved in one kind or another of foreign work, does present opportunities for Soviet military and civilian intelligence and it would be naive to think that TASS or Novosti is not used for covert operations.[12]

Whatever the relationship between espionage organizations and the Soviet information agencies, the latter overtly and quite legally gather information throughout the world on a daily basis and transmit it to Moscow. The Soviet political and government bureaucracies, like their counterparts in every country, must necessarily be alerted quickly and thoroughly to shifts of policy, statements of other political figures, and changes of government. They need to know what the mass media of other countries are reporting. We know that American government officials consider the wire services and major Washington and New York newspapers prime sources of information about international affairs. One reason is that foreign correspondents can sometimes obtain information that diplomatic corps cannot because of the former's unofficial status. A second reason is that they transmit information rapidly (and, in the case of news agencies, continuously), thus serving as an early warning system.[13] We can be fairly certain that Soviet officials also rely on their own and foreign mass media for much information. According to one account of TASS operations, the agency daily prepares three different reports. One is a compilation of world news that is distributed to the Soviet mass media for public dissemination. A second—reportedly called a "white" summary —contains a more thorough and unbiased review of foreign events and is intended to brief Soviet communicators who must be well informed on international developments for their work. Still a third report—the "red" summary—provides the most unvarnished compilations from the foreign media and is written for high-ranking editors and Soviet officials.[14]

Assuming that TASS does prepare such selective summaries, which is entirely plausible, we do not know in what form they reach Soviet leaders and other policymakers. Judging from TASS and Novosti news dispatches and commentaries, as well as those in major national newspapers, the Soviet mass media extract a good deal of their information from the foreign press. That is, Soviet officials probably receive from their own and foreign mass media a thorough, varied, and competent report of international developments. Indeed, given the bond between the bureaucracy and the mass media, the latter are more likely to be deliberately and consciously employed to gather specific information for use by officials than for example the American press, which is under no compulsion to seek information of special use to government officials.

Following this further, we may wonder what effect the Soviet mass media's portrait of the world has on the political bureaucracy. The upper echelons of the Communist Party and government apparatuses undoubtedly have access to far more news of international developments than appears in Soviet national newspapers. But there are thousands of lesser ranking bureaucrats whose notions of foreign political processes must be considerably shaped by information in the mass media, supplemented perhaps by privately circulated reports bearing directly on their work. One can imagine certainly that confidential briefings contain more candid and balanced information about the political situation in western Europe or the United States, for instance, than *Pravda* or *Izvestia* publish. However, if such private reports reach too large an audience, their very purpose, which is to restrict certain information to a select few, is voided. Thus, it would seem logical that TASS, Novosti, and a few large Soviet newspapers are prime sources of foreign information even for Soviet officialdom.

As such, the mass media tend to reinforce already established ideas about the outside world, and to structure new ones. For example, the constant formulation in TASS dispatches that West Germany is partly governed by former Nazis, that it is a militaristic nation and seeks revenge for defeat in World War II, must form the fundamental outlook of successive generations of second-echelon officials throughout the Soviet Union, there being no serious consideration in the mass media of contrary views. In presenting certain consistent themes, the mass media act as a unifying force for foreign policy. The "foreign threat" can be used as justification for high military budgets, for large investment in heavy industry at the expense of consumption, or for political indoctrination campaigns, for instance. While final decisions in these matters rest with the central Communist Party apparatus, implementation of policy depends in large measure on the party and government bureaucracies, which must be presented with some explanation or reason for a general course of action by the leadership.

Similarly, the mass media keep lower echelon officials attuned to foreign policy on a day-to-day basis, without the leadership having to divulge all the details and considerations entering into conduct of foreign relations. After Soviet Premier Kosygin met with President Johnson at Glassboro, New Jersey, in the summer of 1967, the content of their discussions was probably revealed to only a very few Soviet officials. By giving very little public attention to the meeting, however, TASS and the Soviet newspaper press indicated to the Soviet party-government bureaucracy (and to the population at large, of course) that Soviet-American relations were not being altered as a result of the Glassboro talks, and that the Vietnam war remained an obstacle to improvement. In a like manner, the party-government bureaucrats may be informed of the general state of Soviet relations with India, or Communist China or France, or of policymakers' attitudes toward nuclear arms control and disarmament, United Nations activities, or East-West trade and commercial developments.

In fact, because of the official nature of many TASS dispatches, the mass media are probably more useful in some respects than the American press in briefing party and government authorities on foreign affairs. For example, the Soviet newspaper press regularly prints the full texts of important foreign ministry declarations, of major speeches by leaders, or of government proposals for various forms of international agreement and cooperation. These probably serve to orient the Soviet bureaucracy in somewhat the same way that texts of major documents published in *The New York Times* instruct American officials on foreign policy matters beyond their special competence or responsibility.

What the Soviet mass media fail to do in the realm of foreign affairs, however, is to provide a soundingboard for lower echelon reactions to policy or a forum for discussion of policy. The American press, particularly the half dozen or so major newspapers which give extensive space to international affairs, are demonstrably valuable in these respects.[15] The vaguely attributed report ("Pentagon officials," "state department sources," etc.) in the Washington *Post* or *The New York Times* dealing with current policies can be the means by which an official reaches the President and other important policymakers, or by which he generates support for a certain view. The Soviet mass media do not engage in routing inter-ministry memoranda on foreign affairs, chiefly because international matters are not considered open to public discussion as some domestic policies are.

There may be certain advantages in such handling of foreign policy. It is not subject to emotional reactions, as American policies often are. Soviet leaders are substantially free to alter

or initiate foreign policy, certain that the mass media will
promptly explain the change and mobilize opinion to its favor.
Thus, the Soviet state can act swiftly and decisively in the
foreign arena, while the American government may have to
temporize or dilute foreign policy to conform to domestic
opinion in the press.[16] At the same time, the Soviet leadership
may unnecessarily err in conduct of foreign policy precisely
because the mass media fail to moderate or explore the possible consequences of particular decisions. The Soviet dispute
with Czechoslovakia's reform-minded regime in early 1968 is
a case in point. From diplomatic and intelligence reports, the
leadership presumably became convinced that Czechoslovakia's
liberalization threatened Soviet interests. While Czechoslovak
leaders were appealing for Soviet understanding of their viewpoints, the Soviet mass media largely ignored Czechoslovak
arguments and increasingly emphasized dangers to the Communist Party's monopoly of power and the Soviet-eastern
European military alliance, the Warsaw Pact. Thus, all during
critical discussions in the spring and summer of 1968, before
the Soviet-led invasion of Czechoslovakia on August 20–21,
the Soviet mass media tended to emphasize conflict instead of
conciliation between Moscow and Prague. Had the Soviet press
enjoyed some independence of criticism in foreign policy, it is
conceivable that differences of views, even those within the
Soviet political bureaucracy, would have been tempered and
more understanding generated so that military intervention
could have been avoided.[17]

This is to say that a state-managed press, in which both
official and public discussion of some topics can be excluded,
permits a conduct of foreign policy based on long-term national
interests rather than on the popular mood. The disadvantage
of such a system is a tendency to rigid policy, exempt from the
correcting or moderating forces of informed public discussion.

Much of what has been said about the Soviet mass media's
processing of foreign information can be applied also to the
Soviet population. The TASS flow of news from abroad into
the Soviet Union as it finally appears in the Soviet press or
as broadcast reflects a world view conforming to general Soviet
policies. There is competition from the Voice of America, the
BBC, and other foreign broadcasts which probably reach many
millions of people, especially in cities. We cannot know what
influence these broadcasts have in determining opinion in the
Soviet Union. Clearly, the political bureaucracy has been espe-

cially concerned about them. When Soviet-led forces invaded Czechoslovakia, the Soviet Union simultaneously resumed jamming of foreign broadcasts in Russian, obviously to prevent the Soviet people from receiving foreign versions of the invasion and subsequent events in Czechoslovakia.[18]

The attention to foreign information from non-Soviet sources could derive from two discoveries. Either that Soviet citizens do in fact believe a part of what they hear from outside sources; and they do not readily accept information on international events given out by the Soviet mass media. Indeed, the recent emphasis on Soviet foreign affairs reporting is on positive presentation of Soviet interpretations of events rather than on countering foreign views, though the latter has become a standard part of Communist Party counsel to journalists. The second, however, is the negative approach and places the Soviet Union on the defensive. It is more beneficial to policymakers that the mass audience gives credence to Soviet information.

To some extent, the Soviet mass media have an easier time establishing trust in foreign than domestic reporting. Probably less than 1 per cent of the Soviet population has traveled outside the country or has extensive and regular access to foreign publications. Thus, the mass of citizens has no personal experience or knowledge to hold against international information in the Soviet press. Moreover, foreign developments beyond the global crisis events probably do not engage the bulk of the Soviet population. One must imagine not the well-read Leningrad University student or the informed scientist of a Moscow institute, but a peasant living in a village of log cabins, a man with less than an eighth grade education, who has traveled no farther than to Moscow, if that; or the factory worker in a provincial city of 50,000, whose immediate concerns are his job, family, housing, and leisure. These are the more representative of the mass audience. And like their counterparts in the United States, their interest is drawn only to major foreign events (for example, the Vietnam war, the Israeli-Arab war, the Cuban missile crisis); their inclination to spend thought on foreign policy matters is probably slight indeed.

The mass media are therefore presented with both a captive and a disadvantaged audience as far as foreign affairs go. The problem of TASS and Novosti consists of competing successfully against indifference and of sounding believable. A TASS declaration asserting that "all Soviet people approve" of a particular Soviet foreign venture appears contrived on the face of it. By contrast, Soviet commentary on American politics which distinguishes between views of individual officials or candidates (even while alleging that monopolists and the ruling classes manipulate politics) contains an internal claim to credibility.

Although the Soviet leadership defers not at all to the population in forming foreign policy, it is aware of popular opinion and attempts a consensus. For example, as the Vietnam war escalated and the Soviet Union became increasingly and openly committed to the defense of North Vietnam, the mass media, in TASS and newspaper dispatches from Hanoi and in commentary, began regularly to compare American actions with foreign intervention in Russia after the Bolshevik Revolution and with Nazi Germany's destruction in the Soviet Union during World War II. Anyone who has talked with Soviet citizens knows that recollections of the war, with the mass killings and atrocities, are still vivid memories. That is, the mass media were not simply condemning the United States, which they did in several formulations about "imperialist aggression," and "barbaric war": the Soviet press was also attempting to arouse Soviet popular emotion against American actions by a reminder of terrible events during a war still etched on the public mind.

Information—facts, figures, opinions—is obviously an inherent part of foreign news distributed to the Soviet public. We have already emphasized the screening such information goes through so that it conforms to Soviet national objectives and attitudes. Beyond that, however, the Soviet mass media's presentation of world events is notably two-dimensional. Partly, but only partly, this may be explained by lack of space in Soviet newspapers. The long and detailed accounts of international events that one finds in *The New York Times* or the Washington *Post* are infrequent in *Pravda* or *Izvestia*. But the more substantial reason for brief and shallow reporting, as contrasted to interpretation and commentary, is simply to bar a full range of fact and opinion from the population, for without the raw data of events, it is difficult for anyone to reach conclusions of his own, or at least to question conclusions of the mass press. This process should not be exaggerated. The intelligent, resourceful Soviet citizen can assemble from his own press, particularly if he follows the specialized journals, a good deal of information about foreign affairs. However, the major national newspapers provide no more international news on a daily basis than one will find in a small-town American daily paper.

The consequence is that the average Soviet citizen receives

a little information about all major world events or developments in individual countries. But, like the telegraphic summaries of world events and trends used in some American news
magazines or "inside" newsletters, the information skims swiftly
over the surface. It is then supplemented by interpretations
and editorials, which often draw on the foreign press and include selected information not previously reported in the Soviet
mass media. The total impression, as foreigners who have lived
in the Soviet Union have experienced it, is a certain feeling of
elusiveness about the world beyond Soviet borders. It is never
quite whole. It remains separated from real life, in good share
because it is described in generalities and formulas.

The TASS Establishment

As the foreign correspondent, TASS reports from three
fourths of the some 125 countries of the world. Like other of
the Soviet mass media, the agency has expanded rapidly since
the mid-1950's, as the Soviet state has recovered from the
devastation of World War II. In 1955, TASS maintained bureaus
in about 40 countries. By the early 1960's, the number was up
to 65. In 1967, the agency operated 82 bureaus in 79 nations,
and when TASS celebrated its fiftieth anniversary in January,
1968, it had bureaus in 94 countries.[19] In 1967, the TASS international network included 21 bureaus in Europe, including
Communist countries; 26 in Asia, including 2 in both Turkey
and Pakistan; 21 in Africa and 14 in North and South America,
2 of which were in the United States (New York and Washington). What is striking are the large TASS organizations in
both Asia and Africa. While in a given week's time the Soviet
press carries news dispatches or background articles from many
nations in these continents, every country is not regularly
represented. That is, the TASS organization probably gathers
information in Africa and Asia for use as much by the Soviet
government as by TASS subscribers. Do Mali or the Sudan
rate so high in Soviet editors' or readers' interest or needs, for
example, that TASS directors feel compelled to have permanent
bureaus in those two African countries? It is doubtful. But
they do concern Soviet foreign policy and it is important therefore that TASS, being a government agency, should transmit
information from areas where Soviet interests are involved.

The TASS foreign correspondents corps is not the only source
of international news. Other agencies, though not as important

as TASS, contribute to the flow of news from abroad. Press Agency Novosti had 40 overseas bureaus in 1967. The Committee on Radio Broadcasting and Television maintained 22. Among the newspapers, *Pravda* had 37 bureaus in 35 countries (2 in the United States and 2 in India); *Izvestia*, 25 foreign correspondents posts (2 in the United States); *Trud*, the labor newspaper, 5; *Komsomolskaya Pravda*, the youth paper, 3; and *Selskaya Zhizn*, the farm publication, 4. Both *Pravda* and *Izvestia* maintain domestic press bureaus which supply the local press, but they are not much developed or used.[20] Occasionally, other Soviet national newspapers and the larger republic papers send editors or correspondents overseas for special assignments. Now and then, a Soviet writer, scientist, or bureaucrat who has attended a conference or traveled abroad for other reasons writes an essay for a Soviet newspaper or periodical. Finally, adding to the flow of international news to the Soviet Union, TASS and other Soviet media extract information from major foreign news agencies, newspapers, and magazines.

TASS was an early Soviet entrant in the field of foreign reporting, though it was not the first. To review briefly: After the Bolshevik Revolution, the Russian Telegraph Agency—ROSTA—was formed by the merger of the Petrograd Telegraph Agency and the Bolshevik government's press bureau. A 1925 government decree established TASS, and ROSTA was transformed into the news agency for the Russian republic. Ostensibly, it ranked equally with the Ukrainian republic's telegraph agency, RATAU, with the Byelorussian, and Turkmen agencies. In practice, ROSTA was synonymous with TASS, and in January, 1935, a new charter for TASS simultaneously abolished ROSTA altogether.[21] The remaining republic news agencies became subsidiaries of TASS. Eventually, as other republics were added to the Soviet Union, the number of republic news agencies increased to the present 14.[22]

As part of the TASS organization, the republic agencies distribute information about their own republics to the local press, and through TASS facilities, to the entire Soviet mass media. Their dispatches are, however, of secondary importance. Significant news or documents are released by TASS simply because it processes information about the federal government and about the Russian republic. Moreover, the 1935 statute gave TASS authority to approve directors of republic news agencies and to manage all work of the agencies.[23] And they survive today as TASS regional adjuncts.

TASS itself lived through lean times during the formative years of the Soviet state. With a small, permanent staff in Moscow, it relied partly on Soviet diplomatic and trade staffs for coverage of foreign affairs.[24] Along with many Soviet organizations, including the military officer corps and the Communist Party, TASS fell victim to the 1930's purges, and in 1937, Yakov Doletsky, director first of ROSTA and then of TASS, was arrested along with several of his Moscow staff. Not until 1943, when Nikolai Palgunov was appointed director of TASS, did the agency regain the stature and authority it had lost with the Stalin purges.

Under Palgunov, who managed TASS until 1960, efforts were made to modernize agency operations. Partly because of Stalinist habits of revealing as little as possible about the Soviet state and of distorting foreign information, and partly because of the TASS role as government spokesman, the agency was only slowly improved. Even under Dmitri Goryunov—the career journalist and TASS director from 1960 to 1967, when he was replaced by the career diplomat, Sergei Lapin—TASS was repeatedly critized for poor showing against foreign news agencies and for equally poor servicing of the provincial Soviet press.

Although a modern, 26-story headquarters for TASS was under construction in 1968, its offices for many years have been located in an unobtrusive, solid-looking building within 15 minutes walk of the Kremlin. Except for two plaques at the main door with the agency's full title, the TASS building is unidentified. There is nothing secretive about its location, but its internal operations, like those of other Soviet government agencies, are not fully revealed.

In the mid-1950's, TASS had a staff of 700 to 800 editors and writers, 200 of whom worked abroad in the agency's then 40 bureaus.[25] More recent Soviet figures, for 1968, give the TASS domestic staff, including some correspondents in republic agencies, at 500.[26] There may have been a small reduction as a result of a 1960 Communist Party decree, which complained of bloated correspondent networks in TASS, the central newspapers, and the TV and radio industry, and which ordered a cutback of personnel.[27] And the figure of 500 may include only working journalists. In 1966, Goryunov told visiting American editors and publishers that the entire TASS staff totaled 3,500, presumably including technicians, office help, and the like.[28] The present size of the foreign reporting staff is unspecified, but available evidence, including the fact of 94 foreign bureaus, suggests about 500.[29]

The overseas correspondents are attached to the most important of three TASS divisions—the editorial staff for foreign information, sometimes called INOTASS. This division, along with the department for Soviet domestic news and the department for news for abroad (that is, TASS dispatches for foreign subscribers), is immediately under the agency's director. He in turn has three chief assistants and works with a collegium— a board of advisers—established in 1962 and composed of 12 persons.[30] The foreign news department is divided into nine geographical subdivisions—for western Europe, European Communist countries, North America, Latin America, Africa, Arab countries, the Middle East and India, Asian countries, and southeast Asia. Each regional desk is directed by an editor, who is assigned 2 assistants and 5 or 6 subeditors. The foreign news department also has a large staff of interpreters to handle both incoming and outgoing dispatches. Another adjunct is the press bureau, which supplies special reports, such as world news reviews, to the Soviet mass media.

The foreign news department is the operations center not only for the 94 overseas bureaus, but for information flowing from other news agencies. TASS exchanges, on a cost free basis, with the Associated Press and United Press International. It has contractual arrangements with some 40 other foreign agencies, including Agence France-Presse and Reuters.[31]

The TASS domestic news department is organized more by subject matter than by region. Thus, it contains editorial sections for industry-economics, agriculture, and ideology, plus a special section for Moscow news. Each of these sections has its own editor, managing editor, and a staff of 10 to 15. Linked to the domestic news department in recent years were six regional bureaus in the Russian republic, each with about 60 people. The Leningrad bureau, for example, was staffed with 11 correspondents, 7 photographers, plus editors and technicians. In addition to the bureaus, the domestic news desk had about 65 correspondents working in *oblast* offices. Altogether, TASS drew from about 500 correspondents within the Soviet Union. The republic news agencies, each with about 125 people in the home offices plus *oblast* correspondents, also channel information to the TASS domestic news department in Moscow, where it is edited for distribution both domestically and abroad.

ORGANIZATION OF TASS

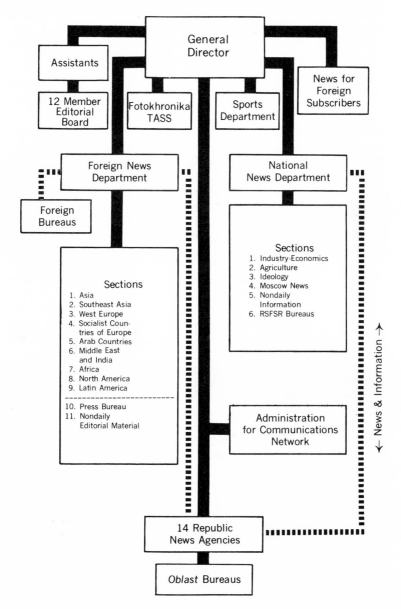

The volume of information arriving daily in the foreign and domestic news departments amounted in the mid-1950's to nearly 700,000 words, according to Palgunov.[32] A 1959 report gave a figure of 600,000 words, 500,000 of which were transmitted to subscribers.[33] And still another source says that TASS processed 2.5 million words daily in 1968, including both incoming and outgoing dispatches. A total of about 1.2 million words was transmitted in all forms to subscribers.[34]

Several other TASS departments should be mentioned briefly. A separate division edits news about the Soviet Union for foreign subscribers, including news agencies and newspapers, in some 70 countries. Dispatches go out in five languages—Russian, French, English, German, and Spanish. The photography division—Fotokhronika TASS—maintains a staff in Moscow of about 100, plus some 70 photographers of its own, and 120 photographers attached to republic news agencies. It supplies both prints and, for the small local Soviet newspapers, engraving plates. The TASS sports department covers athletic events both domestic and foreign, though the Moscow editorial staff numbers only about 15.

TASS services to subscribers are broken down in several ways. First, it should be explained that the agency operates somewhat as a government-franchised corporation. It charges set fees for its news, feature, and photo services, the revenue ostensibly making TASS financially self-sufficient. Neither the entire fee schedule nor the TASS budget have ever been made public, however, so we do not know the details of the agency's finances.[35] TASS has about 5,500 subscribers, most within the Soviet Union, including magazines, local radio and TV stations, and some 3,000 newspapers. About 90,000 miles of TASS-owned and -operated communications lines connect the agency to 187 Soviet cities, and twoway teletype links TASS to 16 foreign capitals.[36] In the mid-1960's, TASS was still transmitting news by radio, at dictation speed, to small Soviet newspapers (specifically the *raion* press). But wire communications evidently are replacing this means of transmission. TASS news dispatches have also been speeded up by increasing use of high-speed teleprinters.

Of the TASS services, the foreign news and the domestic information files are the most important. A TASS promotional pamphlet for 1964 advised Soviet subscribers on the foreign news service: "From 75 countries of the world TASS correspondents will transmit dispatches about the most important, most interesting events. In addition, subscribers will receive all of the more interesting news received by TASS from the major telegraph agencies of the world and agencies of the socialist countries."[37] The foreign news service also included "political commentaries by prominent foreign publicists and the large newspapers of the world, as well as brief TASS commentaries which will help the reader better to understand international events."

The domestic news service promised Soviet subscribers coverage of major developments throughout the country—"TASS will give broad coverage to successes of Soviet industry, agriculture, science, literature and art." Special reports, emphasizing regional developments, were offered to newspapers of central Asia, Siberia, the Caucasus, the far east, and the Urals area.

Besides these major news services, the TASS press bureau— one of the adjuncts of the foreign news department—provided periodic reviews of international events, and political commentary to newspapers and the radio-TV stations. The annual subscription fee for this mail service was 300 rubles ($333). Newspapers of the Komsomol could buy an international commentary service written especially for young people for 180 rubles ($200) a year.

Among several other special TASS news services were those focusing on news of African, Latin American, and Asian countries; of foreign literary and artistic events; of developments in Communist countries; of youth in foreign countries; and of northern European nations. TASS also produced tailored reports for city and evening newspapers, and a supplemental sports news service. These special reports were sent by mail, two to four times a week, some three times a month, for fees ranging from 120 rubles ($133) to 360 rubles ($400) a year.

The quality of TASS services is difficult to assess. Some are beyond judgment; the long, official documents issued through TASS are, like American state department texts, for the record. The one- and two-paragraph TASS news dispatches, which make up a good third of a Soviet newspaper's daily international reporting of immediate events, are best characterized as superficial and biased, but as much in selection of fact (not a fault unique with TASS) as in use of opinion (such as the phrasings, "barbaric war," "aggressive policy," and "peace-loving peoples of the socialist countries").

The more detailed news dispatches and the commentary remain. What has been said to this point about the manage-

ment and objectives of information in the Soviet mass media
applies equally to these products of TASS. That is, they
cumulatively promote the national objectives, foreign and
domestic, established by the political bureaucracy. But two
distinctions should be made. First, TASS engages very little
in the exposé and critique of failings among Soviet institutions. Most articles of that type are found rather in the newspaper press and magazines. TASS is more oriented toward
distribution of immediate and official news or information.
Second, following from the latter point, TASS management
has prodded and cajoled its staff in recent years to speed up
news transmission, in keeping with the atmosphere of urgency
and continuous deadlines that surrounds the operations of other
worldwide news agencies. Even in the 1950's, it was said that
TASS foreign correspondents were obligated to inform Moscow
editorial offices of any news event within 30 minutes after it
occurred.[38] While that may have been the policy, it was not
reflected in TASS service to subscribers. The consistent criticism leveled against TASS is its ponderously slow handling of
news, and its inexpert or inept servicing of the huge local
network of newspapers.[39] But TASS has shown capacity for
change and adjustment. It attempts to provide the provincial
press with specially compiled international events summaries
and commentary. Although TASS is in one sense a government bureaucracy subject to the customary inertia of bureaucracies, it is also a business—albeit virtually a monopoly in the
merchandising of information—and it has some incentive to
please newspaper and broadcasting subscribers.

One of the agency's problems lies in the differences among
the Soviet audience. Very much as with American news agencies, TASS must satisfy readers of varying degrees of knowledge, interests, and sophistication—this beyond the job of
representing Soviet foreign and domestic policies. Or to put
the problem another way, editors of the large national and
republic newspapers seek a somewhat more informed and
professional presentation of world events than do, for example,
editors of rural weeklies, who themselves may not be particularly knowledgeable about foreign affairs. Thus, TASS serves
different customers within the Soviet Union. And it does not
please them all.

For one thing, TASS remains bound by old formulas. While
it has slowly adopted a "news story" approach, it nonetheless
continues with the officious-sounding dispatches that are little

The central editorial offices of the Soviet news agency TASS in Moscow. It is identified on two plaques flanking the entrance.

CIALIST REPUBLIC

● Yakutsk

Lena River

rasnoyarsk

Lake Baikal

Irkutsk ● Chita

Khabarovsk ●

● Vladivostok

ADMINISTRATIVE REGIONS ~ USSR

━━━━━ National Boundaries

············· Republic Boundaries

Miles

0   500   1000

more than reprints of foreign ministry handouts (and some-times just that). Editors have very little choice other than to use TASS, partly because it is the prime source of inter-national news, and partly because they are obliged to dis-seminate official information. But the mass media are the duller for this. A careful study of the Soviet national news-paper *Trud* (circulation 2.4 million at the end of 1967) by Soviet sociologists showed that among the top 10 subjects—according to news inches—official TASS dispatches, such as government statements, ranked first, and TASS foreign news items ranked fifth. When *Trud* readers were asked to select the 10 most interesting subjects, TASS dispatches failed to make the list at all.[40] This may seem hardly surprising to any foreigner who has read TASS articles, but possibly such audience reaction impresses Soviet editors who are just beginning to consider readership as a factor in successful journalism.

One could speculate that TASS lacks appeal to Soviet audi-ences because of inadequately skilled and trained staff. But this seems untrue. TASS correspondents and editors are probably among the Soviet Union's most competent journalists. All TASS staff writers assigned abroad were required to have university educations even in the mid-1950's, when advanced education was a rarer commodity than it is today in the Soviet Union.[41] Foreign correspondents also must know at least two foreign languages.[42] Although TASS does not pay its cor-respondents better than the major Soviet newspapers (TASS staff writers get between 200 and 300 rubles a month—$222 to $333), it does offer opportunities for foreign travel, for association with the sources of power, and for a comfortable life in the large Soviet cities. TASS correspondents also enjoy official prestige. For these reasons, the agency can attract talented men and women from other Soviet media, from spe-cialized centers like the Institute of International Relations, from schools of journalism, and other career fields.

However, they work in a considerably bureaucratized struc-ture. Form and content tend to be dictated by tradition. Writ-ing in 1955, former TASS director Palgunov proposed: "News should both serve and help in the resolution of basic problems of Soviet society and the Soviet people as they make the gradual transition from socialism to communism. News is agi-tation by facts. In choosing the subject of news, the writer should keep in mind that not all facts nor all events must be presented in newspapers."[43] Palgunov also said that news should be timely, brief, written in an understandable way, and should in fact contain something generally unknown to readers. His successor, Dmitri Goryunov, deplored the time (under Stalin) when Soviet journalists lost the ability of "thinking independently, of expressing original judgments," and praised journalism that was "without incantation and shouts, without tedious mastication of commonly known truths, of tiresome moral admonitions and maxims."[44] One senses a difference of tone in the remarks of the two TASS directors, which probably derives as much from general changes of thought in the Soviet Union among journalists as from individual variations in journalistic philosophies. Indeed, in his counsel to TASS correspondents, Palgunov revealed a respect for probing, accurate, and truthful journalism that attempted as much to supply an understandable context for events as to describe events themselves.[45] Such declared ethics have not prevented TASS from gross and deliberate distortion of information, however.

What we come back to is the association of TASS with the government. It is this that seems to prevent innovation in the agency to meet the demands for rapidly transmitted, dispassionate, and thorough news of the world and the Soviet Union. This is not to say that TASS wholly fails in its role as a news agency, but that it does not measure up to the standards that some Soviet journalists, not to mention foreign critics, set for contemporary news coverage. Rather, enmeshed in the Soviet government bureaucracy, TASS is imbued with the caution, tendentiousness, and chauvinism of the Soviet foreign ministry. Its function as a news agency conflicts with its role as government spokesman. And while changes since Stalin have tended to favor the news role, TASS finds it difficult, because of entrenched habits and institutional bonds with the government, to reform very rapidly.

Novosti: The Soviet USIA

In one sense, Novosti (the word means "News") was an effort to circumvent TASS in reporting of foreign news within the Soviet Union, and in supplying information to foreign media about the country. An obvious question is why establish an entirely different organization to do what TASS was already set up to do? A report on a conference held in February, 1961, to found Novosti noted that world interest in the Soviet Union had enlarged considerably, which "raises the question of the necessity of significantly expanding and improving information" about the country abroad—a not very subtle criticism of TASS.[46] Alexei Adzhubei, then editor of *Izvestia* and already noted for his innovations in Soviet journalism, was among those chosen for the new agency's board of directors. It must have been decided that TASS, associated abroad as it was with the Soviet government, gained little credence as a channel of unbiased information about the post-Stalin Soviet society. Moreover, the argument must have gone, TASS was unsuited by its nature as a news agency and its resistance to radical change to embark on imaginative forms of journalism. The solution was a new "public organization" with no direct government ties. Thus, Press Agency Novosti was the child of the Union of Journalists, the Union of Writers, the Union of Soviet Societies for Friendship and Cultural Contacts with Foreign Countries, and of the National Union for Dissemination of Political and Scientific Knowledge.[47] These, too, were "public organizations"—that is, ostensibly voluntary unions of people with like interests. While such organizations in the Soviet Union have no formal links with either the Communist Party or the government, they cannot be considered independent social agencies. Rather, they form the Soviet substructure of social control mechanisms under the guidance of the party-government bureaucracy, by virtue of the latter's command of executive boards. Thus, Novosti could and does claim to be an independent agency, though in reality it is no more divorced from the political establishment that the USIA is in the United States.

Formally created on April 3, 1961, Novosti's declared purposes were: (1) To prepare written and photographic material concerning domestic and foreign affairs of the Soviet Union for the foreign mass media; (2) to supply the Soviet mass media with material on political, economic, scientific, and cultural developments in foreign countries; and (3) to publish magazines, newspapers, and brochures designed to acquaint foreign readers with the Soviet Union. As the Soviet version of USIA, Novosti differed in two respects. It was intended to be a domestic as well as foreign information service; and it was confined largely to the printed media.

Novosti maintains a network of correspondents throughout the Soviet Union. Their duties are twofold: first, to supply feature and background reports for distribution to Soviet domestic subscribers; and, second, to contribute to Novosti's foreign service. Novosti's domestic customers receive daily reports on both Soviet and foreign events, and separate dispatches on sports (twice a week) and culture and art (once a week). In 1964, subscribers numbered 515 magazines, television and radio stations, and newspapers, the last including those from the *oblast* level and up. By mid-1965, Novosti had about 700 newspaper subscribers alone, each paying a token $1 a month for the Novosti service.[48]

Novosti's foreign service is by far the most important of the agency's work, however. Within the Soviet Union, it works with resident and visiting foreign journalists, supplying photographs and feature articles. It arranges for interviews with Soviet officials and tours of institutions, and it seems to have a monopoly on arrangements with foreign television agencies filming special programs in the Soviet Union. Novosti photographs and other services have appeared or have been evident in such publications as *Life* and *The New York Times*, and in several recent documentaries by major American broadcasters on the Soviet Union.[49]

Editorial offices of Press Agency Novosti are located in this Moscow building.

Beyond Soviet borders, Novosti rapidly established services and outlets for its information. In 1965, it was publishing 35 foreign language magazines and newspapers and 64 information bulletins. It maintains its own teleprinter network, which connects to offices in Asia, Africa, Europe, and Latin America. With its own representatives in 56 countries and 40 established bureaus (in 1967), Novosti counted 3,500 foreign newspapers and magazines, 70 information agencies, and 80 publishing houses among its customers in 1965.[50] As an example of its swift growth, Novosti had 2 representatives in Africa in 1961, and 16 by the end of 1964. That same year, Novosti established a television section, which aids foreign TV companies as well as supplying Soviet TV films abroad. Also in 1964, the agency set up its own book publishing organization, which subsequently established working relations with 100 foreign publishing houses.[51]

The scope of Novosti's work is indicated by the fact that it has published books on everything from Soviet sociology to Soviet history to science and engineering. Its magazine section puts out *Soviet Land* in India, in 12 languages; *Soviet Weekly* in England; *Soviet Union Today* in Japan; and *Soviet Life* in the United States. A recent addition (in 1967) was *Sputnik*, a monthly digest of translations from the Soviet press.

Compared with other Soviet institutions, particularly those dealing with foreign organizations, Novosti ranks among the most flexible and imaginative, if not obliging. Its efforts to please and satisfy foreign subscribers and customers, while typical of public relations programs in the United States, represent a singular change of attitude in the Soviet Union. Novosti is also capable of talented work. *Soviet Life*, the English language monthly published in the United States, contains some of the best photography and most stimulating journalism in the Soviet Union. Its format and obvious attempt to attract and interest readers with varied content exceeds all but a few Soviet periodicals. Novosti has a peculiar advantage over domestic Soviet mass media. With its assigned job of "selling" the Soviet Union to the world, Novosti apparently can and does argue that bureaucracy-oriented journalism, so omnipresent in the Soviet Union, is of little worth, and that its material must be competitive with the consumer-directed journalism of the West if it is to enjoy any degree of success. Novosti issues its share of Soviet Communist Party decrees and government declarations; its portrayals of Soviet society are frequently enough painted in bright hues. But compared with other Soviet mass media, Novosti's products are strikingly free of ponderous, official journalism. If one were to contrast TASS and Novosti in style and tone of propaganda and information, one might say that TASS is of the Soviet iron age, and Novosti of the nuclear era.

CHAPTER 8

THE PEOPLE'S PRESS AND THE PEOPLE

I‍T IS EASY to be cynical about Soviet journalistic ethics and ideals. The "people's press"—the now huge apparatus of newspapers, magazines, radio, and television—is demonstrably managed by a political bureaucracy for special interests. Censorship, either by *Glavlit* or by journalists themselves, is far more extensive than necessary to protect national security. The important segments of the mass media have grown large and in many ways distant from their human audiences.

It is not only that truth and honesty are violated, but that they are espoused as ideals of Soviet journalism while the most deliberate deception and distortion are undertaken. Not by all Soviet journalists, and not always willingly, but the false is presented as the truth all the same. This is not, one needs to remember, a peculiarly Soviet failing. The same reasoning that leads American public officials to put out "cover stories"—to protect the national interest—and that leads American journalists to report only part of what they know or to write what they know is not quite true—this same resoning is an entrenched habit in the Soviet press.

In the Soviet case, it derives from the Bolshevik revolutionary past, from the Stalinist era, and from the "class nature of truth" concept. All conditioned the press to subordination to a social movement, to shaping attitudes in accordance with a social doctrine, rather than to finding social meaning in human events.

The result was that the concept of the democratic press, accessible to all and serving all, became in good measure rote. And as that process occurred, the press increasingly lost contact with the masses. The two phenomena are intertwined, but let us deal with them separately.

The "People's Press"

From the very beginning of the Soviet state, participation of the rank-and-file worker and peasant in the press was considered a basic principle. We have already seen how the idea of public ownership of newspapers never matured beyond an embryonic stage. It sounded progressive and wholly in accord with a socialist society. But even after the Communist Party consolidated power in the 1920's, and when it was in a position to experiment, the press was organized largely within the party structure. However, the involvement of the masses in the press remained an objective. The *rabselkor* movement became one index of popular participatory journalism. Letters to the editor as a link between leaders and the led became a second.

Originally conceived as a mass educational program, the *rabselkor* organization was transformed during the 1930's into an indiscriminating champion of state policies. After Stalin's death in 1953 and the denunciation of Stalinism in 1956, there were some efforts to revive authentic mass participation in the work of the press. That the *rabselkor* movement had by then lost its momentum was emphasized in a Communist Party decree of August, 1958. The first major document on the *rabselkor* since 1931, the decree commanded all local party organizations to establish instructional courses for worker-peasant correspondents, to assign the better correspondents to jobs on newspapers, and to hold meeting in factories and on farms to explain the work of the *rabselkor*. Party committees were to recruit more correspondents and to encourage the so-called raids, in which teams of citizens descended on a particular agency to conduct a thorough investigation of operations. Finally, local party leaders were to stimulate more letters from correspondents to editors, and journalists themselves were actively to seek contributions from people outside the press.[1]

Two years later, in 1960, the *rabselkor* corps was said to have grown to "more than 5 million" persons. The central party press administration thereupon issued another decree, in June, 1960, intended to enlarge amateur journalist ranks even more. It applauded the establishment of so-called nonstaff departments and authors' councils in newspapers, magazine, and radio and television editorial offices, and ordered that these adjuncts be introduced throughout the mass media. They were to include "leading factory workers and collective farmers, representatives of the intelligentsia, the party, local governments, trade unions and Komsomol organizations."[2] The scheme was, in effect, to set up readers' councils, which would both contribute to the press and act as a soundingboard for editors. Conceivably, the councils would draw readers into mass media operations, as well as develop a closer bond between professional journalists and their audiences.

The attempt to involve the citizenry in the mass media occurred amid a general campaign to stimulate public participation in social institutions. With Stalin dead and Stalinism denounced, Khrushchev was searching for ways to stimulate popular dedication and commitment to the "building of communism." It may have seemed eminently sound at the time, when a cynicism and disenchantment had become widespread, to undertake a grandiose scheme for drawing the masses into society's administration. In any case, the attempt was made. Comrades' courts, composed of laymen, and empowered to try minor offenses of fellow citizens, were reactivated in 1959. People's police units—called the *druzhina*—blossomed in the early 1960's. A Party-State Control Commission—a revival of the old Workers' and Peasants' Inspection—was established in 1962 to function as a check against bureaucracy, inefficiency, and corruption. In 1961, at the 22nd Communist Party Congress, Khrushchev unveiled a new party program which forecast the Soviet great society within 20 years.

It was in this context that the Soviet mass media were prodded to envelop the rank-and-file reader in their work. Part of the reason may have been purely economics. The late 1950's witnessed a drive to reduce government subsidies of the press and to trim editorial costs.[3] But mostly, the political bureaucracy seemed intent on creating the appearance, if not the reality, of a mass media responsive to popular control or guidance.

"Raids" by squads of citizens working with newspapers became increasingly common. Teams would arrive at a factory or government institution, question officials and workers, and then write a critique, usually with some scathing observations. These appeared on special pages of major newspapers, under the general title of "People's Control." As well, editors were repeatedly told to pay more attention to readers' "signals," the equivalent of news tips in American newsrooms.

In addition to the worker-peasant correspondents, whose official stature had been elevated, editorial offices formed their unpaid *aktivs* of nonprofessionals. For example, the large *oblast* newspaper, *Leningradskaya Pravda*, established an advisory group of specialists in chemical technology in 1963, after the Soviet chemical industry had been given priority. Composed of nine members, the panel advised editors on coverage of the newspaper's local campaign on the chemical industry and checked over articles for technical accuracy.[4]

On paper, at least, citizen involvement in the press made large strides under Khrushchev. It is difficult to say what existed in practice. The whole apparatus of *rabselkor*, citizens' groups, and Party-State Control Commission raids (in conjunction with newspapers) was never quite subject to statistical analysis or tabulation. But there was and is a good deal of discussion about popular participation in the press, and editorial staffs remain under constant pressure to maintain close contact with readers. Thus, on any given day, even the large Soviet newspapers will carry an article by a factory brigade foreman, or a collective farm tractor operator, or government office worker. Letters to the editor are standard features. But there is little evidence that the rank-and-file reader has much influence over his local newspaper or radio station, let alone the republic or national mass media.

There is evidence, however, to the contrary: that is to say, the press is managed by professional journalists who, while many may see their work as a public service, do not really want citizens counseling them on how to run their business. This is especially true among larger newspapers. As the education, training, and professional ability of a newspaper's staff increases, the less likely is it that it will accept the advice of the average reader, who is judged to know little about journalism.

Consider the situation in the United States. The readers of the small-town weekly newspaper can easily get a news item printed. Indeed, weekly editors are eager for contributions, rightly concluding that gossipy news notes attract subscriptions. But large American newspapers rely on professional journalists for the great majority of their information. Most readers have nothing to say directly about the content of their newspaper.

The Soviet press does not seem to operate much differently. The *raion* newspaper editor is relatively close to his readers, although unlike his American counterpart he is obligated to publish a good deal of information that satisfies the local political bureaucracy and the demand to promote national

policies. At the top of the mass media pyramid, the national
newspapers are relatively immune to popular reaction.

Again caveats are in order. Soviet newspapers enlist outside
contributors, they publish readers' criticisms within acceptable
limits, and they now are increasingly searching out audience
reaction. But this is not the same as direct public involvement
in the editing of the newspaper, or public control of the press.
Newspapers, as one Soviet journalist has observed, "prefer
publishing the material of specialists and of persons in positions
of responsibility."[5] There is nothing illogical in this. American
daily newspapers are not inclined either to print the observations or comments of readers except in letters to the editor
columns. Despite the urging to close ranks with readers, Soviet
editors, too, disdain the nonprofessional. "They are oriented
toward professional journalism," a Soviet journalism educator
complained more than a decade ago, in criticizing editors' indifference to worker-peasant correspondents.[6]

The despair of editors with amateur journalists, along with
the compulsion to manage public opinion, encourages the practice of extensive rewriting or even ghostwriting of what sup-
posedly are the raw outpourings of the Soviet citizen. Thus, an
Izvestia reporter tells of a political article appearing in one
newspaper under one worker's name and then reappearing in
another factory newspaper word for word under a different
name.[7] This sort of lip service to the ideal of spontaneous expression of public opinion in the public press extends to numerous instances of contrived journalism, ranging from workers'
messages applauding a new Communist Party decision to a
unanimous denunciation by a writers' organization of "imperialist aggression."

Of course, the *authentic* contributions of amateur journalists *do* need editing and rewriting. And that is just the point.
Soviet journalism, at least the upper levels of the mass media
that count, has developed far beyond the talents of the mass
audience. To understand the theoretical, if not real, problem
one must keep in mind that the Soviet mass media are ostensibly public property and are supposed to be the product not of
an elite, but of the common man. In theory, the Soviet press is
closer to the public bulletin board on which anyone may tack
his notices, announcements, and grievances, than to the structured, mechanized printed newspaper formed by well-educated
and experienced specialists who screen and shape information
presented to the public. The latter is the reality of the Soviet

mass media, while the former is the articulated ideal. There is nothing quite comparable to the ideal in the American press tradition unless it is the small-town weekly newspaper. But that is private property and the reader-citizen psychologically does not consider the local weekly a communal possession, as he does the streets or the schools. By contrast, Soviet journalists and their audiences are ever reminded that the mass media belong to the public, precisely as do the schools.

In recent years, as sociological research has documented substantial indifference or boredom on the part of the mass audience with the press, and as greater attention has been focused on the effects of the mass media in society, Soviet journalists accordingly have given some serious thought to the old ideals of popular participation in the press. Thus, one Soviet editor proposed that the concept of the worker-peasant correspondent be consigned to the past. Newspapers, he argued, should develop qualified part-time correspondents, which is saying in effect that the Soviet press should recognize its own professionalism.[8] A rejoinder (in the pages of *Zhurnalist*) quoted a statement by Mikhail Kalinin, the early Bolshevik leader, who had written in 1924: "The relationship between the editorial staff and readers is not, for instance, the relationship between a professor and his students. Rather the newspaper is an enormous parliament or conference in permanent session where the people learn and teach one another."[9] The rejoinder went on to say that comparing Soviet population growth with increase in newspapers, there was less newspaper space available to the reader in the mid-1960's than before World War II. Further, Soviet journalists had virtually ostracized the once glorified *rabselkor*. What was needed, the author concluded, was a "return to letters as the prime source, the wellspring of information, the most reliable means of contact with the masses."[10]

The underlying point in such discussions, whether or not they eventually lead anywhere, is that within their own system and traditions, Soviet journalists are grappling with a problem not unlike that of the major American mass media—the impersonality of the big press and its consequent separation from the mass audience. In the United States, one reaction has been the establishment of an "underground" press, a blossoming of radio programs that provide an outlet for listeners' opinions and proposals for readers' councils. In the Soviet Union, where the recognized alienation of the mass audience is primarily a political rather than an economic issue, the reaction has never-

theless been along the same lines. The sporadic and largely
unpublicized underground press—though the mimeographed or
typewritten literary and information bulletins barely deserve
the name—emerged because the official mass press did not encompass all viewpoints. The political bureaucracy's demands
upon the media to draw the masses into editorial work were,
on the other hand, acknowledgment that an important means
of mass persuasion and social control was falling into disuse.

Letters to the Editor

Letters have occupied a sacrosanct position in the Soviet
press, particularly in the opinion of political leaders. But the
word "letters" here carries too narrow a connotation; in Soviet
usage, what is meant is any sort of communication from the
masses. It therefore may state an opinion, provide a news item,
issue a personal grievance, or point up a flaw in the mechanism of society. From this follow the several functions which
the institution of letters serves. First, and most obviously,
it is an outlet for popular dissatisfaction and frustrations. The
discontented citizen, feeling that he has been treated unjustly
or that public institutions are being mismanaged, is encouraged
to appeal to newspapers. Particularly when the citizen has been
rebuffed elsewhere in the vast Soviet bureaucracy, the newspaper provides an alternative source of satisfaction. It is in a
sense a court of appeals. Second, the flow of letters offers some
measure for political authorities of the popular mood. Third,
letters alert authorities to problems, particularly at the local
level, in the individual factory or farm.

The Soviet fixation on letters goes back to the formative
years, and particularly to the early *rabselkor* movement. The
two were almost identical: the "signal" or news item from
the worker-peasant correspondent was synonymous with a
letter. Thus, in a 1924 Communist Party decree on various
techniques of attracting readers, editors were instructed to
maintain a record of letters and items received from their correspondents and of results achieved.[11] A detailed content plan
for local newspapers in 1922 advised that editorial departments
should include an information bureau to answer readers'
letters.[12] There followed a series of central party declarations,
a major one in 1936, another in 1949, then in 1951, 1954, and
1964, all dealing with the processing of readers' letters.[13] The
dates are not particularly important, but the frequency with

which the political apparatus stressed the significance of letters, which in the whole of mass media management would seem a small item, indicates their high priority.

But in editorial offices, the flood of letters was often enough considered a nuisance. The 1949 decree on letters, making an example out of one newspaper, asserted that "the editorial staff views the work with workers' letters as of little importance, a third rate business. . . ."[14] A 1954 central party statement, again using one newspaper as a whipping boy, decried the "intolerable" bureaucratic attitude toward letters from readers, and charged that the paper had "fenced itself off" from its audience.[15] And in 1967, *Pravda* castigated a particular *oblast*'s newspapers where "editors had permitted themselves to take a scornful attitude toward letters from the working people."[16] A few months later the Communist Party emphasized: "Editorial boards of central and local newspapers and magazines are obligated to systematically publish readers' letters and the decisions taken on complaints. . . ."[17]

What seems evident is a preoccupation by the political bureaucracy with channeling complaints and grievances to collection points where they can be processed, and a considerable lack of enthusiasm among journalists with the task of handling readers' letters.

All Soviet mass media, including broadcasting editorial boards, have letter departments whose staffs are supposed to keep a card file recording letters received, to what organization complaints were forwarded, and what action was taken. The sender then is supposed to be notified of the results. A decree of the Supreme Soviet presidium in April, 1968, provided a detailed procedure for handling citizen complaints, including those received by newspapers and magazines. The government directive not only made a response mandatory, from whatever public agency was involved, but required a resolution of the complaint within fifteen days.[18]

This job, if carried out to the letter, is a formidable task. It is not unlike the "action" columns that have appeared recently in American newspapers and which answer readers' complaints and questions and intervene with the local bureaucracy in behalf of a citizen. On Soviet newspapers, the influx of readers' communications is enormous. In recent years, *Pravda* has received as many as 360,000 letters annually, and *Izvestia* 500,000.[19] At the other extreme, there is the lament of a young journalism school graduate working on a Soviet *raion* news-

paper: "You say five letters a day [in the paper]. If there were
five! In the last few days not a one has been received."[20] But
that complaint seems more the exception. The Soviet press on the
whole attracts a steady stream of communications from readers.

As to the content of grievances and requests, and the handling
of them by the press, a study carried out in Leningrad provides
unusual information. The study focused on two Leningrad newspapers, *Leningradskaya Pravda*, the official *oblast* publication
of the Communist Party and government, and *Vechernii
Leningrad*, the city's evening newspaper. The newspapers had
this record of letters received and published:[21]

Newspaper				Years		
Leningradskaya	1960	1961	1962	1963	1964	1965
Pravda						
Letters received	49,932	50,728	49,623	49,006	43,227	49,127
Letters published	1,568	2,185	2,129	2,875	2,765	3,709
Vechernii						
Leningrad						
Letters received	13,997	12,553	15,398	25,105	30,568	36,290
Letters published	3,444	3,621	4,503	9,830	9,830	12,986

The most conspicuous fact is that Leningrad's major newspaper, *Leningradskaya Pravda*, published less than a tenth
(usually far less) of the letters received, while the less official
Vechernii Leningrad printed about a third. This is not unusual. In 1966, the national newspaper *Sovetskaya Rossiya*
received 69,454 letters and printed 9,376. The central broadcasting studios in Moscow received 439,000, of which 24,000
were read over the air.[22]

From a fourth to a half of all letters received by Leningrad
papers were thank you's for favors or services, a large number
expressing gratitude to doctors. Further, the study revealed
a considerable repetition of themes from year to year. For
example, in the summer and spring of both 1964 and 1965, the
newspapers received many complaints about noise in the city,
inaccurate schedules for trains to the countryside, difficulties
in buying train tickets, and poor organization of vegetable and
fruit sales and supplies. The winter months prompted complaints about public transportation and heating.

Another portion of letters were simple requests for information. How does one find work in Leningrad after discharge
from the armed forces? How is a reservation made at a hotel?

Where can one find a photographer F. Shalyapina? How does one find the address of M. Usambaeva?

Still another category of communications were literary contributions, news items, memoirs, and photographs submitted for publication. In the last six months of 1964, for instance, *Leningradskaya Pravda* rejected 250 poems and 350 other news or literary items.

In addition, a large number of complaints went unpublished. Instead, they were sent to various public agencies which had authority or responsibility to deal with them. In 1964, *Leningradskaya Pravda* forwarded 65 per cent of all communications, or about 28,000, to other organizations for action. *Vechernii Leningrad* sent on about 50 per cent of its letters that same year. The bulk of complaints centered on consumer services— housing, public transport, services, and retail trade. These themes appeared in about half of all letters received by *Leningradskaya Pravda* in 1964, and in about 25 per cent of those sent to *Vechernii Leningrad.*

The published results of the Leningrad study suggest two things. First, a large number of letters from readers deal with rather ordinary, daily life problems, and indeed many are not complaints or grievances, but requests for information or statements of appreciation. The global issues, the philosophical quandaries or political matters (though no letters on these subjects were reported in the Leningrad study) seem to be in a minority position. Second, although the Leningrad newspaper staffs were credited with helping many readers, the study faulted both newspapers for not giving enough attention to grievances and not following up on them.

This is to say that the Soviet procedure for the venting of citizens' complaints through the mass media is far from perfect. But it is not to deny that the press is effective. To mention once more the "action" columns that have appeared recently in American newspapers, it is indisputable that a large metropolitan newspaper can, for example, move government bureaucracy when an individual citizen cannot. The Soviet press is in an equally powerful position, perhaps more powerful than American newspapers. Soviet editors, after all, are usually members of the local Communist Party executive committee; their newspapers are extensions of Soviet political power. The department store manager, the factory director, or the collective farm chairman has good reason to be apprehensive of an investigation by a newspaper and its published criticism.

The Soviet press system is such that, however routine and dreary the job of dealing with citizen grievances may be, Soviet editors are rated the higher for performing well in representing the public. Thus, Soviet newspapers have an incentive for taking a critical stance toward inefficiency and bureaucracy. Newspapers regularly publish exposés of badly managed services and production facilities, and the better ones religiously report the reaction and action of the accused. *Pravda* exposés, some originating with readers' complaints, have resulted in criminal prosecutions, censures, or disciplinary action against Communist Party members or pledges by authorities to remedy a particular deficiency.[23] In other instances, acting on the complaints of readers, newspapers undertake their own investigations. A resident of Kiev was unhappy with the time lost standing in lines to buy food. *Komsomolskaya Pravda* assigned a reporter to check into the matter. From this came an interview with the Ukrainian republic's Minister of Trade, who proposed several ways to eliminate lines (more self-service stores, for example).[24] *Krokodil* came across some letters complaining of inadequate social centers in villages of the Byelorussian republic. An article generated immediate action by the republic Komsomol organization to revive flagging village clubs and social life.[25]

As the investigator and critic of social institutions, the Soviet mass media are by no means playacting. The satirists, essayists, and commentators do not direct their fire at the center of the Soviet system, the political hierarchy. That is to say, the corporation house organ does not criticize the board of directors. However, the performance of lower echelon Communist Party members, of government bureaucrats, industrial and farm management is under constant surveillance by the press, and the citizenry is encouraged to take an active part in the continuous checking.

That the Soviet press often enough does its job well in this sphere is attested by attempts on the part of bureaucrats to suppress criticism in the press, or by the protective silence with which press criticism is often greeted. For example, a local newspaper in the Kharkov *oblast* published seven articles within two years on mismanagement of a maintenance and construction organization. The author, a Communist Party member, eventually became the target of the local party bureau until higher authority intervened.[26] The studied indifference to criticism of public institutions was the subject of a Communist Party decree in September, 1962. It was prompted by such facts as these: *Trud,* the national labor newspaper, published 218 articles in the first half of 1962 criticizing various state enterprises and obtained responses from only 129; *Gudok,* another national newspaper, met dead silence with all of 74 critical articles.[27]

The situation remains essentially the same today, which is not surprising. The inclination of businessmen and civil servants everywhere, whether in capitalist or socialist societies, is to avoid unfavorable publicity. The Soviet press is especially propelled by an obligation to expose waste and corruption in financial and economic affairs, and to reveal instances of bureaucracy riding roughshod over citizens. Obviously there are gross exceptions. Privileged groups—the military, the higher echelons of politicians, the security police—are immune by and large from press criticism. No letters to the editor in Soviet newspapers wonder why the defense budget is as high as it is, or why political leaders enjoy benefits that the rank and file do not, or by what right the KGB arrests demonstrators.[28]

It may be deceptive to generalize about the Soviet mass media as outlets for the Soviet citizenry. But perhaps it is not too far off to compare the Soviet press and citizens' complaints with the company employee suggestion box. Management may receive some audacious and pungent criticism of company operations and personnel and a private reading of these communications is useful in assessing morale. Quiet action can be taken to salve the worst or more frequent grievances. The ones that finally reach the pages of the company newspaper or that receive the awards are, however, the ones with which management agrees or on which it is prepared to act. Such a system probably gives most employees a sense that they have some channel to management and some voice in their company. But it is not by any means a system allowing for unrestricted critiques of the company. Nor are the Soviet mass media, attentive as they are to citizens' complaints and needs, an unregulated channel of public opinion.

Is Anyone There?

From the birth of Soviet power, the mass media have been occupied generally with shaping public opinion. This of course, means acknowledgment by the political bureaucracy that public opinion not only exists but constitutes a force in society to be dealt with. Yet opinion has proved difficult to shape.

The Soviet citizen does not think, feel, and react wholly in accord with the mass media. One reason, of course, is that the press, as we know, is not all powerful in determining public opinion. Further, mass media in the Soviet Union were too often misused.

As a generalization, what happened was that the Soviet press, being managed by a centralized political group, tended toward satisfying the political management rather than the mass audience. Because during Stalin's years very little attention was paid to public opinion, a sort of intellectual incest took place. Editors structured content according to what the political leadership considered the most effective form in propagandizing national goals and thought. The political leadership concurred in what was disseminated; but no one bothered to discover whether the message was reaching the audience. As a consequence, the managed press engendered indifference, disbelief, and cynicism among its audience.

It is ironic perhaps that the effects of the mass media should have gone so long unattended. For, beginning with Lenin's Bolsheviks and continuing throughout Soviet history, the importance of the press in forming mass attitudes has always been recognized. Lenin's discussion of the press as organizer, agitator, and propagandist is one instance. Yet, unlike American advertisers attempting to merchandise products, the Soviet political bureaucracy devoted amazingly little attention to the effectiveness of its political messages.

The rediscovery of public opinion as a proper subject of study was one of many consequences of Khrushchev's denunciation of Stalin in 1956. Hesitantly and carefully after that date, Soviet scholars encouraged—mostly in obscure academic journals—the revival of sociology and sociological research in a society that had seen both stagnate during Stalin's regime. The immediate obstacle was the Communist Party apparatus. To the bureaucratic mind steeped in Marxism-Leninism, exploration of the human and institutional structure of society was an immediately perceived danger. Sociological research focused on what was, rather than what should be. Sociology was therefore proposed by Soviet scholars as a helpmate of social management. By the 1960's, sociology had moved to the point where field studies (known euphemistically as "concrete sociological research") were being conducted on such topics as labor mobility, divorce, education, crime, and the mass media.[29]

As various Soviet researches touched on the press, there were three factors to be considered. What place did public opinion occupy in society? How effectively were the mass media reaching their audiences? And, finally, what influence were the mass media having on popular attitudes?

The first of these—the anatomy of public opinion—no less than the others was a moribund subject under Stalin. Indeed, there was a public opinion, but artificially created. Stalin's concept of the press as a "transmission belt" essentially defined a oneway system of communications. So far as public opinion appeared in the mass media, it was by and large a mirror image of established political attitudes. The mass media were not alone. Other means by which public opinion is ordinarily expressed—civic organizations, lobbies, demonstrations, petitions, and political factions—also were carefully managed in the Soviet Union to prevent public expression of attitudes contradictory to official policies.

Public opinion in the sense of varied ideas openly contending was therefore submerged during the Stalin years. Yet there was an awareness, even in prerevolutionary days among the Bolsheviks, that opinion formation was a significant function of political activity, and moreover that to influence opinion required an analytic approach. Thus, by the 1920's, when the Soviet press structure was being developed, newspapers were arrayed to reach particular segments of the mass audience— the workers, peasants, Communist Party members, youth, intelligentsia, and the military. While this was a natural structuring of the press, it also recognized a diversity of attitudes depending on people's positions in society: that is, one could not write for the worker as for the peasant.

We may touch briefly on one other characteristic of Soviet political management—oral agitation. The corps of Soviet professional propagandists and agitators has been one means by which, in addition to the mass media, popular support has been generated for national policies. Especially in the years immediately after the Bolshevik Revolution, when illiteracy still was widespread, the Soviet political leadership put great stock in face-to-face political communications. Alex Inkeles has written: "The conception of the ideal agitator that emerged in this period [the 1920's] was that of the ordinary Communist, an activist and a man of deep personal convictions, who by means of direct contact with the populace in the course of his everyday affairs, and by means of his own shining example, brought the masses around to the side of the Bolsheviks."[30]

The professional agitator remains a permanent fixture in Soviet mass persuasion campaigns—for efficient harvesting, early completion of production plans, increase in labor productivity, reduction in crime rates, and the like. Since Khrushchev's fall from power, the agitator corps has been supplemented by *politinformers*, who are somewhat like advanced propagandists.[31]

The significance of person-to-person political communications in the Soviet Union is that the system operates according to what is known in American opinion research as the "two step flow of communication." In this design, the mass media inform and educate opinion leaders, who then relay information to a wider audience.[32] Whether by design or intuition—the latter seems more the case—Soviet political leaders have institutionalized this rather sophisticated form of influencing public opinion. They have not been wholly successful, but they have revealed a sensitivity to the shape and flow of public opinion.

In recent years, primarily in the 1960's, more attention has been given in the Soviet Union to the process by which popular attitudes are formed and changed. Following from this, Soviet researchers have inveighed against the "average" reader or television viewer. They have argued that public opinion is a many-faceted object. Levels of education, career patterns, and differences of generations all determine how a given person or group of persons will react to information and how they receive the mass media. One Soviet researcher, working in the Academy of Social Sciences in Moscow, emphasized in a discussion of the mass media's formation of attitudes:

> Of course, the reader is amenable, inquisitive and literate, but he simply does not exist in nature by dint of the abstract modeling of a standard "average" reader. The mass reader varies, by age, by experience, by civic maturity and activity, according to his work and other interests. . . .
>
> The reading audience constantly changes its structure. External signs (age, education, skills, etc.) often seem to determine the perception of the written word.[33]

From rediscovery or recall of individuality and variety of public opinion, Soviet essayists in mass communications have gone on to suggest how public opinion is born. One must keep in mind that the concept in the Stalin era was essentially of a gray and malleable mass, to be sculptured by the press (among

other forms of political education). Against this concept, recent Soviet writings on public opinion formation are remarkably
sophisticated, though in many cases elementary by American
standards.

An initial admission is that the publication or airing of information is not equivalent to creation of public opinion. As
proposed by one Moscow University journalism instructor,
there are three stages in opinion formation: (1) The publicizing
of an idea; (2) the filtering of that idea into the "public psychology," where it inspires either approval or rejection, expressed in letters to newspaper editors, at which time the idea
becomes a "material force"; and finally (3) the gauging of public
opinion and the extent to which an idea has "entered the consciousness of the masses, has found allies and has received
support."[34] Along these same lines, another Soviet student
of mass communications has argued that the "press is in
equal measure a product of and a creator of public opinion"
and that public opinion itself "may be looked on as an expression, and one of the most reliable, of the state of the public
consciousness." Moreover, "The influence of economic circumstances, of the development of production relations and
of the practical experience of the masses on the formation
of public opinion is so great that no sort of propaganda or discussion can change it, if it [the propaganda or discussion] does
not relate to existing economic circumstances or to the masses'
practical experience." And, a last point, public opinion may be
considered a system of information in itself that is constantly
interacting with the public consciousness. That is, what may be
called "primary information" is absorbed gradually by people,
depending on individual characteristics, and forms public
opinion. Public opinion then influences the public consciousness,
which in turn yields "primary information," which once more
changes public opinion. Thus, there is a continuous interplay
between what might be called the general public psychology
and the more narrowly focused and expressed public opinion.[35]

These rather abstract and theoretical Soviet discussions
have contributed to an increasingly complex portrayal of
opinion formation. They tend to challenge the simplistic view
that information presented in the Soviet mass media automatically becomes the mass attitude. And they raise questions
about the actual ways by which public opinion is formed. Soviet
students of mass communications seem to be at the point
of saying, as Bernard Berelson did in 1948: "Some kinds of

communication on some kinds of *issues,* brought to the attention
of some kinds of *people* under some kinds of *conditions,* have
some kinds of *effects.*" [36]

Given the level of communications research in other countries, the Soviet inquiry has not advanced far. Given approximately a quarter century of lost time in exploring the effects
of mass media and the formation of public opinion, Soviet
researchers are working earnestly and intensely to move
abreast of developments. Although still confronted with
political obstacles, they are attempting to analyze precisely
how the mass media function in a society. One result has been
a burgeoning—in the Soviet context—of audience research.

The Mass Audience

Possibly the most important event in Soviet mass communications in the 1960's, if not since Stalin's death, has been
the resurrection of audience research. Even the limited and
relatively elementary studies so far have turned the attention
of journalists and politicians to the public. More than the Communist Party directives to editors commanding greater integration of press and people, audience studies seem to have
impressed Soviet mass media managers with the fact that they
have indeed diverged from the interests of the people. But, of
course, the directives primarily stimulated editors and journalists to satisfy political leaders. The readership and viewing
studies have stirred the press corps to ponder the nature of its
vast and varied audience.

Purely Soviet audience research dates back to the 1920's
when some enterprising efforts were made to provide statistical
profiles of reader interests and needs.[37] The first major readership study was undertaken by *Rabochaya Gazeta* in 1925.
From 7,500 questionnaires, the newspaper determined, for
example, that its audience consisted mostly of men, and about
55 per cent factory workers and 27 per cent office employees.
An analysis also yielded a classification of groups, ranging
from the well-informed, inquisitive reader to the barely literate
subscriber to whom a newspaper was an unfamiliar source of
information. A 1929 study by *Rabochaya Moskva,* a Moscow
newspaper with a circulation of 300,000, indicated that the paper
had almost no influence on the little-educated, poorly paid
segment of workers. Another experimental study in 1923 in one
region suggested that a local peasant newspaper was ignored by
a good share of its intended audience.

Amid reports of such findings, there was considerable discussion in specialized Soviet journals on the question of structuring the press to conform to the existing audience, which, it should be recalled, was heavily weighted with illiterate peasants. Moreover, there was some attempt to form models of audience characteristics and information flow. For example, one hypothesis contended that there were "reader dominants" that governed an individual's interests. The dominant interest acted as an incentive to reading, and was the basis on which other, secondary reader interests could be developed.

The point in mentioning these early and, in Soviet history, pathbreaking studies is simply to emphasize that sociological investigation of the press is not exclusively a contemporary phenomenon. Audience research failed to mature in the 1920's for the same reason that experimental literature, art, and architecture did—that is, the Stalin era of traditional, conservative, and repressive policies gripped the nation.

The revival of audience studies accompanied the general reemergence of sociology. Interestingly enough, American listeners of Radio Moscow's foreign broadcasts were the initial objects of research. In 1960, Americans who had at one time or another written to Radio Moscow were sent postcards containing seven questions on program preferences and listening habits.[38] This cautious and modest Soviet attempt at audience study led to an investigation in 1962–63 in the Moscow area of radio listeners.

Studies of the printed press seem to have been undertaken about that same time. A Moscow University School of Journalism project in 1963 focused on newspaper readers in the cities of Novosibirsk and Krasnodar. In the first, 200 workers in a metallurgical plant and, in the second, more than 100 textile plant workers were given 10 questions concerning newspapers and reading habits.[39] Workers were asked what publications they subscribed to, what they liked and did not like in them, whether they used information from the press, how many persons in their families read the newspapers, whether they wrote for the newspaper, their education, and work. The survey showed that technicians and the more educated workers subscribed to three to four newspapers (for example, *Pravda*, *Izvestia*, the local *oblast* paper, and the city evening paper) and two or three magazines. About 15 per cent of subscribers wrote for local newspapers, according to preliminary data.

The results of these early studies were not so important as

the surveys themselves. They were breaking ground again. In subsequent years up to the present, techniques were improved and studies enlarged considerably. Mass media research now is centered at Leningrad and Moscow Universities, and at Novosibirsk where the Siberian branch of the prestigous Academy of Sciences is headquartered. A sociological research laboratory affiliated with Leningrad University and the university's school of journalism have done some work on the mass media.[40] In addition to these, research has been undertaken by newspapers and central broadcasting in Moscow. Occasional small-scale studies have also been made by some of the 40 sociological institutes or laboratories connected with lower level Communist Party organizations.[41]

It should be noted that Soviet mass communications research is only one part of sociological investigation. And it is only one segment of public opinion study, a young and still underdeveloped discipline in the Soviet Union. The best-known practitioner of the latter is the Public Opinion Institute, set up in 1960 by the national youth newspaper *Komsomolskaya Pravda*. Beginning with a 1961 survey of youths' opinions of youth,[42] the institute has conducted more than a dozen additional surveys. Other sociological research centers have also engaged in public opinion polls to collect data. As regards audience research, Soviet studies can be separated into two sections, one dealing with newspapers, the other with radio and television.

The Newspaper Audience

One of the most ambitious newspaper readership studies focused on *Izvestia*. Undertaken in 1966 by sociologists in Novosibirsk, the project was intended to produce profiles of *Izvestia* readers and to measure their reaction to the newspaper.[43] Information was gathered at 211 locales in the Soviet Union by means of 8,000 personal interviews and 150,000 mailed questionnaires, of which 18,000 were returned.

A separate survey was also conducted, in which about 100 economists, journalists, and scientists were asked to estimate public reaction to questions about readership and *Izvestia* news coverage. The acknowledged purpose of this was to show how erroneous human judgments could be when held against electronically computed mass responses to identical questions.

The reported results are interesting for two reasons. First, they reveal what educated and professionally trained Soviet citizens think of the public attitude toward the press, specifically *Izvestia*. Second, they show what opinions a cross section of *Izvestia*'s subscribers—26,000 out of a total circulation of about 7 million—hold.

IZVESTIA READER OPINIONS

Do the papers fully and objectively reflect the following:

Forecasts of public reaction by	Economic problems? (per cent)				Problems of the development of Soviet democracy? (per cent)				Problems of international affairs? (per cent)			
	Yes	Not fully	No	Don't know	Yes	Not fully	No	Don't know	Yes	Not fully	No	Don't know
Sociologists and economists	30	33	17	20	29	29	21	21	44	28	14	4
Journalists	19	26	15	40	34	29	16	21	45	28	13	14
Well-known	30	40	25	5	50	25	15	10	55	30	15	10
Lesser known	20	30	20	30	20	30	20	30	40	40	20	00
Scientists	34	42	18	6	28	38	18	16	51	25	17	7
Computed survey results	44	18	3	7	45	17	3	5	64	17	1	10

SOURCE: *Zhurnalist*, No. 2 (February, 1968), p. 24.

IZVESTIA READER REACTIONS

Forecasts of public reactions by	Can you recall an occasion when you didn't agree with the paper? (per cent)			How carefully do you read editorials? (per cent)		
	Yes	No	Don't recall	Completely	Partially	Don't read them
Sociologists and economists	34	34	32	16	36	48
Journalists	22	39	35	16	32	52
Well-known	5	85	10	25	55	20
Lesser known	30	30	40	15	25	60
Scientists	49	29	22	39	38	23
Computed survey results	11.9	25.5	54.3	30	53.3	9.4

SOURCE: *Zhurnalist,* No. 2 (February, 1968), p. 23

In the first collection of statistics, the small sample of about 100 specialists invested *Izvestia*'s reading public with considerably more negative reaction to the newspaper than seems to exist. Actually, only about 12 per cent of the readership could ever recall disagreeing with what they had seen in the newspaper. And a majority, about 54 per cent, seem not to have much reaction at all when asked if they ever disagreed with the newspaper.

The specialists further anticipated that a high percentage of *Izvestia*'s audience ignored editorial articles or read only parts of them. In fact, the survey showed that nearly 85 per cent of the mass audience read such articles partially or entirely. Similarly, when questions were asked of specialists and *Izvestia*'s other readers about coverage, there were divergencies. The specialists, probably reflecting their own attitudes as much as describing those of the mass audience, tended to be critical. On *Izvestia*'s coverage of economic and political ("Soviet democracy") events, less than a third usually thought the newspaper "fully and objectively" reflected what was the true state of affairs. On international information, about half were of that opinion. However, *Izvestia*'s general reading public on the whole gave higher ratings to the newspaper's thoroughness and objectivity. Thus, about 45 per cent were confident that economic and political events were well covered, and 64 per cent thought the same of international affairs. One must take these figures with great caution, however. In some instances, figures do not add up to 100 per cent (but more or less) and Soviet reports of the *Izvestia* survey do not explain why. But they are useful as broad guides to audience reaction.

The *Izvestia* survey also attempted to rate the popularity of various categories of information. When subscribers were asked to check the types of articles they read regularly, the results were:

Category	Read Regularly (per cent)
Social issues	75
Unusual stories	71
International reviews	69
"In the Family Circle"	66
Satiric, humorous articles	64
Events in Asia, Africa, Latin America	55

Category	Read Occasionally (per cent)
People, the collective, and society	52
Science	49
Sports	47
Meetings with interesting people	47
Events in Communist countries	47
The world of the intellectual	45
Legal questions	44
Literature and art	37
Education	30
Editorials	30
Economics	23
Political articles	18
Local government	17

When asked if they read articles in the following categories "occasionally," the *Izvestia* subscribers responded differently:

Category	Read Occasionally (per cent)
Editorials	53
Local government	52
Economics	52
Political articles	49
Literature and art	48
Events in Communist countries	47

The first set of responses is the more significant, of course. Two general categories of information seem to attract *Izvestia* readers: light, humorous articles and international news. The articles in which substantial, and often complicated, issues are presented seem to attract little popular following. Thus, only 23 per cent of *Izvestia*'s subscribers regularly read articles on economics, although such reports and essays contain a good deal of information essential both to the Soviet political bureaucracy and to the rank and file in managing an industrial state. Editorials and political articles, which propagate Soviet government and Communist Party policies, also get little attention. Reports on local government are scarcely read at all.

A possible explanation is that articles in the latter categories tend to be repetitive and often shallow. A new policy of importance not only appears in newspapers, but is announced by radio and television, and then discussed at factories and offices. Then it may be the subject of successive articles. Further, editorials and political and economic articles often deal with weighty theoretical problems of concern mostly to specialists. Thus, it does not take much reading of such articles by the citizenry to extract what is needed in dealing with one's daily personal affairs.

By comparsion, articles concerned with people confronted with ordinary problems draw the interest of many of *Izvestia*'s readers. These are the feature articles, the human interest stories, and the bizarre occurrences that also rate high among American newspaper readers. The demonstrably strong attraction of *Izvestia* subscribers to international news arises conceivably from two factors: (1) a growing curiosity after so many years of Stalinist isolation (and with rising educational levels) about the outside world; (2) the stimulus of foreign radio broadcasts. But these can only be suppositions.

The *Izvestia* study did, however, suggest several other influences on readership. As a rule, *Izvestia* readers subscribe additionally to three or more newspapers and to three magazines. A frequent combination of newspapers is *Izvestia*, *Pravda*, a sports or trade union newspaper, and the local newspaper. Further, about 75 per cent of *Izvestia*'s subscribers have radios and/or television sets; 80 per cent "learned the news" from radio before reading it in *Izvestia*, and 40 per cent from television. Along with this, the "average" *Izvestia* subscriber reads only about half the newspaper, and a small 10 per cent spend more than an hour with the newspaper daily. Such statistics led researchers to the conclusion that *Izvestia* is faced with considerable competition from other media and that *Izvestia* editors cannot assume that they are the sole educators of their newspaper's subscribers.

As to the readers themselves, the study of *Izvestia* revealed that 44 per cent have some higher education or completed higher education. Nearly 30 per cent have a least 10 years of schooling. That is, *Izvestia* subscribers tend to be the better educated segments of the Soviet population. The largest group of *Izvestia* readers—about one third—are employed in industry, construction, transport, and communications. By contrast, only about 5 per cent are engaged in agriculture. The bulk of *Izvestia*

A typical front page of *Izvestia*, leading official newspaper of the Soviet government.

readers are, not surprisingly, in the twenty-five to fifty-five age group. Of all subscribers, about 15 per cent are between twenty-five and thirty years old; 27 per cent from thirty-one to forty, and about 27 per cent from forty-one to fifty-five.

For parallel data and, in some instances results supporting the *Izvestia* study of readership, we should deal in more detail with a second Soviet research project. This one concerned the national labor newspaper, *Trud*, with a circulation of 3 million. The results of the *Trud* study, conducted by sociologists of the Academy of Sciences Siberian division in Novosibirsk among an undisclosed number of subscribers, were reported in mid-1968.[44] The findings, much like those of the *Izvestia* audience survey, emphasized the popularity of features, human interest stories, and international affairs. More than 50 per cent of *Trud*'s subscribers regularly read newspaper accounts dealing with problems of everyday life. From 30 to 50 per cent regularly read foreign affairs news, articles on science and technology, on literature and art, and on trade union affairs. Less than 30 per cent regularly read editorial statements, or articles dealing with industrial products and official politics.

Ranking by Column Inches	Readers' Ranking
TASS official news	Satiric, humorous articles
Sports	Everyday affairs, social issues
Entertainment	Legal problems
Industrial problems	Sports
TASS foreign news	Articles of a critical nature
Articles on leading worker collectives	News of capitalist countries
Literature and art	Science and technology
Editorials	Medicine
Political articles	Trade union news
Trade union news	Articles about advanced production techniques and "socialist competition"

As a test of *Trud*'s editorial judgments, researchers categorized information appearing in the newspaper for the first four months of 1967, ranking themes and types of news by column inches. Then they ranked articles or information categories according to popularity. The results showed interesting differences:

Thus, when readers were in effect asked to edit *Trud*, they chose different types and categories of news, and ranked them differently than *Trud*'s editors in terms of interest and importance. TASS official dispatches—formal announcements and proclamations, for example—rank first according to *Trud*'s editors (who are obligated to publish long official decrees). But *Trud*'s readers would prefer light, entertaining articles. Likewise, editorials and political articles, which are given considerable space in *Trud*, would get much less if readers were editing the newspaper. As far as sports, trade union, and foreign affairs news are concerned, however, *Trud*'s editors and readers are reasonably close in their judgments.

Trud's readers, like those of *Izvestia*, also turn to other sources for their news. The average *Trud* reader subscribes to more than three newspapers (*Pravda*, *Izvestia*, *Komsomolskaya Pravda*, in addition to *Trud*, are the most common) and two out of three take the local newspaper. Most also subscribe to three magazines. On the average, the *Trud* subscriber spends 40 minutes on the newspaper, although tests showed that about 1 hour 40 minutes was required to read the whole newspaper. What distracts readers? Cards, dominoes, studies, civic affairs, sports, and hobbies, according to study of *Trud* readers' leisure time use.

A third of *Trud*'s readers are women (who make up about half of the Soviet labor force), and they tend to be more interested in literature and art, and articles on medicine and health. Men turn to sports, international affairs, science and technology, and legal matters. The average age of *Trud*'s readers is thirty-nine, and the "most typical" ages are between thirty-one and forty. The educational level of *Trud*'s subscribers was said to be higher than the national average for factory and office workers, and a third was said to be active in civic affairs.

These two major newspaper audience studies—on *Trud* and *Izvestia*—have been complemented by less ambitious surveys. Reported results of these help, in sum, to fill in a still far from complete profile of the Soviet mass audience. One study is of particular interest because it was carried out in an agricultural town (Kamyshlov, population less than 50,000) and seems to reflect rural readership habits. Undertaken by the Sverdlovsk *oblast* Communist Party organization in cooperation with the Urals branch of the Academy of Sciences, the study drew on 1,733 questionnaires.[45]

Results showed that only 13.3 per cent of those questioned read the local newspaper's section on international affairs (though it is not clear whether "read" meant partial or com-

plete readership). Other categories of information and readership reported were these: daily life and problems, 10 per cent;
local news, 9.3 per cent; humor and satire, 8.4 per cent; features
on interesting people, 8.2 per cent; moral issues, 7.3 per cent;
practical advice and counsel, 7.1 per cent; sports, 6.9 per cent;
literature and art, 6.9 per cent; Communist Party affairs, 4.5
per cent; economic information, 3 per cent; and rural life,
2.7 per cent. Along with this, about three fourths of readers
questioned answered a query on whether their opinions agreed
with those expressed in the newspaper; about 26 per cent
reported disagreement.

The survey results are striking for the apparent low readership of most of the local newspaper's content. They also generally parallel the *Trud* and *Izvestia* studies in that the solid
political and economic information and propaganda rank
lowest in reader interest. Most popular among readers in this
survey were articles on foreign affairs, local and personal news,
and humor.

The question of the influence of economic information on
readers produced a special study in 1965 or so in Siberian industrial regions. Essays and discussions of economics receive
high priority in the Soviet press. Particularly since the adoption in 1965 of economic reforms encouraging decentralized
management and personal incentive, the Soviet mass media
have poured out vast amounts of educational and propagan-
distic information to aid industrial reorganization. A chief problem
has been the reorientation of workers, and this problem motivated the study of four newspapers' effectiveness in reaching
their audiences with economic information.[46] The research
was done by the Communist Party's Academy of Social Sciences
journalism department and the Union of Journalists. An undisclosed number of interviews supplemented information from
7,000 questionnaires. Responses were divided into four categories—workers doing skilled mental labor, unskilled mental
labor, skilled physical labor, and unskilled physical labor.

The chief questions were whether information on economics
helped daily work. The most important, if not predictable, finding was that unskilled manual workers scarcely were interested
in economics. Thus, of one group of 547 unskilled laborers,
85 per cent said such economics information was of no help to
them, while only about 70 per cent of workers in the other three
categories answered negatively. As a check, 350 workers in a
factory requiring developed skills were asked the question about

usefulness of economics material. About 80 per cent said it was helpful in their work. Of 350 workers in a plant where manual labor was the norm, about 25 per cent agreed. The obvious conclusion was that the newspapers under study were not reaching a considerable segment of their reading audiences with information considered to be of some importance. Other results indicated that not only did readership vary by education and training, but also by career. Communist Party officials complained that *Sovetskaya Sibir*, the major newspaper in the Siberian industrial city of Novosibirsk (containing 1.3 million people in 1967), did not publish sufficient detailed information about party affairs. State and collective farm chairmen criticized the inadequate analysis of agricultural problems.

A similar misjudgment by editors of the effectiveness and popularity of their newspaper was revealed in a study of a youth newspaper, *Leninskaya Smena*, in the city of Gorky.[47] A majority of readers—65 per cent—were fifteen- to twenty-one-year-old high school students, workers, or farmers. They, too, tended to shun the ponderous economics material. A running feature, "Comrade of the Economy," was read by hardly anyone, although more specific, concrete information attracted readers. Noticeably popular was another feature—"Teen-agers—Society—and You"—which was read by 47 per cent of *Leninskaya Smena*'s readers, and half of those from fifteen to eighteen, although the feature was chiefly intended to help adults in rearing their teen-agers. On the basis of the readership survey, conducted in 1966, editors introduced new features. One called "Opponent" discussed student life, and another, "Footlights," was for those interested in the arts. Presumably because of these innovations, circulation increased from 55,000 to 80,000 within a year.

Reader reaction to a second youth newspaper, *Smena* (circulation 166,000), was studied in Leningrad. Results indicated that although 40 to 60 per cent of the paper's space was devoted to social-esthetic material, young readers were interested in international affairs, science and technology, literature and art, sports, and social-esthetic questions—in that order.[48] However, the reader preferences seem to be closely related to the characteristics of a newspaper's audience. Precisely the same readership questionnaire distributed among subscribers to 10 Leningrad *raion* newspapers produced different results. These readers, largely adults, showed little interest in their newspapers' information on science, technology, or culture. One explanation put forward was that the papers "write about these subjects infrequently and incompetently." When asked what reaction they most often experienced after reading their *raion* newspaper, 53 per cent of subscribers said "satisfaction" or "pleasure"; 6 per cent said "disappointment"; 6 per cent "in-

Major newspapers are posted on outdoor boards throughout the Soviet Union as one means to increase their exposure to a mass audience. This display in the central Asian city of Tashkent includes all major republic daily newspapers.

difference"; and 24 per cent had no thought one way or the other.[49]

Several things may be said in summary about these studies of Soviet newspaper audiences. First, the results must be accepted with some reservations. Survey techniques are not sufficiently described in Soviet sources that we may be sure of the accuracy or representativeness of the findings. The *Izvestia* and *Trud* studies seem to have been conducted according to contemporary methods of polling. Yet there is no mention of a margin of error in results. The other surveys described here are even less explicit as to techniques, size of sample (in some cases), or indeed as to what questions were asked.

Despite these reasons for caution, we may look on the surveys as rough guides to the success of Soviet newspapers in reaching their audiences. What generally has been found is a divergence of interests. Soviet editors and journalists are publishing much material on politics and economics that is ignored by their readers. If editors composed their newspapers according to their readers' wants, there would be considerably more information on international affairs. Moreover, content would be lighter, more entertaining, and concerned with down-to-earth human problems and issues.

But care is necessary here. The more educated Soviet readers want and will absorb, it seems, the more complex, analytical material, particularly if their work requires them to have certain information. The less educated reader prefers material demanding little intellectual effort. Finally, it should be noted that none of the readership studies deals with one of the prime issues—that is, the matter of content management and censorship. The surveys have been undertaken more to discover how existing types of information are received by readers than whether they desire information currently restricted from the printed media. Soviet studies are mostly designed to aid in improving, not revolutionizing content. Despite this, however, sociological research is turning editors' and journalists' attention to the mass reading audience, and effecting some changes in editing practices.

Radio and Television Audiences

A similar process is occurring in the electronic communications field. There, too, studies are probing the tastes and reactions of audiences. Such research has had to begin at the most elementary level, specifically with listening and viewing-time habits of audiences. The earliest reported research of this type was done in the spring of 1963 by the state Committee for Radio Broadcasting and Television and the Moscow University School of Journalism.[50] Their main objective was to establish the effect of rapidly growing television viewing on radio listenership. For this purpose, 2,722 Moscovites, 204 Leningraders, and 62 persons from two small towns were interviewed—almost entirely an urban sample. The most important result, it seems, was the fact that from 7 to 9 P.M., about 43 per cent of the sample listened to the radio, the largest percentage during the day.

RADIO LISTENERSHIP IN LENINGRAD AND MOSCOW

Listen to Radio Broadcasts	Number	Percentage of Total
From 6 to 9 A.M.	1,028	34.4
From 9 to noon	589	19.7
From noon to 5 P.M.	371	12.4
From 5 to 7 P.M.	971	32.5
From 7 to 9 P.M.	1,275	42.7
From 9 P.M. to midnight	1,026	34.3
From midnight to 2 A.M.	195	6.5

SOURCE: Vestnik Moskovskogo universiteta, Seriya XI, Zhurnalistika, No. 1, 1966, p. 34.

From these results it was asserted that television had some influence on radio listenership, though the latter remained substantial. But it also was discovered that the radio audience varies by group depending on time of day. While this is hardly unexpected, it was new to Soviet researchers. Housewives and retired persons made up a consistently high percentage of radio listeners. In morning hours and from 5 P.M. to 9 P.M., workers, office employees, engineers and technicians, and students comprised fairly large segments of the audience. But from noon to 5 P.M., very few of these four groups listened to their radios.

Studies of this sort have led to more sophisticated surveys of radio and television audiences. One of the most significant attempted to assess popular reaction in 1967 to foreign news and information, purportedly the first such undertaking in the Soviet Union.[51] Moreover, the sample of 5,232 was drawn

COMPOSITION OF LISTENERS OF CENTRAL RADIO BROADCASTS
(PER 100 PERSONS POLLED IN EACH SOCIAL GROUP)

Listen to Radio Broadcasts	Workers	Engineers-Technicians	Workers	Housewives, Pensioners	Students
From 6 to 9 A.M.	25	47	45	21	29
From 9 A.M. to noon	26	9	16	43	19
From noon to 5 P.M.	11	7	7	38	11
From 5 to 7 P.M.	32	24	27	37	35
From 7 to 9 P.M.	40	47	46	40	44
From 9 P.M. to midnight	27	38	42	31	44
From midnight to 2 A.M.	6	4	9	7	11

SOURCE: *Vestnik Moskovskogo universiteta, Seriya XI, Zhurnalistika,* No. 1, 1966, p. 35.

from both rural and urban regions, at 30 different points, according to a statistical model of the Soviet population. The study thus was offered as a national survey.

An initial inquiry was into daily sources of information on international policies. Results indicated that the printed press was the prime source, followed by radio, then television, and finally lectures by political propagandists. Researchers then

SOURCES OF FOREIGN INFORMATION
(IN PERCENTAGES) *

Group	Press	Radio	Television	Lectures
Workers	64.9	56.2	44.1	14.8
Engineers-technicians	78.7	50.0	35.7	14.7
Collective farmers	63.7	52.0	38.0	30.6
Students	70.4	34.7	30.2	14.0
Communist Party and government officials	82.5	50.0	45.0	31.3

SOURCE: *Zhurnalist,* No. 8 (August, 1968), p. 61.

*Percentages across add up to more than 100 because more than one category was checked by respondents.

turned to audience tastes in radio and television foreign affairs information. A consistently large percentage of the sample audience—from nearly 50 per cent of collective farmers to 81 per cent of Communist Party and government officials—rated timeliness as the most important criterion influencing their interest in international news. At the same time, from about 25 to 40 per cent of the audience groups indicated that Soviet radio and television were doing a competent job in this regard. To arrive at these conclusions, Soviet researchers queried people on their preferences in international news among three categories—(1) timely, immediate information; (2) factual news dispatches (not necessarily timely); and (3) commentary and interpretation. Then they rated listenership and viewing of radio and TV programs that corresponded to these three categories. By ranging the two sets of figures side by side, researchers came up with statistical indications of audience

INTERNATIONAL INFORMATION:
PREFERENCE OF RADIO/TELEVISION AUDIENCE
(in percentages)*

Groups	Factual Dispatches		Interpretation and Commentary		Timely Information	
	Preference	"Satisfied" with program	Preference	"Satisfied" with program	Preference	"Satisfied" with program
Workers	49	29	28.9	28.1	56.6	25.2
Engineers-technicians	62.9	18	40.2	18.0	72.4	23.4
Collective farmers	40.0	60.2	27.5	46.6	49.3	52.7
Students	53.8	21.6	38.7	22.1	74.9	27.8
Communist Party and government officials	61.3	28.7	55.0	36.2	81.2	40.0

SOURCE: *Zhurnalist*, No. 8 (August, 1968), p. 62.

*Percentages do not add up to 100 because respondents checked more than one category.

preferences, compared with actual listening/viewing. A curious contradiction occurs in the statistics for collective farmers. Their preferences for any kind of international news are statistically lower than any other group; but they also tend to be more satisfied with existing foreign news programs than all other groups. Apparently these results are related to educational levels, which are relatively low in Soviet rural areas. By contrast, Communist Party and government officials show more interest in international news, but are less satisfied with foreign news broadcasts. Students and engineers-technicians, who also would be more knowledgeable and better educated than collective farmers, exhibit somewhat the same pattern.

Perhaps the most significant conclusions to be drawn from the statistics (which must be taken as only approximations of Soviet audience tastes) are an apparent dislike for commentary and a general dissatisfaction with foreign news coverage. Commentary and interpretation in Soviet journalism are the chief vehicles of the political leadership's point of view. Such radio and TV programs rate low among the mass audience, with the exception of Communist Party and government officials. Understandably, these men have a vested interest in keeping abreast of official interpretations of world events. But neither they nor most other audience groups are particularly content with radio-TV programs on international developments. This leads to the conclusion that the Soviet broadcasters' presentation of the world lacks some credibility among their audience.

The conclusion gains further support from results of a detailed survey of Leningrad's TV audience. This study, made in the spring of 1967, drew on a selected sample of 1,916 persons eighteen years and older, and equally divided between men and women. In depth and scope, the investigation was the most advanced of any in the Soviet Union for television.

Respondents were predominantly skilled and/or experienced factory and office workers, with grade school and often some vocational school education. All but 200 read two or more newspapers (*Pravda, Izvestia*, and the local Leningrad newspapers—*Leningradskaya Pravda, Vechernii Leningrad*, and *Smena*—being the favorites). Nearly 65 per cent listened to the radio daily, and 30 per cent "from time to time."[52] That is, the sample was a reasonably well-educated, informed group representing Leningrad's total population of about 3 million.

Of persons interviewed for the study, 1,646 had television sets in their homes, and half of these had purchased sets in

Press Agency Novosti

A Moscow family watching television in the living room of their apartment.

1962 or earlier. Of the total of 1,916 respondents, nearly 28 per cent watched television daily, 34 per cent three or four days a week, and the remainder two days or less. On weekdays, the majority—75 per cent—watched television for 1 to 3 hours, while on Saturdays and Sundays, from 55 to 60 per cent looked at television 2 to 3 hours. On a weekly basis, Leningrad TV viewers were divided into four groups: very moderate viewing (less than 3 hours a week)—31 per cent; moderate (3 to 10 hours)—37 per cent; enthusiastic (10 to 15 hours)—16 per cent; and very enthusiastic (15 to 27 hours)—16 per cent. Analyzing information on the education of these groups, researchers documented that as a person's education increased, hours spent watching television declined. Of the "very moderate" viewers, for example, 30 per cent had gone beyond secondary school. Of the "very enthusiastic" viewers, only 9 per cent had more than a secondary education.

Program preferences among Leningrad viewers ran especially to entertainment and sports. In conformity with other studies of the mass media, including the printed press, political mate-

rial ranked among the least popular with the Leningrad TV
audience. Among Leningrad TV offerings, serious music and
opera and education programs also received low audience ratings.

PROGRAM RATINGS OF LENINGRAD TV AUDIENCES
Type of Program

Type of Program	Satisfying (per cent)	Don't evoke criticism or praise (per cent)	Unsatisfying (per cent)	Hard to say, rarely see them (per cent)
Reporting of sports events	84.0	5.3	1.2	9.5
KVN and like programs*	81.2	8.6	2.4	7.8
Concerts and variety shows	70.9	19.5	1.8	7.8
Films	66.5	22.5	4.3	6.7
Television spectaculars	61.1	17.5	1.9	19.5
"Horizon" and other programs for youth	58.1	18.0	3.9	19.8
Theatrical and literary programs	45.0	24.0	4.0	27.0
News and current events	38.0	20.0	27.0	18.0
On-the-spot reporting	36.2	24.5	6.7	32.6
Programs on political themes	16.4	21.0	8.6	54.0
Educational shows	16.0	16.0	7.0	61.0
Serious music and opera	15.0	14.0	25.0	47.0

SOURCE: *Zhurnalist*, No. 12 (December, 1967), p. 44.

*KVN is the Russian abbreviation for "Club of Cheer and Wit," the panel quiz
show.

As a check on audience reaction, a second method of rating
popularity was used in the Leningrad study. Respondents were
asked whether they watched particular programs or types of
programs "regularly," "occasionally," or not at all. Regular
viewing scored 2 points; "occasional," 1 point; and "don't
watch," no points. From calculations using weighted results,
an index of popularity for each of 31 programs or types of
programs was produced.

POPULARITY OF LENINGRAD TV PROGRAMS

Highest popularity (watched regularly by 50–70% of viewers)

Programs	Index of popularity
Films	1,730
KVN	1,665
Serial films	1,600
"The Blue Flame"	1,565
Variety shows	1,540

High popularity (30–50% regular viewing)

Spectaculars	1,415
Concerts by master artists	1,365
Theatrical presentations	1,360
Documentary films	1,300
Popular science films	1,285

Average popularity (15–30% regular viewing)

Satirical shows	1,275
Stories of heroism and the like	1,235
Theatrical encounters	1,210
Shows on literary and artistic masters	1,160
Amateur concerts	1,135
Informational shows	1,105
Telenews from Central Television	1,100
Educational shows	1,080
News bulletins	1,075
The world today	1,065
Social-political shows	982
Shows on the themes of social duty, morals, and the family	962
Conversations about the theater	926

Low Popularity (2–15% regular viewing)

News from the Leningrad TV studio	920
Literary theater	883
Interview-67	857
Nevskii Torch	775
Shows on the history of the government	720
Pages of Poetry	700
Shows on economic themes	394
Shows on school programs	162

SOURCE: *Zhurnalist*, No. 12 (December, 1967), p. 44.

By this assessment, too, it seems apparent that Leningrad viewers consider television chiefly a source of entertainment. The weightier, the more serious and "educational" the program, the lower its index of popularity. When asked directly, 70 per cent of the Leningrad audience sample said TV was a source of amusement and relaxation; 60 per cent said it also was a source of general information; and 46 per cent looked on TV as a "means of expanding knowledge and cultural horizons."

To American communicators, to say TV is primarily an entertainment medium as far as the mass audience is concerned is to say the obvious. And perhaps Soviet broadcasters were aware instinctively that this was true, but the suspicion was not statistically proved until the advent of audience surveys.

It is worth quoting segments of the summary report of the Leningrad study since it is based on the complete survey results:

Television spectaculars are most popular with the extreme age groups and among people with an education from the 4th to the 9th grades. Viewers with a higher education gave these shows the lowest rating.

Educational shows were rated equally well by all age groups up to fifty years old. They were most popular with viewers over fifty years old, and also among viewers with an education up to the 5th grade. They found their least popularity among viewers with a 5th or 6th grade education.

Serious music and opera were rated lowest by viewers younger than eighteen, and the highest by viewers over fifty. The rating increases with the amount of education.

News and current events. Interest in these shows grows with age. Rating falls with the increase in education, but the least satisfaction is noted in the group with an education up to the 5th grade.

On-the-spot reporting is most popular among viewers up to eighteen years old. It is rated lowest by viewers from twenty-six to thirty years. The evaluation falls as the amount of education increases.

Films and television films were most popular with viewers up to twenty-five years old, and also those over fifty. Ratings fall as amount of education increases.

Programs on the history of the government were least popular among the youngest viewers. They were most popular among viewers from fifty to fifty-nine years old. The evaluation falls as the amount of education increases.

Concerts and variety shows were rated highest by youth up to eighteen years old.

Shows on socio-political themes evoke the least satisfaction from youth up to eighteen years old. The rating falls with increase in education.

KVN and like shows were most popular among viewers with a 7th to 9th grade education. The rating falls with increased age.

Theatrical and literary shows were most popular among viewers with an education up to the 5th grade and among the extreme age groups.

"Horizon" and other programs for youth—ratings fall with an increase in education; however, it is highest for viewers with a 7th to 9th grade education. They are most popular among viewers up to twenty-five years old.

General comments—The most favorable attitude toward television is found in the groups of viewers with 5th to 6th and 7th to 9th grade educations. Those people with an education up to the 5th grade tend to be "harder" in their rating of socio-political broadcasts and TV information shows. They are more satisfied than the other groups with programs which give an understanding of trends (educational programs on literature and art). They rate movies highest of all.

The most critical attitude toward television is found among viewers with an education higher than average.

Age indicators—There is noticeable "enthusiasm" on the part of youth up to eighteen years old in their ratings of amusement shows and a negativism in their ratings of programs with a serious intellectual content. The most critical attitude to the majority of shows is found in the age group from twenty-six to thirty years. The elderly significantly prefer educational shows, news, and programs on socio-political and historical-revolutionary themes.[53]

Forming Opinions

Various Soviet studies of both printed and electronic media produced patterns in many ways similar to those reported by Alex Inkeles and Raymond Bauer from interviews conducted in western Europe shortly after World War II with displaced Soviet citizens. The communications behavior Inkeles and Bauer described, referring chiefly to prewar years, indicated that Soviet citizens preferred the printed press as a source of information to radio.[54] In addition, use of the printed press declined as educational levels dropped,[55] which is generally what Soviet research has demonstrated.

Further, Inkeles and Bauer reported substantial reliance on word-of-mouth information to supplement the official mass media. This channel of information ranked second to the printed press among more educated groups (intellectuals and white-collar employees, for example) and first with the least educated (collective farmers).[56] Soviet published research has not dealt with this matter at all, though Soviet journalists, politicians, and researchers should be as aware of the phenomenon as are foreign students of Soviet society. Another topic avoided by Soviet sociologists, but investigated by Inkeles and Bauer, is the correlation between exposure to and use of the mass media and political alienation. Allowing that disaffected Soviet citizens would tend to be anti-Soviet, they reported a tendency for the more anti-Soviet person to be less exposed to the mass media. By contrast, the greater a person's participation in Soviet society, and the less his hostility toward the government, the greater the exposure.[57]

If we can apply this pattern to the present, taking into account recent Soviet research on the mass media, we may suppose that collective farmers remain the most disaffected group in Soviet society. In the study on foreign news, for example, collective farmers were the most infrequent users of radio or television, whereas skilled workers and political officials were relatively avid radio listeners and TV viewers.[58] It also seems true today, as several decades ago, that the more career-oriented Soviet citizens make greater use of the mass media than those who have little or no ambition to advance in Soviet society. However, we cannot compare or contrast the Inkeles and Bauer results too extensively with Soviet research. The studies proceeded along different lines, seeking different answers.

Soviet research has, however, yielded some detail on audience reaction to categories of information. Thus, as we have seen, the political and economic material in the mass media rate consistently low with the mass audience, whereas information on social issues generally enjoys high popularity. That is, the Soviet audience seems to be selective in what it accepts and wants from the mass media.

Perhaps the core question is what effect do Soviet mass media have on the attitudes and opinions of the Soviet population? Obviously, the political leadership charges the Soviet press primarily (though not exclusively) with changing and creating mass opinion in accord with national policies. If the mass media had been successful, there would today be an entirely different Soviet society. There would be no "remnants of bourgeois thought," for example, nor any hostility toward the Communist

Party, nor any surviving religious belief. But if the mass media had failed in their tasks entirely, there probably would be no sense of patriotism, or belief in the socialist system or mass literacy, or broad acceptance of mass public education and health care.

The means of influencing attitudes are demonstrably large. Every Soviet citizen is exposed to the mass media daily. A 1966 Soviet survey of 10,000 persons between the ages of sixteen and thirty revealed this pattern: between 77 and 85 per cent subscribed to newspapers and magazines; 47 to 62 per cent owned radios; and 27 to 45 per cent owned television sets.[59] In an unusual survey, nearly 2,000 Soviet youths in eight cities answered a Gallup poll on newspaper readership (among other topics); 94 per cent said they read daily newspapers, and three fourths of those read two or more papers a day. However, 42 per cent rarely or never watched television.[60] Another study, one on international news, reported that 50 to 55 per cent of Soviet adults regularly listened to the radio, and 30 to 45 per cent regularly watched television.[61] Among the 1,916 respondents in the Leningrad TV study, 97.5 per cent read at least one newspaper a day; 90 per cent listened to the radio daily or at times; and 84 per cent watched 3 or more hours of television a week.[62]

These figures represent an urban, relatively well-educated segment of the population. In the Soviet countryside, among the peasantry, exposure to the mass media seems considerably less. In 1967, Soviet national magazine and journal circulation totaled 82.3 million, of which less than a third (23.8 million) was drawn from rural areas.[63] Another comparison: in the two major Soviet cities, Leningrad and Moscow, for every 1,000 persons, 1,500 magazines and newspapers were purchased in 1967. In rural areas throughout the country, 820 publications were circulated per 1,000 persons the same year.[64]

Even with the differences between the Soviet urban (more educated) population and rural (less educated), it is true that the mass media reach most of the people most of the time. But, returning to the key question, with what effect? One Soviet study into the influence of propaganda on religious belief focused on 819 former "believers" in the region of Voronezh. Analyzing the various influences on their conversion to atheism, 55 per cent of the 819 mentioned schooling; 50 per cent also referred to oral propaganda and agitation; 50 per cent radio broadcasts; 36 per cent periodicals and books; and a little over

13 per cent mentioned opinions of relatives.[65] A study by an American political scientist produced different claims. Drawing from material in the Soviet press, this study concluded that "believers" seldom read atheist literature and that Soviet anti-religious propaganda did not enjoy credibility among "believers."[66] These conclusions were based on the fact that religious practices (baptism, church attendance) remain widespread in the Soviet Union after a half century of concerted state propaganda and persecution of "believers." The conclusions also relied on frequent Soviet press articles on the ineffectiveness and misconstruction of atheist propaganda. Further, applying what is known of opinion change in the United States, it seems that Soviet citizens do resist propaganda directed at deepseated beliefs or customs. Certainly, religious beliefs fall into this category. And the mass media have not been able to alter such beliefs among a segment of the population.

Studies of American advertising may also help gauge the effectiveness of the Soviet mass media in creating political and philosophic views among a mass audience. In a sense, Soviet press material on politics attempts acceptance of an idea in the same way as does American advertising. The Soviet mass media theme, "The Communist Party wisely leads and benefits the masses," is an emotional appeal analagous to "Ford Has A Better Idea" or "You Expect More from Standard and You Get It." All are slogans. And we know from some studies that a mass audience mentally turns away from slogans after they are repeated a relatively few times. "While the usual effect is to increase retention under some circumstances, too frequent repetition [of information] without any rewards leads to loss of attention, boredom and disregard of the communication."[67] Soviet studies have yielded the same conclusion.[68] This may partly explain why audience reaction to the Soviet mass media's political information is, as Soviet research documents, a combination of indifference and dissatisfaction. Political articles tend to be repetitious and often enough make claims (on the Soviet standard of living, or civil rights, for example) that are not borne out in practice. Thus, the citizenry comes to ignore them.

By the same token, the Marxist-Leninist world view propagated by the Soviet mass media has not been uniformly absorbed by the population. This is reflected in continuous demands by the political leadership to "improve" and "strengthen" ideological education, particularly among youth. "Socialist realism," though presented by the press as the basic guide to Soviet literary and artistic creation, finds its antagonists in Soviet society. Government bureaucrats extract subservience from subordinates and gifts and favors from those who receive services, though the mass media denounce the practice.

This is to say that the values and ideals for so long propagated by the press have not taken root everywhere in Soviet society. And for that the press (and schools, worker collectives, lectures, and books) have failed to create the "Soviet man." It is neither a surprising nor a damning failure. It is simply to say that the Soviet mass media have their defects in the art of persuasion no less than American advertising campaigns.

But like the latter, the Soviet press does have an effect. No one who has talked with Soviet officials or rank-and-file citizens can conclude otherwise. There exists a mass awareness of Soviet national power and achievement that has, in part, been formed by the mass media. The Soviet citizen's concept of world imperialism stems partially from the press. The youth committed to service to mankind, to building a new social order, and to Marxism-Leninism, has been influenced to some degree by the press.

The problem is that we cannot determine precisely what role the Soviet mass media have played in forming these attitudes. It is reasonable to note that they are repeated in the press and that Soviet citizens reflect them in their opinions, and that therefore some cause-and-effect relationship exists. Yet, an exact analysis of the relationship escapes us for lack of competent research. What specifically do various segments of the Soviet population think of the Communist Party? Or, as a conceivable research topic, how many Soviet citizens accepted the official press version of the reasons for Khrushchev's fall from power? Do Soviet press and radio-TV audiences believe from exposure to the mass media that West Germany is a "militarist" and "revenge-seeking" nation? These are the types of questions that have not been explored. Answers to them would tell us substantially more about the influence of the Soviet state-managed press in forming or changing mass opinion.

What we can be relatively certain of is that the contemporary Soviet press is not nearly so effective as the political leadership would like. The Soviet sociological research into the mass media substantiates what perhaps already was known or suspected. However, it would be a misconception to view the

Soviet mass media in such simple terms of a commanding political bureaucracy spoon-feeding docile, childlike masses with a pablum of propaganda. Political education of the population is but one role of the press. It engages as well in controversy and decisionmaking, in entertainment, in establishing a sense of national unity, in popularizing technology among an increasingly urban society, and in teaching such values as personal hygiene, industriousness, the worth of learning, and the virtue of equality.

Looked upon as one institution in a developing society, the Soviet mass media have contributed to the transformation of an illiterate, peasant society into an educated, industrial nation. The mass media's own development would have been different, as would that of other institutions, had the Stalin era not dictated its growth. Though the press championed industrialization under Stalin, and then victory in World War II, it also may have retarded Soviet society's development by restricting the flow of information and the interplay of ideas and opinion.

In large part, the history of the Soviet press since Stalin's death in 1953 has been a struggle to shed a Stalinist psychology, including the overriding inclination to shield the Soviet citizenry from unfavorable or unpleasant information. Change has been partly dictated from above (Khrushchev) and partly demanded by the evolution of Soviet society. The Soviet population has become more discriminating and critical of information as it has become more educated. The role of the press has been altering as the Soviet Union has faced the problems of an established, industrialized nation, in which simple commands no longer suffice as political management tools. Far more today than in the past, mass media are required to experiment with and criticize ideas before they become national policy. A greater need exists for the press to be a dispassionate critic and a loyal opposition.

Not least, the Soviet press has still far to go to reestablish credibility among the mass audience. Trust and belief were the two greatest losses suffered by the press during the Stalinist years. Among journalists and editors, the virtue of truthful, honest writing was the chief victim. The research and discussion of mass communications occurring today in the Soviet Union are chiefly valuable for their public exposure of the mass media's failings and weaknesses. From this should come further and important modernization of the press.

Yet, since the press is but one institution in a highly organized, managed society, it would be naive to expect it to change radically unless the whole society does. As a model, we may recall the revolutionary change in the Czechoslovak press from January to August, 1968. It broke through established norms and methods, not least official censorship, only when radical political reform was being initiated. Simultaneously, the Czechoslovak press became a prime instrument of that reform.

We should not expect the Soviet mass media to function differently. Managed by the Soviet political bureaucracy, the press cannot change independently of the political system. However, the Soviet mass media constitute a center of power and influence of their own, in the sense perhaps of a subsidiary of the Soviet corporate society. Achievement of this status is probably the dominant event of the Soviet press in the 1960's. If we were to project trends—admittedly a precarious practice —we might expect the Soviet mass media to become a more powerful vehicle of opinion and criticism in the 1970's.

NOTES

CHAPTER 1

1. V. I. Lenin, *Sochineniya* (35 vols., 4th edn., Moscow, 1941–1952), Vol. 5, p. 9. For the American history of the press as political spokesman see, for example, Edwin Emery, *The Press and America: An Interpretive History of Journalism* (Englewood Cliffs, N.J.: Prentice-Hall, Inc., 1962), Chapters 6 and 10. All translations from the Russian are by the author.

2. T. M. Reshetnikov, *Partiya o pechati* (Sverdlovsk, 1934), pp. 16–17.

3. *Pervyi vsesoyuznyi sezd zhurnalistov: stenograficheskoi otchet* (Moscow, 1960), pp. 11–12.

4. N. G. Bogdanov and B. A. Vyazemskii, *Spravochnik zhurnalista* (Leningrad, 1965), p. 28.

5. See, for example, Hyman H. Goldin, "Commercial Television," in *Public Television: A Program for Action—The Report and Recommendations of the Carnegie Commission on Educational Television* (New York: Harper & Row, Inc., 1967), pp. 227–234.

6. See, for example, Nikolai Prusakov, "*Prioritet zakona*," *Zhurnalist*, No. 3 (March, 1967), pp. 43–45. A deputy chairman of the Russian republic's supreme court, Prusakov asserts that judges must be spared inaccurate and emotional reporting of trials in progress if courts are to render fair decisions.

7. Gunther Anders, "The Phantom World of TV," in Bernard Rosenberg and David Manning White (eds.), *Mass Culture: The Popular Arts in America* (New York: The Free Press of Glencoe, paperback, 1964), p. 363.

8. See, for instance, Wilbur Schramm, *Mass Media and National Development: The Role of Information in the Developing Countries* (Stanford, Calif.: Stanford University Press and UNESCO, 1964), pp. 149–157, in which radio broadcasting is discussed as a means of education among illiterate populations.

9. A Communist Party Central Committee statement criticized the Turkmen republic press, for example, for failing to give the "necessary attention to propagating the ideas of proletarian internationalism and friendship of the peoples of the USSR." See *Sovetskaya Pechat*, No. 2 (February, 1964), p. 2.

10. *Pechat SSSR v 1966 godu* (Moscow, 1967), pp. xviii and xix.

11. For discussion of the religious press, see Martin E. Marty, *et al.*, *The Religious Press in America* (New York: Holt, Rinehart and Winston, Inc., 1963), pp. 51–52 and pp. 101–109. These pages focus especially on problems of editorial freedom within church organizations.

12. See, for instance, A. Yakovlev, *"Televideniye: problemy i perspektivy,"* *Kommunist,* No. 13 (September, 1965), pp. 70–80, in which he discusses expansion of international television broadcasting, and then foresees the "open clash of two ideologies in the airwaves."

13. See, for example, D. P. Goryunov's report to the 1966 National Journalists' Conference in *Vtoroi sezd zhurnalistov SSSR,* supplement to *Sovetskaya Pechat,* No. 11 (November, 1966), pp. 15–16.

14. This interpretation is adapted from a stimulating essay by Jay W. Jensen, "A Method and a Perspective for Criticism of the Mass Media," *Journalism Quarterly,* Vol. 37, No. 2, pp. 261–266. See also Theodore Peterson, "Why the Mass Media Are That Way," in Charles S. Steinberg (ed.), *Mass Media and Communication* (New York: Hastings House Publishers, Inc., 1966), pp. 56–71.

15. Boganov and Vyazemskii, *Spravochnik zhurnalista,* pp. 37–49.

16. *Lenin o pechati* (Moscow, 1959), p. 139. The exact sentence: "A newspaper is not only a collective propagandist and a collective agitator, but a collective organizer as well."

17. See *"Nauchnaya konferentsiya po problemam zhurnalistiki,"* in *Sovetskaya Pechat,* No. 2 (February, 1966), p. 56. The characteristics were suggested by A. Mishuris, of Moscow University's School of Journalism at a Moscow conference on laws of the development of the press in socialist society.

18. The late President John F. Kennedy, for example, acknowledged the valuable role of a critical press in a democratic society. But, as all Presidents in the age of mass communications, he saw the press as a means of rallying public support for his policies. See, for example, Theodore C. Sorensen, *Kennedy* (New York: Bantam Books, Inc., 1966), p. 349.

19. Schramm, *Mass Media and National Development,* p. 214. Italics in original.

20. *Ibid.,* p. 114.

21. See, for example, *Mass Media in Developing Countries* (Paris: UNESCO, 1961), pp. 15–16, and pp. 37 ff. The latter section suggests a program of media development integrated with general economic planning.

22. Daniel Lerner suggests a correlation between communication development and urbanization, for example, in "Communication Systems and Social Systems," in Wilbur Schramm (ed.), *Mass Communications* (Urbana, Ill.: University of Illinois Press, 1960), pp. 131–140.

23. This was true in World War I and II, less so during the Korean War, and almost not at all as the Vietnam war progressed.

24. James Reston, *The Artillery of the Press* (New York: Harper & Row, Inc., 1966), p. 64.

25. Richard E. Neustadt discusses some of the complexities in this process in *Presidential Power* (New York: New American Library, Signet Books, 1964), particularly pp. 99–104, where he talks about the President's need to "teach" the public.

26. *Sovetskaya Pechat,* No. 7 (July, 1964), p. 9.

27. Liberman's article appeared in *Pravda*, September 9, 1962; Trapeznikov's in *Pravda*, August 17, 1964. See Margaret Miller, *Rise of the Russian Consumer* (London: Institute of Economic Affairs, 1965), pp. 13–67, for a summary of Soviet economics discussions.

28. A running debate on family law reform, for example, is described by Peter H. Juviler, "Family Reforms on the Road to Communism," in Peter H. Juviler and Henry W. Morton (eds.), *Soviet Policy Making* (New York: Frederick A. Praeger, Inc., paperback, 1967), pp. 29–60.

29. For one diligently researched case study of high-level controversy in the press—over Khrushchev's agricultural policies—see Sidney I. Ploss, *Conflict and Decision-Making in Soviet Russia* (Princeton, N.J.: Princeton University Press, 1965).

30. See *Radio Liberty Dispatch*, December 27, 1967, for a summary and analysis.

31. Priscilla Johnson traces one such debate in her essay, "The Politics of Soviet Culture, 1962-1964," in Priscilla Johnson and Leopold Labedz (eds.), *Khrushchev and the Arts* (Cambridge, Mass.: The M.I.T. Press, 1965), pp. 1–89.

32. Schramm, *Mass Media and National Development*, p. 44.

CHAPTER 2

1. *Lenin o pechati.*

2. See Michael T. Florinsky, *Russia: A History and an Interpretation* (2 vols., New York: The Macmillan Company, 1955), Vol. II, pp. 1186 and 1238-1239.

3. *Lenin o pechati*, pp. 578–580. Italics are Lenin's. The statements are from an article that appeared September 28, 1917, in *Rabochii Put.*

4. Lenin, *Sochineniya*, "*Chto Delat?*", Vol. V, pp. 348, 349. All references are to the 4th edition.

5. *Rabochaya Gazeta*, No. 1, 1897: reprinted in *Bolshevistskaya pechat: sbornik materialov* (Moscow, 1959), Vol. I, pp. 97–99. This sentence is on p. 99.

6. *Sochineniya*, "*Nasha Programa*," Vol. IV, p. 129.

7. *Sochineniya*, "*Nasha Blizhaishaya Zadacha*," Vol. IV, pp. 198–199.

8. *Sochineniya*, Vol. IV, p. 304.

9. *Sochineniya*, Vol. IV, p. 329.

10. *Sochineniya*, "*S Chego Nachat?*", Vol. V, p. 11.

11. In 1899, Lenin proposed that the words of the "veteran German Social-Democrat Liebknecht serve: '*Studieren, propagandieren, organisieren*' —teach, propagandize, organize; only a *party organ* can and must be the central point of this activity." See *Sochineniya*, Vol. IV, p. 200.

12. *Sochineniya*, Vol. V, p. 11.

13. For general background, see Leonard Schapiro, *The Communist Party of the Soviet Union* (New York: Random House, Inc., 1960), Chapters 2 and 3.

14. See *Russkaya periodicheskaya pechat* (Moscow, 1957), which lists many of the newspapers and journals published in Russia between 1895 and November, 1918, along with editors and circulation. There are 141 entries for Lenin, either as editor or contributor.

15. See Florinsky, *op. cit.*, Vol. II, p. 1186.

16. *Lenin o pechati*, in the article *"Partiinaya organizatsiya i partiinaya literatura,"* p. 330.

17. *Lenin o pechati*, p. 334.

18. Beginning in July, 1913, *Pravda* was repeatedly closed by police, and then reappeared under different names, eight in all. See *Russkaya periodicheskaya pechat*, pp. 197–201, for a brief history. A useful general history is *Leninskoi Pravde—50 let: sbornik dokumentov i materialov po istorii gazety (1912–1962)* (Moscow, 1962), published in observance of *Pravda's* fiftieth anniversary.

19. See A. Berezhnoi, *K istorii partiino-sovetskoi pechati* (Leningrad, 1956), pp. 12 ff., hereafter cited as Berezhnoi; and A. K. Belkov, *et al.*, *Partiinaya i sovetskaya pechat v borbe za postroeniye sotsializma i kommunizma* (2 vols., Moscow, 1961), Vol. I, pp. 18–19, hereafter referred to as Belkov.

20. *Dekret o pechati*, reprinted in *Dekrety sovetskoi vlasti* (2 vols., Moscow, 1957), Vol. I, p. 25. The decree was signed November 9, but not published until the next day.

21. *Dekrety*, Vol. I, pp. 55–57.

22. *Dekrety*, Vol. I, pp. 432–434.

23. James H. Meisel and Edward S. Kozera (eds.), *Materials for the Study of the Soviet System* (Ann Arbor, Mich.: The George Wahr Publishing Co., 1953), p. 93.

24. See *Dekrety*, Vol. I, p. 549, for an order for the arrest of 12 men of the "slanderous newspaper" *Revolyutsionnyi Nabat* for trial before the Revolutionary Tribunal.

25. *Dekrety*, Vol. II, p. 569.

26. *Lenin o pechati*, pp. 661–662.

27. *Dekrety*, Vol. I, p. 24.

28. *Lenin o pechati*, p. 592. For a lively account of debate on the press decree see John Reed, *Ten Days That Shook the World* (New York: The Modern Library, Inc., 1935), pp. 267–272.

29. *Dekrety*, Vol. I, pp. 43–44.

30. *Lenin o pechati*, p. 591.

31. *Dekrety*, Vol. II, p. 553.

32. *Lenin o pechati*, p. 598.

33. *Lenin o pechati*, pp. 600–602.

34. *Dekrety*, Vol. II, p. 50.

35. *O partiinoi i sovetskoi pechati; sbornik dokumentov* (Moscow, 1954), pp. 211–212 contain the resolution.

36. See *KPSS v resolyutsiyakh i resheniyakh* (Moscow, 1954), Vol. I, pp. 88–89, for the 3rd Congress; and pp. 463–465 for the 1919 party rules on press management.

37. Berezhnoi, *op. cit.*, pp. 17, 50, 54.

38. *Pechat SSSR za sorok let: 1917-1957* (Moscow, 1957), pp. 4, 107, and 123. A 1917 estimated population of 143 million is used to calculate the number of newspapers per 1,000 in 1918.

39. Berezhnoi, *op cit.*, pp. 67ff., and Belkov, *op. cit.*, pp. 43, 49–50.

40. Berezhnoi, *op. cit.*, p. 67, and *Leninskoi Pravde—50 let*, p. 373.

41. Berezhnoi, *op. cit.*, pp. 52 ff.

42. Belkov, *op. cit.*, pp. 38–41.

43. This section is based on N. G. Palgunov, *Osnovy informatsii v gazete: TASS i ego rol* (Moscow, 1955), pp. 25–27, and on *O partiinoi i sovetskoi pechati*, pp. 180–181.

44. *Sovetskaya pechat v dokumentakh* (Moscow, 1961), p. 212.

45. *Lenin o pechati*, p. 633.

46. Berezhnoi, *op. cit.*, p. 63.

47. *Lenin o pechati*, pp. 644–645 and 764 n.

48. For the congress order, see *O partiinoi i sovetskoi pechati*, p. 356.

49. *Stalin o pechati* (Sverdlovsk, 1932), pp. 14–18.

50. *Sovetskaya pechat v dokumentakh*, pp. 45–57, and Belkov, *op. cit.*, pp. 61–62.

51. Reshetnikov, *op. cit.*, p. 22.

52. I. V. Stalin, *O pechati* (Izdatelstvo Proletarii, 1925), p. 13; also Reshetnikov, *op. cit.*, pp. 16–18.

53. Reshetnikov, *op. cit.*, p. 24.

54. *Stalin o pechati*, p. 18.

55. Reshetnikov, *op. cit.*, pp. 10–11.

56. For a more detailed account see Merle Fainsod, *How Russia Is Ruled* (Cambridge, Mass.: Harvard University Press, 1953), Chapter 6.

57. See *KPSS v resolyutsiyakh i resheniyakh*, Vol. I, p. 513. This reference, at the 9th conference of the Russian Communist Party (Bolsheviks) in September, 1920, is the first official mention of *Agitprop*. It probably was established after the 9th Congress in March–April, 1920.

58. *O partiinoi i sovetskoi pechati*, pp. 239–240.

59. *Resheniya partii o pechati* (Moscow, 1941), pp. 62–63.

60. The decree reorganizing press departments and describing specific authority is contained in L. G. Fogelevich (ed.), *Deistvuyushcheye zakonodatelstvo o pechati* (Moscow, 1927), pp. 3–4.

61. See *Voprosy Istorii KPSS*, No. 7, 1965, pp. 116–122, for a well-documented article on the information department.

62. This section is drawn from Fogelevich (ed.), *op. cit.*, and Fogelevich (ed.), *op. cit.* (3rd edn., Moscow, 1931), p. 60. As Maurice Friedberg has noted, *Glavlit* was precisely the title for the czarist censorship agency existing from 1865 to 1917. See his "Keeping Up with the Censor," *Problems of Communism*, No. 6 (November–December, 1964), p. 23.

63. On the Cheka and censorship, see Merle Fainsod, *Smolensk Under Soviet Rule* (New York: Vintage Books, Inc., 1963), pp. 155–156.

64. Fogelevich (ed.), *op. cit.*, p. 4.

65. This section is drawn from Fogelevich (ed.), *op. cit.*, 3rd edn., pp. 218–219, and L. G. Fogelevich, *Osnovnye direktivy i zakonodatelstva po pechati* 6th edn., (Moscow, 1937), pp. 288–289. The criminal code article on propaganda was 58.10. Insult was covered in Article 160, and slander in Article 161.

66. *O partiinoi i sovetskoi pechati*, pp. 347–349. and Fogelevich, *Osnovyne direktivy*, p. 63.

67. For details, see: *Sovetskaya pechat v dokumentakh*, pp. 47, 51, 56, 67; Fogelevich (ed.), *Deistvuyushcheye zakonodatelstvo*, pp. 122 and 129–130; Belkov, *op. cit.*, pp. 62–67; and V. V. Uchenov, *Partiino-sovetskaya pechat vosstanovitelnogo perioda* (Moscow, 1964), pp. 5–12, and *Pechat za sorok let*, p. 123. Newspaper statistics conflict, noticeably for 1925. Belkov inexplicably gives a total of 589, with a circulation of 7.5 million, for that year.

68. For details, see *Sovetskaya pechat v dokumentakh*, pp. 42–45; and Belkov, *op. cit.*, pp. 60–61.

69. Belkov, *op. cit.*, p. 67.

70. *Resheniya partii o pechati*, p. 99.

71. *Sovetskaya pechat v dokumentakh*, p. 41.

72. See Vyacheslav Molotov's report to the December, 1925, 14th Party Congress in *O partiinoi i sovetskoi pechati*, p. 355.

73. *Sovetskaya pechat v dokumentakh*, p. 42.

74. See *Sovetskaya pechat v dokumentakh*, p. 69; and *Resheniya partii o pechati*, p. 112.

75. *Resheniya partii o pechati*, pp. 105–107.

76. *Ibid.*, pp. 37–39.

77. *Ibid.*, pp. 75–79.

78. Berezhnoi, *op. cit.*, p. 76.

79. *Resheniya partii o pechati*, pp. 24–25.

80. This section is drawn from Ye. L. Khudyakov, "*Universitetskoye obrazovaniye zhurnalistov*," *Vestnik Moskovskogo universiteta: istoriko-filologicheskaya seriya*, No. 1, 1959, pp. 5–6; *Sovetskaya pechat v dokumentakh*, pp. 51–52, 57, 69; and Berezhnoi, *op. cit.*, p. 70.

81. *Resheniya partii o pechati*, p. 24; information on the *rabselkor* is mainly from *ibid.*, pp. 89–92, 192–103; and Fogelevich (ed.), *Deistvuyushcheye zakonodatelstvo* (3rd edn.), pp. 206–216.

82. Berezhnoi, *op. cit.*, p. 78.

83. Belkov, *op. cit.*, p. 70. This section is mostly drawn from *Resheniya partii o pechati*, pp. 80–81, 94–95, and *Sovetskaya pechat v dokumentakh*, p. 64.

84. *Pechat SSSR za sorok let*, p. 107.

85. For sketchy histories of Soviet magazine publishing, see *Bolshaya sovetskaya entsiklopediya* (50 vols., Moscow, 1949–1958,) 2nd edn., Vol. 16, pp. 248–251; and Uchenova, *op. cit.*, pp. 9–12.

86. Quoted by L. N. Fedotova in "*Stanovleniye reportazha na radio*," *Vestnik Moskovskogo universiteta, Seriya XI, Zhurnalistika*, No. 6, 1967, p. 17.

87. For a chronological account of the Soviet radio development in the 1920's and after, see M. Gleizer (ed.), *Radio i televideniye v SSSR: 1917-1963* (Moscow, 1965), and the appropriate months and years.

88. Central Statistical Board, *Forty Years of Soviet Power* (Moscow, 1958), p. 265.

89. *Pechat SSSR za sorok let*, p. 123.

90. R. A. Ivanova, *Partiinaya i sovetskaya pechat v gody vtoroi pyatiletki: 1933-1937* (Moscow: 1961), pp. 4-5.

91. *Pechat SSSR za sorok let*, p. 107.

92. *Forty Years of Soviet Power*, p. 265.

93. For details see Fogelevich (ed.), *Deistvuyushcheye zakonodatelstvo* (3rd edn.), pp. 61-62, 65-66, and 230-231.

94. This summary is based on Fainsod, *Smolensk Under Soviet Rule*, Chapter 19. Other accounts of the censorship mechanism are in A. Finn, *Experiences of a Soviet Journalist* (New York: East European Fund, Inc., 1954), pp. 5-6; and *U.S. News and World Report*, January 13, 1956, pp. 68-75, which contains an interview with two Soviet journalists who left their country in 1946.

95. Fogelevich, *Osnovnye direktivy*, p. 219; and *Deistvuyushcheye zakonodatelstvo* (3rd edn.), pp. 128-130.

96. See Fainsod, *How Russia Is Ruled*, pp. 167-170.

97. *Resheniya partii o pechati*, pp. 182-185.

98. Reshetnikov, *op. cit.*, p. 43.

99. Berezhnoi, *op. cit.*, p. 85.

100. Information in this section is drawn from Alex Inkeles and Raymond A. Bauer, *The Soviet Citizen: Daily Life in a Totalitarian Society* (Cambridge, Mass.: Harvard University Press, 1959), pp. 159-188.

101. S. S. Sevastyanovich (ed.), *Istoriya sovetskoi konstitutsii: 1917-1956* (Moscow, 1957), p. 744.

102. See Belkov, *op. cit.*, Chapter 6, for a summary of the press during the war years. Also useful is the monograph by N. M. Kononykhin, *Partiinaya i sovetskaya pechat v period velikoi otechestvennoi vainy* (Moscow, 1963).

103. *Zhurnalist*, No. 2 (February, 1968), p. 17.

104. Edward Crankshaw, *Khrushchev: A Career* (New York: The Viking Press, Inc., 1966), p. 270.

105. *Pravda*, October 27, 1963.

106. *Sovetskaya Pechat*, No. 4 (April, 1964), p. 6.

107. See, for example, Khrushchev's lecture to republic and *oblast* editors in *Pravda*, December 1, 1953.

108. Quoted in *Sovetskaya Pechat*, No. 4 (April, 1964), p. 7.

109. *Sovetskaya pechat v dokumentakh*, pp. 286-287.

110. For a good resume of Adzhubei's career to 1963, see William J. Eaton, "Red Editor: Aleksei Adzhubei," *Nieman Reports*, No. 2 (June, 1963), pp. 12-19.

CHAPTER 3.

1. See *Freedom of Information Center Report*, No. 181, School of Journalism, University of Missouri, May, 1967.

2. See, for example, *Pravda*, January 30, 1966, where a trio of authors criticized wide use of the phrase "period of the personality cult" which, the authors said, "led to the belittling of the heroic efforts of the party and the people in the struggle for socialism and to the impoverishment of history."

3. See *Report of the National Advisory Commission on Civil Disorders* (New York: Bantam Books, Inc., 1968), pp. 363–366.

4. This section on the American mass media is drawn mainly from Fred S. Siebert, *et al.*, *Four Theories of the Press* (Urbana, Ill.: University of Illinois Press, 1956), Chapters 2 and 3.

5. James Reston, *The Artillery of the Press*, pp. 63–64.

6. Nicolas Berdyaev, *The Russian Idea* (Boston: Beacon Press, 1962), p. 254.

7. Wright W. Miller, *Russians as People* (New York: E. P. Dutton & Co., Inc., 1961), p. 107.

8. Hugh Seton-Watson, *The Russian Empire, 1801–1917* (London: Oxford University Press, 1967), pp. 447–478.

9. For a summary of Russian journalism history, see Jay Jensen and Richard Bayley, "Highlights of the Development of Russian Journalism, 1553–1917," *Journalism Quarterly*, No. 3, 1964, pp. 403–415.

10. Thornton Anderson, *Russian Political Thought: An Introduction* (Ithaca, N.Y.: Cornell University Press, 1967), p. 364.

11. Seton-Watson, *op. cit.*, p. 524.

12. *Pravda*, July 27, 1965, in *Current Digest of the Soviet Press*, Vol. XVII, No. 30, p. 34.

13. Bernard Pares, *A History of Russia* (New York: Alfred A. Knopf, Inc., 1956), p. 181.

14. For a summary, see Florinsky, *op. cit.*, Vol. II, pp. 727–728, 812–815, 1055–1056, and 1111–1112.

15. Fogelevich (ed.), *Deistvuyushcheye zakonodatelstvo* (3rd edn.), p. 230.

16. Fogelevich, *Osnovnye direktivy,* pp. 137–139.

17. Fogelevich (ed.), *Deistvuyushcheye zakonodatelstvo* (3rd edn.), pp. 65, 230–231.

18. Vladimir Gsovski, *Soviet Civil Law* (2 vols., Ann Arbor, Mich.: University of Michigan Press, 1948), Vol. I, pp. 65–66.

19. See *Slovar sokrashchenii russkogo yazyka* (Moscow, 1963), p. 126, under the "*Glavlit*" entry; and the supplement to *Sovetskaya Pechat*, No. 11, 1966, p. 45, where Pavel K. Romanov is identified as "director of the Chief Administration for Protection of State Secrets in the Press."

20. See Leonid Vladimirov, *The Russians* (New York: Frederick A. Praeger, Inc., 1968), p. 97. A former Soviet journalist, Vladimirov provides a description of *Glavlit*'s contemporary operations on pp. 94–100. His description indicates that *Glavlit* has not changed radically since the 1930's.

21. *Ugolovnoye zakonodatelstvo soyuza·SSR i soyuznykh respublik* (2 vols., Moscow, 1963), Vol. I, p. 108. Each of the 15 Soviet republics has its

own criminal code. Except for differences of article numbers and minor differences of wording, they are identical. References here will be to the Russian republic code, which is the model for all others.

22. For a complete translation of the decree, see Robert Conquest (ed.), *The Politics of Ideas in the U.S.S.R.* (New York: Frederick A. Praeger, Inc., 1967), pp. 61–63.

23. See Max Hayward (tr.), *On Trial* (New York: Harper & Row, Inc., 1966) pp. 64–65, for example, where a largely verbatim transcript of the trial refers to a *Glavlit* investigation.

24. Solzhenitsyn's letter has not been published in the Soviet press, but it appeared in European and American newspapers. See *The New York Times*, June 5, 1967, for the text.

25. The first issue of 1967 was delayed, for instance, because of apparent dispute over part of its contents. Its editor, Alexander Tvardovsky, so implied in an editorial note in *Novy Mir*, No. 1, 1967.

26. Fainsod, *Smolensk Under Soviet Rule*, p. 269.

27. Author's interview with a Soviet editor in Kiev, October 5, 1967.

28. Interview by the author at editorial offices of *Vostochno-Siberskaya Pravda* in Irkutsk, September 18, 1967.

29. Interview by the author at *Leningradskaya Pravda* in Leningrad, February 21, 1964.

30. *Ugolovnoye zakonodatelstvo,* p. 108.

31. The four were Alexander Ginzburg, Yuri Galanskov, Vera Lashkova, Alexei Dobrovolsky.

32. U. S. Statutes at Large, "The Sedition Act," I, Sec. 2, p. 596, quoted in Edwin Emery, *The Press and America: An Interpretative History of Journalism* (2nd edn., Englewood Cliffs, N.J.: Prentice Hall, Inc., 1962), p. 55.

33. Emery, *op. cit.*, p. 595.

34. *Ugolovnoye zakonodatelstvo*, p. 108.

35. *Ibid.*, p. 143.

36. *Radyanske Pravo* (March, 1965), p. 55.

37. Conquest (ed.), *op. cit.*, p. 59. The decision appeared in *Byulleten verkhovnogo suda SSSR*, No. 4, 1963, p. 26.

38. *Molodoi Kommunist* (August, 1966), pp. 35–37.

39. *Zhurnalist*, No. 2 (February, 1967), p. 3. The advice came from the chief of the newspaper sector of the Communist Party's department of propaganda.

40. *Ugolovnoye zakonodatelstvo*, p. 121.

41. *Ibid.*

42. Based on interviews conducted by the author in the Soviet Union.

43. *Izvestia*, January 19, 1965, in *Current Digest of the Soviet Press,* Vol. XVI, No. 3, p. 27.

44. *Izvestia*, September 5, 1964, in *Current Digest of the Soviet Press*, Vol. XVI, No. 36, p. 22.

45. See accounts in *The New York Times*, February 3, 1968, p. 21, and the Washington *Post*, February 4, 1968, p. 17.

46. A resume of the case appears in Kazimierz Grzybowski, "Soviet Criminal Law," *Problems of Communism*, XIV, No. 2, 1965, p. 61. *Izvestia*'s report of the suit appeared in the December 19, 1964, issue.

47. The press law was encouraged by Alexander Bek in *Zhurnalist*, No. 2 (February, 1967), p. 15. Czechoslovakia's press law was translated in *Zhurnalist*, No. 6 (June, 1967), pp. 48–49.

48. For information on creation and duties of the press committee, see *Spravochnik zhurnalista*, p. 141, and *Ekonomicheskaya Gazeta*, November 11, 1964, p. 37. For Pavel Romanov's appointment as committee chairman, see *Sovetskaya Pechat*, No. 8 (August, 1963), p. 6; for his career and appointment as *Glavlit* chief, see *Portrait of Prominent USSR Personalities*, Institute for the Study of the USSR, No. 134, and note 19 above. For Nikolai Mikhailov's appointment see *Directory of Soviet Officials*, Vol. I. *USSR and RSFSR* (February, 1966), p. I-B44.

49. *Spravochnik zhurnalista*, p. 181.

50. Information here is drawn from *Spravochnik zhurnalista*, pp. 678–689; and B. P. Stepanov, *Rasprostraneniye, ekspedirovaniye i dostavka gazet i zhurnalov v SSSR* (Moscow, 1955), especially pp. 3–14

51. *Rasprostraneniye Pechati*, No. 6 (July, 1967), p. 4.

52. *Spravochnik zhurnalista*, p. 686.

53. *Rasprostraneniye Pechati*, No. 12 (December, 1967), p. 4.

54. *Rasprostraneniye Pechati*, No. 7 (July, 1960), pp. 13–15.

55. *Pechat SSSR za sorok let*, pp. 108 and 123; and *Pechat SSSR v 1966 godu*, pp. 56 and 66.

56. *Rasprostraneniye Pechati*, No. 2 (February, 1967), p. 5.

57. *Pravda*, October 18, 1964; and *Rasprostraneniye Pechati*, No. 8 (August, 1966), p. 4. For information on the quota system, see *Spravochnik zhurnalista*, pp. 687–688.

58. *KPSS v resolyutsiyakh i resheniyakh*, Vol. III, p. 238.

59. *Spravochnik zhurnalista*, p. 51.

60. Fainsod, *Smolensk Under Soviet Rule*, p. 367. Sergei Kirov was Leningrad's party leader, who was assassinated in 1934, very possibly on Stalin's orders.

61. *O partiinoi i sovetskoi pechati*, p. 534.

62. For these changes, see *Directory of Soviet Officials*, Revisions to Vol. I, *USSR and RSFSR* (February, 1966), p. I-A3; Vol. I, p. I-A5; and Vol. II, under entry for department of propaganda and agitation in sections on each republic.

63. *The New York Times*, October 17, 1964. *Izvestia* officially announced the change in its October 24, 1964, issue.

64. *The New York Times*, November 4, 1964.

65. *Directory of Soviet Officials,* Vol. I, p. I-C28.

66. *Ibid.*, p. I-B44.

67. See Wolfgang Leonhard, "Politics and Ideology in the Post-Khrushchev Era," in Alexander Dallin and Thomas B. Larson (eds.), *Soviet Politics*

Since Khrushchev (Englewood Cliffs, N. J.: Prentice-Hall, Inc., 1968), pp. 44 ff.

68. *Sovetskaya Pechat*, No. 2 (February, 1965), p. 3, refers to an official of the party Central Committee's "ideological commission." *Sovetskaya Pechat*, No. 6 (June, 1965), p. 11, refers to "department of propaganda and agitation."

69. *Sovetskaya Pechat*, No. 5 (May, 1966), p. 2, mentions the "department of propaganda and agitation" but *Sovetskaya Pechat*, No. 8 (August, 1966), p. 30, refers to "department of propaganda."

70. *Sovetskaya Pechat*, No. 11 (November, 1966), p. 3.

71. See, for example, *Sovetskaya Pechat*, No. 10 (October, 1966), p. 42, where there is a reference to "department of propaganda and agitation" of the Ukrainian republic Central Committee; and p. 43, a reference to the "sector for press, radio and television" of the Vladimirsk *oblast* party committee.

72. *Sovetskaya Pechat*, No. 2 (February, 1964), pp. 2–3.

73. See *Sovetskaya Pechat*, No. 10 (October, 1964), pp. 18–19.

74. *Zhurnalist*, No. 10 (October, 1967), p. 78.

75. *Pravda*, November 25, 1967.

76. *Zhurnalist*, No. 12 (December, 1967), p. 44.

77. *Zhurnalist*, No. 2 (February, 1968), p. 24.

78. *Sovetskaya pechat v dokumentakh*, p. 478.

79. See Priscilla Johnson, "The Politics of Soviet Culture, 1962–1964," in Johnson and Labedz (eds.), *op. cit.*, p. 57 n.

80. *Pravda*, November 16, 1966, in *Current Digest of the Soviet Press*, Vol. XVIII, No. 46, pp. 34–35.

81. *Pravda*, January 8, 1965, in *Current Digest of the Soviet Press*, Vol. XVII, No. 1, pp. 30–31.

82. *Partiinaya Zhizn*, No. 1 (January, 1968), pp. 77–79.

83. *Partiinaya Zhizn*, No. 14 (July, 1965), pp. 74–75.

CHAPTER 4

1. *Sovetskaya pechat v dokumentakh*, p. 477.

2. *Itogi vsesoyuznoi perepisi naseleniya 1959 goda SSSR* (Moscow, 1962), p. 165 gives a total of 73,771 "writers, journalists and editors" in the Soviet Union at the time of the 1959 census. One does not know how many of this category were professional writers of prose and poetry in contrast to professional journalists. The 60,000 figure appeared in *The Democratic Journalist*, No. 12, 1968, p. 268.

3. *Zhurnalist*, No. 1 (January, 1968), pp. 4–9, contains these remarks along with a general critique of mechanical writing in the Soviet press.

4. *Pravda*, December 4, 1967.

5. *Sovetskaya Pechat*, No. 10 (September, 1966), p. 41.

6. *Sovetskaya Pechat*, No. 7 (July, 1964), p. 16.

7. *Ibid.*, p. 16.

8. See, for example, Ya N. Zasurskii, "*Itogi i perspectivy razvitiya univers-itetskogo zhurnalistskogo obrazovaniya v SSSR*," in *Vestnik Moskovskogo universiteta, Seriya XI. Zhurnalistika,* No. 5 (September-October, 1967), pp. 14–15.

9. Ye. L. Khudyakov, *Teoriya i praktika partiino-sovetskoi pechati* (Moscow, 1957), p. 13.

10. *Zhurnalist,* No. 9 (September, 1967), p. 34. The writer was Yefim Lazebnik, a doctor of philosophy and editor of the Ukrainian republic newspaper *Rabochaya Gazeta.*

11. This section on early journalism training is taken largely from Khudyakov "*Universitetskoye obrazovaniye zhurnalistov,*" pp. 3–17; see also *Bolshaya sovetskaya entsiklopediya* (2nd edn.), Vol, 16, p. 243.

12. See *Resheniya partii o pechat,* pp. 130–132, for the Communist Party directive.

13. Fogelevich, *Osnovnye direktivy,* p. 63.

14. V. Grammatnikov (ed.), *Teoriya i praktika bolshevistskoi pechati* (Leningrad, 1934), pp. 3–5.

15. Zasurskii, *op. cit.,* p. 13.

16. Data compiled from *Spravochnik dlya postupayushchikh v vysshiye uchebnye zavedeniya SSSR v 1963* (Moscow, 1963), *Vestnik Moskovskogo universiteta, Seriya XI, Zhurnalistika,* No. 6, 1966, p. 90, and Zasurskii, *op. cit.,* p. 14.

17. For the Communist Party decree, see *O partiinoi i sovetskoi pechati,* pp. 558–562.

18. *Pravda,* July 17, 1964.

19. See *Zhurnalist,* No. 6 (June, 1968), p. 43.

20. See *Spravochnik zhurnalista,* pp. 227–333. For proceedings of the first congress see *Pervyi vsesoyuznyi sezd zhurnalistov.*

21. Supplement to *Sovetskaya Pechat,* No. 11 (November, 1966), p. 17.

22. *Zhurnalist,* No. 1 (January, 1967), p. 10.

23. *Sovetskaya pechat v dokumentakh,* p. 275.

24. Information supplied to the author at the Moscow University School of Journalism, March 23, 1964.

25. Zasurskii, *op. cit.,* p. 17, and *The Democratic Journalist,* No. 5 (May, 1968).

26. Khudyakov, "*Universitetskoye obrazovaniye zhurnalistov,*" pp. 7–8.

27. See *Sovetskaya Pechat,* No. 12 (December, 1965), p. 12.

28. *Sovetskaya Pechat,* No. 9 (September, 1965), p. 1.

29. *The Democratic Journalist,* No. 2 (February, 1968), p. 28.

30. *Komsomolskaya Pravda,* July 16, 1966.

31. *Zhurnalist,* No. 1 (January, 1967), p. 10.

32. Taken from *Uchebnyi plan; spetsialnosti, zhurnalistika* of Moscow University, 1957.

33. Information supplied in writing to the author by the Moscow University School of Journalism in April, 1968.

34. See, for example, S. M. Gurevich, *Teoriya i praktika partiino-sovetskoi pechati* (Moscow, 1968), a study aid for journalism correspondence students which gives required and suggested reading.

35. For a discussion of these see, for example, *Spravochnik zhurnalista*, pp. 312–348.
36. See supplement to *Sovetskaya Pechat*, on the Second Congress of Journalists, No. 11 (November, 1966), p. 16.
37. Khudyakov, "*Universitetskoye obrazovaniye zhurnalistov*," p. 7.
38. Supplement to *Sovetskaya Pechat*, No. 11 (November, 1966), p. 10.
39. *Pechat SSSR v 1966 godu*, pp. 67–68.
40. *Sovetskaya Pechat*, No. 1 (January, 1966), p. 19.
41. *Zhurnalist*, No. 1 (January, 1967), p. 10.
42. *Zhurnalist*, No. 9 (September, 1967), p. 79; No. 2 (February, 1968), p. 79; No. 3 (March, 1968), p. 77 and No. 4 (April, 1968), p. 79.
43. These figures were supplied to a group of visiting American editors and publishers in 1966. See Buren H. McCormack, *et al.*, *A Study of the Printing and Publishing Business in the Soviet Union* (New York: American Newspaper Publishers Association, 1967), p. 47.
44. Information supplied to the author in Leningrad in 1964.
45. *Zhurnalist*, No. 4 (April, 1967), p. 74.
46. *Zhurnalist*, No. 12 (December, 1967), p. 61.
47. *Zhurnalist*, No. 1 (January, 1967), p. 38.
48. *Ibid.*
49. *Zhurnalist*, No. 2 (February, 1968), p. 78.
50. *Zhurnalist,* No. 6 (June, 1967), p. 3.
51. TASS International Service, April 12, 1967, and *The New York Times*, April 12, 1967.
52. See *Sovetskaya Pechat*, No. 4 (April, 1966), pp. 5–6, and No. 7 (July, 1966), p. 7.
53. See Ploss, *Conflict and Decision-Making in Soviet Russia*.
54. Palgunov, *op. cit.*, p. 35.
55. *Voprosy zhurnalistiki* (Moscow, 1962), p. 79.
56. *Pravda*, June 14, 1967, in *Current Digest of the Soviet Press*, Vol. XIX, No. 24, p. 14.
57. See, for example, Warren Breed, "Social Control in the News Room," in Schramm (ed.), *Mass Communications*, pp. 178–194; and Walter Gieber, "News Is What Newspapermen Make It," in Lewis A. Dexter and David M. White (eds.), *People, Society and Mass Communications* (New York: The Free Press of Glencoe, 1964), pp. 173–180.
58. In a conversation with the author in Moscow, November 1967.
59. *Pravda*, December 7, 1965, in *Current Digest of the Soviet Press,* Vol. XVII, No. 49, p. 33.
60. *Pravda*, April 26, 1966, in *Current Digest of the Soviet Press*, Vol. XVIII, No. 18, p. 36.
61. *Resheniye partii o pechati*, p. 188.
62. *Pravda*, July 14, 1966.
63. An example was a conflict of views among military men over nuclear war. See William R. Kintner and Harriet Fast Scott (trs. and eds.), *The Nuclear Revolution in Soviet Military Affairs* (Norman, Okla.: University of Oklahoma Press, 1968), pp. 101–103 and pp. 340–341, for editors' notes, and pages following each section for translations of Soviet articles.

64. These have been adapted from Chilton R. Bush, "A System of Categories for General News Content," *Journalism Quarterly*, Vol. 37, No. 2, 1960, pp. 208–210.
65. *Zhurnalist*, No. 7 (July, 1967), p. 3.
66. *Sovetskaya Pechat*, No. 6 (June, 1966), pp. 39.
67. *Zhurnalist*, No. 1 (January, 1968), p. 8.
68. *Zhurnalist*, No. 4 (April, 1967), p. 22.

CHAPTER 5

1. *Pravda*, March 10, 1966, from a report of the Communist Party's central inspection commission at the 23rd Congress.
2. McCormack, *et al.*, *op. cit.*, p. 15.
3. The profit figure was given to the author by *Leningradskaya Pravda* editors in an interview January 30, 1964.
4. In an interview with *Smena* editors December 1, 1963.
5. For the decree, see *Sovetskaya pechat v dokumentakh*, pp. 301–304. Figures are recalculated in new rubles after 1961, when there was a 10 to 1 devaluation of the ruble.
6. *Sovetskaya Pechat*, No. 12 (December, 1962), p. 44.
7. For the decree, see *Pravda*, September 15, 1968.
8. Alex Inkeles, *Public Opinion in Soviet Russia: A Study In Mass Persuasion* (Cambridge, Mass.: Harvard University Press, 1951), p. 270; see also James W. Markham, *Voices of the Red Giants* (Iowa City, Iowa: State University Press, 1967), pp. 87–93, for a brief discussion of Soviet mass media and advertising.
9. *Vechernii Leningrad*, October 10, 1963.
10. *Sovetskaya Torgovlya*, February 4, 1964.
11. *The New York Times*, March 7, 1968, p. 2.
12. *Moscow News*, No. 26 (July 16–23, 1968), p. 10.
13. *Izvestia*, April 20, 1965, in *Current Digest of the Soviet Press*, Vol. XVII, No. 16, p. 36.
14. *Pravda*, May 4, 1965, in *Current Digest of the Soviet Press*, Vol. XVII, No. 18, p. 33.
15. See McCormack *et al.*, *op. cit.*, pp. 17–18, for a description of the campaign, as told to visiting American editors and publishers.
16. *Zhurnalist*, No. 3 (March, 1967), pp. 74–75.
17. Unless otherwise noted, information on the newspaper network is drawn from *Pechat SSSR v 1968 godu* (Moscow, 1969), pp. 65–71 and 175–195. Press run and circulation are used interchangeably here. However, frequent complaints about distribution indicate that Soviet newspapers do not always circulate their entire press run.
18. *Editor and Publisher International Yearbook* (New York, 1968), p. 17, and *Ayer Directory of Newspapers and Periodicals* (Philadelphia: N. W. Ayer and Son, Inc., 1968), p. xix.
19. *Rasprostraneniye Pechati*, No. 3 (March, 1968), p. 2.

20. Calculated from nationalities figures in *Itogi vsesoyuznoi perepisi naseleniya 1959 godu SSSR,* p. 184, and newspaper circulation figures in *Pechat SSSR v 1959 godu* (Moscow, 1960), p. 163.

21. Roman Szporluk, "The Press in Byelorussia," *Soviet Studies*, No. 4 (April, 1967), pp 486–493.

22. *Pechat SSSR v 1955 godu* (Moscow, 1956), p. 175.

23. *Pechat SSSR v 1959 godu* (Moscow, 1960), p. 154.

24. *Sovetskaya pechat v dokumentakh*, pp. 157–158.

25. *Pravda,* September 15, 1968.

26. *Sovetskaya pechat v dokumentakh*, pp. 86–87.

27. Based on information collected by the author in 1964 in the USSR.

28. The decrees are in *Sovetskaya pechat v dokumentakh,* pp. 284–285 and p. 305.

29. *Spravochnik zhurnalista*, p. 102, and *Voprosy ideologicheskoi raboty* (Moscow, 1961), p. 316.

30. For detailed information on wall newspapers see S. Ilin, *Kak organizovat stennoi gazety* (Yuzhno-Sakhalinsk, 1962).

31. *Ibid.,* p. 13.

32. Information on the wall newspapers from the author's personal observation in 1964 in Leningrad.

33. Ilin, *op. cit.*, p. 53.

34. This point was raised, for example, at a meeting of the Estonian Komsomol Central Committee; see *Noukogide Opetaja,* December 17, 1966, noted in *Soviet Studies Information Supplement* (July, 1967).

35. Figures are from *Sovetskaya Pechat,* No. 4 (April, 1964), p. 11; No. 2 (February, 1965), p. 47; No. 2 (February, 1966), p. 4; and *Zhurnalist,* No. 2 (January, 1967), p. 18 and No. 2 (February, 1968), p. 21.

36. Except where otherwise noted, information on *Pravda* is drawn from *Rasprostraneniye Pechati,* No. 1 (January, 1967), pp. 26–27, and the author's visit to the newspaper on March 20, 1964, and to the Pravda Publishing Plant on November 2, 1967.

37. See the interview with K. Ya. Sergeichuk, first deputy Minister of Communications, in *Trud,* December 27, 1967, in *Current Digest of the Soviet Press*, Vol. XX, No. 2, p. 8.

38. *Zhurnalist*, No. 1 (January, 1967), p. 77. By comparison, *The New York Times* had an average of 290 columns of news space daily in 1967. News and editorial department employees totaled 775, including 27 correspondents in the *Times* Washington bureau, 13 full-time regional correspondents in the United States, and 42 foreign correspondents in 32 bureaus. See *The New York Times,* January 21, 1968.

39. Leningrad's *Smena*, a Komsomol newspaper, pays fees in this range according to its editor, in an interview with the author December 1, 1963.

40. See also *Spravochnik zhurnalista*, pp. 246 ff., for brief descriptions and discussion of the internal organization of various Soviet newspapers.

41. See *O partiinoi i sovetskoi pechati*, pp. 533–534, for the 1945 decree, and p. 602 for the 1948 directive.

42. *Spravochnik zhurnalista*, p. 247.

43. This section is based on the author's discussions with *Leningradskaya Pravda* editors on January 30, 1964, and February 21, 1964.

44. See the monograph by S. M. Gurevich, *Secretariat redaktsii gazety* (Moscow, 1961), for a description of the managing editor's and the secretariat's responsibilities.

45. *Zhurnalist*, No. 10 (October, 1967), p. 78.

46. *Zhurnalist*, No. 3 (March, 1967), p. 14, reports an annual total of "half a million."

47. S. M. Gurevich, *Planirovaniye redaktsii gazety* (Moscow, 1961), p. 27. See also pp. 4–22 for a discussion of Soviet newspaper planning.

48. *Smena* editors estimated in 1964 that they published 25 per cent of TASS dispatches.

49. This issue of the paper was discussed in detail with the author by *Leningradskaya Pravda* editors.

50. Information based on an interview in Bratsk with the editor, September 20, 1967.

51. *Pechat SSSR v 1968 godu,* pp. 56–64, give basic statistical data on Soviet magazines.

52. *Zhurnalist*, No. 1 (February, 1968), p. 21.

53. *Spravochnik zhurnalista*, p. 120.

54. *Rasprostraneniye Pechati*, No. 4 (April, 1967), p. 4, gives a circulation of national magazines as 94.3 million, and republic, 27.6 million.

55. The 1957 circulation figures are from *Sovetskaya Pechat*, No. 5 (May, 1957), p. 55.

56. *Voprosy Ekonomiki*, No. 6 (June, 1965), pp. 20–30.

CHAPTER 6

1. *Kommunist*, No. 13 (September, 1965).

2. *Zhurnalist*, No. 4 (April, 1967), p. 39.

3. *Ibid.*

4. *Sovetskaya Kultura*, September 9, 1965, in *Current Digest of the Soviet Press*, Vol. XVII, No. 39, p. 11.

5. *Pravda*, September 14. 1965.

6. *Zhurnalist*, No. 12 (December, 1967), p. 44.

7. *World Communications* (2nd edn., Paris: UNESCO, 1966), p. 367.

8. *Ibid.*, p. 368.

9. *Pravda*, June 28, 1968.

10. See, for example, an article on this topic in *Soviet Life,* December, 1965, pp. 24–25.

11. *Zhurnalist,* No. 6 (June, 1968), pp. 18–20.

12. *Report of the National Advisory Commission on Civil Disorders*, pp. 362 ff., generally expresses the point of view that disorders connected with civil rights activities must be presented by the mass media with an understanding of the impact such reporting has on public attitudes. On p. 375, the commission suggests more positive—using the word in quotations—news about Negro ghettos.

13. *Sovetskaya pechat v dokumentakh*, p. 134.

14. *Zhurnalist*, No. 5 (May, 1968), p. 28.

15. *Zhurnalist*, No. 6 (June, 1968), p. 14.

16. *Ibid.*, p 15.

17. Gleizer (ed.), *op. cit.*, p. 3.

18. *Spravochnik zhurnalista*, pp. 173–174.

19. Quoted in L. N. Fedotova, "*Stanovleniye reportazha na radio*," p. 17.

20. See, for example, *Sovetskaya Pechat*, No. 6 (June, 1965), p. 1, where 1,200 hours of daily program are equated with "about 300 4-page newspapers of a large format."

21. *Forty Years of Soviet Power*, p. 265, gives the number of receivers. According to the 1926 census, 26.3 million people out of a population of 147 million lived in cities. See *Itogi vsesoyuznoi perepisi naseleniya 1959 goda; SSSR*, p. 13.

22. Gleizer (ed.), *op. cit.*, p. 51, and *USSR Today and Tomorrow* (Moscow, 1959), p. 285.

23. As late as 1966, 24 per cent of all farm workers' *homes* were without electricity. *Selskaya Zhizn*, April 26, 1966. For the Central Committee decree, see *Zhurnalist*, No. 5 (May, 1967), p. 28.

24. Inkeles, *Public Opinion in Soviet Russia*, p. 251.

25. See Gleizer (ed.), *op. cit.*, p. 265, for these and other statistics in this section.

26. *Narodnoye khozyaistvo SSSR v 1960 godu* (Moscow, 1961), p. 576.

27. *Ibid.*, pp. 576 and 528.

28. *Ibid.*, p. 576, and *Ezhegodnik bolshoi sovetskoi entsiklopedii* (Moscow, 1967), p. 89.

29. See these newspapers for May 7, 1968.

30. *World Communications*, pp. 33 and 364; *Pravda*, May 7, 1968.

31. See Gayle Durham Hollander, "Recent Developments in Soviet Radio and Television News Reporting," *Public Opinion Quarterly* (Fall, 1967), pp. 362–364, for this information, and for amount of news programming on radio and television.

32. *World Communications,* p. 367.

33. V. N. Yaroshenko, "*Izucheniye radioauditorii*," *Vestnik Moskovskogo universiteta, Seriya XI, Zhurnalistika*, No. 1, 1966, p. 29, mentions "abolition of subscriber fees," in the context of radio development in the early 1960's. For evidence that subscriber fees still seem to apply to wired loudspeaders, see *Zhurnalist*, No. 5 (May, 1967), p. 28.

34. *Ibid.*, pp. 29–30.

35. *Kommunist*, No. 13 (September, 1965), p. 70.

36. TASS International Service, May 5, 1968, and *Pravda*, May 7, 1968.

37. Gleizer (ed.), *op. cit.,* pp. 60 and 86.

38. *Forty Years of Soviet Power*, p. 265.

39. *Ibid.*, and *Narodnoye khozyaistvo SSSR v 1960 godu* (Moscow, 1961), p. 576.

40. *Sovetskaya Pechat*, No. 5 (May, 1960), p. 25.

41. *Sovetskaya pechat v dokumentakh*, p. 136.

42. *Ezhegodnik* (Moscow, 1962), p. 78, and *Pravda*, May 7, 1968.

43. *Kommunist*, No. 13 (September, 1965), p. 70, and *Pravda*, May 6, 1968.

44. Moscow Radio, April 12, 1968, translated in *Foreign Broadcast Information Service (FBIS)*, April 15, 1968, p. D5; *TASS International Service*, December 27, 1967, in *FBIS*, December 29, 1967, pp. BB18–19.

45. Washington *Post*, May 16, 1968, p. 23.

46. *Izvestia*, August 11, 1968, and *Zhurnalist*, No. 10 (October, 1968), p. 38.

47. *Zhurnalist*, No. 12 (December, 1967), pp. 16–17.

48. *Sovetskaya Pechat*, No. 11 (November, 1959), p. 37.

49. This section, unless otherwise noted, is based on *Spravochnik zhurnalista*, pp. 181–186 and 212–215.

50. *Ibid.*, pp. 184–185.

51. *Ekonomicheskaya Gazeta*, No. 19 (May, 1968), p. 23.

52. *See Yaroshenko, "Izucheniye radioauditorii,"* p. 27. In an elementary survey, American listeners who wrote to the American Department of Radio Moscow were sent postcards asking listeners to note preferences for various programs.

53. See Associated Press dispatch from Moscow, January 17, 1968.

54. Translated in *The Soviet Press* (Madison, Wis.: University of Wisconsin Press), Vol. V, No. 1, 1966, pp. 7–9.

CHAPTER 7

1. Bernard C. Cohen, *The Press and Foreign Policy* (Princeton, N.J.: Princeton University Press, 1963), pp. 160 ff., and pp. 151–152 and 198–203.

2. Anita Mallinckrodt Dasbach, "U.S.-Soviet Magazine Propaganda: *America Illustrated* and *USSR*," *Journalism Quarterly* (Spring, 1966), pp. 73–84. *Amerika*, the United States Russian language magazine which circulates in the Soviet Union, similarly emphasized a cultured, dynamic, technologically advanced American society, but played less on the peace theme than *USSR*.

3. See Theodore E. Kruglak, *The Two Faces of TASS* (Minneapolis: University of Minnesota Press, 1962), Chapter 2.

4. See "Soviet News Media and the Middle East Crisis," *Radio Liberty Research Paper*, No. 16, 1967, in which *Pravda*'s and *Izvestia*'s reports on the Arab-Israeli crisis are matched against recorded events. TASS transmitted summaries and excerpts from both newspapers.

5. Don D. Smith, "Radio Moscow's North American Broadcasts: An Exploratory Study," *Journalism Quarterly* (Autumn, 1965), pp. 643–644.

6. Estimates in 1962 varied between more than $100 million and less than $1 billion for all Communist countries for foreign propaganda, the Soviet share being about 40 per cent. See Frederick C. Barghoorn, *Soviet Foreign Propaganda* (Princeton, N.J.: Princeton University Press, 1965), p. 306.

7. See Vladimirov, *op. cit.*, pp. 87–88.

8. Both quotations from *The New York Times*, February 15, 1967.

9. See *Pravda*, June 28, 1968.

10. *The New York Times*, February 21, 1967.

11. See Kruglak, *op. cit.*, Chapter 12, for a discussion of TASS as an intelligence organization in postwar years.

12. Col. Oleg Penkovsky, a Soviet intelligence officer executed in 1963 for supplying information to western countries, listed TASS among 26 Soviet organizations to which military or civilian intelligence agents were assigned. It is not clear from his reports whether Novosti was exempted, or whether Penkovsky's list preceded Novosti's founding in 1961. See Oleg Penkovsky, *The Penkovskiy Papers* (Garden City, N.Y.: Doubleday & Company, Inc., 1965), pp. 66–67.

13. See Cohen, *op. cit.*, pp. 136–142.

14. See Vladimirov, *op. cit.*, pp. 91–92. The existence of a special TASS report for confidential use has been referred to also by Leo Gruliow in "The Soviet Press: 'Propagandist, Agitator, Organizer,'" *Journal of International Affairs*, No. 2, 1956, pp. 159–160.

15. See Cohen, *op. cit.*, pp. 219–230, for a discussion of newspapers' role in circulating foreign policy ideas among American officials and legislators.

16. Zbigniew Brzezinski and Samuel P. Huntington make this point in *Political Power: USA/USSR* (New York: The Viking Press, Inc., 1964), pp. 386–388, where they discuss American policy toward Cuba, and Soviet actions in Hungary in 1956.

17. See *ibid.*, pp. 405–406, where Brzezinski and Huntington suggest that American-French differences in the early 1960's were eased somewhat by open debate, partly in the press, whereas the Soviet-Chinese controversy during the same period resulted in a sharp split, partly because policy decisions in both Moscow and Peking were not subject to discussion.

18. *The New York Times*, September 25, 1968, noted that the jamming was continuing, though English language broadcasts were not disturbed.

19. Figures from Palgunov, *op. cit.*, p. 29; *World Communications*, p. 366; *Zhurnalist*, No. 1 (January, 1967), p. 77; and *TASS International Service*, January 8, 1968.

20. *Zhurnalist*, No. 1 (January, 1967), p. 77.

21. Palgunov, *op. cit.*, p. 27.

22. TASS serves as both the Soviet national news agency and the Russian republic agency. Other republics and their agencies: Azerbaidzhan—AzTAG; Armenia—ArmenTAG; Moldavia—ATEM; Byelorussia—BelTAG; Georgia—GruzTAG; Kazakhstan—KazTAG; Kirgizia—KirTAG; Latvia—LTA; Ukraine—RATAU; Tadzhikstan—TadzhikTAG; Turkmen—TurkmenTAG; Uzbekistan—UzTAG; Lithuania—ELTA; Estonia—ETA; *Spravochnik zhurnalista,* p. 161.

23. Palgunov, *op. cit.*, p. 28.

24. Kruglak, *op. cit.*, pp. 27–28.

25. Palgunov, *op. cit.*, p. 30, gives a figure of "more than 800" in the entire TASS apparatus; Khudyakov, in *Teoriya i praktika partiino-sovetskoi pechati,* p. 112, says "about 700." Both agree that about 200 persons were assigned overseas.

26. *TASS International Service*, January 9, 1968.

27. *Sovetskaya pechat v dokumentakh*, pp. 318–322.

28. McCormack, *et al.*, *op. cit.*, p. 51.

29. *Ibid.* Goryunov said that in the 10 years before 1966, the foreign staff had been increased 2.5 times. In the mid-1950's, the foreign staff totaled about 200. Thus the 500 estimate. Figures on the size of the TASS staff must be accepted cautiously, however. One source reports 500 TASS correspondents in all, domestic and foreign. See *The Democratic Journalist*, No. 12, 1968, p. 271.

30. Unless otherwise noted, information in this section is from *Spravochnik zhurnalista*, pp. 157–166; and Palgunov, *op. cit.*, pp. 29-32 and 49–56. *Sovetskaya Pechat*, No. 2 (February, 1964), pp. 20–27, also provides some material on TASS.

31. McCormack *et al.*, *op. cit.*, p. 52.

32. Palgunov, *op. cit.*, p. 49.

33. *Sovetskaya Pechat*, No. 10 (October, 1959), p. 47.

34. *Izvestia*, January 10, 1968.

35. In 1930, some TASS rates were published. Large republic and *oblast* newspapers were charged 2 per cent of subscription income for TASS general political material, excluding telegraph charges. For smaller republic and *oblast* newspapers, the fee was $1\frac{1}{2}$ per cent of subscription income, and for *raion* and national language newspapers, 1 per cent. See Fogelevich, *Deistvuyushcheye zakonodatelstvo* (3rd edn.), p. 148. Also reported are ROSTA rates.

36. *Izvestia*, January 10, 1968, and *Soviet Life*, No. 2 (February, 1966), p. 40.

37. From *TASS podpiska na 1964 g*, a pamphlet describing TASS services for 1964.

38. Khudyakov, *Teoriya i praktika partiino-sovetskoi pechati*, p. 113.

39. See for example *Sovetskaya Pechat*, No. 1 (January, 1966), pp. 35–36, where a TASS editor responds to some criticisms of *raion* newspaper editors.

40. *Zhurnalist*, No. 7 (July, 1968), p. 48.

41. Palgunov, *op. cit.*, p. 32.

42. McCormack *et al.*, *op. cit.*, p. 55.

43. Palgunov, *op. cit.*, p. 35.

44. See the supplement to *Sovetskaya Pechat*, No. 11 (November, 1966), p. 11.

45. See Kruglak, *op. cit.*, Chapter 6, for a good summary of Palgunov's attitudes as expressed in *Osnovy informatsii v gazete: TASS i ego rol.*

46. *Sovetskaya Pechat*, No. 3 (March, 1966), p. 50.

47. See also *Spravochnik zhurnalista*, pp. 166–171, for information on the founding of Novosti. The last of the four sponsoring organizations is currently called the National Society of Knowledge. The Society for Friendship and Cultural Contacts was abolished in 1968 and its functions incorporated into the Soviet foreign ministry.

48. *World Communications*, p. 367; and *Spravochnik zhurnalista*, p. 171; *Izvestia*, July 13, 1965.

49. Novosti makes something of a business of these services. See William S. Rumeyser's report in the *Wall Street Journal*, September 20, 1966, for information on Novosti fees. However, Novosti seems more to charge what the market will bear, rather than according to a fee schedule.
50. *Za Rubezhom*, No. 2, 1965, and *Zhurnalist*, No. 1 (January, 1967), p. 77.
51. *Soviet Life* (June, 1966), p. 24.

CHAPTER 8

1. *Sovetskaya pechat v dokumentakh*, pp. 200–202.
2. *Ibid.*, pp. 204–205.
3. See *ibid.*, for Communist Party directives: in 1958, exposing excessive bonuses, pp. 295–296; in 1959, ordering newspapers and magazines to operate at a profit, pp. 301–306; and in 1960, commanding reductions of staff correspondents in *oblast* bureaus, pp. 318–322.
4. Based on the author's interview with *Leningradskaya Pravda* editors, January 30, 1964.
5. *Zhurnalist*, No. 4 (April, 1967), p. 22.
6. Khudyakov, *Teoriya i praktika partiino-sovetskoi pechati*, p. 157. Khudyakov was on the Moscow University School of Journalism staff for many years.
7. *Zhurnalist*, No. 4 (April, 1968), p. 19.
8. See *Zhurnalist*, No. 2 (February, 1967), pp. 9–11.
9. M. I. Kalinin, *O korrespondentakh i korrespondentsiyakh* (Moscow, 1958), p. 37.
10. *Zhurnalist*, No. 4 (April, 1967), pp. 21–23.
11. *Resheniya partii o pechati*, p. 77.
12. *Ibid.*, pp. 38 and 39.
13. See *Spravochnik zhurnalista*, pp. 268-270.
14. *Sovetskaya pechat v dokumentakh*, p. 196.
15. *Ibid.*, p. 199.
16. *Pravda*, January 7, 1967.
17. *Pravda*, September 17, 1967. The most recent attention to readers' complaints probably was motivated by a flurry of petitions and letters denouncing trials of Soviet dissidents and charging violations of civil rights. For examples, see *Problems of Communism*, Nos. 4 and 5, 1968.
18. *Izvestia*, April 26, 1968.
19. *Pravda*, January 1, 1966; *Izvestia*, January 1, 1966.
20. *Zhurnalist*, No. 12 (December, 1967), p. 23.
21. Results of the study are in *Vestnik Moskovskogo universiteta, Seriya XI, Zhurnalistika*, No. 4, 1966, pp. 43–50.
22. *Zhurnalist*, No. 4 (April, 1967), p. 23.
23. See Bernard A. Ramundo, "They Answer (To) *Pravda*," in Wayne R. LaFave (ed.), *Law in the Soviet Society* (Urbana, Ill.: University of Illinois Press, 1965), pp. 113–124, for a good discussion of the investigative functions of the Soviet press.
24. *Current Abstracts of the Soviet Press*, Vol. I, No. 1, 1968, p. 11.

25. For an account of *Krokodil's* operations see Theodore Shabad, "Behind the Smile on Krokodil," *The New York Times Magazine,* June 7, 1964.
26. *Pravda,* August 28, 1965.
27. *Sovetskaya Pechat,* No. 13 (October, 1962), pp. 1-2.
28. But the letters are received, as *Komsomolskaya Pravda* acknowledged after the trial in January, 1968, of four dissidents. The newspaper said that persons who had written letters defending the convicted persons has been misled. It published none of the letters. Associated Press dispatch from Moscow, February 28, 1968.
29. See Alex Simirenko, *Soviet Sociology: Historical Antecedents and Current Appraisals* (Chicago: Quadrangle Books, 1966), for the history and development of Soviet sociology, particularly the essay by Paul Hollander. The monograph by George Fischer, *Science and Politics: The New Sociology in the Soviet Union* (Ithaca, N.Y.: Cornell University Center for International Studies, 1964), is a good summary of developments in Soviet sociology to about 1963.
30. Inkeles, *Public Opinion in Soviet Russia,* p. 75.
31. See *Pravda,* December 14, 1967.
32. See Elihu Katz, "The Two Step Flow of Communication," in Schramm (ed.), *Mass Communications,* pp. 346-365.
33. *Vestnik Moskovskogo universiteta, Seriya XI, Zhurnalistika,* No. 6, 1966, pp. 43-53.
34. *Ibid.,* No. 4, 1966, pp. 21-22.
35. For this discussion see *ibid.,* No. 6, 1966, pp. 31-41.
36. Bernard Berelson, "Communications and Public Opinion" in Schramm (ed.), *Mass Communications,* p. 531.
37. This information is drawn from the well-documented essay by R. F. Ivanova, "*Pervyi opyt konkretnykh sotsiologicheskikh issledovanii sovetskoi pechati,*" in *Vestnik Moskovskogo universiteta, Seriya XI, Zhurnalistika,* No. 2, 1967, pp. 43-55. Soviet researchers were not, however, innovators. In 1899, for example, an elementary study was carried out in a Moscow factory to determine reading habits of workers. See *Rasprostraneniye Pechati,* No. 8 (August, 1968), p. 47.
38. See *Vestnik Moskovskogo universiteta, Seriya XI, Zhurnalistika,* No. 1, 1966, p. 27. The questions are reprinted on p. 37.
39. Information supplied the author during interviews at the Moscow University School of Journalism, March 24 and 31, 1964.
40. The Leningrad School of Journalism staff exhibited an early though unpublicized interest in audience research. In the 1964-65 academic year, a seminar was conducted on the "sociology of the press and the psychology of the journalistic creativity." In 1966, a "methodological council" was set up, drawing on local Communist Party officials, journalism staff, and professional journals, to develop media research. See *Vestnik Moskovskogo universiteta, Seriya XI, Zhurnalistika,* No. 4, 1966. pp. 84-86.
41. The figure of 40 is reported in *Partiinaya Zhizn,* No. 4 (February, 1968),

p. 56. Judging from available evidence, most of these are not significantly large centers. Moreover, they engage in research other than on the press.

42. See *The Soviet Review* No. 11 (November, 1961), pp. 3–24, for results.

43. Information on the *Izvestia* poll is drawn from *Izvestia*, July 11 and 12, 1968; *Nedelya*, *Izvestia*'s Sunday supplement, No. 11, 1967; and *Zhurnalist*, No. 2 (February, 1968), pp. 23–25.

44. See *Zhurnalist*, No. 7 (July, 1968), pp. 46–48.

45. See *Zhurnalist*, No. 4 (April, 1967), p. 22, for information on the survey.

46. The four papers involved in the study were *Uralskii Rabochii, Omskaya Pravda, Sovetskaya Sibir,* and *Vechernii Novosibirsk.* Information on the study is in *Vestnik Moskovskogo universiteta, Seriya XI, Zhurnalistika*, No. 6, 1966, pp. 42–53; see also the article by N. Gerasimov in *Partiinaya Zhizn*, No. 16 (August, 1967), which deals with a section of the same study, on *Sovetskaya Sibir.*

47. Results are in *Zhurnalist*, No. 7 (July, 1967), pp. 32–33.

48. *Zhurnalist*, No. 1 (January, 1967), pp. 8–10.

49. *Ibid,* p. 9. Reported results do not account for 11 per cent of subscribers asked for reactions.

50. *Vestnik Moskovskogo universiteta, Seriya XI, Zhurnalistika*, No. 1, 1966, pp. 33–35, contains the findings.

51. Preliminary results are in *Zhurnalist*, No. 8 (August, 1968), pp. 61–62.

52. Results are from *Zhurnalist*, No. 12 (December, 1967), pp. 42–45.

53. *Ibid.,* p. 45.

54. Inkeles and Bauer, *op. cit.,* p. 168.

55. *Ibid.,* p. 167.

56. *Ibid.,* p. 167 ff.

57. *Ibid.,* pp. 168–169.

58. *Zhurnalist*, No. 12 (December, 1967), p. 62.

59. *World Marxist Review*, No. 6 (June, 1968), p. 58. The higher percentages were engineers, technicians, and researchers; the lower, collective farmers. Factory workers and office workers fell between the two.

60. *Soviet Life*, No. 11 (November, 1965), p. 13.

61. *Zhurnalist*, No. 8 (August, 1968), p. 62.

62. *Zhurnalist*, No. 12 (December, 1968), p. 43.

63. *Rasprostraneniye Pechati*, No. 4 (April, 1967), p. 4.

64. *Rasprostraneniye Pechati*, No. 11 (November, 1967), p. 5; No. 9 (September, 1967), p. 2.

65. *Current Abstracts of the Soviet Press*, Vol. I, No. 2 (May, 1968), p. 18.

66. David Powell, "The Effectiveness of Soviet Anti-Religious Propaganda," *Public Opinion Quarterly* (Fall, 1967), pp. 366–380.

67. Quoted by Donald F. Cox, "Clues for Advertising Strategists," in Dexter and White (eds.), *op. cit.,* p. 367. Cox also draws from other studies to indicate that sheer repetition does not guarantee acceptance of an advertiser's message.

68. See *Zhurnalist*, No. 6 (June, 1968), p. 16.

SOVIET NEWSPAPERS AND PERIODICALS

National Newspapers

All national Soviet newspapers have their editorial offices in Moscow and most are printed there. A few—*Pravda, Izvestia,* and *Komsomolskaya Pravda*—are printed from matrices flown to regional plants. Circulation figures are for 1967–68.

Ekonomicheskaya Gazeta (Economics Gazette). Published by the Communist Party Central Committee. A tabloid-size weekly; deals with economics, industry, and finance. Founded in 1960. Circulation, 460,000.

Gudok (Whistle). Published by the Ministry of Transportation and Railroad Workers' Union. General information, with particular focus on railroads and railwaymen. Daily except Monday. Founded in 1920. Circulation, 641,000.

Izvestia (News). Organ of the presidium of the Supreme Soviet (parliament). General news and information with special emphasis on government actions and administration. Second-ranking Soviet newspaper for authoritative views. Daily except Monday. Founded in 1917. Circulation, 7,700,000.

Nedelya (The Week). Izvestia's tabloid-size Sunday supplement. Essays, feature articles, illustrations on general topics. One of the most popular Soviet publications. Circulation, 1,800,000.

Komsomolskaya Pravda (Komsomol Truth). Published by the Central Committee of the Young Communist League—the Komsomol. Particular attention to youth, but also general news and information. Daily except Monday. Founded in 1925. Circulation, 6,700,000.

Krasnaya Zvezda (Red Star). Published by the Ministry of Defense. Most important of military newspapers, reflecting views of Soviet high command. Daily except Monday. Founded in 1925. Circulation, 2,400,000.

Literaturnaya Gazeta (*Literary Gazette*). Published by the national Union of Writers. A weekly newspaper containing general information, with special emphasis on literature, art, and culture. Founded in 1929. Circulation, 500,000.

Meditsinskaya Gazeta (*Medical Gazette*). Published by the Ministry of Public Health and Trade Union of Medical Workers. Emphasis on health and medical information. Twice weekly. Circulation, 1,000,000.

Pionerskaya Pravda (*Pioneer Truth*). Published by the Central Committee of the Young Communist League. Tabloid size; content oriented toward members of the Pioneers, an organization for grade school children. Founded in 1925. Twice weekly. Circulation, 9,200,000.

Pravda (*Truth*). Published by the Communist Party Central Committee. Most authoritative Soviet newspaper, reflecting Soviet foreign and domestic policies of leadership. Daily. Founded in 1912. Circulation, 7,500,000.

Selskaya Zhizn (*Rural Life*). Published by the Communist Party Central Committee. Leading newspaper on agricultural and rural themes. Daily except Monday. Founded in 1929. Circulation, 6,400,000.

Sovetskaya Kultura (*Soviet Culture*). Published by the Ministry of Culture and Trade Union of Cultural Workers. Popular culture. Three times a week. Founded in 1953. Circulation, 190,000.

Sovetskaya Rossiya (*Soviet Russia*). Communist Party Central Committee. Formerly (until 1966) organ of the Russian republic bureau of the Central Committee. General news and information, reflecting accurately the political leadership's views. Daily except Monday. Founded in 1956. Circulation, 2,900,000.

Sovetskaya Torgovlya (*Soviet Trade*). Published by the Union of Trade Workers. Deals with commerce and retail and wholesale trade. Three times a week. Founded in 1939. Circulation, 665,000.

Sovetskii Sport (*Soviet Sports*). Published by the Central Council of Trade Unions and the Sports Committee of the Council of Ministers. Sports news. Tabloid size; twice weekly; founded in 1933. Circulation, 2,600,000.

Trud (*Labor*). Organ of the Central Council of Trade Unions. Content oriented toward labor and industry. Daily except Monday. Founded in 1921. Circulation, 2,300,000.

Republic Newspapers

All republic newspapers listed below are jointly published by the Central Committee of the republic's Communist Party organization and the republic's Council of Ministers and Supreme Soviet. They appear daily except Monday. In the following list, the republic capital where the newspaper is published appears in parenthesis. The first newspaper listed is printed in the Russian language; the second, in the national language of the republic. Circulations are given when available.

Armenia (Yerevan)
  Kommunist (*Communist*)
  Sovetikan Ayastan (*Soviet Armenia*): Circulation 90,000.

Azerbaidzhan (Baku)
  Bakinskii Rabochii (*Baku Worker*)
  Kommunist (*Communist*): Circulation, 125,000.

Byelorussia (Minsk)
  Sovetskaya Byelorussia (*Soviet Byelorussia*)
  Zvyazda (*Star*): Circulation, 115,000.

Estonia (Tallinn)
  Sovetskaya Estonia (*Soviet Estonia*)
  Rahva Haal (*Peoples Voice*): Circulation, 100,000.

Georgia (Tbilisi)
  Zarya Vostoka (*Dawn of the East*)
  Kommunist (*Communist*): Circulation, 175,000.

Kazakhstan (Alma-Ata)
  Kazakhstanskaya Pravda (*Kazakhstan Truth*)
  Sotsialistik Kazakhstan (*Socialist Kazakhstan*): Circulation, 75,000.

Kirgizia (Frunze)
  Sovetskaya Kirgizia (*Soviet Kirgizia*)
  Sovettik Kyrgyzstan (*Soviet Kirgizia*): Circulation, 50,000.

Latvia (Riga)
  Sovetskaya Latvia (*Soviet Latvia*)
  Cina (*Struggle*): Circulation, 215,000.

Moldavia (Kishinev)
  Sovetskaya Moldavia (*Soviet Moldavia*)
  Moldova Socialiste (*Socialist Moldavia*)

Tadzhikstan (Dushanbe)
  Kommunist Tadzhikstana (*Tadzhikstan Communist*)
  Tochikistoni Soveti (*Soviet Tadzhikstan*)

Turkmen (Ashkhabad)
  Turkmen Iskra (*Turkmen Spark*)
  Soviet Turkmenistany (*Soviet Turkmen*)

Ukraine (Kiev)
  Pravda Ukrainy (*Ukraine Truth*): Circulation, 440,000.
  Radyanska Ukraina (*Soviet Ukraine*): Circulation, 500,000.

Uzbekistan (Tashkent)
  Pravda Vostoka (*Truth of the East*)
  Sovet Uzbekistoni (*Soviet Uzbekistan*): Circulation, 423,000.

Periodicals

The following magazines and journals are representative of the Soviet periodical press, although it is not a full listing. All are published in Moscow. Circulation figures are for 1968.

Kommunist (*Communist*): Published by the Communist Party Central Committee. Leading political and theoretical party journal. Founded in 1924 as *Bolshevik*, renamed *Kommunist* in 1952. Issued 18 times yearly. Circulation, 760,000.

Krokodil (*Crocodile*): Published by the newspaper *Pravda*. Popular magazine of satire, contains critical essays and cartoons. Three times monthly. Founded in 1922. Circulation, 4,600,000.

Krestyanka (*Peasant Woman*): Popular magazine for rural women, publishes essays, feature articles, and illustrations. Monthly. Founded in 1922. Circulation, 5,400,000.

Novy Mir (*New World*): Published by the Union of Writers. Contains fiction, poetry, literary criticism, and general social essays; considered "liberal" in viewpoint. Monthly. Founded in 1925. Circulation, 121,150.

Ogonek (*Little Flame*): Publishes popular social, political essays, literature, illustrations. Founded in 1923. Weekly. Circulation, 2,000,000.

Oktyabr (*October*): Published by the Russian republic Union of Writers. Prints literature and social essays; considered "conservative" in outlook. Monthly. Founded in 1924. Circulation, 140,000.

Partiinaya Zhizn (*Party Life*): Published by the Communist Party Central Committee. Focuses on party administration, ideology, and experience. Published twice monthly. Founded in 1919. Circulation, 920,000.

Politicheskoye Samoobrazovaniye (*Political Self-Education*): Published by the Communist Party Central Committee. Deals with official politics. Monthly. Founded in 1957. Circulation, 1,400,000.

Rabotnitsa (*Woman Worker*): Most popular illustrated magazine for women, containing cultural and political information. Monthly. Founded in 1914. Circulation, 10,000,000.

Smena (*Young Generation*): Published by the Young Communist League Central Committee. Focuses on essays, fiction, features of interest to youth. Twice monthly. Founded in 1924. Circulation, 1,000,000.

Voprosy Ekonomiki (*Problems of Economics*): Published by the Academy of Sciences Institute of Economics. Most important journal for discussion of economics. Issued monthly. Circulation, 49,850.

Za Rubezhom (*Abroad*): Published by the Union of Journalists. Contains translated excerpts from the foreign press. Weekly. Circulation, 1,100,000.

Zdorovye (*Health*): Published by the Ministry of Health of the USSR of the Russian republic. Popular magazine on health and medical care. Monthly. Founded in 1955. Circulation, 8,000,000.

Zhurnalist (*Journalist*): Published by the Union of Journalists. Emphasizes professional journalistic subjects, along with ideology. Monthly. Founded in 1955 as *Sovetskaya Pechat* (*Soviet Press*); name changed in 1967. Circulation, 130,000.

BIBLIOGRAPHY

$\mathbb{O}$F THE AVAILABLE Soviet material on the mass media, various collections of Communist Party and government documents, decrees, resolutions, and the like remain the most valuable and useful sources. Three stand out: *Sovetskaya pechat v dokumentakh*, published in 1961; *O partiinoi i sovetskoi pechati*, 1954, and *Resheniya partii o pechati*, 1941. All bring together official documents on the press specifically, and although there is considerable duplication, all must be consulted since they reflect different political periods. The laws and regulations assembled and edited by L. G. Fogelevich are indispensable for study of the Soviet press in the 1920's and 1930's. Lenin's writings on the press are conveniently contained in *Lenin o pechati*; Stalin's in *Stalin o pechati* (Sverdlovsk); and Karl Marx's and Friederich Engels's in *K. Marks i F. Engels o pechati*. Beyond these, *Spravochnik zhurnalista* is, in my opinion, the best single reference for the contemporary Soviet mass media. A thorough history of the Soviet press has yet to be written in the Soviet Union. In its absence the 2-volume *Partiinaya i sovetskaya pechat v borbe za postroeniye sotsializma i kommunizma* is a helpful general survey, though it primarily summarizes official documents.

These and other Soviet books and monographs which to my mind are most valuable or essential in studying the Soviet mass media are given first in the listing below. The secondary sources are chiefly monographs and pamphlets dealing with particular facets of the Soviet press, but which contain illuminating detail amid much repetitive information.

Of Soviet periodicals on the press, *Zhurnalist* (formerly *Sovetskaya Pechat*) is the most rewarding. Also very useful, however, is *Vestnik Moskovskogo universiteta, Seriya XI, Zhurnalistika*. Published by the Moscow University School of Journalism, it offers discussions of the mass media and research results.

Among English language sources, Alex Inkeles's *Public Opinion in Soviet Russia* deserves special reading. So does Merle Fainsod's *Smolensk Under Soviet Rule*, which provides unique material on political management and the censorship of the Soviet press in the 1930's. There is a vast library available in English on the Soviet Union. I have listed only those books to which specific reference has been made.

SOVIET SOURCES

Books and Monographs

1. *Primary*

   Atlas razvitiya khozyaistva i kultury SSSR, Moscow, 1967.

   Belkov, A. K., *et al.*, *K. Marks i F. Engels o pechati*. Moscow, 1963.

   ———, *Partiinaya i sovetskaya pechat v borbe za postroeniye sotsializma i kommunizma*. Vol. I, Moscow, 1961. Vol. II, Moscow, 1963.

   Berezhnoi, A., *K istorii partiino-sovetskoi pechati*. Leningrad, 1956.

   Bogdanov, N. G., and B. A. Vyazemskii, *Spravochnik zhurnalista*. Leningrad, 1965.

   Bolshaya sovetskaya entsiklopediya. 2nd edn., 50 vols., Moscow, 1949–1958.

   Bolshevistskaya pechat: sbornik materialov. Vol. I., Moscow, 1959.

   Dekrety sovetskoi vlasti. 2 vols., Moscow, 1957.

   Ezhegodnik bolshoi sovetskoi entsiklopedii. Moscow, 1968. Also editions for the years 1960, 1961, 1962, 1963, 1964, 1965, 1966, and 1967.

   Fogelevich, L. G. (ed.), *Deistvuyushcheye zakonodatelstvo o pechati*. 1st edn., Moscow, 1927. 3rd edn., Moscow, 1931.

   Fogelevich, L. G., *Osnovnye direktivy i zakonodatelstva po pechati*. 6th edn., Moscow, 1937.

   Forty Years of Soviet Power. Central Statistical Board, Moscow, 1958.

   Gleizer, M. (ed.), *Radio i televideniye v SSSR: 1917–1963*. Moscow, 1965.

   Gsovski, Vladimir, *Soviet Civil Law*. 2 vols., Ann Arbor, Michigan, University of Michigan Press, 1948.

   Gurevich, S. M., *et al.*, *Teoriya i praktika partiino-sovetskoi pechati*. Moscow, 1968.

   Itogi vsesoyuznoi perepisi naseleniya 1959 goda SSSR. Moscow, 1962.

Khudyakov, Ye L., *Teoriya i praktika partiino-sovetskoi pechati.* Moscow, 1957.

KPSS v resolyutsiyakh i resheniyakh. 4 vols., Moscow, 1954 and 1959.

Lenin o pechati. Moscow, 1959.

Lenin, V. I., *Sochineniya.* 4th edn., 35 vols., Moscow, 1941–1952.

Leninskoi Pravde—50 let. Moscow, 1962.

Narodnoye khozyaistvo SSSR v 1960 godu. Moscow, 1961, and for the years 1961, 1962, 1963, 1964, and 1965.

O partiinoi i sovetskoi pechati: sbornik dokumentov. Moscow, 1954.

Palgunov, N. G., *Osnovy informatsii v gazete: TASS i ego rol.* Moscow, 1955.

Pechat SSSR za 50 let: statisticheskiye ocherki. Moscow, 1967.

Pechat SSSR za sorok let: 1917–1957. Moscow, 1957.

Pechat v SSSR v 1968 and for the years 1955, 1959, 1960, 1961, 1962, 1964, 1966, and 1967.

Pervyi vsesoyuznyi sezd zhurnalistov: stenograficheskoi otchet. Moscow, 1960.

Resheniya partii o pechati. Moscow, 1941.

Reshetnikov, T. M., *Partiya o pechati.* Sverdlovsk, 1934.

Russkaya Periodicheskaya Pechat. Moscow, 1957.

Sovetskaya pechat v dokumentakh. Moscow, 1961.

Stalin, I. V., *O pechati.* Izdatelstvo Proletarii, 1925.

Stalin o pechati. Sverdlovsk, 1932.

Ugolovnoye zakonodatelstvo soyuza SSSR i soyuznykh respublik. 2 vols., Moscow, 1963.

USSR Today and Tomorrow. Moscow, 1959.

2. *Secondary*

Bogdanov, N. G., *et al.*, *Raionnaya gazeta.* Leningrad, 1957.

Grammatnikov, V. (ed.), *Teoriya i praktika bolshevistskoi pechati.* Leningrad, 1934.

Gurevich, S. M., *Planirovaniye redaktsii gazety.* Moscow, 1961.

———, *Secretariat redaktsii gazety*, Moscow, 1961.

Ilin, S., *Kak organizovat stennoi gazety.* Yuzhno-Sakhalinsk, 1962.

Ivanova, R. A., *Partiinaya i sovetskaya pechat v gody vtorio pyatiletki: 1933–1937.* Moscow, 1961.

Kalinin, M. I., *O korrespondentakh i korrespondentsiyakh.* Moscow, 1958.

Kononykhin, N. M., *Partiinaya i sovetskaya pechat v period veli-koi otechestvennoi voiny.* Moscow, 1963.

Lunenko, G., *Partiinaya organizatsiya i pechat*, Moscow, 1962.

Mishuris, A. L. (ed.), *Iz istorii partiinoi i sovetskoi pechati.* Moscow, 1957.

Romanov, A. V., *Stroitelstvo kommunizma i pechat.* Moscow, 1963.

Slovar sokrashchenii russkogo yazyka. Moscow, 1963.

Spravochnik dlya postupayushchikh v vysshiye uchebnye zavedeniya SSSR v 1963. Moscow, 1963.

Stepanov, B. P., *Rasprostraneniye, ekspedirovaniye i dostavka gazet i zhurnalov v SSSR.* Moscow, 1963.

Uchebnyi plan: spetsialnosti, zhurnalistika. Moscow University. 1957.

Uchenova, V. V., *Partiino-sovetskaya pechat vosstanovitelnogo perioda.* Moscow, 1964.

Vitakhov, S. P., and L. N. Andreeva, *Nasha ezhednevnaya stennaya gazeta.* Leningrad, 1961.

Voprosy ideologicheskoi raboty. Moscow, 1961.

Voprosy zhurnalistiki. Moscow, 1962.

Yurov, Yu, *Tvoya zavodskaya gazeta.* Moscow, 1960.

Newspapers and Periodicals

Ekonomicheskaya Gazeta

Izvestia

Kommunist

Komsomolskaya Pravda

Leningradskaya Pravda

Moscow News

Novy Mir

Partiinaya Zhizn

Pravda

Rasprostraneniye Pechati

Smena

Sovetskaya Pechat

Sovetskaya Torgovlya

Soviet Life

TASS

Vechernii Leningrad

Vestnik Moskovskogo universiteta: Istoriko-filologicheskaya seriya

Vestnik Moskovskogo universiteta, Seriya XI, Zhurnalistika

Voprosy Ekonomiki

Voprosy Istorii KPSS

Za Rubezhom

Zhurnalist

NON-SOVIET SOURCES

Books and Monographs

Anderson, Thornton, *Russian Political Thought: An Introduction.* Ithaca, N.Y., Cornell University Press, 1967.

Ayer Directory of Newspapers and Periodicals. Philadelphia, N. W. Ayer and Son, Inc., 1968.

Barghoorn, Frederick C., *Politics in the USSR.* Boston, Little, Brown and Company, 1966.

———, *Soviet Foreign Propaganda.* Princeton, N.J., Princeton University Press, 1965.

Berdyaev, Nicolas, *The Russian Idea.* Boston, Beacon Press, 1962.

Brzezinski, Zbigniew, and Samuel P. Huntington, *Political Power: USA/USSR.* New York, The Viking Press, Inc., 1964.

Carnegie Commission on Educational Television. *Public Television, A Program for Action.* New York, Harper & Row, Inc., 1967.

Cohen, Bernard C., *The Press and Foreign Policy.* Princeton, N.J., Princeton University Press, 1963.

Conquest, Robert (ed.), *The Politics of Ideas in the U.S.S.R.* New York, Frederick A. Praeger, Inc., 1967.

Crankshaw, Edward, *Khrushchev: A Career.* New York, The Viking Press, Inc., 1966.

Dallin, Alexander, and Thomas B. Larson (eds.), *Soviet Politics Since Khrushchev.* Englewood Cliffs, N.J., Prentice-Hall, Inc., 1968.

Dexter, Lewis A., and David M. White (eds.), *People, Society and Mass Communications.* New York, The Free Press of Glencoe, 1964.

Directory of Soviet Officials. Vol. I, Vol. II, and revisions to Vol. I, Washington, 1966.

Dizard, Wilson P., *Television: A World View.* Syracuse, N.Y., Syracuse University Press, 1966.

Editor and Publisher International Yearbook. New York, 1968.

Emery, Edwin, *The Press and America.* 2nd edn., Englewood Cliffs, N.J., Prentice-Hall, Inc., 1963.

Fainsod, Merle, *How Russia Is Ruled.* Cambridge, Mass., Harvard University Press, 1953.

———, *Smolensk Under Soviet Rule.* New York, Vintage Books, Inc., 1963.

Finn, A., *Experiences of a Soviet Journalist,* New York, East European Fund, Inc., 1954.

Fischer, George, *Science and Politics: The New Sociology in the Soviet Union*. Ithaca, N.Y., Cornell University, Center for International Studies, 1964.

Florinsky, Michael T., *Russia: A History and an Interpretation*. 2 vols., New York, The Macmillan Company, 1955.

Hayward, Max (tr.), *On Trial*. New York, Harper & Row, Inc., 1966.

Inkeles, Alex, *Public Opinion in Soviet Russia: A Study in Mass Persuasion*. Cambridge, Mass., Harvard University Press, 1951.

Inkeles, Alex, and Raymond A. Bauer, *The Soviet Citizen: Daily Life in a Totalitarian Society*. Cambridge, Mass., Harvard University Press, 1959.

Johnson, Priscilla, and Leopold Labedz (eds.), *Khrushchev and the Arts: The Politics of Soviet Culture, 1962-1964*. Cambridge, Mass., The M.I.T. Press, 1965.

Juviler, Peter H., and Henry W. Morton (eds.), *Soviet Policy-Making. Studies of Communism in Transition*. New York, Frederick A. Praeger, Inc., 1967.

Kintner, William R., and Harriet Fast Scott (trs. and eds.), *The Revolution in Soviet Military Affairs*. Norman, Oklahoma, The University of Oklahoma Press, 1968.

Kotlyar, A., *Newspapers in the U.S.S.R.—Recollections and Observations of a Soviet Journalist*, East European Fund, Inc., New York, 1955.

Kruglak, Theodore E., *The Two Faces of TASS*. Minneapolis, University of Minnesota Press, 1962.

LaFave, Wayne R. (ed.), *Law in the Soviet Society*. Urbana, Illinois, University of Illinois Press, 1965.

Markham, James W., *Voices of the Red Giants*. Iowa State University Press, Iowa, 1967.

Marty, Martin E., John G. Deedy, Jr., David Wolf Silverman, and Robert Lekachman, *The Religious Press in America*. Chicago Holt, Rinehart and Winston, Inc., 1963.

Mass Media in Developing Countries. Paris, UNESCO, 1961.

McCormack, Buren H., *et al., A Study of the Printing and Publishing Business in the Soviet Union*. American Newspaper Publishers Association, New York, 1967.

Meisel, James H., and Edward S. Kozera (eds.), *Materials for the Study of the Soviet System*. Ann Arbor, Michigan, The George Wahr Publishing Co., 1953.

Miller, Margaret, *Rise of the Russian Consumer*. London, Institute of Economic Affairs, 1965.

Miller, Wright W., *Russians as People*. New York, E. P. Dutton & Co., Inc., 1961.

Neustadt, Richard E., *Presidential Power*. New York, Signet Books, The New American Library, Inc., 1960.

Pares, Bernard, *A History of Russia*. New York, Alfred A. Knopf, Inc., 1956.

Paulu, Burton, *Radio and Television Broadcasting on the European Continent*. Minneapolis, Minn., University of Minnesota Press, 1967.

Penkovsky, Oleg, *The Penkovskiy Papers*. Garden City, N.Y., Doubleday & Company, Inc., 1965.

Ploss, Sidney, *Conflict and Decision-Making in Soviet Russia*. Princeton, N.J., Princeton University Press, 1965.

Reed, John, *Ten Days That Shook the World*. New York, The Modern Library, Inc., 1935.

Report of the National Advisory Commission on Civil Disorders. New York, Bantam Books, Inc., 1968.

Reston, James, *The Artillery of the Press. Its Influence on American Foreign Policy*. New York and Evanston, Illinois, Harper & Row (published for the Council on Foreign Relations), 1966.

Rosenberg, Bernard, and White, David Manning (eds.), *Mass Culture: The Popular Arts in America*. New York, The Free Press of Glencoe, paperback, 1964.

Schapiro, Leonard, *The Communist Party of the Soviet Union*. New York, Random House, Inc., 1960.

Schramm, Wilbur (ed.), *Mass Communications*. Urbana, Illinois, University of Illinois Press, 1960.

———, *Mass Media and National Development. The Role of Information in the Developing Countries*. Stanford, California, Stanford University Press, 1964.

Seton-Watson, Hugh, *The Russian Empire, 1801–1967*. London, Oxford University Press, 1967.

Siebert, Fred S., *et al.*, *Four Theories of the Press*. Urbana, Illinois, University of Illinois Press, 1956.

Simirenko, Alex, *Soviet Sociology: Historical Antecedents and Current Appraisals*. Chicago, Quadrangle Books, 1966.

Sorensen, Theodore C., *Kennedy*. New York, Bantam Books, Inc., 1966.

Steinberg, Charles S. (ed.), *Mass Media and Communication*. New York, Hastings House, Publishers, Inc., 1966.

Vladimirov, Leonid, *The Russians*. New York, Frederick A. Praeger, Inc., 1968.

World Communications: Press, Radio, Television, Film. Paris, UNESCO, 2nd edn., 1966.

Newspapers and Periodicals

Amerika

Current Abstracts of the Soviet Press

Current Digest of the Soviet Press

The Democratic Journalist

Foreign Broadcast Information Service

Freedom of Information Center Report No. 181. School of Journalism, University of Missouri, May, 1967.

The Soviet Press, University Extension, The University of Wisconsin, Journalism Extension.

Journalism Quarterly

Nieman Reports

The New York Times

Problems of Communism

Public Opinion Quarterly

Radio Liberty Dispatches

Radio Liberty Research Papers

The Soviet Review

Soviet Studies

Soviet Studies Information Supplement

U. S. News & World Report

Wall Street Journal

Washington *Post*

World Marxist Review

ACKNOWLEDGMENTS

The author is grateful for permission to quote from the following publications:

Nicolas Berdyaev. *The Russian Idea.* Beacon Press, Boston, Mass., 1962. By permission of Geoffrey Bles Ltd., London.

Wright W. Miller. *Russians As People.* E. P. Dutton & Co. Inc., New York, 1961.

Thornton Anderson. *Russian Political Thought: An Introduction.* Copyright © 1967 by Cornell University. Used by permission of Cornell University Press.

Hugh Seton-Watson. *The Russian Empire 1801–1917.* Oxford University Press, London, 1967. By permission of the Clarendon Press, Oxford.

Wilbur Schramm. *Mass Media and National Development: The Role of Information in the Developing Countries.* Stanford University Press, Stanford, Calif., 1964.

Segments of Chapter 2 are taken by permission from the author's article, "Lenin, Stalin, Khrushchev: Three Concepts of the Press," which appeared in *Journalism Quarterly,* Vol. 42, No. 4.

INDEX

Advertising: revival of, 50–51; Lenin on monopoly of, 54–55; declared state monopoly in 1917, 62–63; Lenin on state monopoly decree, 63; *Soyuzpechat* campaigns, 136–37; in local press, 185; compared with American, 186–87; types of, 186–88; functions of, 188; organizations for, 188; expenditure on, 188

Adzhubei, Alexei: as editor, 106; replaced as editor of *Izvestia,* 141; on journalism, 150; and Novosti, 292

Aesopian language: in press, 170

Agitation: 309–10

Agitprop: 96; created, 76; instructions on press content, 83–85; and radio broadcasting, 90; renamed, 140; restaffed after Khrushchev, 140–42; sectors for mass media, 142; surveillance of press, 143–44

American press: development and principles of, 112–14; in problem solving, 113; and libel, 132

APN, *see Novosti* and *News agencies*

Audience: Leningrad reaction to TV, 238; and *Trud,* 243; use of media, 334–36

Audience ratings: of *Izvestia* content, 314–19; of *Trud* content, 319–22; of foreign news on radio-TV, 328; of Leningrad TV, 329–34

Audience study: early years, 312–13

Bednota: peasant newspaper, 68

Bias, in the press: 176–77

Bloknot Agitatora: 224–25

"Blue screen": 240

Bolsheviks: 1903 split of Social-Democrats, 58; seize power in 1917, 60; early restrictions on press, 61–63; control of press, 65–68. *See also* Communist Party

Brezhnev, Leonid: appears on television, 240–41

Buchwald, Art: reprinted in Soviet press, 50

Burkov, Boris: director of *Novosti,* 164

Censorship: introduction of, 77–79; of periodicals, 87–88; expanded in 1930s, 93–94; procedure, 94–95; prohibited information, 94–95; under czars, 122; and journalists' views, 127–28 effectiveness, 127–28; and journalists' work, 126–27; and "Smolensk archives," 127; and Committee on the Press, 133. *See also Glavlit*

Central television *see* television

Cheka: and censorship, 78. *See also* Secret police

Chief Commercial Advertising Administration: 188

Circulation: 134–38; per capita, 190; of Pravda, 209; of newspapers, 68, 203, 336–37; of periodicals, 336. *See also Soyuzpechat*

City newspapers, *see* Local press

Cold war, and radio broadcasting, 247–48

Collective farmers, use of media, 327, 328

Collective farm newspapers *see kolkhoz* newspapers

Collectivization, begun 91

Commissariat for Press Affairs: Bolshevik agency, 62–63; closes newspapers, 62–63

Commissariat for Education, and *Glavlit,* 77

Committee on Radio Broadcasting and Television: and government control of press, 133–34; Communist party controls over, 139; directors changed after Khrushchev, 141; created, 254; structure of, 254–55; foreign bureaus, 280; and listenership study, 326

Committee on the Press: 78–79; abolished, 95; recreated, 133; directors, 133; and advertising rates, 185

Communications satellites: 252–53; and international TV, 259–60

Communist Academy, and journalism training, 154

Communist Institute of Journalism, 154

Communist Party: 29–30; and press management, 28–30, 76–81, 95–96; justified in press, 40–41; opinion management, 43–44; debates in press, 44–45; need for critical press, 44–45; 8th congress and press, 66–67; control of press by local party, 66–67; and 3rd congress of Social-Democrats, 66–67; early objectives for press, 70; 11th congress and press, 72; central committee structure, 75; politburo, 75; orgburo, 75; press departments, 76–77; development of press network, 80; 13th congress and press, 82–84; management agencies for mass media, 138–144; appoints editors, 138–39; substructure of, 147; and journalism education, 152–53; categories of news about, 173–76; income from press, 184; subsidies for press, 184–85; regulations on lower press, 203; criticism of prohibited in wall newspapers, 205; editors members of, 213; on development of television, 251; instructs on foreign news, 270–72; on worker-peasant correspondents, 298–99; on letters to editor, 302–03; use of media by officials, 327–28. *See also Agitprop*

Council of Ministers, determines state secrets, 125

Council of People's Commissars, 75; issues Decree on Press, 62–63; split on press freedom, 64

"Counterrevolution": prohibited in press, 62; and the press, 79

Credibility gap, 34, 41, 178–79

Crime: coverage by the press, 175; and television programming, 241–42

382

INDEX

Moscow: TV programming, 259; radio listenership, 326

Moscow News, advertising in, 188

Moscow University: and journalism education, 85, 152; journalism school established at, 153–54; journalism students, 154–55; journalism courses, 155–56; readership study, 313; and listenership study, 326

Myasnikov, Alexander, on press freedom, 71

National Association for Commercial Advertising, 188

National development, and mass media, 46–47

National press, 81–82, 364–66; development of, 194–96

Nationalities, and press structure, 25–26

Nationalities press, 82, 192–93; and periodicals, 225

Nauka i Zhizn, 227

Nedelya, 364

NEP, 70; private publishing plants, 72; controversy over, 90

"New Soviet man", 39–40

News: in Soviet mass media, 48–49; definitions of, 165–66, 290–91; categories of, 173–76; slanting of, 176–180; in *Leningradskaya Pravda,* 219–23; lack of timeliness on radio and TV, 243; sources of for audience, 318–19, 321–22

  international: government management of, 267–68; party instructions on, 271–72; screened by TASS, 273; and mass audience, 276–77; superficiality of, 278–79; sources of, 279–80; and *Izvestia* readership, 314–17; readership of, 321–22; and audience tastes, 327–29; on television, 331

  of economics: in *Izvestia,* 315, 316, 317; in rural areas, 321–22; readership, 322–23

  of politics: readership in *Izvestia,* 315, 316, 317; in *Trud,* 319, 320; in rural areas, 321–22; on television, 331, 332

News agencies: czarist, 68; in republics, 79–80, 280n; compared with foreign, 266; as intelligence agencies, 272–73; and mass audience, 277–78. *See also* TASS, ROSTA and Novosti

Newspapers: Lenin on, as revolutionary center, 56; circulation statistics, 68, 80, 91–94, 203, 336; military, 68; states subsidies, 79–80; structure reorganized, 81–82; content criticized, 83–84; staffing of, 96; during World War II, 99–100; economic bases in Russia, 116–17; party press exempt from censorship, 123; and libel, 130–32; fees for circulation service, 135–36; "quota" subscription system, 136–37; writing style, 156–58; profits, 184–85; number of compared with American, 190; number per nationalities, 192–93; foreign language, 193; staff sizes, 202; editorial structure, 212–13; editorial plans, 216–18; and criticism in, 303–07; readership of, 336; competition among, 318, 321; as source of foreign news, 327. *See also Kolkhoz* newspapers, Local press, Lower press, National press, Nationalities press, *Oblast* newspapers, *Raion* newspapers, Republic press, and Wall newspapers

Newsstands, number of, 134

Nicholas II: as czar, 55; abdicates, 60

NKVD, *see* Secret police

"Nonnews," in Soviet mass media, 49

Novaya Zhizn, Bolshevik newspaper, 59

Novosti: compared with USIA, 267; as intelligence agency, 272–73; foreign bureaus, 280, 293–94; purposes of, 292; creation of, 291–92; and contacts with foreign press, 294; numbers of subscribers, 293

Novoye Vremya, 231

Novy Mir, 229; criticized 109–10; and censorship, 126

Oblast newspapers: 81–82; number and format, 199; staff size, 202; example of, 212–19. *See also* Newspapers

Ogni Angary, format and content, 223–24

Ogonyek, 227, 367

OGPU, and censorship, 78. *See also* Secret Police

Oktyabr, 368

Orbita, ground stations, 253

Orgburo. See Communist Party

Ostankino, Moscow TV station, 254

Palgunov, Nikolai, on definition of news, 165, 290–91; appointed TASS director, 281

Partiinaya Zhizn, 232, 368

Pasternak, Boris, 102

"People's press," 18; Lenin's view, 54–55; and Khrushchev, 104–05; and Marxist thought, 117–18; and amateur journalists, 297–99, 300–01; and letters to editor, 302–05

Periodicals, 367–68; early development, 87–88; compared with newspaper press, 88; party's attitude toward, 88; circulation statistics, 93, 224–26, 336; during World War II, 99–100; fees for circulation service, 135–36; for nationalities, 226; political guidelines, 227–28; special audiences, 228, 230; as critics, 230, 232, 234–35

"Personality cult," *see* Stalinism

Phoenix 66, underground literary journal, 129

Pionerskaya Pravda, 365; founded, 81; circulation of, 193

Planyerka, on newspapers, 217–19

Politburo, see Communist Party

Political leadership: management of press, 24; references to in press, 110; and television, 239–41; informed by mass media, 272–75; use of media, 327, 328, 329

Politicheskoye Samoobrazovaniye, 227, 368

Politinformers, 310

Popov, Alexander, Russian scientist, 244

Pornography: prohibited in press, 122; penalties for publication of, 129–30

Pravda, 207–12, 365; and "economics debate," 43; on Khrushchev's removal, 49; founding in 1912, 59; ordered to direct provincial press, 66; in civil war years, 67, 68; circulation of, 82, 209; and "review of press," 97; editors changed after Khrushchev, 141; salaries paid on, 160, 210; on definition of news, 166; on ideology in press, 177–78; description of, 207–12; printed from matrices, 209; editorial structure, 210–12; letters to editor, 216, 303; as instrument of foreign policy, 271–72; foreign bureaus, 280

Pravda Ukrainy, 199

Press, and the people, 18

Press Agency Novosti, *see* Novosti and News agencies

Press freedom, *see* Freedom of the press

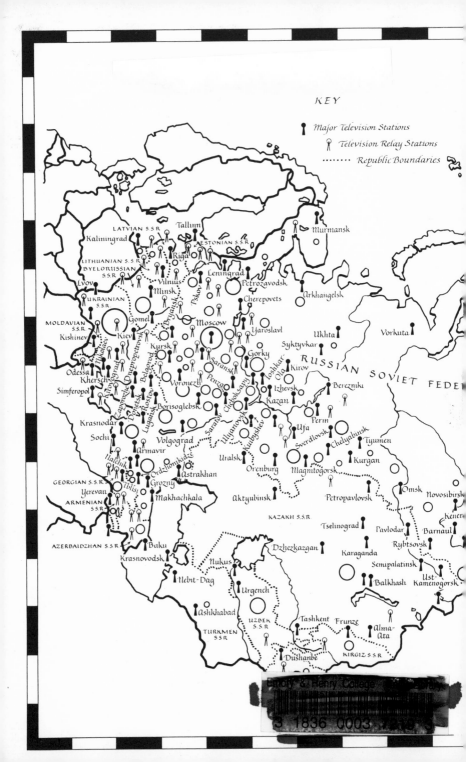

KEY

Major Television Stations
Television Relay Stations
.... Republic Boundaries

LATVIAN S.S.R.   Tallinn   Murmansk
Kaliningrad   ESTONIAN S.S.R.
LITHUANIAN S.S.R.   Riga
BYELORUSSIAN   Leningrad   Petrozavodsk
S.S.R.   Vilnius Pskov
Lvov   Minsk   Arkhangelsk
UKRAINIAN   Cherepovets
S.S.R.   Gomel   Vorkuta
MOLDAVIAN   Kiev   Moscow   Ukhta
S.S.R.   Kursk Yaroslavl   Syktyvkar   RUSSIAN   SOVIET FEDE
Kishinev   Nikolaev Belgorod   Gorky   Kirov
Odessa   Dnepropetrovsk Saransk Yoshkar-   Berezniki
Khersch   Voronezh Penza Cheboksary Ola
Simferopol   Donetsk Rostov   Izhevsk
           Lugansk Borisoglebsk   Kazan
Krasnodar   Saratov   Perm
Sochi   Volgograd Ulyanovsk Ufa
           Armavir Kuibyshev   Sverdlovsk Chelyabinsk Tyumen
GEORGIAN S.S.R. Nalchik Ordzhonikidze Uralsk   Kurgan
Yerevan Tbilisi Grozny Astrakhan   Orenburg Magnitogorsk   Omsk   Novosibirsk
ARMENIAN   Makhachkala   Petropavlovsk   Kemer
S.S.R.   Aktyubinsk   Barnaul
AZERBAIDZHAN S.S.R. Baku   KAZAKH S.S.R. Tselinograd Pavlodar Rybtsovsk
Krasnovodsk   Dzhezkazgan   Karaganda   Semipalatinsk
        Nebt-Dag   Nukus   Balkhash Ust-
                    Urgench   Kamenogorsk
        Ashkhabad   UZBEK   Tashkent Frunze
        TURKMEN   S.S.R.   Alma-
        S.S.R.   Ata
                Dushanbe   KIRGIZ S.S.R.